THE SILAPPADIKARAM

THE SILAPPADIKARAM

VISHNAMPET R. RAMACHANDRA DIKSHITAR

GYAN

Published by

Gyan Publishing House
5, Ansari Road
Daryaganj, New Delhi-110002
Phone: 011-47034999, 9811692060
E-mail: books@gyanbooks.com

Distribution Network
gyanbooks.com
India, USA, Canada, UK, Australia

ISBN: 978-93-7316-031-3 (PB)

First Published, 1939

2nd Impression 2025

Printed at: Gyan Press, Delhi.

THE SILAPPADIKARAM
Arthur: VISHNAMPET R. RAMACHANDRA DIKSHITAR

The
Śilappadikāram

PATTIṈI DĒVĪ

Reproduced by permission of the British Museum and Dr A. K. Coomaraswamy

The Śilappadikāram

TRANSLATED
WITH AN INTRODUCTION AND NOTES
BY

V. R. RAMACHANDRA DIKSHITAR, M.A.
Lecturer in Indian History and Archaeology
University of Madras

WITH A FOREWORD BY
JULES BLOCH

INDIAN BRANCH
HUMPHREY MILFORD
OXFORD UNIVERSITY PRESS
1939

TO THE MEMORY OF

PROFESSOR M. A. CANDETH

AND

PRINCIPAL REV. FR. F. BERTRAM, S.J.

FOR THEIR ABIDING INTEREST IN AND LOVE OF SOUTH INDIAN CULTURE

FOREWORD

I BELIEVE there is no need to introduce Mr V. R. Ramachandra Dikshitar to the public, which knows him already and favourably. If, however, I have accepted the honour of writing a foreword to the present book, it is to lay stress on its special character, and to plead for more works of a similar nature.

Its significance will clearly appear if we follow the progress of the author's researches. At the start, as a research scholar in history, Mr Dikshitar devoted his first studies to the old Hindu administrative institutions; his ambition was to give a synthetic survey of them, including the theories of Kauṭalya and the traditional law-books, and also the actual practices of the sovereigns. Here, of course, Aśoka comes into prominence. Mr Dikshitar in this connexion happily considers old Tamil institutions. But he finds this last-mentioned subject in itself worthy of further and deeper investigation; to quote Mr Dikshitar's own words, he 'felt more and more the need for an intrinsic study of the priceless literary treasures of Tamil'. Hence a set of essays which formed the basis of his useful book, *Studies in Tamil Literature and History* now in its second edition. Here general statements and hypotheses are not altogether lacking, and therefore the author does not completely escape from criticism. But, happily, facts and an analysis of contents find a large place, and there is a progressive disappearance of the historian behind the materials of history. In praising this book at the time, I regretted that instead of short notices of the contents, especially of the more archaic works, we were not also offered long or even complete translations. Now Mr Dikshitar himself has come to that same necessary conclusion ; the historian has resorted to the more difficult and often ungrateful, but also more beneficent, task of translation. Let the reader have the plainest possible access to the text ; help him with all the needed current explanations, and reserve personal inductions for the introductory survey. This will be a boon not only to the student of history but also to the literary man and to everybody interested in Tamilian culture. And this means many people at a time when so much is being done, not only to assert India's culture before the world, but also to make India known to herself, and to show in their true light the various original civilizations which all together form Indian civilization.

Among them the Tamil country can boast of an antique and original culture. A picture of India, historical or literary, will not be complete if due importance is not attached to it ; no more than a physical description of India will be complete if rocky Deccan and southern deltas or backwaters are omitted.

But how many are there who have access and are able to enjoy or usefully consult Tamil literary works, especially the older ones? It is a matter of common knowledge that only a few can do so even among those born in the Tamil country. On those few lies the responsibility of helping their compatriots to appreciate those works which are the particular glory and the inspiration of their country, and to give outsiders a faithful rendering of them.

Scholars themselves will be benefited by that work. Need I recall what progress in Sanskrit studies has been due to translations from Sanskrit into European languages, and primarily into English? And to those interested in furthering the cultural unity of India, need I recall that those periods of history when translations were most numerous were also periods of unification and progress?

This is my plea, and the reason why I have great pleasure in recommending this present new departure of a historian. Let me also take advantage of this opportunity to mention that already in 1900 Prof. Julien Vinson, in his *Légendes Bouddhistes et D'Jains*, rendered into French the analysis given by Mahamahopadhyaya Swaminatha Aiyar of both the *Śilappadikāram* and the *Maṇimēkalai* and added his own full translation of three cantos[1] of the former.

I could dilate longer on this and similar topics. Better do I invite readers to take advantage of this beautiful poem and treatise in its present garb, and compatriots of Mr Dikshitar to emulate him in translating fully as many old poems as possible, especially those of the Śangam, where there probably is still much to be discovered.

Collège de France JULES BLOCH
March 1939

[1] Cantos xvi-xviii, and also *padikam*.

PREFACE

Some time after the publication of my book *Studies in Tamil Literature and History*, in 1930. Mr F. J. Richards, formerly of the Indian Civil Service, wrote to me suggesting that I should undertake the writing of a handbook on the History of Tamil Literature. He also pointed out the desirability of publishing a series of critical editions of the Tamil classics with English translations and annotations. He wrote : 'I have no hesitation in pressing for English editions, for the reason that Tamil is almost a sealed book to all who are not Tamilians, and it is a pity that the rest of India does not realize the importance of the Tamil contribution to Indian culture. We can only be made to do so by publishing for a wider circle of readers, and English is the most handy medium for this publicity both in India and elsewhere.' This letter of Mr Richards induced me to undertake the rather stupendous task of attempting an almost literal translation of the most difficult of Tamil classics, the *Śilappadikāram*.

The translation is based on Mahamahopadhyaya Dr V. Swaminatha Aiyar's Tamil edition of the *Śilappadikāram*. I have to acknowledge my indebtedness to this scholarly and critical work of the Mahamahopadhyaya. I have also derived immense benefit from Rao Sahib Pundit M. Raghava Aiyangar whom I have had to consult frequently in the course of preparing this work. My thanks are also due to several colleagues in the departments of the University and other friends who have been of help to me in one way or another.

To Professor Jules Bloch I acknowledge my particular indebtedness for the Foreword he has written.

I must also express my gratitude to the Madras School-book and Literature Society for their generous contribution towards the publication of the book.

I shall feel my labour amply rewarded if the book helps to spread Tamil culture in India and abroad.

V. R. RAMACHANDRA DIKSHITAR

Madras
20 April 1939

CONTENTS

CANTO		PAGE
	INTRODUCTION	1
	Book I : PUHĀRKKĀṆḌAM	
I.	MANGALAVĀḶTTUPPĀḌAL	87
II.	MAṈAIYAṞAMPAṬUTTAKĀDAI	92
III.	ARANGĒṞṞUKĀDAI	97
IV.	ANTIMĀLAIŚŚIṞAPPUCCEYKĀDAI	106
V.	INDIRAVIḶAVŪREḌUTTAKĀDAI...	110
VI.	KAḌALĀḌUKĀDAI	122
VII.	KĀṈALVARI	131
VIII.	VĒṈIṞKĀDAI	145
IX.	KAṈĀTTIṞAMURAITTAKĀDAI	151
X.	NĀḌUKĀṆKĀDAI	156
	Book II : MADURAIKKĀṆḌAM	
XI.	KĀḌUKĀṆKĀDAI	171
XII.	VĒṬṬUVAVARI	180
XIII.	PUṞAÑCĒRIIṞUTTAKĀDAI	190
XIV.	ŪRKĀṆKĀDAI...	199
XV.	AḌAIKKALAKKĀDAI	209
XVI.	KOLAIKKAḶAKKĀDAI	219
XVII.	ĀCCIYARKURAVAI	228
XVIII.	TUṈBAMĀLAI...	239
XIX.	ŪRŚŪḶVARI	242
XX.	VAḶAKKURAIKĀDAI	246
XXI.	VAÑJIṈAMĀLAI	251
XXII.	AḶAṞPAṬUKĀDAI	255
XXIII.	KAṬṬURAIKĀDAI	262
	Book III : VAÑJIKKĀṆḌAM	
XXIV.	KUṈṞAKKURAVAI	275
XXV.	KĀṬCIKKĀDAI	283
XXVI.	KĀLKŌṬKĀDAI	292

Contents

CANTO		PAGE
XXVII.	NIRPPAṬAIKKĀDAI	304
XXVIII.	NAḌUKAṞKĀDAI	316
XXIX.	VĀḶTTUKKĀDAI	327
XXX.	VARANTARUKĀDAI	337
	APPENDIXES	347
	INDEX	375

ABBREVIATIONS

Aham.	*Ahanāṉūṟu*
Anc. Ind.	*Ancient India*
An. Rep. Ep.	*Annual Report for Epigraphy*
Ar. Śās.	*Artha Śāstra*
A.S.I.	*Archaeological Survey of India*
Bhāga. pur.	*Bhāgavata purāṇa*
C.A.	*Ceylon Antiquary*
C.I.I.	*Corpus Inscriptionum Indicarum*
Ep. Ind.	*Epigraphia Indica*
Ep. Z.	*Epigraphia Zeylancia*
I.H.Q.	*Indian Historical Quarterly*
Ind. Ant.	*Indian Antiquary*
Jīvaka	*Jīvakacintāmaṇi*
J.I.H.	*Journal of Indian History*
J.O.R.	*Journal of Oriental Research*
J.R.A.S.	*Journal of Royal Asiatic Society*
Kali.	*Kalittogai*
Kalinga.	*Kalingattuparaṇi*
Maṇi.	*Maṇimēkalai*
M.A.S.C.	*Memoirs of Archaeological Survey of Ceylon*
Mhb.	*Mahābhārata*
Padiṟṟu.	*Padiṟṟuppattu*
Puṟam.	*Puṟanāṉūṟu*
Puṟa. Veṇbā.	*Puṟapporuḷveṇbāmālai*
Perumpāṇa.	*Perumpāṇāṟṟupadai*
Raghu.	*Raghuvamśa*
Śila.	*Śilappadikāram (Tamil Edition)*
S.I.I.	*South Indian Inscriptions*
Tolk.	*Tolkāppiyam*
T.A.S.	*Travancore Archaeological Series*
Vis. pur.	*Vishṇu Purāṇa*
Z.I.I.	*Zeitschrift der Indologie und Iranstick*

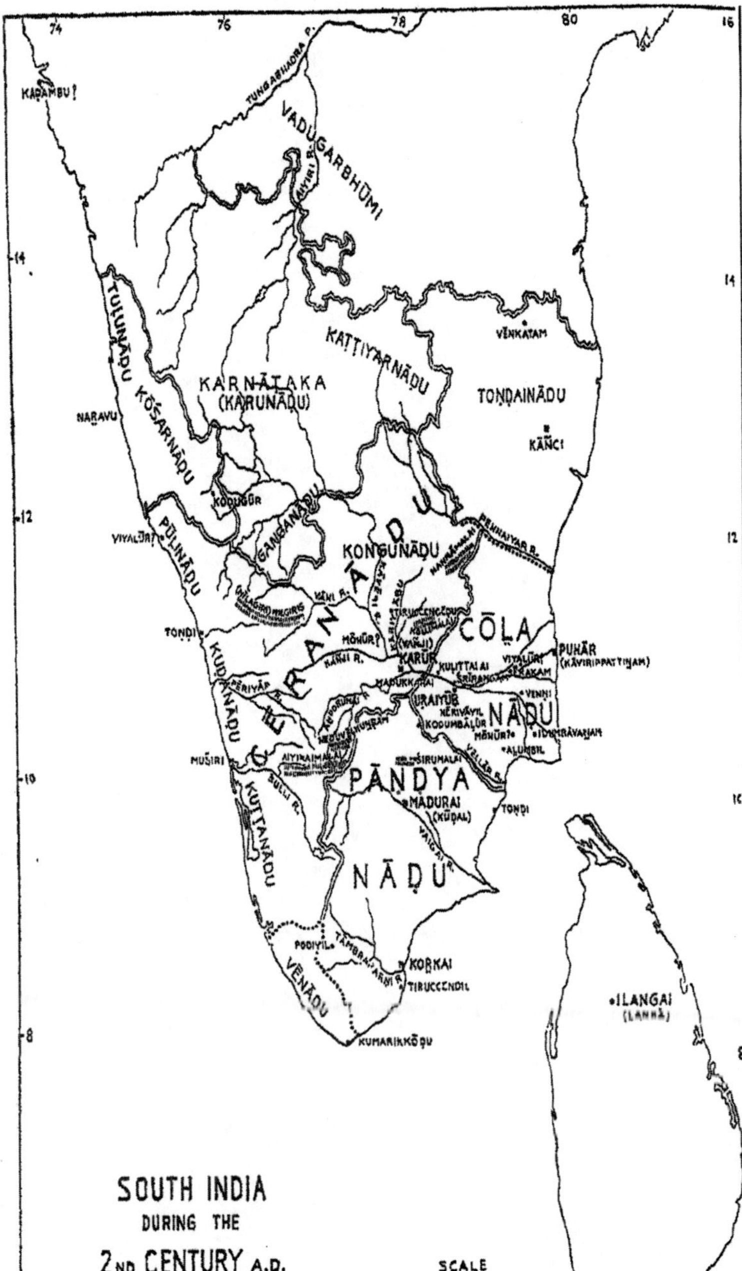

SOUTH INDIA
DURING THE
2ND CENTURY A.D.

INTRODUCTION

I

THE NAME

THE term *Śilappadikāram* is made up of two words, *śilambu* and *adikāram*. Literally the title means 'the story that centres around a *śilambu* or anklet'. The hero and the heroine of the story, Kōvalaṉ and Kaṇṇaki, set out for Madura to dispose of a *śilambu* and thereby raise the capital needed to pursue a trade. In the bazaar street of Madura Kōvalaṉ meets the state goldsmith. The state goldsmith who has stolen the queen's anklet (similar to that in Kōvalaṉ's hand) reports to the king that he has found the thief. The king blindly believes the goldsmith and has poor Kōvalaṉ executed. The heroine proves to the king her husband's innocence by breaking open her other anklet and showing that the contents of her anklets are different from those of the queen. The Pāṇḍyan king dies of grief on realizing his blunder in having ordered the execution of Kōvalaṉ without proper investigation. Kaṇṇaki destroys the city of Madura by fire to avenge the execution of her husband, and is finally proclaimed the goddess of chastity. As the story thus centres round the *śilambu*, it can appropriately be named the Epic of the Anklet.

One among the five *perumkāppiyams* (*mahākāvyas* of Sanskrit literature), the *Śilappadikāram* may come under the category of *toṭarnilaicceyyuḷ* and in it we find *iyal*, *iśai*, and *nāṭakam* as its chief characteristics. *Iyal*, *iśai*, and *nāṭakam* mean, respectively, Literary Tamil, Music, and the Drama. There will be no two opinions about the excellence of the literary Tamil of the epic; and as regards the other two characteristics, *iśai* and *nāṭakam*, the work may be described as a model of ancient Tamil musical and dramatic composition. A wealth of material is found scattered throughout the work. One is struck with wonder at the *iśaippāṭṭu* or the lyric songs in which the author not infrequently indulges. The songs of Kōvalaṉ and Mādavi on the seaside (*kāṉalvari*) are full of lyric charm. Equally charming are the songs sung in honour of the deity at the Aiyyaikōṭṭam, the songs of the *āycciyar* (cowherdesses) in their *kuravaikkūttu*, and the songs of the hill-women in honour of Murugaṉ (Subrahmaṇya).

Though *iyal* and *iśai* are prominent in the pages of the work, the epic contains positive elements which go to make up a dramatic composition, with the result that it can also be styled, appropriately, a *nāṭakakkāppiyam*. Adopting the modern terminology for the classification of dramatic literature, we may say that this epic is a tragi-comedy. The tragic elements preponderate in the story. The separation of Kaṇṇaki from her husband, her ominous dream, the equally fearful dream of Kōvalaṉ, the journey of the couple through wild forests, the unjust execution of Kōvalaṉ, and Kaṇṇaki's inconsolable distress, the Pāṇḍyan's great grief at the injustice perpetrated by him, the plucking out by Kaṇṇaki of one of her breasts, the burning of the city, the death of the Pāṇḍyan king and queen, are all tragic elements in the story. Notwithstanding these tragic elements which evoke the reader's sympathy and tears, the ending is happy. Both the wronged persons attain Heaven in a celestial car surrounded and celebrated by gods.

THE FORM

The form adopted is that of the *kāvya* or *kāppiyam* of Tamil literature. There are excellent descriptions of rivers like the Vaigai and the Kāvēri, of cities like Puhār and Madura, of forms of dancing like the *kuravaikkūttu*, of gods like Viṣṇu, of wild forests, of the celebration of marriages, etc., all affording data for reconstructing the ancient Tamil social life. Iḷangō-Aḍigaḷ himself calls the work in his preface (*padikam*) *pāṭṭuḍaicceyyuḷ* or *uraiyiḍaiyiṭṭa pāṭṭuḍaicceyyuḷ*. This Tamil phrase is a free rendering of the Sanskrit term *campu*. Compositions like this contain at frequent intervals *uraippāṭṭu* (rhetorical prose). A good example of *campu* literature in Tamil is the *Bāratam* of Perumdēvaṉār.

II

THE STORY

In the fifties of the second century A.D. there lived in the city of Puhār, which was the capital city of the great Karikālaccōḻaṉ, two merchant princes who had respectively a son and a daughter. The son went by the name of Kōvalaṉ, and the daughter by that of Kaṇṇaki. At their respective ages of sixteen and twelve, their parents had them married according to the fire-rites prescribed in Vēdic literature. Soon a separate establishment was set up for them and the young couple spent some time together happily. One day when Kōvalaṉ was passing through the busy streets of Puhār, he happened to cast his eyes upon Mādavi, a charming courtesan of the city, who had just won her laurels from the king of the land. Kovalaṉ having fallen in love with her, left his home and lived with the courtesan until he had wasted upon her the whole of his wealth. There then came the festival sacred to Indra, the God of Heaven. All Puhar celebrated it with pomp and splendour. The lovers spent their evenings in the park on the seashore entertaining themselves with music. A song of Mādavi made Kōvalaṉ suspect that she had thoughts of another lover. This caused a change in his feelings towards her. With wounded pride he left her, as he intended, for good. He came home and opened his heart to his sorrow-stricken wife.

He explained the circumstances he was in, and told her of his resolution to leave the city for Madura to earn his livelihood. Kaṇṇaki who was a strict observer of the rules laid down for chaste wives, and who practised them to their very letter, welcomed the suggestion, and sought permission to follow him wherever he might go. He spoke to her of the difficulties of traversing on foot forest belts and mountain-tracts full of wild animals and haunted by evil spirits bent on mischief. All this could not persuade her to stay at home. Her only desire was to share his weal and woe, and he finally assented to her earnest wish.

With Kaṇṇaki, whose only remaining jewels were the pair of anklets, he set out for Madura early before daybreak so that no one might come to know of their whereabouts. His idea was to dispose of a *śilambu* in the bazaar at Madura, and with the capital raised thereby to set up some business. Kōvalaṉ and Kaṇṇaki passed along the northern bank of the Kāvēri towards the west and reached a grove. Here they met Kavundi, the celebrated woman ascetic doing penance, and bowed to her. She offered to accompany them and show them the right path to Madura and they gladly accepted her kind offer. All the three crossed over to the southern bank of the Kāvēri by boat and reached Uṟaiyūr, the other capital of the Cōḻa kingdom.

Having stayed a day there, the three proceeded towards Madura. On the way Kōvalaṉ met a certain Kauśikaṉ who was bringing a message of regret from Mādavi to Kōvalaṉ. Kauśikaṉ communicated to Kōvalaṉ Mādavi's protestations of her love for him. But Kōvalaṉ sent the messenger to his own parents and asked him to deliver the same letter to them so that they might be relieved of their poignant distress at his secret departure. Passing on, the couple and Kavundi reached the river Vaigai and crossing it by boat, they reached the outskirts of the city of Madura. Here they came upon Mādari, a cowherdess of the city, to whom Kavundi introduced Kōvalaṉ and Kaṇṇaki. She was requested to accommodate them until Kōvalaṉ was able to stand on his own legs. To this Mādari agreed, and the couple repaired to her cottage. Kavundi chose to stay outside the city discussing questions of religion and philosophy with sages residing there.

Mādari left Kaṇṇaki in the company of her daughter Aiyai. Helped by Aiyai, Kaṇṇaki prepared dinner for herself and her husband of which the couple partook. Kōvalaṉ then took one of her anklets and went towards the bazaar to sell it. It was an inauspicious hour when he started, but of this he was not aware. In the bazaar he met the state goldsmith to whom he showed the anklet and offered to sell it for a fair price.

This goldsmith, who had stolen the queen's anklet sometime before, thought it a good opportunity to accuse Kōvalaṉ of the theft of the queen's jewel and proclaim himself innocent. He therefore readily consented to Kōvalaṉ's proposal, and leaving him in his cottage, went post-haste to the palace, informed the king that he had found out the thief who had stolen the queen's anklet, and handed it over to the king. Without bestowing a moment's thought on the matter, the king ordered his executioners to behead the thief. Followed by the goldsmith, the executioners came to the cottage where Kōvalaṉ was. Moved by his innocent looks they hesitated at first to carry out the king's order, until the goldsmith treated them to a lecture on the theory and practice of thieving. Thereupon one among the party of executioners, more cruel than his companions, beheaded Kōvalaṉ.

In the meantime Mādari, who noticed evil omens portending danger, arranged for a *kuravaikkūttu* in honour of Viṣṇu and Piṉṉai. The *kūttu* being over, Mādari went to the river for her bath. There she heard people talking about the slaughter of the innocent Kōvalaṉ. She shook with fear, ran home and informed her kith and kin. Noticing the sorrow-stricken faces, and hence feeling uneasy, Kaṇṇaki asked them to give her news of her husband. Though none of them had the heart to break the shocking news, her persistence made one of them yield to her repeated entreaties. The rude shock, and the agony which she could hardly endure distracted her. She raved like a mad woman, fell down on the earth, rose up and sobbed aloud in anguish. Though it was late in the night she went to the bazaar to have a look at her husband. She found him in a pool of blood gushing out of his wounds. Her grief knew no bounds. She cried till she seemed to see Kōvalaṉ rise up to go to Heaven saying to her 'Stay here'.

She could no longer endure the wrong done to her innocent husband. All her grief was now turned into anger against the king. She went to the palace and demanded proper justice at his hands. She narrated her case, proved by her other anklet how the one supposed to have been stolen by Kōvalaṉ was hers and not the queen's, and showed how the goldsmith had deceived him. At this the just and repentant king fell into a swoon which ended in his death. It was no consolation to poor Kaṇṇaki whose innocent husband had been irretrievably wronged. She plucked out her left breast and threw it over the city cursing that the city be consumed by flames. The god of fire brought destruction to all except the Brahman sages, cows, chaste women, children and the aged. The guardian deity of Madura at this time presented herself before Kaṇṇaki and narrated to her how in his previous birth Kōvalaṉ was Barataṉ, in the service of Vasu, king of Śingapura, who had killed an innocent merchant, Śangamaṉ by name, suspecting him to be a spy, and that was why he now had this fate.

Asked as to Kaṇṇaki's future, the deity replied that on the fourteenth day from that hour she would go to Heaven invited by her husband in a celestial car.

Kaṇṇaki thereupon left Madura and proceeding west to the Malaināḍu reached Murugavēḷ-kuṉṟam (the hill sacred to Muruga) which she ascended. There she stood under the shade of a *vēngai* tree to the wonder of the people of the place, most of whom were Kuṟavas. When every one of them was looking at her, Kaṇṇaki left the place in the celestial car for Heaven. This they reported to Śenguṭṭuvaṉ, their king. The poet Śāttaṉār, who was there, narrated the events that had happened in Madura. The queen desired that a temple should be set up in honour of Kaṇṇaki. Śenguṭṭuvaṉ who had been thinking for a long time of leading a military expedition to the north to subdue the refractory chieftains there, resolved to secure a block of stone from the Himalayas to carve out an image of the Pattiṉikkaḍavuḷ as they called her. So he started on his northern expedition through the Nilgiris.

In the meantime there was a famine in the Pāṇḍyan kingdom due to continuous drought. Iḷamjeḻiyaṉ, the Pāṇḍyan at Koṟkai, offered a sacrifice of 1,000 goldsmiths to the Pattiṉikkaḍavuḷ, and the country had plentiful showers of rain. Hearing this, the kings of Kongumaṇḍalam, of Ceylon, and of Uṟaiyūr dedicated temples to Kaṇṇaki and instituted daily worship and festivals. At this time, it may be noted, Gajabāhu was the king of Ceylon and Perunaṟkiḻḻi was the Cōḻa king at Uṟaiyūr.

After defeating the northern kings Kaṉaka and Vijaya. Śenguṭṭuvaṉ brought a stone from the Himalayas and after bathing it in the Ganges returned home. A temple was consecrated to the Pattiṉikkaḍavuḷ and was endowed for daily worship. The consecration ceremony was attended by eminent kings including those of Mālva and Ceylon. After this, on the advice of the Brahman Māḍalaṉ, the king engaged himself in the performance of Yajñas or

Vēdic sacrifices and spent the evening of his life in peace and prayer.

III

ITS PLACE IN THE ŚANGAM WORKS

To find a way out of the tangled forest of South Indian chronology is a very intricate task. This is especially true of the Śangam works. The question of the dates of the Śangam works has been discussed.[1] Roughly speaking the Śangam epoch may be assigned to a period commencing with the fifth century B.C. and ending with the fourth century A.D. The *Śilappadikāram* belongs to this epoch and is an accredited Śangam work, as is also the other work of that class, the *Maṇimēkalai*. Both these belong to the category of the great Epics (*mahākāvyas*) of which five are distinguished. These twin epics, the *Śilappadikāram* and the *Maṇimēkalai*, can be likened in certain respects to the *Rāmāyaṇa* and the *Mahābhārata*, and are invaluable sources for re-contructing the history of the ancient Tamil land.

The date of the classic deserves an independent examination. This epic, which is very ancient in age, is quoted as an authority even by ancient commentators like the commentator of the *Iṟaiyaṉār Ahapporuḷ* and Uraiyāśiriyar (Iḷampūraṉar). In the use of choice words and in terseness of expression the book is unrivalled. Yet the style is simple though polished. Ornate in expression, it has also grace and simplicity. It has already been mentioned that this epic is a treatise on the threefold classification of the Tamil language — Literary Tamil, Music and the Drama. Beginning with the drama, we have *uraippāṭṭu* or rhetorical prose compositions. The varied forms of musical composition such as *kāṉalvari* (sea-song), *vēṭṭuvavari* (hill-song), *āṟṟuvari* (river-song),

[1] V. R. R. Dikshitar, *Studies in Tamil Literature and History*, 2nd ed., 1936.

ūśalvari (song to accompany swinging), and *kandukavari* (song sung by girls while playing with balls) are worthy of note in the pages of the work. The distinguishing traits of the literary Tamil—*veṇbā* and *ahavaṟpā* or *ahaval* —are prominently seen. Of all the metres used in the poem, *ahavaṟpā* or blank verse is the metrical form most frequently used.[1] Thus the *Śilappadikāram* is an excellent example of *ilakkiyam* or Tamil poetry. It may be noted in this connexion that the early works on music and drama have been lost beyond recovery. The *Śilappadikāram* may, however, be said to represent in a way the earlier musical and dramatic pieces. It thus takes a legitimate place among the extant Śangam works and is very valuable to the historian of South India. But the most conclusive argument in respect of the epic's place in the Śangam category is that the friend and companion of the author of the *Śilappadikāram*, Kūlavāṇikaṉ Śīttalai Śāttaṉār, is a Śangam celebrity. And this Śāttaṉār is the reputed author of the *Maṇimēkalai*, which is a continuation of the theme contained in the *Śilappadikāram*. A futile attempt has recently been made to prove that these epics were post-Śangam works.[2] But this militates against the fact that the author of the *Maṇimēkalai* belonged to the same age as poets like Paraṇar[3] and Kapilar. We know that these two are among the most distinguished names mentioned in connexion with the traditional third Śangam. This, above all, assigns to the *Śilappadikāram* a rank among the Śangam works.

One conclusive evidence for the second century A.D.

[1] *Śila.*, preface p. 9; *Tolk.* 'Ceyyul', the gloss of Iḷampūraṇar on *sūtra* 157.

[2] E.g. P. T. Srinivasa Aiyangar's *History of the Tamils*, ch. XXIX; K. N. Sivaraja Pillai's *The Chronology of the Early Tamils*, p. 42. The latter says that he is mainly guided by the literary test.

[3] For Paraṇar's reference to Senguṭṭuvaṉ see *Padiṟr.*, fifth Ten; *Puṟam.*, st. 369; *Aham.*, st. 212, etc.

as the date of the *Śilappadikāram* is the complete silence of the epic with regard to the Pallavas of Kāñci. This epic as well as the *Maṇimēkalai* speaks of Kāñci in more than one place, but does not mention anywhere the Pallavas themselves or any of their kings. The earliest of the Pallava charters—the records in Prākrit—are three in number: the Mayidavolu plate, the Hirahaḍagalli plates, and the British Museum plates. These have been published in the volumes of the *Epigraphia Indica*, and range over a period *circa* A.D. 200-350. This means that we have inscriptional evidence of the early Pallavas and the earliest of them could be dated from A.D. 200.[1] The evidence of Śangam literature shows that, up to the occupation of the city by the Pallavas, Kāñci was one of the northern outposts of the Cōḻa kingdom, and was the capital of the Cōḻa Viceroy. In the age of the *Śilappadikāram* the Cōḻa Viceroy was Toṇḍamāṉ Iḷam-Tiraiyaṉ celebrated in the *Perumpāṇāṟṟuppaḍai* by Uruttiraṉ Kaṇṇaṉār. Iḷam-Tiraiyaṉ was a chief of the Tiraiyar who preceded the Pallavas at Kāñci, and who were subordinate to the Cōḻas in the second century A.D. Thus the *Śilappadikāram* which actually refers to Kāñci, does not mention the Pallavas even indirectly, while subsequent literature represented by the *Tēvāram* and the *Divyaprabandham* often makes references to the Pallava kings. The inference is therefore conclusive that the Pallava kings came to reign at Kāñci after the composition of the *Śilappadikāram*. Otherwise it is difficult to understand the silence of the epic and other Śangam works on the Pallavas or any member of that dynasty.[2]

[1] *Ep. Ind.*, Vol. XV, pp. 246-55, 'Two Pallava Copper-plate Grants', ed. H. Krishna Sastri.

[2] R. Gopalan, *The Pallavas of Kāñci*, p. 9 ff., (Madras University, 1928).

IV

THE DATE OF CERAN ŚENGUṬṬUVAN

A stanza in the *Puṟanāṉūṟu*[1] and a few in the *Ahanāṉūṟu*[2] compared with a reference in the *Śilappadikāram*[3] show that the early history of the Cēras can be carried back to an epoch before the Mahābhārata war. For we hear of one Udiyaṉcēral, a Cēra king who acted as the host to the combatants of that war. An analytical study of the *Padiṟṟuppattu*, so far as the political data contained in it are concerned, furnishes us with ample material to reconstruct the chronology of the three ancient South Indian dynasties, and particularly that of the early Cēras. Of the ten Tens (*Padiṟṟuppattu*), the first and the last have not been traced, and we must congratulate the talented editor, Dr. V. Swaminatha Aiyar, for presenting us with the available eight Tens, all very important as preserving in a nutshell an account of the ancestry of the Cēra kings, to whom these poems have been dedicated. The following is the list of kings as they occur in the *Padiṟṟuppattu*.

1. Imayavarambaṉ (also Kuḍavar Kōmāṉ and Kuḍakkō) Neḍumcēralātaṉ
2. Palyāṉaic-celkeḻu-kuṭṭuvaṉ
3. Kaḷangāykkaṇṇi Nārmuḍiccēralātaṉ
4. Kaḍalpiṟakkōṭṭiya Śenguṭṭuvaṉ
5. Āḍukōṭpāṭṭuccēralātaṉ
6. Śelvakkaḍungō-Vāḻiyātaṉ
7. Perumcēral-Irumpoṟai
8. Iḷamcēral-Irumpoṟai

As regards their relationship the following information is available from the epilogue attached to each of the respective eight Tens. Imayavarambaṉ Neḍumcēralātaṉ is the son of Udiyaṉcēral and Veḷiyaṉ-Vēṇmāḷ Nalliṉi. Palyāṉaic-celkeḻu-kuṭṭuvaṉ is said to be the younger brother

[1] St. 2. [2] St. 65, 168, and 233. [3] Canto xxiii, ll. 55-60.

of Imayavaramban̲. Nārmuḍiccēralātan̲ is the son of Cēralātan̲ and Vēḷāvikkōmān̲ Padumaṉdēvi. Śenguṭṭuvan̲ is said to be the son of Kuḍavarkōmān̲-Neḍumcēralātan̲ and Naṟcōṇai, daughter of Cōḻan̲ Maṇakkiḷḷi. Āḍukōṭpāṭṭuccēralātan̲ is the son of Kuḍakkō-Neḍumcēralātan̲ and Vēḷāvikkōmān̲dēvi. Śelvakkaḍungō is said to be the son of Anduvan̲ and Poṟaiyan̲perumdēvi, that is, the daughter of Orutandai or Orūutandi. Perumcēral is the son of Śelvakkaḍungō and Vēḷāvikkōmān̲ Padumaṉdēvi. Iḷamcēral is said to be the son of Kuṭṭuvan̲ (Perumcēral) Irumpoṟai[1] and Vēṇmāḷ-Anduvan̲ Ceḷḷai, the daughter of Maiyūrkiḻān̲, perhaps the minister of Iḷamcēral.[2]

The genealogy as mentioned in these *padikams* has made Professor S. S. Bharati draw the conclusion that Marumakkattāyam was an ancient practice of the old Cēra monarchs, and the present practice is only a relic of the ancient custom.[3]

As against this inference, Pandit M. Raghava Aiyangar has made out a strong case and proved how the interpretation does not admit of Marumakkattāyam but only of Makkattāyam, of son succeeding father, as in the other parts of the country.[4] The *Śilappadikāram*[5] mentions Vēṇmāḷ as the wife of the Cēra king Śenguṭṭuvan̲, and the full name seems to be Iḷangō-vēṇmāḷ. According to a note to the *padikam* of the fifth Ten, Śenguṭṭuvan̲ had a son by name Kuṭṭuvan̲cēral who was given to Paraṇar, the noted Śangam celebrity, as a gift, in addition to other

[1] Iḷamcēral is the son and not the brother. The expression is similar to Iḷampañcapāṇḍavas meaning, sons of the Pāṇḍavas.

[2] From the *padikam* of the ninth Ten it is seen that a certain Maiyūrkiḻān̲ was the minister of Iḷamcēral. The same *padikam* speaks of a Maiyūrkiḻān̲ as his grandfather. Either the two Maiyūrkiḻān̲s are different, or the grandfather of Iḷamcēral was also his minister.

[3] *Sentamil*, Vol. XXVII, No. 4; see also M. Srinivasa Aiyangar, *Tamil Studies*, p. 103 ff.

[4] *Cēravēndartāyavaḻakku* in Tamil (1930); see also 'Marumakkattāyam and the Sangam Literature', *Z.I.I.*, Vol. IX, No. 3, p. 255 ff.

[5] Canto xxv, l. 5.

presents. Collating all these available materials we can arrive at a tentative genealogy of the early Cēras, and the following table is drawn up for purposes of ready and easy reference.

Paternal line of Śeṅguṭṭuvaṉ

Udiyaṉcēral
- Imayavaramban Neḍumcēralātaṉ =Naṛcōṇai (daughter of Cōḻa king Maṇakkiḷḷi)
  - Seṅguṭṭuvaṉ = Iḷaṅgō-vēṇmāḷ
    - Kuṭṭuvaṉcēral
- Palyāṉaic-celkeḻu-kuṭṭuvaṉ

Maternal line of Śeṅguṭṭuvaṉ

Maṇakkiḷḷi (Cōḻa)
- Naṛcōṇai (daughter) = Imayavaramban Neḍumcēralātaṉ
  - Seṅguṭṭuvaṉ
    - Kuṭṭuvaṉcēral
  - Iḷaṅgō-Aḍigaḷ

Maternal line of other Cēras

Vēḷāvikkōmāṉ
- daughter (No. 1) = Imayavarambaṉ Neḍumcēralātaṉ
  - Nārmuḍiccēral
  - Aḍukōṭpāṭṭuc-cēralātaṉ
- daughter (No. 2) = Selvakkaḍuṅgō-Vāḻiyātaṉ
  - Perumcēral-Irumpoṟai (or Kuṭṭuvaṉ-Irumpoṟai) = Vēṇmāḷ-Anduvaṉ Celḷai
    - Iḷamcēral-Irumpoṟai

Proceeding to find a solution for fixing the date of Śeṅguṭṭuvaṉ, we find that Perumcēralātaṉ (probably Imayavarambaṉ Neḍumcēralātaṉ) was defeated and wounded in the chest at Veṇṇi, otherwise Veṇṇil,[1] by Karikāla.[2]

[1] Identified with Kōyilveṇṇi, a village near modern Mannargudi.

[2] *Aham.*, st. 55; *Puṟam.*, st. 65 (colophon) and st. 66.

The defeat was so crushing that the Cēra king abdicated his throne.[1] The reference in the *Ahanāṉūṟu* is positive evidence for establishing the contemporaneity of Karikāla and Imayavarambaṉ, and Karikāla could not therefore have been the contemporary of Śenguṭṭuvaṉ. In other words, the theory that Karikāla and Śenguṭṭuvaṉ were contemporaries has little to support it. Imayavarambaṉ must have died in the early half of the second century A.D. We know from the *Padiṟṟuppattu* that Imayavarambaṉ and Śenguṭṭuvaṉ reigned for fifty-eight and fifty years respectively. It would appear that Imayavarambaṉ had two queens and four sons, and one of them, Śenguṭṭuvaṉ, was his successor. His brother Iḷangō-Aḍigaḷ became an ascetic. Of the other two, Nārmuḍiccēralātaṉ seems to have been in charge of the northern part of the Kongu kingdom, the region where was the hill Naṉṟā,[2] while Āḍukōṭpāṭṭuccēralātaṉ was in charge of the Kuṭṭanāḍu. The last two were princes ruling under the suzerainty of the emperor reigning from Vañjikkaruvūr.

For purposes of fixing the date of the epic a beginning must be made from the year A.D. 172 or 173 which is the probable year of the foundation of the Pattiṉi temple at the Cēra capital; for Gajabāhu, the king of Ceylon, who attended the consecration ceremony of the temple, came to the throne only in A.D. 171, and we have to assume that he must have visited India after he became king. The question of the Gajabāhu synchronism has not found acceptance with the learned author of the *History of the Tamils*.[3] One argument is that the alternative reading for the word Kayavāgu is Kāval, and if the latter reading were adopted, the edifice based on the Gajabāhu synchronism would fall to the ground. We must emphasize the word *if*.

The editor, who has consulted no fewer than eleven

[1] The term *vaḍakkirundaṉaṉ* in the texts is translated 'committed suicide' by P. T. Srinivasa Aiyangar in *History of the Tamils*, pp. 335-7.

[2] *Padiṟṟ.*, *padikam* to the seventh Ten.

[3] p. 375, ff.

manuscripts of the text and fourteen manuscript copies of the commentary, and whose scientific precision and punctillious care in collating the manuscripts cannot be questioned, has not only adopted Kayavāgu as the correct reading, but has also shown how there are two Gajabāhus mentioned in the *Mahāvamśa* differing in age by a thousand years,[1] and how Gajabāhu I must be the king of Ceylon mentioned in the *Varantarumkādai* as having been present at the festivities held in honour of Pattiṉikkaḍavuḷ by Śenguṭṭuvaṉ.

The *Mahāvamśa*[2] says : 'After Vankanāsikatissa's death, his son Gajabāhukagāmaṇi reigned twenty-two years.' He founded a number of *vihāras* and *stūpas*. Dr. Wilhelm Geiger, the learned translator of the *Mahāvamśa*[3] has furnished in his introduction a list of the ancient kings of Ceylon with the length of their respective reigns both in the Buddhist era and the Christian era. In this list Gajabāhukagāmaṇi figures as the forty-sixth king, ruling from A.D. 171-193.[4] This must have been the Gajabāhu who is celebrated in the *Śilappadikāram*.

It is asked[5] how a devout follower of the Buddha could embrace a new cult like the Pattiṉi cult. The answer is simple. In those days the religion followed by monarchs was cosmopolitan in character. There was not much of sectarian rancour. To the people then, God was one and

[1] For an inscription of Gajabāhu I, 171-193 on the elephants' stables or Ratanapāsāda, see *M.A.S.C.*, Vol. I, No. 2. See also chronological table in B. G. Singe's translation of the second part of the *Mahāvamśa*, p. 20. According to this, Gajabāhu II ascended the throne in A.D. 1142. Cf. *M.A.S.C.*, Vol. II, No. 1.

Cf. *Ep.* Z., Vol. III, No. 1, 'Ceylonese chronology', p. 9. Also H. W. Codrington's *Short History of Ceylon*, pp. 24, 26-34; *C.A.*, Vol. X, p. 115.

This is also the view of investigators on the subject like Seshagiri Sastri, Kanakasabhai, Krishnaswami Aiyangar, and Nilakanta Sastri. It may be noted that Dr. S. K. Aiyangar (*Ancient India*, p. 350) has answered the points raised by E. Hultzsch in *S.I.I.*, Vol. II, No. 3, p. 378, with regard to this question.

[2] Canto xxxv. pp. 254-5.

[3] Pāli Text Society, 1912.

[4] *Dīpa.*, st. 22, 14 and 28. *Mahāvamśa*, Intro. p. xxxviii.

[5] *History of the Tamils*, p. 380.

might be worshipped in any shape or form. In the epoch when there was no nice distinction between the established religion of the land and the dissenting sects like the Jains and the Buddhists, it is no wonder that Gajabāhu built a temple in honour of the Pattiṉikkaḍavuḷ. Among the popular deities in Ceylon, Pattiṉi Dēvi figures as the guardian of female chastity. 'Two wooden images of her and her husband in a cave at the Nikawaewa monastery are supposed to date from the eleventh century.'[1] The most notable of the images of the goddess Pattiṉi Dēvi is an image in bronze, 4 feet 9½ inches in height, discovered in Ceylon and presented to the British Museum in 1830.[2] To deny totally a tradition which receives corroboration from an unexpected quarter, like the Pāli literature of Ceylon, and thus to shake the corner-stone of early South Indian chronology, would be a breach of the historical and critical method. For various reasons into which we need not enter here, the reference in the *Śilappadikāram* cannot be to Gajabāhu II who figures in the history of Ceylon nearly ten centuries after the time of Gajabāhu I. Thus the Gajabāhu synchronism is explained, and the date of the composition of the *Śilappadikāram* settled once for all. It was in the second half of the second century after Christ.

At that time (*circa* A.D. 172) Śenguṭṭuvaṉ was fifty years of age.[3] Therefore, when he started for the north he was forty-seven, as he had spent three years there. In the light of the statement in the *Padiṟṟuppattu* that he ruled for fifty years, it may be taken roughly that he ascended the throne when he was twenty years of age and must have died about A.D. 192. Śenguṭṭuvaṉ must, therefore, have led the northern expedition about A.D. 168, though these estimates cannot be accepted rigidly.

[1] V. A. Smith, *A History of Fine Art in India and Ceylon*, 1911, p. 248. Also H. Parker, *Ancient Ceylon*, Fig. 272.

[2] See frontispiece.

[3] Canto xxviii, ll. 129-30.

That Śenguṭṭuvaṉ took nearly three years for his North Indian expedition is evident from the following. While he was still in the north a certain Brahman, Māḍalaṉ by name, sought the audience of His Majesty, and after his conversation with him, the royal astrologer informed him that it was thirty-two months since the latter left his capital.[1] Again two years before Śenguṭṭuvaṉ left for the north, Maṇimēkalai was in Puhār, and when she returned to Vañji after a five years' tour, it is said that it was three years since Śenguṭṭuvaṉ had left for the north. Without going into further details, we may conclude that Imayavarambaṉ ruled from *circa* A.D. 80-140 and Śenguṭṭuvaṉ from *circa* A.D. 140-192.

V

ŚENGUṬṬUVAṈ'S ACHIEVEMENTS

The fifth Ten of the *Padiṟṟuppattu* is sung in praise of Cēraṉ Śenguṭṭuvaṉ by the poet Paraṇar. Śenguṭṭuvaṉ became the greatest of the Cēra monarchs. From the *padikam* can be gathered some knowledge as to his achievements. These can be categorically mentioned here.

(1) The success over the northern kings in his campaign to the Himalayas to get a stone thereof to carve out an image of the Pattiṉikkaḍavuḷ.

(2) The lifting of cattle from the Iḍumbil forest tracts. It is said that on his return from the northern expedition the king spent some time on the outskirts of this forest.[2]

(3) The defeat of Naṉṉaṉ Vēṇmāṉ or simply Naṉṉaṉ, the chieftain of the Vēḷir, and the occupation of his capital Viyalūr.[3]

[1] Canto xxvii, l. 149. [2] Canto xxviii, l. 118.
[3] Canto xxvii, l. 115; *Aham.*, st. 97, 'Māmūlaṉār'.

(4) The overthrow of a confederacy of nine Cōḻas at Nērivāyil[1] which was near the southern gateway of the ancient Uṟaiyūr.[2]

(5) The overthrow of seven kings and the wearing of their respective seven garlands in his crown in commemoration of his heroic deed.[3]

(6) His success over the Kongar[4] who can be identified with the Gangas, also called Kongudeśarājākkaḷ. During this encounter Koḍuhūr was completely devastated as the *Padiṟṟuppattu* has it.[5] There is a Koḍuhūrnāḍu today in the division of Puṉṉāḍu of the Mysore state.[6]

(7) His successful naval engagements and specially the battle of Mōhūr[7] where the *vēmbu*[8] or margosa tree of Paḻaiyaṉ was destroyed. It may be noted in passing that his naval engagements were so striking and decisive that he earned the title of Kaḍalpiṟakkōṭṭiya Vēlkeḻukuṭṭuvaṉ.[9] This can appropriately be compared with the statement[10] made at different places in the *Śilappadikāram*.

Most of these are corroborated by the *Śilappadikāram* which gives a detailed account of his expedition to the

[1] Cantos xxviii, ll. 116-7: xxvii, ll. 118-23.

[2] *Anc. Ind.*, p. 95; also the commentary of Arumpadavuraiyāśiriyar on *Sila.*, canto xxviii, l. 117.

[3] Canto xxviii, l. 169; *Padiṟr.*, st. 45. In these places he is called Eḷumuḍimārpa.

[4] Canto xxv, ll. 152-5.

[5] *Padikam* to the fifth Ten.

[6] See M. Raghava Aiyangar, *Cēraṉ Śenguṭṭuvaṉ*, pp. 28-9; also *Ind. Ant.*, 1889, p. 369.

[7] Canto xxvii, ll. 124-6. *Padiṟṟ.*, st. 44, 49.

[8] The reference to the wearing of the garland of margosa goes to prove that Mōhūr Paḻaiyaṉ was an ally of the Pāṇḍyan king and more probably a general of his. (*Maduraikkāñji*, ll. 507-8. *Aham.*, st. 346.)

[9] *Padiṟṟ.*, st. 41, 45, 46.

[10] e.g. முந்நீரி னுட்புக்கு மூவாக் கடம்பெறிந்தான் canto xvii, 'Uḷvarivāḻttu', 3. See canto xxviii, l. 135; canto xxix, 'Ūsalvari', st. 1.

north to secure a block of stone to make the image of the Goddess of Chastity, and if we are to believe the account in the epic, this was the last of his achievements; for Māḍalaṉ has drawn attention[1] to all the six achievements mentioned above.

The poet Paraṇar refers to five of these seven achievements. The two, which are not mentioned by him, are his northern expedition to get a stone for the Pattiṉi, and his success at the battle of Nērivāyil. If we place his achievements in chronological order these two were his last, and the northern expedition was the last of all. It would be appropriate to say that when Paraṇar sang of this Cēra, he had not undertaken these things. These deeds were done after Paraṇar sang the *Padiṟṟuppattu.* From the absence of any mention by Paraṇar of these last two of his achievements, an endeavour has been made to distinguish Vēlkeḻukuṭṭuvaṉ from Śenguṭṭuvaṉ.[2] And in this the correspondence of the five incidents, which marked the earlier activities of the king, has been ignored, with what valid reasons we cannot see. In the writer's opinion, Vēlkeḻukuṭṭuvaṉ is another name for Śenguṭṭuvaṉ.

VI

AN ESTIMATE OF HIS CHARACTER

Bold and powerful, Śenguṭṭuvaṉ was able to bring under his control not only his own neighbours, the Pāṇḍya and the Cōḻa, but also to carry his conquest so far north as to earn the title of Imayavarambaṉ (literally 'one, the territorial limits of whose empire extended to the Himalayas'). We know his father had carried his arms up to the distant Himalayas and hence came to be distinguished as Imayavarambaṉ Neḍumcēralātaṉ. Already mention has been made of the achievements which

[1] Canto xxviii, ll. 114-22.

[2] *The Chronology of the Early Tamils*, pp. 124-5.

Senguṭṭuvaṉ had to his credit, and which entitle him to be ranked with the great emperors of Ancient India. We shall here call attention to a few outstanding traits of his character.

The rather horrid detail of his having made the women-folk of Paḻaiyaṉ drag the margosa tree with a rope made of their twisted hair[1] may be dismissed as a poetic exaggeration, though there may be truth in the statement that he made the northern kings carry the stone for the Pattiṉi on their heads. These details and especially the fact of his making prisoners of the vanquished and the retreating foes, which evoked scathing comments from the Pāṇḍya and the Cōḻa sovereigns of his time, go to prove that Śenguṭṭuvaṉ was too severe an avenger of wrongs. The above incidents smack of the *asura* form of warfare so eloquently described in the *Kauṭalīya Arthaśāstra*.[2]

Notwithstanding these incidents we find the king to be God-fearing and possessing a religious bent of mind. He was superstitious and had faith in astrology and astronomy. This is borne out by the fact that he set out on his northern expedition at an auspicious hour. That he was religious is seen from his prayers in the temples of Śiva and Viṣṇu on the eve of his historic march to the north.[3]

Besides, he was a patron of arts and letters. He spent his time in amusements which consisted of dancing and singing. It is said that a number of these dancers went along with him to the north. That this was an ancient war-practice is seen from the *Rāmāyaṇa*, where it is said that actors and dancing-masters followed the army of Śatrughna.[4] He rewarded learned men with presents, some of which were invaluable. The gifts received by Paraṇar and Māḍalaṉ may be quoted as instances in point. Śenguṭṭuvaṉ had a fine artistic mind as is seen from the

[1] *Padikam* to the fifth Ten.

[2] For details see *Ar. Śās.*, Bk. xii, §1; also V. R. R. Dikshitar, *The Mauryan Polity*, 1932, p. 129.

[3] Canto xxvi, ll. 54-66.

[4] Bk. vii, ch. 64, st. 3.

fact that he went all the way to the Himalayas in order to fetch a good stone to carve out an image of Kaṇṇaki.[1] That he was a follower of the established religion of the land and that he was a Kṣatriya by caste are evident from the fact that he engaged himself in the performance of Vēdic sacrifices, after the temple was constructed and consecrated to Kaṇṇaki. From this time until his death it appears that he took to a life of ease and peace, penance and prayer, his mind being centred on the study and practice of *dharma*.[2]

He was a great soldier and a bold warrior. The prowess of his arms was felt throughout the Tamil land, the Cōḻa and Pāṇḍya being his tributary allies. He carried his sword as far as the Ganges, and brought the whole of India under his suzerainty. According to the *Harihara Caturanga*, a manuscript on War written by the minister of Pratāparudra, the Kabanda engages in a dance, usually known as the devil dance, whenever a thousand *śūras* fall dead on the field of battle, or when a *śūra* kills one thousand able heroes in a battle. Viewed in this light, and from the fact that the Kabanda danced his dance in glee, blessing Śenguṭṭuvaṉ for the sumptuous food for him and his companions, it transpires that Śenguṭṭuvaṉ was a *śūra* and a *vīra*. With unlimited power at his disposal and being a vigorous ruler, Śenguṭṭuvaṉ was able to keep peace in his vast and diversified empire for a full half-century. This would in itself be ample proof of his greatness. No doubt he is the most memorable figure in the history of ancient Tamil India.

VII

KARIKĀLA IN THE *ŚILAPPADIKĀRAM*

Another king much celebrated by Iḷangō-Aḍigaḷ next only to Śenguṭṭuvaṉ, is the Cōḻa king Karikāla. If we

[1] Canto xxv, ll. 115-31.

[2] Canto xxx, ll. 170 ff.

are to believe the account in the *Porunarāṟṟuppaḍai*[1] Karikāla was a posthumous child and son of Uruvappahrēr-Iḷanjēṭcenni. He began to reign when he was a mere child. It is said that in the battle of Veṇṇi, Imayavaramban was wounded and the victory was won by the boy Karikāla.[2] His was a benevolent form of administration.[3] His interest in irrigation and consequently in agriculture is seen from his construction of embankments for the Kāvēri as testified to by the Leyden grant.[4] For this work, it is said that thousands of Ceylonese labourers were employed.

The text of the *Śilappadikāram* contains three references to Karikāla.[5] The first reference is to his military prowess. Here he is called Tirumāvaḷavan, which term, it is worthy of note, occurs in the *Paṭṭiṉappālai* (l. 299) of Kaḍiyalūr Uruttirankaṇṇanār who was the recipient of 1,600,000 gold pieces at the hands of Karikāla (ll. 19-21). This internal evidence establishes beyond doubt the contemporaneity of the poet and the king, a chief plank in determining the date of Karikāla. The second reference gives him the full name of Karikālvaḷavan by which term the *Puṟanāṉūṟu 66* mentions him. In the third reference in the text referred to above, we have the story of Karikāla's daughter who, finding her husband, the ruler of Vañji, being washed away by the floods, plunged courageously into the waters and rescued him by the power of her chastity. It is unfortunate that we have no more details about this incident, not even the names of that daughter and her husband.

An instance of his military prowess can be said to be the carving of the bow emblem on the Himalayas and the consequent overthrowing of the Arya monarchs of the

[1] ll. 130-48. [2] *Aham.*, st. 246; cf. *Maṇi.*, canto iv, ll. 107-8.

[3] *Paṭṭiṉappālai*, ll. 283-4.

[4] J. Burgess and Natesa Sastri, *Tam. and Sans. Ins.*, No. 29, pp. 204-24. See also *Anc. Ind.*, p. 349.

[5] Cantos v, ll. 90-104; vi, ll. 159-60; xxi, l. 11 ff.

north. This march was prompted by the fact of the intrusion of the northern kings into South India. As if to corroborate this statement the *Śilappadikāram* elsewhere evidences the fact that Śenguṭṭuvaṉ was an ally of Avanti (Ujjain in Mālva), and of the kings of Vajra and Magadha. We have records, literary and epigraphical, which testify to such invasions during the epoch of the Nandas and the Mauryas. There was a reaction. Powerful southern kings like Karikāla, Imayavaramban Neḍumcēralātaṉ and Śenguṭṭuvaṉ led expeditions to the north and their unqualified victories stemmed the tide of political invasions from the north for the time being; for we know Samudragupta carried his victorious arms to the very south. The extant commentaries on the epic regard Karikāla as the contemporary of Śenguṭṭuvaṉ, the hero of the Vañjikkāṇḍam of the epic. The commentators say that the Cōḻa king under reference in the Puhārkāṇḍam and even later was Karikālaccōḻaṉ.[1] But this militates against the indications furnished by the text of the *Śilappadikāram*. That a certain king by name Karikāla lived, and that he was an ancient monarch is testified to us by the anthologies of the *Puṟanāṉūṟu* and the *Ahanāṉūṟu*, besides other Śangam works. Here are celebrated the achievements of the Cōḻa Karikāla, and if we compare these achievements with those referred to in the *Śilappadikāram*, it is just possible that the Cōḻa under reference is no other than Karikāla.

In describing the two achievements of Karikāla—the march to the Himalayas, and the festival of bathing in the first freshes[2] of the Kāvēri, the poet refers to them as past incidents by the significant expression *annāḷ*, making us infer that Karikāla lived a little before the epic was composed, and not very far removed from the date of its composition. The next question arises as to who this

[1] *Arumpadavurai*, canto iii, l. 11; also gloss of Aḍiyārkkunallār on cantos i, ll. 65-8, v, l. 212, and vi, l. 15.

[2] Canto vi, ll. 159-60.

Karikāla was, and what was his relationship to Cēraṉ Śenguṭṭuvaṉ. In the *padikam*, the prologue to the poem, Śenguṭṭuvaṉ's mother is said to be a daughter of the Cōḻa king, and her name was Naṟcōṇai. According to the *Padiṟṟuppattu* (the fourth Ten) there was one Cōḻa Maṇakkiḷḷi. His daughter must be the mother of Śenguṭṭuvaṉ and her name was Naṟcōṇai. Maṇakkiḷḷi in his turn must have been the son of Karikāla. In the light of this relationship, Karikāla must have been the maternal great-grandfather of Śenguṭṭuvaṉ and not his grandfather as some scholars would have it. If the latter relationship can be accepted, Maṇakkiḷḷi would stand by himself, and it would be difficult to find for him a proper place in the genealogical list. Hence it stands to reason that Karikāla must have lived a generation before the age of Śenguṭṭuvaṉ, and could not therefore have been his contemporary.[1]

Incidentally we may remark that the Karikāla of the *Śilappadikāram* or of the Śangam works has nothing to do with the Karikāla represented to be a contemporary of Trilōcana Pallava and Cālukya Vijayāditya of the early fifth century A.D.[2] It is still a moot question who this Trilōcana was and when he lived.[3] Even if his date and identity were established, and there is no reliable testimony to establish it, there is nothing to prevent another Karikāla having flourished in Puhār a few centuries later. If the reference in the *Akanāṉūṟu*[4] has any significance at all, it shows, as has already been said, the contemporaneity of Imayavarambaṉ Neḍumcēralātaṉ and Karikāla. Though

[1] Prof. K. A. Nilakanta Sastri in his learned study of Karikāla accepts that the figure of Karikāla is, to start with, thoroughly realistic and historical, and indicates his view that Senguṭṭuvaṉ came at least half a century after Karikāla, if not earlier. (*Studies in Cōḻa History and Administration*, pp. 37, 49-50.)

[2] *Contra* P. T. Srinivasa Iyengar, *History of the Tamils*, pp. 382-7; Dr. N. V. Ramanayya, *Trilōcana Pallava*.

[3] For Krishna Sastri's opinion, see *Ep. Ind.*, Vol. X, p. 58, n. 2.

[4] St. 55.

we cannot definitely mark out the chronological limits of Karikāla's career, it is reasonable to assume that he lived at the commencement of the second century A.D. It seems to be certain that at the accession of Śenguṭṭuvaṉ to the Cēra throne (*circa* A.D. 140) Karikāla was dead, and Maṇakkiḷḷi was reigning. For, according to the account preserved in the *Śilappadikāram*, Śenguṭṭuvaṉ had to interfere in the disputed election to the throne of the Cōḷas,[1] and it needs no stretch of the imagination to deduce that this was the consequence of the death of Maṇakkiḷḷi's son. The conclusion is irresistible that the duration of the reigns of Karikāla and Maṇakkiḷḷi was comparatively short. According to the evidence cited by the *Uraipeṟu-kaṭṭurai* it was Perumkiḷḷi or Perunaṟkiḷḷi that succeeded Maṇakkiḷḷi, or probably his son Neḍumkiḷḷi, and was reigning at Uṟaiyūr at the time of the consecration of the Pattiṉi temple.

From this foregoing evidence the following genealogical list of the early Cōḷas of the first and second centuries A.D. can be drawn.

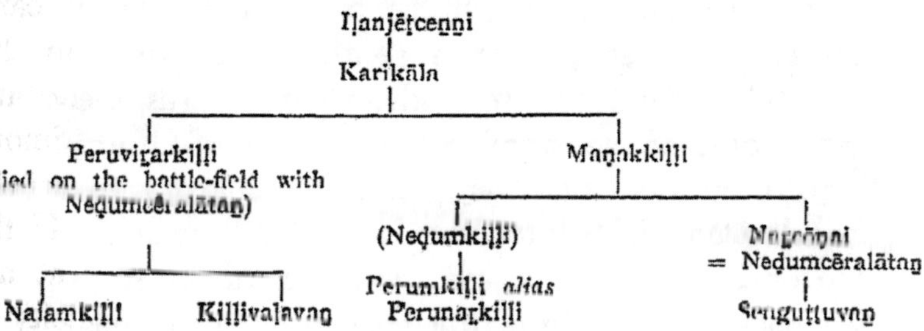

VIII

THE POLITICAL CONDITION OF NORTH INDIA

The *Śilappadikāram* also gives an insight into the political condition of North India in the first three centuries of the Christian era. This was the dark period of

[1] Canto xxvii, ll. 118-23.

Indian History so far as North India was concerned. But the recent researches of Dr. K. P. Jayaswal in his *History of India, A.D. 150-350,* have shed much light and lifted up the veil of gloom. It was only under the Guptas that North India regained its old position of prestige and pre-eminence. During that period, which extended for more than two centuries, there was no towering personality of prowess and valour to meet a strong foe like Śenguṭṭuvaṉ. The whole region was divided into a number of petty principalities over each of which was a chieftain. It is said that there were as many as one thousand chieftains whom Śenguṭṭuvaṉ had to encounter single-handed.[1] Though this number is an exaggeration, it demonstrates that there were a good number of small and independent states. Apparently, these different chiefs were enjoying autonomy. The principal kingdoms mentioned in the epic were Avanti, Vajra, Magadha and Mālva.[2] We know by their gifts of choice presents that the first three acknowledged the overlordship of Karikāla. The king of Mālva was an ally of Śenguṭṭuvaṉ. Some of them became jealous of the arms of the neighbouring monarchs. Hearing that a south Indian king like the powerful Śenguṭṭuvaṉ was advancing towards their kingdoms, some of the prominent minor rulers, Uttiraṉ, Vicittiraṉ, Uruttiraṉ, Bairavaṉ, Cittiraṉ, Śingaṉ, Tanuttiraṉ, and Śivētaṉ, joined together under the common leadership of Kaṉaka and Vijaya, and went to meet Śenguṭṭuvaṉ encamped far from the north of the Ganges.[3] The scene of action mentioned is Kuyilāluvam.

The political situation in the north was quite favourable to the south Indian conqueror. The Āndhras were in the position of allies. Kaniṣka, the other powerful king, was already dead. The smaller chieftains were not strong enough to offer a bold front to the strong arms of

[1] Canto xxv, ll. 160-6.

[2] Canto v, ll. 99 ff.

[3] Canto xxvi, ll. 180-6.

a conquering monarch like Śeṅguṭṭuvaṉ. The result was a crushing defeat for the northerners. Excepting those who had been slain and who had fled from the field of battle in fear and in different disguises, other important leaders were captured as prisoners of war, taken to the distant south as a mark of humiliation, and thrown into prison after being shown to Śeṅguṭṭuvaṉ's brother-monarchs, the Pāṇḍya and the Cōḻa.

It would not be out of place to refer here to the Yavana-nāḍu and the Mālva region which find mention in the *Śilappadikāram*. According to the *padikam* of the second Ten of the *Padiṟṟuppattu*, Imayavarambaṉ put the Yavanas to disgrace by pouring ghee over their heads. The Yavanas are mentioned frequently in Tamil literature including the *Śilappadikāram*.[1] These were originally foreign traders with whom the Tamils had commercial transactions. But by the time of Śeṅguṭṭuvaṉ they had settled in India and, according to the *Śilappadikāram*, had their own flourishing and independent *nāḍu*, probably the Indus region.[2] They seem to have been very wealthy for diamonds formed part of the tribute paid by them. It appears that they acknowledged the over-lordship of Śeṅguṭṭuvaṉ by paying tribute to him.

Mention is again made of the aid given by Nūṟṟuvar-Kaṉṉar. The late Mr. Kanakasabhai identified them with the Śātakarṇi.[3] According to the version in the epic these were apparently a class of people having their residence in the Ganges tracts. It is said that they helped Śeṅguṭṭuvaṉ with boats to cross the Ganges.[4] The context does not warrant it to be the action of a particular individual but a group of persons. If the reference is to a certain

[1] Canto xxix, 'Ūśalvari', st. 3; and canto xxviii, l. 141.

[2] See in this connexion V. A. Smith, *The Early History of India*, 4th ed., revised by S. M. Edwardes, 1924, pp. 462-3.

[3] *The Tamils 1800 Years Ago*, p. 7.

[4] Canto xxvi, l. 176.

Śātakarṇi[1] it must be Śiva Śrī Pulumāyi (A.D. 163-170). In fact the neutrality or rather the alliance of the Āndhras was a preliminary condition for the success of the northern expedition of the Cēra monarch. That the Āndhras conquered Magadha and established an All-India empire cannot be gainsaid. Light comes from an unexpected quarter which helps us to identify Bālakumāra and Vijaya. In this connexion Ptolemy's reference to Baleokourous is of capital importance. Baleokourous is perhaps a corrupt form of Bālakumāra. Him Ptolemy refers to as a contemporary ruling prince about A.D. 160. From the fact that Bālakumāra belonged to a collateral line of the Āndhras it can be inferred that he was an ally of Śenguṭṭuvaṉ. A certain Śātakarṇi was the imperial ruler at this time. He was perhaps Yajñaśri Śātakarṇi or Pulumāyi. According to the account of the *Matsya Purāṇa*, Yajñaśri was succeeded by Vijaya, a usurper. If we are to believe the epic account, this Vijaya was the son of Bālakumāra. What is remarkable is the coincidence of dates, which fixes Śenguṭṭuvaṉ in the latter half of the second century A.D.[2]

Before we close this section attention may be drawn to the futile attempt made by some scholars to identify Kaṉaka and Vijaya with Kaniṣka and Vijayakīrti of Khotan. According to Tibetan sources, shortly after A.D. 120, an expedition against India was undertaken by Kanika in connexion with Vijayakīrti king of Khotan and the king of Guzan. This Kanika is identified with Kaniṣka; but as Prof. F. W. Thomas points out[3] this is in conflict with Tārānātha's statement. According to the Professor, Kaniṣka lived in the Mauryan epoch. If on

[1] According to Pandit M. Raghava Aiyangar the king of Mālva is under reference especially from the fact that he was present at the installation of the Pattiṉidēvi. (For a temple of Pattiṉi in E. Mālva, see T. G. Aravamudhan, *The Kāvēri, the Maukharis and the Sangam Age*, pp. 41-2.)

[2] See K. G. Sesha Iyer, *I.H.Q.*, Vol. I.

[3] *Ind. Ant.*, Vol. XXXII, 1903, p. 349.

the other hand, Kaniṣka is identified with king Kanika, then Kanika 'must have started on his career from the Khotan country'. The evidence of the *Kalpanāmaṇḍiṭikā* and of the *Mahārājakanikalēkha* points in the same direction. It is also to be noted that at the time of the expedition of Vijayakīrti to India, the ruling prince in Khotan was Vijayasimha. Last but not least is the tradition that Kaniṣka left India after his conquest and went back to Khotan. Excepting the accidental identity of the names Kaṉaka and Vijaya, other events connected with them have no bearing on the historical data furnished by the *Śilappadikāram*.[1] Vāsiṣka had succeeded[2] Kaniṣka in A.D. 152. If Chinese historical sources which mention the history of western countries down to A.D. 125 are to be believed, we have to take it that Kaniṣka rose to power after A.D. 125; for he is not mentioned in the Chinese books. It is impossible by any stretch of imagination for a Khotan prince to invade, conquer India up to the Ganges—for according to the *Śilappadikāram* the battle was fought on the banks of the Ganges—and to found an empire. It could not stop with this. Having firmly established himself, he heard of the distant Tamil kings and spoke slightingly of their prowess. All this in the course of less than twenty-five years is an impossibility. Hence this identification cannot stand a critical examination.

IX

THE POLITICAL CONDITION OF SOUTH INDIA

From the foregoing account we have a rough estimate of the political condition of the Tamil land at the beginning of the Christian era. The three powerful kings were the Cēra, the Cōḻa, and the Pāṇḍya. The Pallavas of

[1] *C.I.I.*, Vol. II, Pt. I, 1929, 'Kharōshṭhī Inscriptions', by Sten Konow, Intro., p. lxxvff.

[2] According to inscriptional evidence; ibid. p. lxxviii.

Kāñci were yet to come. Wars among these states were frequent. Often two kingdoms joined together against the third.

THE CĒRA KINGDOM

In the section on geographical data an attempt has been made to locate the *nāḍus* of the ancient Cēra kingdom. These were broadly classified into the *malaināḍu* and the *kaḍalmalaināḍu*. The *malaināḍu* (literally, mountainous country) was the Kongunāḍu, a part of which comprised the territory now occupied by the Salem and Coimbatore districts. Here was the famous capital city Vañjikkaruvūr. Here the Kollis and the Ānamalai range are the chief hills, and it may be remarked in passing that the Ānamalais are said to contain lofty peaks. The districts of Malayāḷa (the territory covering modern Malabar) were known as *kaḍalmalaināḍu* (region of seas and mountains). Here the chief divisions were Kuṭṭanāḍu,[1] Kuḍanāḍu and the Pūḻināḍu. The term *kuṭṭa* means lowlands and apparently the reference is to the backwaters of the Malabar region. Probably it extended from Cranganore to modern Trivandrum. The Kuḍanāḍu covered the territory from opposite the Palghat gap to South Kanara and Coorg. The region of the Poṟaiyaṉ, (literally, small hilly tracts), extended from Palghat to the Kongunāḍu proper.

The Cēra king was known generally as Kuḍavarkōmāṉ or the lord of the western region. His other titles were Kuṭṭuvaṉ, Kongaṉ, Pūḻiyan, Poṟaiyan, etc. This extensive Cēra kingdom, infested here and there by lofty hills, could not have been ruled directly by the central authority. If we analyse the available data, the inference forces itself on us that these different *nāḍus* were the various divisions of the empire, each division under the charge of a governor or viceroy who was appointed by and

[1] *Padiṟṟ.*, glossary, p. 168.

who owed allegiance to the Cēra king reigning at Vañjikkaruvūr. From the nature of the materials before us, it is not possible to say when these *nāḍus* were conquered and by whom. But at the time when the *Śilappadikāram* was composed, or even long before it, these *nāḍus* formed part and parcel of the Cēra kingdom. By extending their mighty empire, the Cēras occasionally earned the titles of Puhār-Śelva and Imayavaramba. The Cēra state had international relations, or more appropriately inter-state relations, not only with its immediate neighbours, but also with distant rulers. The enemy kings were conquered, and often their states were annexed. Sometimes the defeated monarchs were reinstated under certain conditions. At the time of which we are speaking, the Cēra kingdom was the most powerful and the most wealthy of the Tamil kingdoms.

THE CŌḶA KINGDOM

At the commencement of the story in the *Śilappadikāram*, the ruler of the Cōḷa kingdom was Kuṇavarkōmāṉ, and the kingdom had two capitals Uṟaiyūr and Puhār. The ruler of Uṟaiyūr was Maṇakkiḷḷi or more probably his son Neḍumkiḷḷi. According to the *Maṇimēkalai*, Māvaṉkiḷḷi or Kiḷḷivaḷavaṉ was the ruler of Puhār. His younger brother was Iḷamkiḷḷi (also Nalamkiḷḷi). There was a civil war between the Uṟaiyūr and Puhār Kiḷḷis. The most important battle was fought at Kāriyāṟu where Neḍumkiḷḷi was slain by Iḷamkiḷḷi. Neḍumkiḷḷi, it may be remembered, was the uncle of Śenguṭṭuvaṉ, and he had a son Perumkiḷḷi or Perunaṟkiḷḷi. The succession was disputed, and Śenguṭṭuvaṉ had to interfere. In this connexion he had to overthrow a confederacy of nine Cōḷas, and ultimately he succeeded in enthroning his uncle's son Perumkiḷḷi. From this it is reasonable to assume that, besides the two capitals, there were other small semi-independent states within the Cōḷa kingdom where minor chieftains reigned, but all of whom acknowledged the overlordship of the Cōḻa at the capital. It is worthy of note that the Cōḻamaṇḍalam extended as far as Kāñci, which belonged to Karikāla as provided by independent testimony.[1]

The importance of Puhār was not long-lived. Anticipating the forthcoming devastation of the city, the Būta at the Būtacatukkam, which was brought from Indra's abode by Mucukunda, was removed to Vañji by the Cēra king.[2] The destruction of Puhār by the erosion of the sea was effected during the period between the time when Maṇimēkalai left Puhār on a tour to Maṇipallavam and other places, and her return after nearly five years. This was probably in the year A.D. 170. Notwithstanding the ruin of the city, Puhār continued to be the capital, though diminished in importance. Once more Uṟaiyūr rose to prominence as the chief seat of the Cōḻa monarchs. At the time of the establishment of the Kaṇṇaki temple at Vañji, the Cōḻa ruler was Perunaṟkiḷḷi (also Perumkiḷḷi)[3] who also had a temple built for her at Uṟaiyūr, his capital.

THE PĀṆḌYAN KINGDOM

Proceeding to speak about the Pāṇḍyan kingdom, Madura was flourishing as the capital of Āriyappaḍaitanda Neḍuñjeḻiyaṉ.[4] It was a busy centre of trade and commerce and attracted even people like Kōvalaṉ and Kaṇṇaki. But the city was not to flourish long. Neḍuñjeḻiyaṉ ordered the unjust execution of the innocent Kōvalaṉ and this cost the king's life and the destruction of the city. The ancient Pāṇḍyan kingdom had another capital at Koṟkai. From the *Uraiperukaṭṭurai* it is seen that at Koṟkai, was reigning Veṟrivēṟceḻiyaṉ (also Iḷamjeḻiyaṉ) at the time when Śeṅguṭṭuvaṉ was in the north.

[1] *Maṇi.*, canto xxviii, ll. 168-72. [2] *Sila.*, Canto xxviii, ll. 147-8.

[3] *Uraiperukaṭṭurai*, l. 4.

[4] *Kaṭṭurai* at the end of the 'Maduraikkāṇḍam'; also Āriyappaḍaitanda Neḍuñjeḻiyaṉ.

Iḷamjeḻiyan was the younger brother of Āriyappaḍaitanda Neḍuñjeḻiyaṉ or simply Neḍuñjeḻiyaṉ. The latter was a man of letters,[1] and was a patron of literature. During his reign Koṟkai was the seat of the Yuvarāja who was the king's own brother. The latter was crowned king while Śenguṭṭuvaṉ was absent in the north.[2] Finding his country suffering from a disastrous famine, he ordered the sacrifice of a thousand goldsmiths as an offering in honour of the Goddess of Chastity installed in his capital. He was also known as Veṟṟivēṟceḻiyaṉ.[3] It is believed that after he became king he took the title of Naṉmāṟaṉ. Naṉmāṟaṉ had a son Neḍuñjeḻiyaṉ of Talaiyālangāṉam fame and a grandson of Ukkirapperuvaḻudi.[4] This Peruvaḻudi with the attribute *Kāṉappērtanda* was a friend and contemporary of Perunaṟkiḷḷi (Rājasūyamvēṭṭa) and the Cēra Mārivenkō.[5]

OTHER KINGDOMS

In the above outline of the political condition of South India mention has been made of the three chief Tamil kingdoms. But a study of the Śangam works, especially the *Puṟanāṉūṟu* and the *Ahanāṉūṟu*, points to a number of petty kingdoms ruled by chieftains of minor importance besides these three major kingdoms. There is not enough material to deal in detail with these chiefs. But a reference has to be made to the Kongiḷamkōśar, or simply the Kōśar, whose country went by the name of Tuḷunāḍu;[6] and these Kōśar can be identified with the Satyaputras of the Aśōkan inscriptions.[7] According to

[1] See his verse in *Puram.*, st. 183.

[2] Canto xxvii, ll. 114-38.

[3] ibid., ll. 127-34.

[4] *Puṟam.*, st. 76 ff.; *Aham.*, st. 36. Cf. the Siṉṉamanūr copper-plate.

[5] *Puṟam.*, st. 367 where the poetess Avvaiyār celebrates these three kings.

[6] *Aham.*, st. 15.

[7] See paper by V. R. R. Dikshitar on 'The Kōśar' read to the All-India Oriental Conference, Patna, 1930, also his article in *Indian Culture*, Vol. I, Pt. I., Calcutta, 1934; also in Pt. III, the contribution entitled 'Who were the Satyaputras?'.

3

the testimony of literature, there was one Kongunāḍu which seems to have been comprised of the Cēra kingdom, the Tuḷunāḍu, and the country of Gangar and Kaṭṭiyar.

Our investigation would be incomplete if we did not mention other countries and peoples, mostly of South India, which were antagonistic to Śenguṭṭuvaṉ. These are the Kalingar, the Karunāṭar, the Bangalar, the Gangar, and the Kaṭṭiyar.[1]

The Kalingar were the people of Kalinga, whose history can be traced back by independent testimony to the later Vēdic and epic periods. It continued to be a powerful kingdom during the time of the Nandas and the Mauryas. We get a glimpse of the ancient history of Kalinga in the *Śilappadikāram*. There were two famous cities, Śingapura[2] and Kapilapura, ruled over respectively by Vasu and Kumara, of cognate relationship. Civil wars between them were common.[3]

The Karunāṭar, on the other hand, were the Kaṉṉaḍa people who are described as being hard-hearted and fierce. Karunāḍu means elevated country. Possibly the reference is to the people who occupied the plateau which was above sea-level. It may possibly refer to the region now occupied by the Mysore country.[4] The Śangam literature knows again of a people called Vaḍukar who are also partly identified with the Kanarese people and partly with the Telugus. The term simply means 'people of the north' and hence must be the north of Tamiḻagam. Who the Bangalar were it is difficult to say; but it may be that they were the people of Bengal. We know from the

[1] Canto xxv, ll. 156-7.

[2] R. D. Bannerji relates a legend that led to the foundation of Singapura which became the capital of northern Kalinga. He is inclined to identify this city with the village of Singur in the Hooghly district of SW. Bengal. *History of Orissa*, Vol. I, p. 49.

[3] Canto xxiii, l. 138 ff. See also *Maṇi.*, canto xxvi, l. 15 ff.

[4] For the derivation of Karunāṭar see *Mysore Gazetteer*, Vol. I, pp. 254-7.

Buddhist legends that there was intercourse by sea between Bengal and Ceylon at least from the fifth century B.C. when Vijaya is said to have landed here. It is reasonable to suppose that the route lay through the Coromandel coast. No doubt its effects were felt by the Tamil countries as well. The Gangar can be said to be the people of Gangavāḍi whose capital was Talakad. The Kaṭṭiyar are often mentioned in the Śangam works,[1] and they seem to have occupied the territory lying to the south of the Vaḍukarbūmi. Apparently these were small chieftains who enjoyed independent rule. During the days of the Vijayanagar empire their descendants were ruling over the territory now occupied by the Salem district.[2]

CEYLON

The mention of Gajabāhu, the king of Ceylon, as having been present at the installation ceremony of the Goddess of Chastity is significant from more than one standpoint. It shows the frequent intercourse between Ceylon and South India. According to the *Mahāvamśa* the invasions by Tamil kings into the kingdom of Ceylon were pretty frequent, and were resented by the Ceylonese. We hear of an old woman complaining to Gajabāhu that among the 12,000 persons taken away by Karikāla for making an embankment on the Kāvēri, was her only son. Notwithstanding this, the Ceylon king's relations with Śenguṭṭuvaṉ were cordial. As became an ally, he was present at the celebration of his victorious march to North India. 'South India and Ancient Ceylon' is a fascinating subject of study for a student of South Indian History, and it is hoped that a fuller treatment of the subject will be undertaken in the future.[3]

[1] *Aham.*, st. 44 and 226, and *Kuṟuntogai*, st. 11.

[2] See M. Raghava Aiyangar, *Cēraṉ Senguṭṭuvaṉ*, pp. 112-3.

[3] An attempt has already been made by Mr. C. Rasanayagam in this direction in his book *Ancient Jaffna*, 1926.

X

SOME FEATURES OF THE ADMINISTRATION

Long and laborious research in ancient Indian polity has tended to remove the misconception generally prevalent that all ancient Indian monarchies were autocracies. The consensus of opinion among scholars of the modern day is that the ancient Indian monarchs were not autocratic, but were subject to the laws of the land both customary and statutory. There were democratic institutions in the country which kept the king under control and prevented him from acting unduly on his own initiative. Such institutions were common both in North India and South India.[1]

But confining ourselves to South Indian polity we may make the statement that the king was benevolent and cared for the promotion of the welfare of his subjects. We know how the Cōḻa king Karikāla converted jungles into regions of fertility and wealth and how he undertook large irrigation schemes. There are stories told of his even-handed justice.[2] So was known the Pāṇḍyan Neḍuñjeḻiyaṉ who gave up his life when he heard that he had meted out unjustifiable punishment to the innocent Kōvalaṉ. These instances are enough to prove that the king was no autocrat.

ASSEMBLIES

In the conduct of his administration the king was assisted by the assembly of five (*aimperum-kuḻu*) which consisted of the minister, the *purōhita*, the commander-in-chief, an ambassador and a spy, and by a group of eight officials (*eṇpērāyam*), the superintendent of the accounts, the head of the executive, the officer of the treasury, the chamberlain, the representatives of the citizens, the commander,

[1] For an elaborate study of these institutions see V. R. R. Dikshitar, *Hindu Administrative Institutions*, 1929.

[2] *Paḻamoḻi*, st. 6; *Maṇi.*, canto iv, ll. 107-8.

the chief of the elephant-warriors and of the horse-warriors.[1]

To illustrate; King Śenguṭṭuvaṉ was served by Villavaṉkōdai, the commander of the land forces, and Aḷumbilvēḷ, the superintendent of income and expenditure. Sañjaya and Nīla were the chief messengers. Sañjaya was the head of the Kañjuka-mākkaḷ. The spies are described as wandering in different disguises in the capitals of the other kingdoms while the spies of other kings were going about in Vañji. The king consulted his officials before he undertook any business. That the queen attended such a council and had her say in the questions debated upon can be presumed from the fact that Śenguṭṭvaṉ's queen Iḷangōvēṇmāḷ was present in the Council Chamber and took part in the discussion when the question of erecting the temple to Pattiṉi Dēvi was decided.[2] The monotony of state business was often enlivened by dancing and music by the class of Śākkaiyar whose head was Kūttuḷpaṭuvōṉ.[3] The kingship was generally hereditary,[4] and the king reigned according to the laws of the land. As has been pointed out already the theory of Marumakkattāyam as prevalent among the Cēras is not supported by the *Śilappadikāram*. On the other hand its evidence nullifies any such theory. The king knew the evil effects of tyrannical rule[5] and hence endeavoured to do justice.

FLAGS, ETC.

The three kings of the Tamil land had as their respective standards, the bow, the fish, and the tiger. They

[1] Cantos iii, l. 126; v, l. 157; xxvi, l. 38. Also *Maṇi.*, canto i, l. 17. The *eṇpērāyam* is also interpreted in a different way as *eṇperumtuṇaivar* (*Tamil Lexicon*, Vol. I, p. 520). These were professional people who catered for the needs of the royal household. We hear Mādari the cowherdess saying that she had to send ghee to the palace the next day (canto xvii, l. 7).

[2] Cantos xxv, ll. 107-14; xxviii, l. 50.

[3] Canto xxvi, l. 125.

[4] Canto xxvii, l. 134.

[5] *Maṇi.*, canto vii, l. 12.

were further distinguished by garlands of palmyra, margosa, and *atti* leaves and flowers. We search the texts in vain for a national flag, for politically India was then divided into many nations each called after the name of their respective tribes.

CONDUCT TOWARDS PRINCES

Refractory sons were severely dealt with. The examples of Manunītikaṇḍa Cōḷa, and Kiḻḻivaḷavaṉ are furnished by the epic. When it was feared that some prince would stand in the way of the legitimate heir succeeding to the throne, the former took to a life of renunciation. Iḷangō-Aḍigaḷ, the brother of Śenguṭṭuvaṉ, is a case in point.

INTERREGNUM

Sometimes it so happened that there was an interval between the decease of the reigning king and the appointment of his successor. This was what happened at the death of Neḍuñjeḻiyaṉ by the curse of Kaṇṇaki. Then the council was in charge of the kingdom till Iḷamjeḻiyaṉ, the Imperial Viceroy at Koṟkai, was elected to the throne.[1]

ROYAL AMUSEMENTS

Among the royal amusements were dancing and music by professionals. The king often retired to what may be called a pleasure resort, *ilavandikaippaḷḷi*. He was generally accompained there by his queen. It is said that Śenguṭṭuvaṉ spent some time in that park in the company of his queen Iḷangōvēṇmāḷ.[2]

RELEASE OF PRISONERS

Among the festivities of the state figured the king's birthday. It is called *Perunāḷ* (also *Perumangalam*) when there was a general release of prisoners. Such general

[1] Canto xxvii, ll. 132-8.

[2] Cantos x, l. 31; xxv, l. 4.

amnesty was also granted on other similar occasions. For example, on the occasion of the founding of the temple of Pattiṉi Dēvi, Śeṅguṭṭuvaṉ ordered the release of prisoners.[1]

TULĀBĀRADĀNAM

The *tulābāradānam* was a redeeming feature of the royal festivities. It was a gift of gold to the deserving, generally a *śrōtriya*, equal to the donor's weight. It figures as one of the sixteen *mahādānas* as prescribed by the Purāṇas like the *Matsya* and the *Linga Purāṇas*.[2] It is said that Śeṅguṭṭuvaṉ made this gift to the Brahman Māḍalaṉ[3] on the banks of the Ganges after he had had the stone intended for the image of Kaṇṇaki bathed in the sacred river.

DEPARTMENT OF FINANCE

The department of finance was under the control of a body of officials who went by the name Kāvidimākkaḷ. Perhaps the Kāvidi was the chief finance minister who looked after the collection of revenues in the right season and in the proper way. He was one of the five officials whose advice was sought on questions of state finance by the king. His establishment went by the name *āyakkaṇakkar*,[4] which, it is said, announced a remission of taxes when the temple of Kaṇṇaki was founded.

COMMERCE, A SOURCE OF REVENUE

As a source of revenue commerce came only next to agriculture. There was active trade by land and sea. It is said that bales and cartloads were numbered and marked (*kaṇṇeḻuttu*). The merchants were the wealthiest community in the land and the king befriended them by honouring them with titles. Eṭṭi[5] was one such title.

[1] Canto xxviii, ll. 204-5.
[2] See V. R. R. Dikshitar, *Matsya Purāṇa*, 1935, p. 96.
[3] Canto xxvii, ll. 175-6. [4] Canto xxviii, ll. 204-6. [5] Canto xv, l. 163.

TREASURE TROVE

We hear of an Eṭṭi Śangamaṉ, a flourishing merchant at Madura.[1] Treasure trove was generally the property of the state, and tended to swell the royal exchequer. But so far as the Pāṇḍyan kingdom was concerned we hear that the Pāṇḍyan Neḍuñjeḻiyaṉ issued a proclamation to the effect that treasure and other legitimately acquired wealth belonged by right to the discoverer.[2]

This proclamation was the result of a representation made to the king by a poor young poet who was punished by the subordinate officials. Thus this was an exception and not the rule. The presents of the hillmen (like those at the Nilgiris) to Śenguṭṭuvaṉ[3] and the tributes by subjugated monarchs were other sources of revenue, though the income from these items could not have been much.

The chief item of expenditure was connected with the civil and the military establishments of the state. An idea of the military expenditure will be apparent from the number of the fourfold army and commissariat which followed Śenguṭṭuvaṉ on his northern expedition.[4]

Chariots	100
Elephants	500
Horses	10,000
Carts and carriages	20,000
Kañjukar	1,000
Dancing-girls	102
Musicians	208
Jesters	100

WARFARE

We have seen that the army of the ancient Tamils consisted of a fourfold classification of chariots, elephants, cavalry and infantry. The chief defence was by means

[1] Canto xv, l. 196. [2] Canto xxiii, ll. 128-9. [3] Canto xxv, ll. 35-55.
[4] Canto xxvi, ll. 128-40. See also M. Raghava Aiyangar, op. cit., p. 134.

of well furnished fortifications. The battlements and ramparts were mechanically provided with efficient mechanisms containing curious devices in the shape of monkeys, kingfishers, sows, vultures, serpents, horses and swans.[1]

Before the king left his capital he entertained his soldiers with a grand feast and sent his sword and umbrella on the state elephant in advance, on an auspicious day. After having prayed to the gods in the temples of his city and in the Yajñaśālas the king actually left his town. This was what Śeṅguṭṭuvaṉ did on the eve of his northern expedition.[2] Such of the heroes as showed a bold front to the end and died, were honoured with Vīrakkal or Naḍukal, monuments raised in commemoration of their deeds of valour of which a good number are even now brought out by the spade of the archæologist. Before the actual operations, an ultimatum was generally sent to the enemy king to the effect that those who did not voluntarily surrender would have to submit to the horrors of war.[3]

A number of musical instruments were displayed on the field of battle. These were *koḍumpaṟai*, *neḍuvayir*, *muraśam*, *pāṇḍil*, etc. The kings who still opposed him in open war were taken prisoners after their defeat and released on their submission. The wars were so fierce that the soldiers sometimes cast off their arms and escaped in the guise of ascetics, musicians and dancers, Brahmans and other non-combatants.[4] This points to the prevalence of ethical standards in ancient warfare in South India.

DEPARTMENT OF JUSTICE

Passing on to the department of justice we notice that the chief magistrates who sat in the hall of justice (*Aṟakkaḷam*) when they disposed of cases were Brahmans. The idea

[1] Canto xv, ll. 206-16.
[2] Canto xxvi, ll. 52-66.
[3] Canto xxv, ll. 183-94.
[4] Canto xxvii, l. 179 ff.

was that those dispensing justice must be versed in the law codes.[1]

Though the kings were actuated by the best of motives in meting out justice there was sometimes a miscarriage as we note in the case of Kōvalaṉ.[2] There were jails and superintendents of jails.[3] As already noticed there was a periodical release of prisoners. Usually capital punishment was awarded in cases of theft. Among others the six chief offenders according to the laws of the state were false witnesses, pseudo-*sannyāsins*, unchaste women, disloyal ministers, adulterers, and tale-bearers.[4]

VILLAGE ADMINISTRATION

Already we have seen that the empire was divided into *nāḍus* (perhaps answering to modern provinces) and a subdivision of the *nāḍu* was the *kūṟṟam* (district). But the village was the unit of administration.

Every village had a *maṉṟam* or the village *sabhā*, where the elders transacted the business of the village. There were certain tribal settlements in the hills and forests. The Eiyṉar settlement may be cited as an example. Excepting these settlements, the villages in general were not isolated groups far away from the link of humanity. There was active intercourse, political and commercial, between village and village and between village and city. Learned men and pious Brahmans of one kingdom felt at home in alien kingdoms. To cite an instance, the Brahman of Mānkāḍu, a village in the Cēra *nāḍu*, visited sacred places as far as Cape Comorin through the Cōḷa and Pāṇḍya kingdoms. In spite of the gloomy trail through woods and jungles the roads were safe. There were officials appointed by the state to look after the welfare of the villages, and these were to a large extent responsible

[1] Cantos xxii, l. 8; xxvi, l. 246; xxviii, l. 222.
[2] Canto xvi, l. 148 ff.
[3] Canto xxiii, l. 103. *Maṇi.*, canto xix, l. 133.
[4] Canto v, ll. 128-34.

for the peace and security of the rural parts. They were often aided by the village assembly.

XI

GEOGRAPHICAL DATA

The celebrated commentator Naccinārkkiniyar divides the whole Tamil land into four divisions: Malaimaṇḍalam, Cōḻamaṇḍalam, Pāṇḍyamaṇḍalam, and Toṇḍaimaṇḍalam. In the days of the *Śilappadikāram* there was no Toṇḍaimaṇḍalam division as such. There were then only three divisions. Malaimaṇḍalam was already referred to as the Cēra kingdom. It may be noted in passing that the term *maṇḍalam* in the sense of a province or kingdom does not occur in the Sangam works.

The ancient Cēranāḍu was constituted by modern Salem, Coimbatore, and the Nilgiri districts besides the whole of Malabar and a part of Travancore (Vēḷnāḍu). This kingdom occupied five of the twelve divisions which comprised all the Tamiḻagam. The five of the Cēramaṇḍalam were Kuṭṭanāḍu, Kuḍanāḍu, Kongunāḍu, Pūḻināḍu and Malāḍu (Malaināḍu). Some of the titles of the Cēras like Kuṭṭuvan and Pūḻiyan are coined from the names of these territorial divisions. The ancient Kongunāḍu comprised the modern districts of Salem and Coimbatore. The chief rivers of the Cēra kingdom were Āṉporuṉai (Amarāvati), Kuḍavanāru, Kāñji (Noyyil), Kāriyāṟu, Ṣulliyāṟu,[1] Pēriyāṟu or Poṉṉāṉi, and Bavāṉi or Vāṉi. To this kingdom Śenguṭṭuvan added by conquest Koḍuhūr in the south of the Mysore state. Vañjikkaruvūr[2] was the capital of this great kingdom. Toṇḍi and Muśiri were the chief ports.

We are furnished with a full and detailed description of the capital city, its suburbs, fortifications, streets and roads, public halls, museums, parks, temples and *māṭams* and the palace.[3]

[1] Suḷḷi falls into the western sea; at its mouth is the town Muśiri.
[2] Cantos xxvi, l. 50; xxviii, l. 196.
[3] *Maṇi.*, canto xxviii; *Sila.*, canto xxviii, ll. 48-50.

The late Kanakasabhai surmised that this Vañji might be Tiru-karūr now a deserted village three miles from Kothaimangalam and this view has been adopted by some of the later scholars without bestowing much thought on this all-important question. This theory did not go unchallenged. Pandit M. Raghava Aiyangar first identified Vañji with Karuvūr in Trichinopoly district. Following him Mahāvidvān R. Raghava Aiyangar, whose authority on the Śangam classics cannot be disputed, wrote a book in Tamil entitled *Vañjimānagar*. The long and short of this erudite thesis was to settle once for all the controversy as to the location of the original Cēra capital, and after a critical examination of all the aspects of the question, he came to the only possible conclusion that this Vañjikkaruvūr was the present town Karūr in Trichinopoly district. It is not possible nor is it necessary to traverse the ground again. If epigraphy were pressed into service, the following would be read with interest : 'A damaged record in the Śiva temple here (Nerūr, a village very near Karūr) mentions Karuvūr as Vañjimānagaram which must help to settle the identification of the original Vañji at Karūr and not at Cranganore on the west coast.'[1]

The chief mountains are the Kolli hills, the Ayirai hills (in which the Ayirai river has its source), and the chain of Ānamalais. This river Ayirai[2] must be Poṉṉāni (Pūrṇavāhini). The hill Ayirai (Aivar-Malai) was sacred to the goddess Koṟṟavai, the deity of the Cēras. The other hills of the Kongunāḍu are Naṉṟā and Vaṇḍamalai, the latter south of Karuvūr.

THE PĀṆḌYAN KINGDOM

It would appear that the ancient Pāṇḍyan kingdom extended far into the south where were the Kumari hill and the river Pahṟuḷi both of which had been swallowed up by the sea long before the commencement

[1] *Gazetteer of the Trichinopoly District*, Vol. II, 1931, p. 130.
[2] Canto xxviii, ll. 145-6.

of the Christian era.[1] As if to compensate for the loss of this territory, the Pāṇḍyan king Neḍuñjeḻiyaṉ added by conquest Miḻalaikkūṟṟam[2] and the Muttūṟkkūṟṟam[3] from the Cōḻas, apparently territories in the modern district of Tanjore,[4] and Kuṇḍūṟkūṟṟam[5] from the Cēras. It is only the gloss that gives this indication, and we have no other testimony to confirm it.[6]

If we are to follow the traditional account of three Śangams, and there is no reason why we should not, the ancient capital of the Pāṇḍyan kingdom was also swallowed up by the sea, and this necessitated the moving of the capital to Koṟkai, probably the Kavāṭapuram of Sanskrit literature. From this again the capital was transferred to the modern city of Madura, and this had been effected by the time of Pliny as he refers to it.[7] This became the seat of the great and ancient academy well known as the Śangam. Koṟkai also continued to be a chief city under the charge of the crown prince. The chief hill in the

[1] Canto xi, ll. 17-22; see commentary on canto viii, ll. 1-2.

[2] It is rather difficult to identify this, though South Indian inscriptions often mention this as part of Pāṇḍināḍu. For instance a record in the fourteenth year of the Pāṇḍyan king Jaṭāvarman Sundara Pāṇḍya of the thirteenth century A.D. refers to it. (See also Tamil record No. 67 of 1910.) Tamil records Nos. 460-1 of 1909 refer to two places, Kiḻkūṟṟu and Kaḷakūṟṟu as subdivisions of Milalaikkūṟṟam. Naḍuvīrkūṟṟu is another subdivision according to Tamil records, 130 of 1908 and 425 of 1911.

[3] This is also referred to in a number of inscriptions. Tamil record No. 59 of 1909, dated in the thirteenth year of the Pāṇḍyan King Jaṭāvarman mentions Muttūrkkūṟṟam in Pāṇḍyamaṇḍalam. See also 441 of 1904, 86 of 1905 and 80 and 266 of 1907. In the thirteenth and fourteenth centuries Kappalūr seems to have been an important place in this subdivision (see Nos. 425 and 429 of 1913).

[4] K. A. Nilakanta Sastri, *The Pandyan Kingdom*, p. 28.

[5] This can be indentified with Kuṇḍūrkūṟṟam occurring in the Madura inscription of a Pāṇḍyan king whose name is lost. According to this, Kuṇḍūr was the capital of Kuṇḍūrkūṟṟam, and this *kūṟṟam* formed a part of Aṇḍanāḍu (see *I.M.P.*, Vol. II, p. 1036, ed. by V. Rangachary). According to a record of Trichinopoly district, 460 of 1908, it came to be known later as Rājanārāyaṇa-Caturvēdimangalam.

[6] p. 303.

[7] E. H. Warmington, *The Commerce between the Roman Empire and India*, 1928, p. 167.

kingdom was Podiyil, the residence of the sage Agastya if we are to believe the traditional account, and the important river was the Vaigai which was crossed when in flood by boats and canoes.

The limits of the ancient Pāṇḍyan kingdom may roughly be stated to have comprised the modern districts of Madura, Ramnad and Tinnevelly. The Veḷḷār flowing through the Pudukkottai State formed its northern boundary. The Cōḻa kingdom consisted of a part of the modern Trichinopoly district, as well as Tanjore, Chingleput and South Arcot districts. The Toṇḍaimaṇḍalam which rose to prominence under the Pallavas was an appendage to the old Cōḻamaṇḍalam. It was in its turn divided into a number of *nāḍus* and *kūṟṟams*. Like the Pāṇḍyan kingdom the Cōḻamaṇḍalam had two capital cities Uṟaiyūr (Sans., Uragapuram) in the Trichinopoly district and Kāvērippaṭṭiṉam in the Tanjore district. The latter achieved prominence under Karikālaccōḻaṉ, the son of Iḷamcēṭceṉṉi, but a part of it was destroyed by the sea in the course of two generations. It consequently lost its ancient glory as the principal seat of government.[1]

According to the *Periplus* the capital city Uṟaiyūr was the chief mart for pearls and the well-known Argynitic muslins; Argynitic being an adjective derived from the name Uragapuram. Sixty years later Ptolemy states that Uṟaiyūr was the capital. The Kāvēri was the only important river of the Cōḻa country.

To conclude, 'the traditional meeting-place of the three Tamil kingdoms was the temple of Sellāndi Amman on the banks of the Kāvēri, twelve miles west of Kuḷittalai and three miles below the junction of the Amarāvati and the Kāvēri. The temple was the common place of worship of the kings of the three Tamil dynasties; a bund which runs

[1] For a detailed description of the city, its fortifications, streets and roads, see cantos v and vi.

to the south of the river marks the boundary between the Cōḷa and the Pāṇḍya territories, and the Karaipōttaṉār on the opposite bank of the river was the boundary between the Cōḷa and the Cēra kingdoms.'[1]

XII

RELIGIOUS DATA

Man is a religious animal and invokes the assistance of superhuman beings in his weal and woe. This invocation comprises rituals of fasting and feasting, singing and dancing. These are believed to please the deity who in his turn is expected to shower blessings on his worshippers. The chief gods invoked by the ancient Tamils were Śēyōṉ (also Murugaṉ and Vēlaṉ) and Māyōṉ (Kṛṣṇa or the Black God). Other gods worshipped were Śiva, Koṟṟavai or the Goddess of Victory, Balarāma, Varuṇa, Indra, etc. There is a view that some of these were peculiar to the different regions (of which five are distinguished) in the Tamil land.[2] But these are also Vēdic and Purāṇic gods, and their mention in early Tamil poetry shows that the assimilation and the blend of the two cultures, Sanskrit and Tamil, was a thing of the ancient past. The earliest extant work in Tamil, the *Tolkāppiyam* bears evidence of this. Similar ideas are found scattered in the *Śilappadikāram*, and the twin epics betray clear influence of the Buddha and the Jaina cults which had come to stay in the Tamil land.

Side by side with these dissenting sects of which three are mentioned—the Buddha, the Jaina and the Ājīvaka, the established religion of the land was in a flourishing condition. At the outset, it must be remarked that there was no nice distinction between the orthodox religion and the so-called religion of the dissenting sects. The fundamental principles of all these sects were the same, and the

[1] *Gazetteer of the Trichinopoly District*, Vol. II, 1931, p. 67.

[2] See *History of the Tamils*, p. 75 ff.

differences, if any, were minor and trivial. It was in philosophical outlook and speculation that there was any difference, and hence the masses of the people to whom the higher philosophy was a sealed book did not trouble themselves about it. The religious discussions were only among the cultured few, and differences in opinions and views among them were treated with mutual respect. By the orthodox religion we mean Śaivism and Vaiṣṇavism. Even here the bitter hatred of the Śaiva and Vaiṣṇava cults as separate sects, which was only a later growth on the tree of Indian religion, is totally absent in the *Śilappadikāram*. It is not possible to say whether in the days of the epic a certain person was a Śaiva or Vaiṣṇava in his creed, and hence he cannot be marked exclusively a Śaiva or exclusively a Vaiṣṇava. In fine, the sectarian spirit was totally absent, and every person was both a Śaiva and a Vaiṣṇava. Mādari, a devotee of Kṛṣṇa and hence a Vaiṣṇava paid respects to Kavundi-Aḍigaḷ, a Jain *sannyāsini*.

A classic example is Cēraṉ Śenguṭṭuvaṉ himself. Besides his prayers at the Agnihōtraśāla of his palace on the eve of his expedition to the north, the king went to the Śiva temple and bore the feet of the Lord on his head as a mark of respect to Him. At this time the priests of the temple of Āṭakamāṭam, the local Vaiṣṇava temple, gave him the *prasādam* (garland of flowers) which he wore on his shoulders. The commentator has identified Āṭakamāṭam with the Trivandrum Padmanābhasvāmi temple. But as Pandit R. Raghava Aiyangar has ably argued that once the thesis that Karūr was the capital of the Cēras is established, it could not be that priests came all the way from Trivandrum to Karūr, and that therefore we must look for the temple in or near Karūr.[1] Therefore this must be the Ranganātha temple in Karūr, while the

[1] *Vāñjimānagar*; cf. canto xxvi, commentary on l. 62; *T.A.S.*, Vol. V. p. 116.

Śiva temple must have been the Paśupatikōil of that place.[1]

The epic also mentions the great shrines dedicated to Subrahmaṇya like Tiruccendūr, Tiruccengōḍe, Ērakam and Veṇkuṉṟu.[2] The dances *tuḍikkūttu* and *kuḍaikkūttu* are attributed to Subrahmaṇya as the *koḍukoṭṭi* and the *pāṇḍarangam* are to Śiva.

The worship of the Dēvi as the Koṟṟavai or the Goddess of Victory and of Maṇimēkalai as the chief guardian deity of the sea is seen throughout. The idea that Lakṣmī, Sarasvatī and Pārvatī represent different aspects of the same Power is evident from the *veṇbā* in Canto xxii. This reminds us of the Lalitōpākhyāna portion of the *Brahmāṇḍa Purāṇa* where it is stated that the original goddess at Kāñci was Mahālakṣmī who came to be known in latter times as Kāmākṣī. The ritual dance *vēṭṭuva-vari* in honour of Koṟṟavai was often performed by hill tribes like the Maṟavar. The opening lines of Canto xii, in fact the whole canto, describe this dance, and in this connexion we find that among the *bali* (offerings) mentioned, human and bloody sacrifices were not uncommon.[3] The Dēvi is often praised as the destroyer of Mahiṣāsura.

The ritual dance connected with Viṣṇu goes by the name of the *kuravaikkūttu* (probably Sans., Rāsakrīḍa). This kind of dance was largely performed by the female members of the community in honour of the god Kṛṣṇa who, tradition affirms, married the cowherdess Pinnai in the same way that Murugaṉ married Vaḷḷi, a hill girl. When Kōvalaṉ was executed under the orders of the Pāṇḍyan king, the city was visited with a number of ill omens which indicated some disaster to the city and its residents. According to the belief of the times such things could be averted by invoking deities dear to them. Hence

[1] Dikshitar also visited this ancient town and is inclined to confirm the learned pandit's opinion.

[2] Canto xxiv, p. 516.

[3] See in this connexion E. A. Payne, *The Sāktas*, introductory chapter.

a *kuravaikkūttu* was arranged by Mādari and her daughter Aiyai in the presence of Kaṇṇaki. Another *kuravaikkūttu* was performed by the women of the hill tribes on the Neḍuvēḷkuṉṟam, the hill which Kaṇṇaki reached after the conflagration at Madura, and where, as she stood under the *vēngai* tree, a celestial car came down and took her to Heaven. In honour of Kaṇṇaki, these ladies arranged a dance and performed it with success.

Connected with the worship of Kṛṣṇa was the worship of Balarāma, his elder brother. That there was a cult of Balarāma is obvious from the mention of a separate temple to him.[1] Prof. R. G. Bhandarkar is of opinion that the cult of Balarāma was known in Patañjali's time. It is not clear when the cult became extinct.[2] It is remarkable that the worship of Balarāma was in vogue in Tamil South India in the time of the *Śilappadikāram*.[3]

Again, we find evidence in the *Śilappadikāram* of the existence of separate temples to the Sun God, the Moon God, the Kalpa Tree, the Airāvada, the Vajra, Śāttaṉ, and other Pāṣaṇḍa gods.[4] In the cities were found local shrines for the guardian deities. Such definite statements as to the existence of temples bear testimony to the fact that the institution of the temple had a much more ancient origin than that we would at present imagine. Evidence is not altogether lacking that temples existed in India in the fourth millenium B.C. as the recent finds of the Indus Valley indicate. Again, the four Būtams named after the four castes and the Būta at the

[1] Canto ix, l. 10.

[2] See his *Saivism, Vaiṣṇavism, and minor religious systems*, p. 13.

[3] Dewan Bahadur K. S. Ramaswami Sastri drew my attention to a temple of Balarāma at Uḍabhanēśvaram on the seashore at a short distance from Uḍupī, dedicated by Śrī Madhavācārya, worship being conducted there down to the present time.

An image of Balarāma said to be a typical example of the Kushāna period, is one of the acquisitions noted in the *An. Rep.* of the U. P. Provincial Museum, Lucknow, for the year ending 1930.

[4] Canto ix, ll. 9-15.

Būtacatukkam were also offered prayers. Among the Vēdic deities Indra, Varuṇa and Agni are invoked. In more than one place, there are references to Vēdic Brahmans, their fire-rites, and their chanting of the Vēdic hymns. The Brahman received much respect from the king and was often given gifts of wealth and cattle. The *purōhita* (*āśāṉ*) held a high status among the chief officials of the state, and he was a member of the cabinet which the king consulted on matters affecting the state. This is not unnatural as the Tamil kings claimed to be Kṣatriyas and the literary tradition connected them with the Solar and Lunar races.

Among the deities of the heretical sects, viz. the Pāṣaṇḍas, of whom the *Divākaram* distinguishes as many as ninety-six sects, the Śāttaṉ is prominently mentioned. Even now remains of these old Śāsta temples are found in the boundary limits of villages, and people in distress invoke their aid to tide over their difficulties. As now, in olden days the temples of these deities were frequently visited by distressed people and their wishes were granted. These Śāsta temples appear to be indigenous to South India, where they are largely found, especially in the Tamil districts. But in the age of the *Śilappadikāram* owing to the impact of Sanskrit culture the Śāsta cult was apparently treated as heretical in character.[1]

We do not propose to deal fully with the three dissenting sects of Hinduism to which reference has already been made. There are references to the Buddha, the Indravihāra of Puhār, and the Mābōdi,[2] but the references to Buddhism which can be gleaned from the epic are very few. This is probably because the other epic *Maṇimēkalai* gives a full treatment of the subject. In the same

[1] It is interesting to note in this connexion that Śāsta or Mahāśāsta is the son born of Śiva when He embraced Mōhini (Viṣṇu in disguise), and hence he is called Hariharaputra. According to Aḍiyārkkunallār and the *Divākaram* another name for Sāttaṉ is Sātavāhanaṉ.

[2] Canto x, ll. 11-14.

way there are but few references to the Śamaṇa sect, the Ājīvaka, and to know what it is, one has to turn again to the pages of the *Maṇimēkalai*. It may be remarked in passing that all these sects were patronized by Aśōka, the Mauryan Emperor.

Some details about the Jaina practices and customs are also furnished by the *Śilappadikāram*. From a study of Canto xv one is tempted to conclude that Kōvalaṉ and Kaṇṇaki followed the Jain practice of bathing and clothing and eating. In fact they did so at Mādari's house. But the evidence of the *Maṇimēkalai* shows that they were Buddhists. As has already been said the distinctions between the orthodox religion and the other sects were not sharp. While Śenguṭṭuvaṉ was of the orthodox faith, his brother Iḷangō-Aḍigaḷ is at least contended to have been a Jaina, and the poet Kūlavāṇikaṉ Śāttaṉār, their common friend, was a Buddhist. This is not peculiar to South India. We know, for example, that members of Harṣa's family 'acted on their individual preferences in the matter of religion'. While Prabhākaravardhana, Harṣa's father, followed the worship of the Sun, his elder son Rājyavardhana was a Buddhist. Harṣa worshipped the Sun, Buddha and Śiva. And yet there was no conflict of interests among them.[1]

Again while the parents of Kōvalaṉ were Buddhists, those of Kaṇṇaki embraced the Ājīvaka faith.[2] Thus different members of the same household followed different faiths and there was no sectarian spirit among them. Only two explanations can be offered for this. Either the people did not look upon religious distinctions seriously, or there were no fundamental differences between one sect and another. To every one of them, *karma* was a factor to be reckoned with. Man's actions bad or good are

[1] V. A. Smith, *The Early History of India*, 4th ed., revised by S. M. Edwardes, pp. 358-9. See also R. K. Mookerjee, *Harsha* (Rulers of India Series).

[2] Canto xxvii, ll. 90-100.

bound to yield results bad or good. Suffering in this birth may not necessarily be due to unrighteous acts done now but may be the result of past actions. Hence man must do his duty (*svadharma*) if he wants to attain salvation. The people in those days seem to have pinned their faith to this doctrine as many do even now.

Before we close this section it is worth noting that of all the Vēdic gods, the worship of Indra is prominently mentioned. In fact the whole of Canto v of the epic is devoted to a detailed description of the festival of Indra and festivities connected with it. It would appear from the canto that the king interested himself in celebrating that festival with grand success, and to witness it, gods and men came even from remote parts of North India. It was an annual festival lasting for a number of days. It commenced on the full moon day in the month of Cittirai (April), and with the preliminary worship of the guardian deity who was sent by Indra to help an ancient king of the Puhār line, Mucukunda. Sacrifices were offered in the five different *maṉṟams* of the city of Puhār.[1] One feature of the festival was the removal of the drum from the Vajrakkōṭṭam to the Airāvada temple, where it was placed on the nape of the elephant sacred to Indra. The bathing ceremony of Indra was the important day of the festival. We hear of the Indradhvajam festival in Sanskrit literature[2] which can be identified with the ceremony of *talaikkōl* in Tamil literature, but there was no actual celebration of Indra's festival. How the ancient Tamils took to this special form of Indra's worship still remains a puzzle.

XIII

SOCIAL CONDITIONS: TOWNS AND TOWN LIFE

If the *Maṇimēkalai* can be characterized a philosophico-religious work, the *Śilappadikāram* can be said to be a

[1] ll. 140-4.

[2] E.g. *Vīramitrōdaya Rājanītiprakāśa*, pp. 421-33.

treatise on political and social life.[1] Here we have a description of the three capitals with their glowing culture and civilization. In the busy streets of the cities any number of people belonging to various nations were met, most of them having come on commercial and other business. The municipal administration was excellent. The roads and streets were kept in good condition and were lighted. Committing nuisance in public streets was punishable. The houses seem to have been well built and properly provided with ventilation. Seven-storied buildings were not uncommon in the ancient cities, thus pointing to a considerable development of engineering skill in ancient South India. Among the communities the Brahmans received much respect especially for their learning in the sacred lore and for their continuance of the fire-rites. They were often awarded rich presents both in cash and kind. They were left unmolested during times of war, as was the case during Śeṅguṭṭuvaṉ's battle on the banks of the Ganges. Next came the merchant community, and being the wealthiest community its members were honoured with titles by the reigning chieftains of the land.

Life in towns was one of luxury and ease. Some of the amusements of the people were dumb-shows and dancing accompanied by music, both vocal and instrumental. Women freely participated in such amenities of life. They attended temples and took part in the public dances. They decked themselves with costly attire and ornaments and made themselves attractive. Their clothes were of cotton, wool, silk, and even rat's hair.[2] One mode of their decoration was the painting of their bodies with scented pastes and powders and the wearing of garlands of flowers.

The womenfolk in towns can be classified into two divisions: housewives attending to household duties and

[1] As Dikshitar has devoted a long chapter to this question in his book *Studies in Tamil Literature and History* only a bare outline is given here.

[2] Canto xiv, ll. 205-7, comm.

leading pure lives, and prostitutes who were public women living in special quarters where the voluptuous young men of the city thronged. Even married men resorted to these places and wasted all their wealth on these courtesans, caring little for their wedded wives. A typical example is Kōvalaṉ who spent all his fortune on Mādavi the dancing-girl, as a result of which he became so poor that he had to go to Madura to earn a living. Outside the city in the suburbs, were public places which were the residences of ascetics and penance-performers, both orthodox and heterodox.

VILLAGES AND VILLAGE LIFE

If the town life was rich, the village life was equally so. The villagers, of whom the agriculturists, cowherds and shepherds formed the majority, led a simple life attending to their hereditary professions of cultivation and cattle-tending. The villages were not altogether cut off from the activities of town life. There were means of transport which were, primarily, bullock-carts on land and boats on water. Between the villages, or more properly between two great towns, thick forests abounded with wild animals and serpents, streams and springs of water, fruit trees and trees of other kinds, cornfields and flower gardens. Iḷangō-Aḍigaḷ gives us a vivid picture of all this when describing the route from ancient Puhār to Madura.[1]

The monotonous life of the villager was often enlivened by rural amusements of a varied character. Every village had a common dancing-hall (*kaḷam*).[2] Even the village women took part in these public performances like the *tuṇangai*, a kind of dance.[3] Having enough to eat and drink, the villagers led a contented and happy life. Notwithstanding the security and peace afforded by the

[1] Cantos x-xi. [2] *Maṇi.*, canto iv, l. 6. [3] Canto v, l. 70.

kings of the land, theft was not uncommon. The Maṟavar who lived in forests and desert tracts, otherwise known as the Eiyṉar, who were often employed as soldiers in wars by the Tamil kings, had for their chief profession highway robbery.[1] They often deprived the unwary wayfarer of his belongings : cattle lifting was one feature of their thieving. They were addicted to liquor and ate from a common table. They hunted the wild hog, boar and deer, whose flesh they ate, using their skins as clothes and their ivory teeth and nails as ornaments.

MARRIAGE

Another aspect of social life deserving notice is marriage. In the ancient Tamiḻagam two forms of marriage were prevalent, the *kaḷavu* and the *kaṟpu* (i.e. marriage in secrecy and marriage in the open). It was a peculiar custom of the *kaḷavu* that the lover secretly met the unmarried girl of his choice and made overtures of love to her. This roughly corresponds to the *gandharva* form of marriage. The lover usually came bearing a present in his hand as a token of his love. It was one of the divisions of the *kaikkiḷai* form of love.[2] The whole of the canto 'Kāṉalvari' is a dissertation on the different stages of the *kaḷavu* form of marriage.[3] The *kaṟpiyal* form which had already taken the place of the *kaḷaviyal*, from the epoch of the *Tolkāppiyam* if not earlier,[4] had come to stay by the time of the epics. Though there are details of the *kaḷavu* form of marriage, it seems to have been confined to certain communities such as those living near the seaside or those living in the hills. In other words, the people in the lower stages of culture adopted it. In the more civilized parts of the land, the form of

[1] See also Dikshitar's paper 'The Eiyṉar' in *Sentamil*, Vol. XXXI, No. 1.
[2] *Tolk.*, 'Porul', *sūtrams* 104-6.
[3] For further details see canto xxiv, 'Kuṉṟakkuravai'.
[4] *Tolk.*, 'Kaṟpiyal', *sūtra* 4.

marriage was that laid down in the *Dharmaśāstras* and the *Gṛhyasūtras*. The chanting of the Vēdic mantras by the *purōhita*, the circumambulation of fire and similar customs show the profound influence which Sanskrit culture had on the Tamils. If the Tamils took to northern customs of marriage, the northerners who settled in the Tamil land also adopted some of the Tamil practices in their system of marriage. The tying of *tāli* (*māngalyam*) or a sacred thread to the neck of the bride by the bridegroom is an instance in point. There is no warrant in the ancient law-codes for this practice. It is a practice of the Tamils copied in later times by the so-called Aryans. This is another instance of the harmonious fusion of the two ancient cultures.[1]

MUSIC AND DANCING

Passing on, we meet with a wealth of material for an elaborate study of music and dancing. There was ritual singing and ritual dancing. Dancing as a part of religious worship is in evidence among the ancient peoples. It is said[2] that 'in early Christianity bishops led the faithful in the sacred dances both in the churches and before the tombs of the martyrs'. We also hear that the Tarahumare Indians of Mexico regard the dance as 'a very serious and ceremonial matter, a kind of worship and incantation rather than amusement'.

A dance conducted with the intention of moving the deity becomes a real form of prayer and this is in evidence in the Tamil classic. In addition there were dumb-shows ; but there is no evidence of any regular play having been enacted.

The *Silappadikāram* furnishes the legendary origin of

[1] The marriage of Kaṇṇaki and Kōvalaṉ is a description of marriage in high life. See canto i for the preliminaries, the *pandal*, the religious and social functions ending with the *āśīrvāda* rites.

[2] E. Crawley, *The Mystic Rose*, Vol. I, 1927, p. 371.

dancing. Once in the *sabhā* of Indra, his son Jayanta misbehaved with the heaventIy actress Urvaśī, in a manner that enraged the sage Agastya who cursed Jayanta to be born a bamboo stick in the Vindhya hills, and Urvaśī a courtesan on the earth. Hence the name Jayanta is celebrated in the ceremony and worship of *talaikkōl*. It was a bamboo stick symbolical of Jayanta. Often the handle of the umberlla of an enemy-king was used as the *talaikkōl*. It was duly bathed and adorned and carried in procession before it was finally taken to the public theatre. The actress for the day placed it on her head perhaps to serve as an equipoise when regular dancing began.

The worship of Murugaṉ and Māyōṉ included dancing as a relieving feature of the occasion. The former is the war-god and the latter the love-god. But a number of dances are associated with gods like Śiva, Durgā, Indrāṇī, besides Murugaṉ and Kṛṣṇa. Aḍiyārkkunallār informs us that Kṛṣṇa danced ten kinds of dances[1] (of which *alliyakkūttu*, *mallāḍal*, and *kuḍakkūttu* are mentioned in the text) after his victory over Kamsa, Bāṇāsura, and after the release of Aniruddha. Iḷangō-Aḍigaḷ refers to the dances of Śiva, Murugaṉ Kāma, Durgā, Lakṣmī, and Indrāṇī. Śiva is said to have danced the *koḍukoṭṭi* and *pāṇḍarangam* dances after the burning of the Tripura (Three Cities) in the presence of Brahmā who was his charioteer at that time.[2] Murugaṉ is said to have danced the *tuḍi* after exposing the deceit of Śūrāsura; Kāma (the God of Love) the dance of Hermaphrodite; Durgā the dance of *marakkāl* after vanquishing the *asuras*; Lakṣmī (the Goddess of Wealth) the dance of *pāvai* after her victory over the *asuras*; Indrāṇī the *kaḍayam* after defeating Bāṇāsura. But it is difficult to find similar references to these dances in Sanskrit literature. Of the eleven kinds of dancing,[3] two divisions are distinguished: *nilaininṟāṭal* (a dance fixing oneself in a particular station); and *pādam vīḻntāṭal*. Six dances like

[1] Canto vi, l. 46 ff. [2] ibid., l. 39 ff. [3] ibid., l. 65, comm.

the *alliyam* constitute the first division and five like the *tuḍi* the second division.

In addition to these are the *kuravaikkūttu* so elaborately explained in the epic and performed by the women of the cowherd and other communities. It is said that Kṛṣṇa and Piṉṉai once engaged in that kind of dance. There was also the *kūttu* of the Maṟavar in honour of Koṟṟavai. The *Śilappadikāram* shows an advanced state of evolution in the art of dancing. From primitive ritual dancing, it became transformed into a mere form of secular amusement. This must have been due to the profound influence exerted by the classic works like the *Bharatanāṭyaśāstra.* The term *dēśikkūttu* in the 'Arangēṟṟukādai' will itself explain the indigenous as opposed to the alien forms of dancing introduced into the Tamil country. In explaining the technical terms the commentator quotes as authorities such authors as Śeyiṟṟiyaṉār, Mativāṇar, Barataśēṉāpatiyār, Guṇanūluṭaiyār, Jayantanūluṭaiyār.

From a study of relevant portions of our epic, the *kūttus* may be broadly classified into *vēttiyal* and *poduviyal.* Another classification was *śāntikkūttu* and *vinōdakkūttu.*[1] Dancing was always to the accompaniment of music. The *Śilappadikāram* belongs to the class of *iśaittamiḻ* in the sense that it has six cantos on music—'Arangēṟṟukādai', 'Kāṉalvari', 'Vēṉirkādai', 'Āycciyarkuravai', 'Kuṉṟakkuravai' and 'Vēṭṭuvavari'. Melody is fully realized as the basis of Hindu music. The structure of the musical modes or *rāgas* rests invariably on a system of seven notes. W. W. Hunter remarks: 'It is indeed impossible to adequately represent the Indian system by the European notation; and the full range of its effects can only be rendered by Indian instruments, a vast collection of sound producers, slowly elaborated

[1] For details see Aḍiyārkkunallār's commentary, pp. 79-80.

during 2,000 years to suit the special requirements of Hindu Music.'[1]

South Indian music, usually called Karnāṭaka music seems to follow largely the theory, modes and notation of early Sanskrit musicians. But still in many respects it differs from them and maintains a distinct individuality unbroken for centuries together. Refinements were introduced from time to time in the original *rāgas*.[2]

It would be an interesting study to examine the ancient theory of music, and its practice by means of musical instruments in use.[3] But it is so technical in character that it is rather difficult to understand the full significance of the text in spite of elaborate commentaries on it. *Iśai* is the technical term for music and singing, secular and religious, and may be vocal or instrumental or both. Suffice it here to say that the ancient Tamils like the ancient Greeks had a highly developed art of music.[4] There were musicians of both sexes. The male singers were known as *pāṇars* and female singers as *viraḷis* and *pāḍinis*. They went from place to place displaying their musical talents and thus earning their livelihood. In addition to these professionals the ancient Tamils were lovers of music. Four varieties of tunes—*paṇ*, *paṇṇiyaṟṟiram*, *tiṟam*, *tiṟattiṟam*—were developed, appropriate perhaps to each of the four regions into which the whole Tamil land was divided. The 'Arangēṟṟukādai' (canto iii) is a treatise by itself on the various aspects of musical science. Besides the text, the commentary throws welcome light without which it is not possible to make out anything of the ancient modes of Tamil music.

The qualifications of the songster, the drummer, the flutist, and the *vīṇā* player are described in elaborate

[1] *The Imperial Gazetteer of India*, Vol. VI, 'India', p. 111.

[2] See introduction to M. S. Ramaswami Aiyar's *Svaramēḷakalānidhi*.

[3] For a collection of important extracts from the epic see M. Abraham Pandithar's *Karunāmṛtasāgaram*, 1917, pp. 526 ff.

[4] For a short history of music, see W. J. Turner's *Music* in 'The How and Why Series'.

detail. The songster must possess the instinct to group and develop the notes by distinguishing the foreign from the indigenous.[1]

He and his assistants like the drummer must be versed in *nāṭaka* literature which is divided into two parts, one relating to the king and the court, and the other relating to the common people. The drummer had to adjust his performance to that of the songster so that the latter might not feel the strain, nor the audience the monotony of the pure song. He supplied the deficiencies of the vocalist and the instrumentalist by appropriately swelling or reducing the sound of the drum. His skill much depended on the practice of his hand.[2] The flutist was a practised hand in what was known as *cittirappuṇarppu* which was nasalizing the hard consonants in singing a musical piece. He must be an expert in the use of his fingers.[3]

The *vīṇā* player[4] must be versed in fourteen *pālais*, four pertaining to the lower key, seven to the medium and three to the higher. In this way he adjusted the sound.

From a study of Canto iii in the *Śilappadikāram* three kinds of musical performance can be distinguished—the *vīṇā*, the flute and the vocal. The musician exhibited his skill either by playing on the *vīṇā* or flute, or by singing, but in all cases he was accompanied by the low-voiced *mṛdangam* and similar instruments. Four kinds of *vīṇā* are referred to by the commentator—*pēriyāḻ*, *makarayāḻ*, *śakōḍayāḻ*, *śengōṭṭiyāḻ*. The *yāḻ* was distinguished by the number of its strings. The flute was classified into five types according to the material of which it was made: bamboo, sandalwood, bronze, red catechu and ebony. Of these bamboo was the best, bronze middling while sandalwood and the others were inferior. The flute had seven holes for the seven *svaras*—sa, ri, ga, ma, pa, da, ni. Seven fingers were pressed into service when

[1] Canto iii, ll. 30-8.
[2] ibid., ll. 45-55.
[3] ibid., ll. 56-69.
[4] ibid., ll. 70-94.

playing on the flute.[1] The seven fingers are three of the left hand leaving out the thumb and the small finger, and four of the right hand leaving out the thumb.

Of percussion instruments, which were generally hit with a stick and were accompaniments for any performance, thirty-one kinds were distinguished. All of them were made of stretched skins.[2]

A qualified actress went through seven years' training from her fifth year to her twelfth, and exhibited her skill on the public stage to win the appreciation and approval of the king.[3]

XIV

SUPERSTITIONS

The remark has been made already that the ancient Tamils were, like all ancient peoples, god-fearing, simple, superstitious, and almost ready to take things for granted. That they had a number of deities and that they sent their prayers to the gods in their daily life has been indicated in the foregoing pages. It was an age of crude astrology, and its aid was sought whenever any one fell ill and sickness persisted. This was especially so when girls were stricken with love-sickness. Little knowing that their unmarried daughters were under the frenzy of love, their parents treated them for one sickness or another. The final relief came, of course, only with the marriage of the girl. Side by side with this, the ancient Tamils attached much importance to dreams. There was the belief that a dream foreshadowed coming fortune or misfortune. It was believed that a dream, as they remembered it, would come true at some future time. Kaṇṇaki had an evil dream which she communicated to Dēvandi; and the Pāṇḍyan queen dreamt a horrid dream

[1] p. 101. [2] *Studies in Tamil Literature*, p. 299 n.

[3] For the construction of the stage, ibid., pp. 295-6.

on the eve of the conflagration at Madura, of which she informed her husband, the king Neḍuñjeḻiyaṉ.[1] There was in existence a treatise on dreams which foretold the results of dreams, good or bad. Aḍiyārkkunallār quotes from that book in his commentary.[2]

We may draw one or two references from the text to show how the ancient Tamils were superstitious. The *nāṭkōḷ* and the practice of *parasthānam* on an auspicious day on the eve of starting on distant expeditions or other parts of the country may be cited. The appearance of a hump-backed bull from an opposite direction when setting out on any business was supposed to lead to calamity.[3] The following among others were supposed to spell disaster to the State: The falling down of the sceptre and the royal umbrella of their own accord; the appearance of Indra's bow (a rainbow) at night, and the falling of stars during the day-time, were regarded as omens[4] foretelling that some evil was in store for the ruling house and even for the kingdom. They had faith in gods and goddesses flying in the air to give aid to the distressed, such as the shipwrecked, and they also heard with faith the preachings of Cāraṇas, Yakṣas and other divinities whose feet did not of course touch the earth. Faith in the efficacy of mantras like the *pañcākṣara* and *aṣṭākṣara* was widespread. Belief in evil spirits who made a feast of dead and wounded bodies, and also frequented burial grounds, is attested to. The ancient Tamils had their own belief in expiatory ceremonies; for example, Kōvalaṉ helped in her *prāyaścittam* (expiation) the Brahman lady who killed the mungoose. They took purificatory baths in sacred pools of water and gave lavish gifts in cash and kind to the deserving, all of which, it was believed, would stand them in good stead in their lives after death. It is significant that there was a treatise on theft known as *Karavaṭam*, to which the state

[1] Canto xx. ll. 1-12.

[2] p. 408.

[3] Canto xvi, ll. 100-101.

[4] Canto xx, l. 1 ff.

goldsmith referred in his argument with the executioners of Kōvalaṉ.[1]

The existence of a high degree of excellence in the art of painting is clear from the reference to *Ōviyanūl*, to the different aspects and modes of painting, and the large use of it on walls of houses and on stage curtains. In this connexion the commentator furnishes notes from the *Nāṭakanūl*, *Pañcabāratīyam* and other works now lost to us. The carving out of Kaṇṇaki's image and the building of temples, *paḷḷis*, and *kōṭṭams* also substantiate the view that sculpture and architecture were developed to the same high degree as the other fine arts, such as music and dancing. In fact, mention is made of all the sixty-four arts known to the Tamils.[2]

XV

TRACES OF ARYAN CULTURE

The life described in the *Śilappadikāram* is generally permeated by Aryan concepts and Aryan religious ideas. This is also true of Śangam works like the *Tolkāppiyam*, the *Naṟṟiṇai*, the anthologies of the *Ahanāṉūṟu* and the *Puṟanāṉūṟu*. It is evident that the Tamil imagination has been from early times influenced by Aryan culture. It can be safely asserted that in the Śangam age the original Tamil culture was transformed into a synthesis of Sanskrit and Tamil elements. The author of the *Śilappadikāram* must have had first-hand knowledge of the Sanskrit works on drama and music as well as of the Epics, and the Purāṇas. The following among the many may be cited as instances of Aryan influence in South India.

(i) The opening lines of the first chapter are laudatory of Sūrya, Candra, Indra, and Varuṇa of the Vēdic literature.[3]

[1] Canto xvi, l. 189.
[2] Vātsyāyana's *Kāmasūtra*, Bk. I, § 3, st. 14-5, comm.
[3] For similar references see *Tolk.*, 'Porul', *sūtra* 88; *Kalittogai*, st. 141.

(ii) In the first chapter again we find that the marriage rites of Kōvalaṉ and Kaṇṇaki were performed in the Aryan fashion with the help of a learned Brahman *purōhita*.[1] The bridegroom went around the fire as enjoined[2] by the *Gṛhyasūtras* on Vaiśyas, and Kōvalaṉ was a Vaiśya. The fire-cult had been introduced into the Tamil country in much earlier times,[3] and the monarchs of old engaged in Vēdic Yajñas or sacrifices. Instances of this are not lacking. We have the Cōḻa Rājasūyamvēṭṭa Perunaṟkiḷḷi, the Cēra Celkeḻu-kuṭṭuvaṉ, the Pāṇḍya Palyāgaśālai-Mudukuḍumi.[1]

(iii) There is again a reference to the region of Uttarakurus or the *Bhōgabhūmi* of Sanskrit literature in Canto ii of the epic and elsewhere, and the *Padiṟṟuppattu* speaks[5] of Pālai-Gautamaṉār going to Heaven in human form helped by his king Palyāṉaic-celkeḻu-kuṭṭuvaṉ.

(iv) The general description of dancing and music, the dance of Mādavi in particular before the Cōḻa king, and the very names Mādavi, Citrāpati, and Mādari lead us to infer that the author is indebted to Aryan ideas. Though the *yāḻ* is a characteristic Tamil instrument, the art and science of dancing reveal borrowings from an alien culture.

(v) The reference to the *sūta* and the *māgadha*[6] among the establishment of the royal

[1] *Māmudupārppāṉ maraivaḻi kāṭṭiḍa tīvalam ceyvatu*, canto i, ll. 52-3.

[2] *C.H.I.*, Vol. I, p. 233.

[3] *Tolk.*, 'Porul', *sūtra* 92.

[4] *Puṟam.*, st. 6 and 12.

[5] See also third Ten.

[6] Canto v, l. 48. For similar references see the *Maduraikkāñji*, a composition of Māṅguḍi Marudaṉār whose contemporaneity with Talaiyālaṅgānattup-pāṇḍyan is unmistakable. See *Puṟam.*, st. 72.

household may point to the introduction of another Aryan institution.

(vi) The epic mentions deities like Śiva, Baladēva, Subrahmaṇya, Viṣṇu and Indra, and their worship, in more than one place.[1]

To conclude, the dissemination of Aryan culture was largely brought about by that class of wandering mendicant whose business was to spread the light of knowledge from one part of the country to another. The exposition of the Purāṇa is spoken of as *tiṟavōruraikkum-śeyal*[2] and it was expounded by ascetics who made the outskirts of the city their residence.

From the foregoing discussion it can be noted that there is nothing in the *Śilappadikāram* which would mark it off from the cultural point of view as a poem belonging to an age different from that of the *Puṟanāṉūṟu*, *Ahanāṉūṟu*, *Eṭṭuttogai*, *Pattuppāṭṭu* or even the *Tolkāppiyam*. If detailed references are lacking in these works it is due to the difference in the themes of each respective composition. If the *Puṟanāṉūṟu* and *Ahanāṉūṟu* do not furnish us with religious data, it is because they were sung to earn the patronage of chieftains by eulogizing, sometimes unduly, their achievements. There is however the *Paripāḍal*, where a poet like Nallanduvaṉār shows himself versed in Vēdic and Purāṇic lore.[3]

XVI

THE AUTHOR OF THE POEM

Iḷangō was the younger son of king Cēralātaṉ, and his elder brother was the Cēra king Śenguṭṭuvaṉ celebrated in the *Śilappadikāram*. The word Iḷangō means the younger prince, and perhaps it was more a title than a proper name. But what his real name was we cannot say with any certainty. This young prince, who belonged

[1] Cantos v, ix and xiv. [2] Canto v, ll. 179-81.
[3] E.g., the opening lines of poem 8; cf. also poem 5.

to a distinguished family connected by marriage alliances with the other ruling dynasties of South India and who was blessed with fortune and wealth, was destined to give up the pleasures of royalty and to take to a life of renunciation and self-sacrifice. This came to pass as follows.

One day, when the king Cēralātan̲ was sitting in the audience hall, there came to the court an astrologer who predicted the immediate death of the reigning monarch and the passing of the throne to his younger son. It was an age of faith in astrology. The prediction was a rude shock to Śeṅguṭṭuvan̲, the elder son of the king and the heir-apparent to the throne. Iḷaṅgō noticed this, and in order that his brother might enjoy the honour attached to the throne, became a monk so that he could not be king.[1] The assumption of holy orders was to assure his brother that he would not stand in the way of his hopes and aspirations. As a monk should, he left the palace for the *kōṭṭam* (usually situated in a suburb); and his residence came to be called Kuṇavāyir̤-kōṭṭam.[2]

IḶANGŌ, THE HISTORIAN

Iḷaṅgō led a secluded life, but a few scholars visited him now and then. His friend and companion was Kūlavāṇikan̲ Śīttalai Śāttan̲ār, the celebrated Śangam poet and the great author of the *Maṇimēkalai*, another epic of no mean repute to which references have already been made. From the *Padir̤r̤uppattu* and other Śangam works like the *Pur̤anān̲ūr̤u* and *Ahanān̲ūr̤u* anthologies, we gain an idea of the contemporary poets and scholars. Paraṇar to whom is attributed the fifth Ten was a contemporary of

[1] Some biographers of Aśōka have misunderstood the real significance of Indian monastic life, and have wrongly styled him monk-emperor.

[2] Canto xxx, ll. 174-85.

Iḷangō. So also were Kapilar and others. Well qualified for the task as a member of an important royal family of the Tamil land, Iḷangō, in his retirement, wrote what may be called a contemporary history of the three chief Tamil dynasties, and even planned to continue the epic *Maṇimēkalai* himself. But having heard that Śāttaṉār had begun and completed the work, he contented himself with the composition of the *Śilappadikāram*.[1] Like the other poets of his age, he did not go from court to court eulogizing one chieftain after another. Iḷangō's task was to write a history, and if we bear in mind the impartiality with which he has described the Cōḷa and the Pāṇḍya chiefs, one has to conclude that he has in no way exaggerated the achievements of his brother. Thanks, then, to Iḷangō, we have reliable material for reconstructing the history of the period.

HIS RELIGION

We need not enter again into the controversy regarding the age in which Iḷangō lived. From what we have said of Śenguṭṭuvaṉ it follows that Iḷangō also must be assigned to the latter half of the second century A.D. But far more important is the question of his religious faith. The term Kuṇavāyiṟkōṭṭam is interpreted by Aḍiyārkkunallār as Aruhaṉkōil, the name generally given to the Jaina temples. From this and from the term Aḍigaḷ being used as a suffix to his name, the late Mr. Kanakasabhai opined that Iḷangō was a monk of the Nirgrantha sect of the Jains.[2]

But this question is largely interwoven with the faith adopted and adhered to by his brother Śenguṭṭuvaṉ. Aḍigaḷ is a term of respect, and is in use even today among saints, seers and holy men to whatever faith they may

[1] See the *padikam* to the *Silappadikāram*.

[2] See V. Kanakasabhai, *The Tamils 1800 Years Ago*, p. 208.

belong. Again, the term *kōṭṭam* is a general name for temple, and cannot be said to denote particularly a Jaina temple.[1]

While we are examining this question it is necessary to call in the testimony of another datum that goes to establish his religion beyond doubt. This is the fact of Iḷango's attending the Vēdic sacrifice elaborately performed by his brother after his return from his northern expedition. A follower of the Jaina cult, with his watchword of *ahimsā*, could not be expected to attend a function like the Vēdic sacrifice. This, together with his presence on the occasion of the founding of the Pattiṉi cult, conclusively shows that Iḷangō was a follower of the orthodox religion like his brother Śenguṭṭuvaṉ. We have already seen that Śenguṭṭuvaṉ was a follower of orthodox Hinduism. In fact, his very birth was due to special prayers offered to Śiva.[2] But his was not the Śaivism of the rabid type. He worshipped Viṣṇu also. To him there was no difference between Śiva and Viṣṇu. Śenguṭṭuvaṉ's religion was what is known in the Sanskrit texts as the *sanātana-dharma*. He was a tolerant Hindu monarch. He was the originator of the cult of the Pattiṉi, to which Iḷangō not only assented, but heartily co-operated in its accomplishment. One cannot make out any difference in his description between one particular sect and another. It is the view of the learned editor Dr. V. Swaminatha Aiyar that Śaivism was the religion of Iḷangō.[3] While agreeing in the main with this view, we may respectfully point out that at the time of which we are speaking, there were no cut and dried sects like Śaivism and Vaiṣṇavism. It would be therefore more appropriate to say that he was a follower of the established faith of the land, which we may call Hinduism in its broader sense.

[1] Canto ix, l. 9 ff. [2] Canto xxvi, ll. 98-9. [3] *Sila.*, preface, p. 17.

XVII

COMMENTATORS AND COMMENTARIES: ARUMPADAVURAIYĀŚIRIYAR

It is unfortunate that we have not been able to discover the name and age of the distinguished commentator of the *Śilappadikāram,* well known as Arumpadavuraiyāśiriyar. Though no clue is forthcoming for the identification of this commentator, this much is certain that his literary attainments were of a high order, and that his special knowledge of musical treatises was undoubted. This commentary *Arumpadavurai* is the older of the two extant commentaries, the other being that of Aḍiyārkkunallār. The excellence of the commentary is due to the fact that it explains fully the technical terms and phrases in the text, and interprets them in the light of their actual use in the Śangam epoch. Though only words and phrases which require interpretation are pressed into service, the commentary is complete, and throws welcome light on the portion of the text to which the comments of Aḍiyārkkunallār are not available. In this way the commentary is useful and also valuable.

That Aḍiyārkkunallār was indebted to this *Arumpadavurai* is obvious from his own commentary, where in one place[1] he explicitly acknowledges the sources from which he has taken his material. Aḍiyārkkunallār quotes him once by the name Arumpadavuraiyāśiriyar. A study of the two extant commentaries shows how Aḍiyārkkunallār has simply followed him in many places, especially in the cantos which deal with the theory and practice of music. The greatness of the commentary lies in the fact that it furnishes rare and detailed notes on music and dancing. It is no exaggeration at all to say that without them nothing can be made out of the text. For, even with the two commentaries before us, it is difficult to get

[1] Canto v, ll. 157-60, commentary.

at the true interpretation of these technical terms relating to the art of music. Arumpadavuraiyāśiriyar's religion was, so far as can be gathered from the commentary, the established religion of the land, i.e. Hinduism. From the fact that he quotes the extant astrological work *Jinēndramālai* in connexion with *ārūḍams*[1] it may be said that he lived after the author of the *Jinēndramālai*. But when the latter flourished is itself doubtful.

XVIII

AḌIYĀRKKUNALLĀR

The other commentator is Aḍiyārkkunallār, who is supposed to have lived, not without reason, in the fifteenth century A.D. As we have already said, he mentions Arumpadavuraiyāśiriyar in one place and he has followed him in the main, sometimes adopting his very phrases and sentences. His is a commentary where due acknowledgement is made of the authorities from which he has taken his material. That he was a critical scholar and a researcher is seen from the portion of his commentary where he interprets the religion of the different characters in the epic, as also from his endeavour to fix the chronological limits of the exact day and time of Kōvalaṉ's starting for Madura, etc. In pressing into service the astronomical data, though not in a way warranted by the original, the commentator shows himself an able astronomer and, we may add, an astrologer too. That he was an accomplished scholar and had made a special study of the musical treatises is evident from the names of the originals which occur in the commentary. The books quoted from are *Indirakāḷiyam*, *Pañcamarapu*, *Baratasēṉāpatiyam*, and *Mativāṇar-nāṭakattamiḻnūl*. It appears that these treatises, which were available to the commentator in his time,

[1] Canto xvii, p. 443.

have been lost in the course of the last five centuries. The commentator is very meticulous about alien words, words in use in the Malaināḍu and the use of extinct proverbs. Such terms and expressions are interpreted with the care and the caution which they deserve. He also quotes an author Kaviccakkaravirutti.[1] This may be a reference to Jayamkoṇḍāṉ, the author of the *Kalingattu-paraṇi*, or Oṭṭa-Kūttar, the author of a *paraṇi* on Vikrama-cōḻa as testified to us by the commentator on the *Takkayā-gapparaṇi*.

THE COMMENTARY INCOMPLETE

But it is unfortunate that the whole of the commentary is not available. It is not available in respect of the cantos entitled 'Kāṉalvari', 'Vaḻakkuraikādai', 'Vañjiṉamālai', 'Aḻaṟpaṭukādai' and 'Kaṭṭuraikādai', and the whole of 'Vañjikkāṇḍam'.[2]

Two explanations can be offered. One is that he did not write a commentary on these cantos and the other is that these portions have been lost. The latter theory seems more plausible in view of the internal evidence which can be gathered from the commentary. The following may be adduced :[3]

(1) In his gloss on the term *vari* in 'Arangēṟṟu-kādai', he says more details are furnished in Kāṉalvari'.[4]

(2) Again, in the same *kādai*, in his gloss on the *yāḻ* (l. 26) he says that an elaborate examination of it is made in 'Kāṉalvari'.[5]

(3) In commenting on lines 27-8 of 'Vēṉir-kādai' he remarks that he has spoken of it before under *āṇi* etc. This *āṇi* is in the original text of 'Kāṉalvari', l. 3.

[1] Canto v, ll. 76-88, commentary.

[2] Cantos xxiv-xxx.

[3] *Sila.*, preface, p. 20.

[4] ibid., p. 88.

[5] ibid., p. 100.

(4) Again, in commenting on lines 106-7 of 'Arangēṟṟukādai', the remark is made that it would be examined *in extenso* in 'Aḻaṟpaṭukādai'.[1]

(5) Further, in his comment on lines 45-71 of 'Vēṉirkādai' he refers to the fact that additional details are given in 'Kaṭṭuraikādai', and a reference may be made to it.[2]

It is thus established that Aḍiyārkkunallār certainly wrote his commentary on all the *kādais*, and that the work as a complete one is now lost to us. Though we have no internal evidence to substantiate the theory that he also wrote a commentary on 'Vañjikkāṇḍam', yet in the light of his remarks quoted above, and in view of the fact that some portions of the commentary which according to him were actually written were lost, it is reasonable to assume that the commentator wrote a full commentary which is not traceable now. It may be that one day we shall find it in some private library in an out-of-the-way village.

HIS RELIGION

Though there are no definite data regarding the religion of the commentator, the assumption may be made that he was a Śaiva by faith. His leanings towards Jainism can be proved by his interpretation of the common terms as referring to the Jaina in many a place. To quote one example, he makes the *kōṭṭam* in the Kuṇavāyiṟkōṭṭam Aruhaṉkōil, which has afforded some foundation for the theory that Iḷangō-Aḍigaḷ, who made it his residence, must have been a Jain.

VALUE OF COMMENTARIES

In examining the value of these annotations as sources of information of the early history of the ancient Tamil kingdoms, the late P. T. Srinivasa Iyengar was not prepared

[1] p. 116 [2] p. 237

to attach any importance to them.[1] But this view of the learned author cannot stand. It may be true to some extent that the commentary is coloured by personal views, but generally the annotator aims at giving the interpretation handed down by an unbroken tradition, without the help of which no intelligible meaning could be attached to several underlying allusions or references. If this interpretation can be corroborated by an independent source or sources, it compels our acceptance and approval.[2]

Examining the work in this light, and remembering the paucity of the materials for reconstructing the history of early South India, we must ever be grateful to these annotators, whose authority cannot be questioned inasmuch as their works are quoted by the still more celebrated later annotators. Dr. V. Swaminatha Aiyar is inclined to the view that Naccinārkkiniyar was one such annotator who quotes Aḍiyārkkunallār.[3] If this is so, it speaks well of the authority, value and standing of our commentator on the epic.

[1] *History of the Tamils*, pp. 371-2.

[2] See S. K. Aiyangar, *Evolution of Hindu Administrative Institutions in South India*, p. 14.

[3] For example cf. the lines கறை முறை முகல்வன் பேணர் . . . பெருகுப்பன of 'Vēṭṭuvavari' with ll. 40-2 of *Maduraikkāñji*, commentary.

THE ŚILAPPADIKĀRAM

PADIKAM

THE hill-Kuṟavas came in a group before Kuḍakkōc-Cēral Iḷangō[1] who had renounced his royalty and was permanently residing in the hermitage of Kuṇavāyil[2] and said : 'A chaste lady who had lost a breast came to the shade of the *vēngai* tree, rich in its golden flowers ; there the King of the Dēvas appeared, to show her her loving husband, and took her to Heaven before our very eyes. This was verily a wonder. Be gracious to know this !' 1–9

At that time, the great Tamil poet Śāttaṉ,[3] who was 10–36
by his side, exclaimed, 'I know how this happened', and began to narrate the details. 'In the ancient city of undying fame, Puhār, belonging to the Cōḷa wearing the *ātti* garland,[4] there was a merchant, named Kōvalaṉ.[5] He lost his great wealth by dalliance with a dancing-girl who was expert in her art. His wife was Kaṇṇaki. With the intention of selling her tinkling anklet, he went with her to the great Pāṇḍyan city of Madura, highly renowned in literature. When he was taking it for sale in the great bazaar, he happened to show it to a goldsmith who said that it was fit to be worn only by the queen and not by any one else. Asking Kōvalaṉ to stay there, the goldsmith went to, and told, the king that he saw the queen's anklet (which the goldsmith himself had previously stolen) in the hands of the thief. Since that was the moment when Kōvalaṉ's destiny was being fulfilled, the king who

[1] The younger brother of Senguṭṭuvaṉ.

[2] The term in the text is Kuṇavāyiṟkōṭṭam. Aḍiyārkkunallār describes *kōṭṭam* as a Jaina temple. But this does not seem to be correct. The term *kōṭṭam* (Sans., *kōṣṭha*) means any building sacred to any divinity and not particularly to Aruhaṉ, the Jaina deity. Kuṇavāyil (literally, east gate), was the name of the suburb to the east of Vañji.

[3] The Sangam poet and author of the *Maṇimēkalai*.

[4] *Ātti = bauhinia racemosa*. The Tamil kings were distinguished by the garlands they wore. The Cōḷa king had the *ātti*, the Pāṇḍya and the Cēra kings used the margosa and the palmyra respectively

[5] Sans., Gōpāla.

wore the garland of margosa blossoms did not inquire into the matter fully, but ordered his tried watchmen to kill the thief and fetch the anklet. The wife of the murdered Kōvalaṉ having no refuge, shed tears copiously; and because she was so very virtuous, the Pāṇḍya suffered great distress when she plucked out one of her breasts, on which lay a string of pearls, and thereby burnt the great city of Madura. That lady of chastity of high repute is this one (referred to by the Kuṟavas).'

37–62 Hearing this, Iḷangō asked: 'You said that destiny was fulfilled.[1] How was that?'

In reply, Śāttaṉ said, 'Holy man, listen! I lay down at midnight in the Veḷḷiyambalam[2] of the Maṉṟappodiyil, sacred to Lord Śiva who wears the *koṉṟai* flower on His tuft, in the hoary city of Madura of untainted fame. I saw the tutelary deity of Madura appearing before the heroic Pattiṉi who was in deep distress and saying: "O lady, who raised furious flames from your breast! Now it is that the action of your previous birth has become completed. In your previous birth, the wife of the merchant Śangamaṉ of Śingapuram[3] of undying fame laid a curse upon your husband and yourself. O lady of the beautiful tresses of hair! You will see your husband (again) fourteen days from now, not in his human form, but in the divine." This guileless account did I hear. So we shall write a poem, with songs, illustrating the three truths that *dharma* will become the God of Death to kings who swerve from the path of righteousness, that it

[1] This is the central theme underlying the whole epic. The story seems to elucidate the fundamental belief of Hinduism and its dissenting sects, like Buddhism and Jainism, that a man's fortune or misfortune in this birth is the result of his actions, good or bad, in past birth or births.

[2] Veḷḷiyambalam (literally, silver hall) is an open space for the use of the public. Note there are Poṉṉambalam, Maṇiyambalam, etc., referring to particular shrines. The term Maṉṟappodiyil shows that the village assembly usually met in the temple compound, where it is natural to suppose that large and shady trees were planted and allowed to grow.

[3] Singapuram is one of the capitals of ancient Kalinga.

is natural for great men to adore a chaste lady of great fame, and that destiny will manifest itself and be fulfilled; and as these truths centre round an anklet of artistic beauty, the poem (*pāṭṭuḍaicceyyuḷ*) can be named *Śilap-padikāram*. As this story relates to all the three crowned monarchs, it is only proper, O venerable saint, that you should write it.'

In response to this request of Śāttaṉ, the saint of 63-85
extraordinary repute (Iḷaṅgō) composed a poem, consisting of thirty parts, which were the following: The song of benediction; the story about the parents establishing the hero as a householder; the story of the dancing-girl Mādavi receiving royal recognition for her skill on the stage; the chapter in praise of the twilight; the canto narrating the celebration of Indra's festival in the city; the canto describing the sports on the seashore; the section describing the *kāṉalvari* and Mādavi's sorrow at the heat caused by the blazing sun; the canto dealing with the sight of the city (Madura) and that of the forest; the canto dealing with the song of the hunters and the sojourn of Kōvalaṉ with his spouse outside the city; the section dealing with the visit to the city; the section describing the shelter found for the fair lady Kaṇṇaki; the account of the murder of Kōvalaṉ; the canto in which the dance of the cowherdesses is described; that dealing with the distress of the people who heard the news of the burning of the city; the song (*kūdai*) dealing with the entry into the city which was in utter turmoil; the canto describing the manner in which Kaṇṇaki presented her case before the king; the vow, the story of the great conflagration, the facts revealed by the tutelary deity of Madura to Kaṇṇaki; the dance of the hill-damsels wearing fragrant flowers; the story of the seeing, taking and bathing of the slab of stone in the holy Ganges, and the planting of the image; the story of the praise offered to, and the boon obtained from, the Goddess of Chastity.

86–90 These stories which are narrated in poetic form (*uraiyiḍaiyiṭṭa pāṭṭuḍaicceyyuḷ*) by Iḷangō-Aḍigaḷ were heard by Kūlavāṇikaṉ[1] Śāttaṉ of Madura. This is the account of the origin of the poem which elaborates the *trivarga* (*pālvahai*).[2]

[1] This indicates that Sattaṉ belonged to the community of corn-chandlers. The term *vāṇiya* is from the Sanskrit *vaṇik*, a merchant. Though a common name etymologically for all merchants, it is used in practice only in connexion with oil-pressers. Amongst the other *vāṇiyas* there were *ilaivaṇiyas* or betel-sellers and numerous other branches. *Kūlavāṇiyas* are said to have dealt in grain.

[2] The *trivarga* are *dharma* (Tam., *aram*), *artha* (Tam., *poruḷ*) and *kāma* (Tam., *iṉbam*). The expression shows the naturalization of the idea of *puruṣārthas* in the Tamil land.

URAIPEṞUKAṬṬURAI[1]

1. From that day forth the Pāṇḍyan kingdom was deprived of rains, and famine-stricken. This was followed by fever and plague. Veṟṟivēṟceḻiyaṉ[2] reigning at Koṟkai[3] propitiated the Lady of Chastity by sacrificing a thousand goldsmiths, and celebrated a festival when there was a downpour causing fertility to the land. Thereupon the kingdom was rid of disease and distress.

2. Hearing this, the Iḷam-Kōśar[4] of the Kongunāḍu[5] instituted festivities in honour of the Lady of Chastity in their land, and this resulted in plentiful rains.

3. On hearing this, Gajabāhu[6] of Ceylon encircled by the sea, built a shrine for the Lady of Chastity where daily sacrifices were performed. Thinking that she would remove the distress (of his land), he also instituted annual festivals commencing with the month of Āḍi; then the rains came to stay, and increased the fertility of the land so as to produce unfailing crops.

4. At this the Cōḷa king Perumkiḷḷi[7] built at Uṟaiyūr a shrine for Pattiṉikkaḍavuḷ, and instituted daily offerings, thinking that she would shower her blessings at all times.

[1] This was added to the *padikam* by an early editor whose identity is not known.

[2] The successor of Neḍuñjeḻiyaṉ.

[3] Quondam capital of the Pāṇḍyan kingdom. It was the same as Kavāṭapuram (seaport capital) referred to in the *Kauṭalīya Arthaśāstra* and the *Rāmāyaṇa*.

[4] The smaller chieftains of Tamiḻnāḍu. Their services were requisitioned by great kings like the Pāṇḍyan. (See *Maduraikkāñji*, ll. 773-4.)

[5] This is to be identified as the western part of the Kongu region: Tuḷunāḍu, Coorg and parts of Mysore. This may be called Kōśarnāḍu.

[6] The Cēra King Senguṭṭuvaṉ's contemporary in Ceylon.

[7] The contemporary Cōḷa king.

NURSIRAPPUPPĀYIRAM

Veṇbā

THE unexcelled language of the *opus* of the ascetic Cêraṉ, the prince of Kuḍanāḍu, highly spoken of by the people of Kūḍal (Madura), resembles a range of hills with its group of peaks as seen in a mirror.[1]

Kaṭṭaḷaikkalittuṟai

The crown-jewel of the great Cēra composed the *Silappadikāram*, much appreciated by the people of Pūm-puhār, which was the residence of wealthy merchants who formed one of the four famous castes created by the four-faced Lord (Brahmā), and which was the dwelling-place of authorities on Tamil literature.

[1] This and the following stanza appear to be ancient compositions, but it is not possible to trace their authorship.

BOOK I

PUHARKKAṆḌAM

Canto I

MANGALAVĀḺTTUPPĀḌAL

OR

THE SONG OF BENEDICTION

Praised be the Moon![1] Praised be the Moon, for, like 1–12
the cool white umbrella of the king who wears the pollen-spreading garland, He blesses our beautiful world.

Praised be the Sun! Praised be the Sun, for, like the commands of the Lord of the Kāvērināḍu, He revolves round the golden-peaked Mēru.

Praised be the mighty Clouds! Praised be the mighty Clouds, for, like him whose land the frightful sea surrounds, they stand on high, and pour their gifts to men below.

Praised be sweet Puhār![2] Praised be sweet Puhār, for it is as famous as the glory of the (Cōḻa) royal line all over the wide world, encircled by the waters of the sea.

Those who have fully heard and known all that is to be 13–19
heard and known,[3] hold the view that, like the Podiyil hill[4] and the Himalayan range, the unique city of Puhār,

[1] For a similar invocation of the deities see *Takkayāgappparaṇi*, 'Kaḍavul', st. 9, comm. It may be noted that the first deity invoked is the Moon, thus bearing testimony to the prevalence of the moon cult in ancient Tamil India.

[2] Puhār, Kākandi, Kāvirippūmpaṭṭiṇam, and Paṭṭiṇam, are other names for Kāvērippaṭṭiṇam, the ancient capital city of the Cōḻas on the seashore. According to some, it is the *Khaberis Emporium* mentioned by Ptolemy in the first century A.D. The inscriptions secured from the modern Kāvērippattinam and its vicinity leave no doubt as to its identity with Kāvirippūmpaṭṭiṇam alias Puhār. (*An. Rep. Ep.*, 1919, p. 92.)

[3] The term *kēḷvi* in l.19 may also be interpreted as the *Sruti* or the Vēdic lore. It occurs in the sense of the Vēdas in *Padiṟr.*, third Ten, st. 1, l.1.

[4] The Podiyil hill is noted as the residence of the sage Agastya (*Bhāga. Pur.*, Bk. X, ch. 79, st. 16-17). This hill of the Pāṇḍyas can be identified with the Malaya, otherwise known as Chandanādri or Candanācala. Perhaps the epithet Malayadhvaja attributed to the Pāṇḍyan king in the *Mhb.*, Bk. III, ch. 281, st. 44f. (cf. *Ṛaghu*, canto iv, st. 46-9) is after the hill Malaya. The Tamil name Podigai is the original of the Bettigo of Ptolemy (J. W. MacCrindle, *Ptolemy*, 1885, p. 78).

renowned for its generations of unexcelled ancient families, stands immutable as the great ones who live there.

20–29 In that city of Puhār which equalled Heaven in its fame and the Serpent World[1] in its enjoyments, there lived a celebrated sea-captain (*mānāikaṉ*),[2] liberal in his gifts like the rain-bearing clouds. He had a daughter, Kaṇṇaki,[3] who was like a golden creeper and was[4] nearing twelve years old. She had high qualities on account of which women adored and praised her, exclaiming, 'She is Lakṣmī[5] of praiseworthy form, seated on the lotus, and her excellence is that of the faultless northern star (Arundati.'[6]

30–39 In that selfsame city lived an inland merchant prince (*māśāttuvāṉ*) of abounding wealth, who, along with his relations, was placed in the foremost rank of the aristocracy

[1] Nāganāḍu; also Pavaṇam. According to the Jaina scriptures the joys in the Nāgalōka are greater than those in heaven or Svargalōka: cf. *Mhb.*, 'Ādi', ch. 234.

[2] The terms *mānāikaṉ* (Sans., *mahānāyaka*=great leader) and *māśāttuvāṉ* (Sans., *mahāśārtha*) connote respectively 'members of maritime commercial ventures' and 'members of caravan trade': see canto ii, ll. 7-8; also *Studies in Tamil Literature and History*, p. 77, n. 2.

[3] It is to be noted here that the heroine of the story has been mentioned first and then the hero. This is because the story from start to finish centres round the heroine. Or it may point to a custom in ancient India of speaking first of the wife and then of the husband in referring to a married couple (*vadhūvara*), e.g. Sītārāma, Pārvatī Paramēśvara.

[4] The term *ahavaiyāḷ* means that she was not yet twelve years old.

[5] Consort of Viṣṇu and Goddess of Wealth.

[6] Arundati is the wife of the sage Vasiṣṭha, one of the seven celebrated sages who went by the name of Saptarṣis. She was distinguished for her chastity.

Chaste women are generally compared to Arundati (see *Padirr.*, fourth Ten. st. 1, l. 28). The *Bōdhāyana Gṛhyasūtra* rules that a married couple should see the star Arundati and the Pole Star on the first day of their marriage (*Govt. Oriental Series*, Mysore, 1904, p. 124). Legend has it that each of the seven primeval sages had his own wife. Of these, the wives of six sages excluding that of Vasiṣṭha fell in love with Agni and gave their breast-milk to Subrahmaṇya. These six became Kṛttika Nakṣatras which are six in number (the Pleiades); but Arundati stood firm in her chastity and attained an honourable place as an auspicious star fit to be seen by chaste and pure women so that they might ever lead holy lives. (*Mhb.*, 'Vana Parva', ch. 226-30. Also S. Sorenson's *Index*, p. 91.)

by the monarch of that great kingdom. He was, in sooth, the lord of a rich treasure[1] and gave away his earnings to others in need. He had a son, named Kōvalaṉ,[2] nearing sixteen years. Kōvalaṉ's expanding fame made the earth all too small to bear it. Moon-faced maidens, skilled in song and sweet in voice, fondly said to each other, 'O, He is Subrahmaṇya incarnate!'[3] and revealed their excessive love for him when they spoke in praise of him in their own gatherings.

Them, (Kaṇṇaki and Kōvalaṉ), their worthy parents 40–44
longed to see, on a happy day, as a bridal pair. Happy in such thoughts, they sent forth fair maidens, seated on an elephant's neck, to invite to the wedding all those who lived in that great city.

As they went forth into the streets, drums were beaten: 45–53
mṛdangams were sounded: conches were blown: and white umbrellas were lifted high as if in kingly procession. O, how enchanting was their entry into the pavilion, glimmering with pearls beneath the canopy of blue silk and with dazzling pillars, decked with diamonds and beautified by overhanging garlands! That was the day on which the Moon moving in the sky approached the star Rōhiṇī;[4]

[1] It may be interpreted as twofold treasure and the comparison may be to Kubēra, the Lord of Divine Treasure, Saṅkha and Padma.

[2] Note here also the term *ahavaiyāṉ*.

[3] He is the War-God in whose honour Kālidāsa wrote his classic *Kumārasambhava*. He is a very popular deity in Tamil India (see T. A. Gopinatha Rao, *Elements of Hindu Iconography*, Vol. II, p. 415). According to *Tolk.*, he is the tutelary deity of the hillmen (*kuṟiñjimlam*) (*Aham.*, *sūtra* 5). Among the Sangam works the *Tirumurugāṟṟuppaḍal* and one-fourth of the *Paripāḍal* are sung in glorification of Kumāra. Incidentally it may be noticed that the arguments in favour of a later date for the *Paripāḍal* (seventh century A.D.), on the basis of astronomical data, put forward by the late Swamikannu Pillai (see *Indian Ephemeris*, Vol. I, Pt. II, Appendix III; 'The Chronology of Early Tamil Literature', and further examined by K. G. Sankara in *J.R.A.S.*, 1932, pp. 541-5), are not tenable in the light of other and more positive data.

[4] Cf. *Aham.*, st. 136. That Rōhiṇī is an auspicious planet is attested to by Vēdic authority (*Vedic Index*, Vol. I, p. 415), not to speak of the later *Bṛhat-Jātaka* and similar literature. Rōhiṇī, moreover, was the favourite of the twenty-seven wives of the Moon.

when Kōvalan who walked around the holy fire,[1] in accordance with scriptural injunctions as directed by the revered priest, approached his bride, divinely fair, resembling the star Arundati. How fortunate were those who
54–68 enjoyed such a splendid sight! Lovely maidens, bringing spices and flowers, spake and sang, and looked bewitching. Women with full breasts and glowing tresses took with them sandal-paste, frankincense, perfumes and powders. Ladies with lovely teeth bore lamps, vessels, and *pālikai* pots[2] of tender shoots. These maidens, who looked like golden creepers and whose hair was decked with flowers, showered blossoms on the bridal pair, saying: 'May you live a flawless life, with a love that knows no separation, and held in close and unrelaxing embrace!' They then led Kaṇṇaki, the Arundati of this vast world, to the auspicious nuptial bed with the prayer that the royal tiger-emblem, engraved on this side of the Himalayas, might remain for ever on the golden crest of that mountain,[3] and that the Cōḷa king

[1] The fire-rite was already in vogue in the Tamil land for purposes of marriage. It seems to have been a regular institution ever since the age of *Tolk.* Arundati (Sans., Arundhatī) is the star Alcor in the Great Bear. She was the daughter of Kāśyapa, sister of Nārada, and wife of Vasiṣṭha. As the model of conjugal felicity she figures in the Śāstraic literature. The reference indicates the adoption by the Tamil Vaiśyas of the Aryan marital custom and procedure. It is worth noting that Kaṇṇaki was barely twelve at the time of her marriage.

[2] *Pālikai* pots are the chief feature of marriage and other *samskāras* among the Hindus even today. The *Bōdhāyana Gṛhyasūtra* mentions five *pālikais* for purposes of marriage. The technical term *ankurārpaṇa* (p. 328 of the Mysore edition), probably suggests that the married couple should be blessed with good and healthy progeny.

[3] The reference here is to Karikāla's engraving the tiger crest on the Himalayas. For a learned study on the life and achievements of Karikāla see Oolaganatham Pillai, *Karikālaccōḷan*, in Tamil. If we compare these lines with canto v, ll. 90-104, there is the implication that Karikāla was not satisfied with being the overlord of all India and his ambition was to cross the snow-clad hills and to extend his conquests to Tibet, China, etc. (Note the terms *ippāl* and *uppāl*.) But the Himalayas were a stumbling block; he could not proceed further and had to return. Pandit M. Raghava Aiyangar is of opinion that the Cōḷa king's route lay through the passes between Sikkim and Bhutan, leading to the Chambi Valley in Tibet. This is attested

(Śembiyaṉ)[1] who possessed the fierce javelin in battle, might throw his matchless discus[2] all over the world.

to by the fact that even today one of the passes there, and the mountain range as well, go by the name of the Cōḻa Pass and the Cōḻa Range. (*Imperial Gazetteer of India*, 'Sikkim', Vol. X, p. 327, Vol. XXII, p. 365. *Encyclopædia Britannica*, Vol. V, p. 667, s. v. Sikkim, Vol. XX, p. 640) *Kalaimagal* (Madras), Vol. I, p. 56 ff.

[1] Śembiyaṉ is an epithet for the Cōḻa king. The tradition transmitted in Tamil literature bears evidence to the fact that one of the great ancestors of the Cōḻas was Sibicakravarti, and as coming from his family, the Cōḻas claimed the title Śembiyaṉ. If this tradition has any value at all, it demonstrates that the Cōla dynasty is only a branch of a North Indian dynasty of which Sibi was an honoured member. But there are scholars who look upon this dynasty as indigenous to South India.

[2] An emblem of universal sovereignty.

CANTO II

MAṈAIYAṚAMPAṬUTTAKĀDAI

OR

SETTING UP HOME

1–11 THE untold wealth of the seafaring merchants of the rich city (Puhār) made even far-famed monarchs covet it. The varieties of foreign merchandise, rare commodities brought to the city by ships and caravans, were so vast that, even if the whole world, encircled by the roaring seas, flocked into it, its wealth would not become diminished. In the delights which it yielded, and in the presence of noble persons, (the parents of) Kaṇṇaki the lotus-eyed and her loving husband Kōvalaṉ, who were nobly born and blessed with inexhaustible ancestral wealth, the city resembled Uttarakuru,[1] the residence of great penance-performers.

12–25 In the middle story of their lofty mansion, they (Kōvalaṉ and Kaṇṇaki) seated themselves on a gem-legged couch which looked as if it had been made for them by Maya.[2] As they were enjoying themselves, the soft south wind entered, at the proper time with the bees, through the lattice windows ornamented with a series of jewelled hangings, bringing the sweet fragrance of the cool *āmbal*, the close-petalled *kuvaḷai*, the half-opened lotus filled with humming drones, and several other flowers

[1] The Uttarakuru (*Vedic Index*, p. 84) is perhaps the semi-mythical region of enjoyment and bliss Six such places are distinguished also in the Jaina literature. See *Divākaram*, st. 12. For a similar description of the Uttarakuru, see *Mhb.*, 'Sabhā Parva', ch 29, st. 66-71. The *Aitarēya Brāhamaṇa* locates it as a trans-Himalayan country (ch. 8, st. 14). According to Pliny, Bk. VI., c. 17, Amometus wrote a book on the Attacorae (Uttarakuru)). See J. W. MacCrindle, *Megasthenes and Arrian*, 1926, pp. 76-9.

[2] Though Aḍiyārkkunallār interprets the term Mayaṉ as the Carpenter of the Gods, Sanskrit tradition has it that Viśvakarmā was the architect of the Gods, and Maya was the architect of the Asuras,

which blossomed in fields and on the surface of small pools, to wit, the pleasing *tāḻai* and the white wide-mouthed *kōdai*, and blew over them. Along with it came the drones which had partaken of the tiny particles of *mādavi* from the arbour of the *campaka*, and which were in eager search for the sweet-smelling tresses of the charming damsel with her beaming face.

(Bathed in such a breeze), the couple passed out into 26–37
the open terrace where, under the cool rays of the moon, the God of Love sat holding his arrow of flowers. There they laid themselves down in a bed covered with pollen attracting humming bees. Kōvalaṉ amused himself by painting, on the broad shoulders of his lady-love, the sugar-cane[1] and the *valli*,[2] when they looked like the sun and the moon shedding their lustre upon the whole sea-girt world. He wore a garland of jasmine whose sparkling white petals had been opened by the honey-seeking bee. Hers was a garland of the charming close-petalled *kaḻunīr*. With their wreaths intertwined owing to their close embrace, both of unsatiated love grew wearied when Kōvalaṉ looked into the beaming face of Kaṇṇaki, and spoke to her in words of prattling endearment:

'My dear, though Śiva has adorned his tuft of hair by 38–45
placing the beautiful crescent moon[3] in it so that the gods may praise him, He will yet give it away to you so as to make it your forehead: for, was not the moon born along with you?[4]

[1] The bow of the God of Love is said to be of sugar-cane.

[2] *Valli* is evidently the heavenly creeper known as *kāmavalli*. Cf. *Jīvakacintāmaṇi*, st. 365, where the *kāmavalli* is compared to a lovely lady.

[3] This is apparently a reference to the *aṣṭamīcandra*, i.e. the crescent of the eighth lunar day, which is generally compared to the forehead of beautiful ladies. Among the Sahasranāma of the Dēvī, one is *aṣṭamīcandrabibhrāja dalikasthalaśōbhitā*.

[4] The reference is to the legend of the churning of the ocean by the Dēvas and the Asuras for nectar which the former drank and became immortal. With the nectar came also the Moon and the Goddess of Wealth. To Kōvalaṉ, Kaṇṇaki is none else than this Lakṣmī. See *Mhb.* 'Ādi', ch. 17-19 for a fuller description; also S. Sorenson's *Index*, pp. 34-5.

'Likewise the bodyless God of Love will be happy to give you his big sugar-cane bow, so that it may become your dark eyebrows; for, is it not a law of warfare that the vanquished foe should yield up his weapons?

46–52 'Indra too is bound to give you his thunderbolt[1] which protects the Dēvas, saying that it will fittingly become your waist, for, were you not born long before ambrosia?

'Though the six-faced one (Subrahmaṇya) has no cause for doing it, still He has given you his long lance, red as fire, so as to form your two dark, cloudlike, red-cornered eyes; he naturally wishes to see me in distress!

53–61 'By your complexion you have put to shame the gem-tinted peacock with its beautiful black plumes, which hides itself in the woods. O lady of the shining face! By your soft and lovely gait you have put to shame the swan which hides itself amidst the lotuses of the cool tank. The little green parrots are ashamed of themselves when they listen to your charming voice which assumes the character of the flute, *viṇā,* and ambrosia: yet, O lady of stately gait, they love to stay for ever on your flower-like hands.

62–72 'O lady with charming tresses fragrant with flowers! Of what use to you are dressing maids and ornaments other than your flawless *tāli*?[2] Again, beyond a few flowers to be worn on your black hair, what need is there

[1] Like nectar, Indra's Vajra or thunderbolt is said to have sprung from out of the churning ocean. It is a two-headed trident with a slender handle in the middle, which is compared here to the lady's waist. According to the Sanskrit tradition, it was the bone of the sage Dadhīci that was transformed into the Vajra, the war-implement of Indra. (See *Mhb.*, 'Vanaparva', ch. 99; 'Salyaparva', ch. 52.)

[2] The commentators seem to interpret the term *mangalavaṇi* as natural beauty, and this may fit in with the context. The other interpretation of *mangalavaṇi* is *tāli* or *tirumāngalyam,* the wearing of which on the occasion of a marriage seems to have been originally a South Indian custom, later adopted by the followers of the Brahmanical religion. Cf. canto iv, l. 50. See, for instance, the chapter in the *Rāmāyaṇa* describing the marriage of Rāma and Sītā (Bk. I, ch. 73), where there is no mention of *māngalya-sūtram.* The term *sūtram* in the sense of *tāli* occurs in the later *Smṛtis.*

for any splendid wreath of flowers? Nor does your hair require any paste of *kastūri*. Common frankincense is quite sufficient. Likewise with the sandal-paste figures painted on your beautiful breasts, there is no need for a string of pearls. What folly induced them to deck you with so many ornaments causing drops of perspiration on your face, and pain to your slender waist!

O purest gold! O conch-white pearl!
O faultless fragrance! O sugar-cane, honey! 73–83
Unattainable beauty, life-giving nectar!
O noble child of nobly-born merchants!
Shall I say that you are an unborn gem of the hills?
Shall I say that you are nectar not produced from the sea?
Shall I say that you are melody not born of the *yāḻ*?
O my girl of dark and flowing hair!'

Uttering ceaselessly such well-worded speeches, the ecstatic lover with bright garlands, spent with his fair lady-love days and days in deep enjoyment.

One such day, the venerable lady (mother of Kōvalaṉ) 84–90
established the lady of abundant and flowing tresses (Kaṇṇaki) in a house of her own, where she provided her with faithful servants and wealth of all kinds, so as to serve[1] her near and dear ones, ascetics and guests, in a manner appropriate to the householder's life, that thereby her fame might increase.

Some years passed, and Kaṇṇaki in the discharge of her household duties earned a name worthy to be praised.

[1] The chief duties of the lady of a house were the giving of gifts to the deserving, the serving of Brahmans, and the entertaining of ascetics and guests, as evidenced by Kaṇṇaki's own words in canto xvi, ll. 71-3. This is also the prescription of the Dharmaśāstras or law-codes like that of Manu. A student of Tiruvaḷḷuvar's *Tirukkuṟaḷ* will find elaborate prescriptions for the above-mentioned duties of the householder.

VEṆBĀ

They (Kōvalaṉ and Kaṇṇaki), who (respectively) resembled Kāma (God of Love) and Rati (Goddess of Love), enjoyed close embraces like smoke-coloured serpents; they enjoyed all sorts of pleasures as if realizing the instability of life on the earth.[1]

[1] The poet here hints at the coming tragedy.

Canto III

ARANGERRUKĀDAI

OR

THE DEBUT

The great sage (Agastya) of the divine Podiyil hill 1–11
(once) cursed Indra's son[1] (along with Urvaśī)[2], and the latter obtained redemption by displaying her skill on the stage.[3] From that distinguished line of celestial nymphs, was descended Mādavi, noted for her deeds of great distinction, as well as for her broad shoulders and beautiful tresses which scattered the pollen of flowers. In dance and song, and in grace of form,[4] she underwent training for seven years, succeeding in all three; and at the age of twelve she was in a position to display her talents before the reigning king[5] who wore heroic anklets.

Her dancing master knew the characteristics of the 12–16
two schools of the dancing art.[6] He could effectively

[1] Jayanta, the son of Indra, was cursed, together with Urvaśī, by the sage Agastya for misbehaviour. Jayanta was reborn as a bamboo in the Vindhya Hills and Urvaśī as a dancing-girl on the earth. According to the [illegible], a late musical treatise, Urvaśī was born first in the city of Kāñci.

[2] Urvaśī (Tam., Uruppaśi) is a daughter of the Gods (an *apsaras*). For the origin and career of Urvaśī see *Matsya Purāṇa*, ch. 24, st. 25 ff. Cf. Dikshitar, *Matsya Purāṇa—a study*, 1935, pp. 42-3.

[3] The term used is *talaikkōl*. It might be a staff used by the dancer to serve as an equipoise. For details see ll. 114 ff.

[4] The chief requisites are dancing, singing and natural beauty (*aḻahu*). If *aḻahu* is interpreted as an art, it may mean 'proper rhythm'. The period of training was seven years commencing from the age of five.

[5] According to the commentator the king under reference is Karikāla. But a study of the chronology of the early centuries of the Christian era shows that the king referred to must have been a successor to Karikāla. This has been examined in the Introduction.

[6] The two schools are the *dēśi* (secular) and *mārga* (orthodox), which are the two kinds of *kūttu*. There were a number of *kūttus* which came

combine the different dancing poses with the *vilakku* song.[1] He had a clear knowledge of the established rules of the eleven modes of body-movement and limb-movement (*āḍal*), of the songs (*pāṭṭu*),[2] of the resounding instruments (*koṭṭu*), as also of the dance (*āḍal*), of gestures (*pāḍal*),[3] of the measured beats (*pāṇi*),[4] and of time-beats (*tūkku*).[5]

17–25 During the course of the exhibition of the dancing art, composed of the foregoing elements, he knew when only one hand had to be used for gesticulation (*piṇḍi*),[6] and when both the hands had to be used (*piṇaiyal*). He also knew when the hands had to be used for exhibiting action alone (*toḻiṟkai*), and when for graceful effect alone (*eḻiṟkai*). Knowing as he did the conventions at the time of dancing, he avoided the mixing up of the single-hand demonstration (*kūṭai*) with the double-hand demonstration (*vāram*) and vice versa, as also the mixing up of pure gesture with gesticulatory movement and vice versa. In the movements of the feet also, he did not mix up the *kuravai* with the *vari*.[7] He was such an expert.

26–35 Her music teacher was likewise skilled in handling the

under one category or the other. Like *kūttu*, music was also classified as *dēśi* and *mārga*. (See introduction by M. S. Ramaswami Aiyar to his edition of the *Svaramēḷakalānidhi*, Annamalai University, 1932.)

[1] Of the fourteen limbs of *vilakku* three are distinguished, *vēnduvilakku*, *paṭaivilakku* and *ūrvilakku*. For details see Aḍiyārkkunallār's commentary, *Sila.*, p. 82.

[2] The expression *pāttu* here is a reference to the *Aham.* and *Puṟam. nāṭakam*, or dramatic compositions.

[3] The gestures of *pāḍal* are said to be of eight kinds.

[4] This was either with the hands or a metal disk. Was the Tamil technical expression *paṇ* derived from it? The earliest texts of the *Tēvāram* and *Nālāyirapprabandam* classify the psalms according to *paṇs*.

[5] This *tūkku* is said to be of seven kinds. The reverberations are created by the manipulation of time-beats. Probably *pāṇi* and *tūkku* composed a full *tāḷam*.

[6] The *piṇḍi* consisted of twenty-four exhibitions and the *piṇaiyal* of thirteen.

[7] These are the *kuravaikkūttu* and the *varikkūttu*.

yāḻ[1] and the *kuḻal* (flute),[2] in the technique of the *tāḷam* (timing), in the manipulation of the vocal chords, and in the production of the soft low note of the *mṛdangam.*[3] He could make all these sounds harmonize agreeably to the dance (*āḍal*). Knowing what music was appropriate to the *vari* and *āḍal*, he had the discriminating knowledge of all the subtle sounds of the flawless *dēśikam* music. Because of his perfect knowledge he could elaborate upon and classify all varieties of dances and music, and still remain true to the spirit of their composers.

There was, again, the learned composer of songs whose 36–44
knowledge of the Tamil language was complete and known to the whole Tamil land surrounded by the noisy sea.[4] An authority in the art of dramaturgy he had a knowledge of the two branches, *vēttiyal*[5] and *poduviyal,*[6] and exhibited it in his compositions. Realizing the improper expressions employed by others (his rivals), he scrupulously avoided such defects in his own dramatic poetry.[7]

[1] Four varieties of *yāḻ* are distinguished: *pēriyāḻ*, *makarayāḻ*, *śakōṭayāḻ*, and *śeṅgōṭṭiyāḻ* of 21, 19, 14 and 7 strings respectively. (See also *Puṟam.*, st. 152, comment.). It may be pointed out that Sārngadēva's *vīṇā* was of 22 strings, and that it was simplified by Rāmāmātya (16th cent.) into one of seven strings, and by his critic and successor Vēnkaṭamakhi (17th cent.) into one of five strings. We cannot say positively what was the type prevalent in the Tamil country. The *yāḻ* was apparently the *viṇa*, known as such because of the figure of the conventional lion into which the shaft was worked at the end. The terms *makarayāḻ*, etc., give a clue to it. The lute is an instrument going back to Vēdic times.

[2] The *kuḻal* was made of one of five materials, namely, bamboo, sandal, bronze, red catechu, or coromandel ebony. Of these, bamboo was regarded as the best material, bronze middling, and others as distinctly inferior. The flute was as ancient an instrument as the lute and the drum.

[3] This is one of the thirty-one skin instruments of music.

[4] Surrounded by sea on three sides and extending up to Vēngaḍam (modern Tirupati Hills) in the north and the Kumarī in the south was the ancient Tamil land. Here three branches of Tamil literature were current.

[5] The branch relating to *Aham.* in the dramatic composition.

[6] The branch relating to *Puṟam.* in dramatic works.

[7] The technical term Tamiḻ is of three kinds, *iyal*, *iśai* and *nāṭakam*. See V. G. Suryanarayana Sastri, *History of the Tamil Language*, 1930, and Pandit V. Swaminatha Aiyar's *Saṅgattamiḻum Piṟkālattamiḻum*, 1929, pp. 45-52. *Iyal* refers to literary Tamil; *iśai* is that division of Tamil literature which

45-55 He who played upon the *mṛdangam*, knew all forms of dancing and singing, the musical notes, the pure Tamil modes of speech, the melody and the *tāḷam*, the harmony born of differentiated time-beats, as well as the flaws that might result from such manipulations, together with the use of different kinds of expressions (*dēśikam*). In playing upon his instruments, he knew how to combine correctly single beats, how to give time for double beats so as to be heard well, how to make both these kinds of beats melodiously merge with the notes of the lute and the flute, and also with the evenly drawn-out note of the vocal chords. With dexterity he could, wherever necessary, subdue the sound of his instrument, so that the other instruments might be properly heard; at times, he would also fitly drown them with the overpowering sound of his *mṛdangam*. (Such was the high degree of perfection which this master had reached.)

56-69 The flutist was a master of the traditional rules of that art. He knew the two combinations known as *cittira*[1] and *vañjaṉai*,[2] whereby harsh syllables were softened and rendered sweet to the ear. He knew the four *varttaṉas* (involving fingering skill), and with his knowledge of the science of the *pālai* music (*kural* and *iḷi*),[3] he adjusted himself to the sound produced by the *muḻavu*. He could play carefully enough to be in tune with the *mṛdangam* and the *iḷi* strains of the flute. He could observe the notes voiced by the singer and elaborate upon what he heard and at the same time keep himself within the limits of the tune. He exhibited his grasp of melodies[4] by playing note by note so that each separate sound might faultlessly be heard.

consists of verses set to music as distinct from poetry or drama. *Nāṭakam* is dramatic literature. These three divisions constitute the *muttamiḻ*.

[1] The term *cittira-p-puṇarppu* is nasalizing the hard consonants in singing a musical piece (*Tamil Lexicon*, p. 141).

[2] The term *vañjaṉai-p-puṇarppu* is nasalizing the soft consonants in singing.

[3] Also *Paṭṭaṭai* as in *vaṇṇap-paṭṭaṭai* of the line 63.

[4] The technical terms are *vārappāḍal* and *kūḍaippāḍal*.

Then there was the master of the lute of the fourteen 70–79
strings. In order to produce the seven *pālai* notes he would conjointly sound the respective strings in the lute, known as the *tāram*, and the *kural*, and bringing them to the central part of the lute he would tune the *kaikkiḷai* part of the instrument. Similarly, touching the other stout string on the *tāram* side and the other two slender strings on the *kural* side and bringing them to the central part of the lute, he would tune the *viḷari* part of the instrument.

Then proceeding from *uḻai*, the most slender string, up 80–94
to the *kaikkiḷai*, he would play upon all the fourteen strings and thus produce the *śempālai* note. In a definite order the notes would arise, e.g. *paḍumalaippālai* from *kaikkiḷai*, *śevvaḻippālai* from *tuttam*, *kōḍippālai* from *tāram*, *viḷarippālai* from *viḷari*, *mēṟśempālai* from *iḷi*—thus are the combinations effected. In the lute, the notes become lower and lower as they pass over to the left (side of the instrument). It is just the opposite in the flute. The expert in the lute can mix the low and high and the middling notes with a pleasing effect.

The site for erecting the stage was also chosen in 95–114
accordance with well-established traditions,[1] having regard to the nature of the soil. For purposes of the measurement of the stage,[2] the *kōl*, which was a piece of bamboo growing in the sacred high hills, with the length of a span between every two of its joints, and with twenty-four thumb breadths, was the standard. The stage was eight *kōls* in length, seven *kōls* in breadth, and one *kōl* in height. It had two appropriate doors. The plank

[1] The reference to *nūl* in ll. 95-6 shows the authority of the *śilpaśāstra* which was then in vogue. According to *Arumpadavurai* the reference is to dramatic works. This is not very convincing. The choice of the site and the fixing of the stage must follow the prescriptions of the *śilpaśāstra* only.

[2] For a description of the stage see *Suddhānandappirakāśa* quoted by Pandit Swaminatha Aiyar, *Sila.*, pp. 114-5, n. The two doors were intended one for entrance and the other for exit.

platform placed over it was four *kōls* in width. Over the stage were placed painted pictures (of the *bhūtam*)[1] for praise and worship. The graceful lamp illumining the stage was so placed that the pillars did not cast shadows.[2] The single screen and the screen[3] between the two pillars to the right of the stage, besides the overhanging curtain, were well manipulated by ropes. (Added to these) was the canopy painted[4] with many beautiful pictures, from which were hanging loosely, garlands of pearl and others. Such was the novel and attractive appearance which the stage presented.

114–120 The *talaikkōl*, or the staff,[5] was the central shaft of a splendid white umbrella captured in the battle-field from monarchs of great repute. It was covered over by purest *jāmbūnada* gold,[6] its joints bedecked with nine gems. This staff represented Jayanta, Indra's son, and as such was worshipped in the palace of the protecting king of the white umbrella (the Cōḷa).

On the day[7] on which this staff was to be used by the dancing-girl, she had to bathe it with holy waters, brought

[1] This statement shows that the institution of *varṇāśrama* had already come to stay in the Tamil land. The names of the deities or *būtas* worshipped are Vacciradēhaṉ, Vacciradandaṉ, Varuṇaṉ and Irattakēśvaraṉ (*Sila*., p. 115, n. Cf. *Jīvakacintamani*, st. 672). Further details as to the clothing, food, etc., of these four *būtas* are seen in 'Alarpaṭukādai', ll. 2 ff. and ll. 110 ff.

[2] This shows a highly advanced state of engineering skill.

[3] In the *Jīvakacintāmaṇi* these three kinds of screens (*eḻiṉi*) are mentioned (st. 675, comm.). See also *Maṇi*., canto v, l. 3. *Eḻiṉi* is evidently the same as *yavanika*.

[4] Portrait painting was not unknown in the early centuries of the Christian era. Cf. *Maṇi*., canto xviii, l. 46.

[5] ll. 114-5 are repeated in a slightly altered form in canto xxviii, ll. 98-9 of this work.

[6] Four varieties of gold are distinguished, of which the *jāmbūnada* is the purest variety.

[7] Adiyārkkunallār, acting on the authority of Mativāṇaṉār, speaks of the following as the auspicious days: *Pūrāṭam*, *Kārtikai*, *Pūśam*, *Baraṇi*, *Rēvati*, *Tiruvātirai*, *Aviṭṭam*, *Cittirai*, *Viśākam*, and *Makam*. The *rāśis* appropriate to these are *Ṛṣabha*, *Simha*, *Tulām*, *Kaḍakam*, *Vṛścikam*, and *Mitunam*. It must be noted that there is no warrant in the text for such astronomical data.

in a golden pitcher, and afterwards to garland it. Then
it was handed over with a blessing to the State elephant
already adorned with a plate of gold and other ornaments 121–129
on its forehead. To the accompaniment of the drum proclaiming victory, and other musical instruments, the king and his five groups of advisers[1] were to circumambulate the chariot and the elephant and give the *talaikkōl* to the musician-poet on the top of the chariot. Then they went round the town in a procession, and entering the theatre they placed the *talaikkōl* in its appointed position.

After this the instrument-players occupied their allotted 130–49
seats.[2] The dancing-girl (Mādavi) placed her right foot[3] forward, and stepping in, stayed by the side of the pillar on the right, according to the ancient custom. Likewise her older assistants who followed the old custom gathered themselves by the side of the pillar on the left. The two kinds of prayer (*vāram*) were sung in turn so that virtue might increase and vice might disappear. At the close of the prayer all the musical instruments held by the respective players were sounded.[4] The lute was in tune with the flute, and the *mṛdangam* with the lute. The resounding note was in tune with the *mṛdangam*, and the *āmantirikai* with the sound of the pot.[5] Each was in perfect harmony with the other. Two beats made one *maṇḍilam*, and eleven such *maṇḍilams* were executed in conformity with the established theatrical practice. When this

[1] The term *aimperumkuḻu* has been interpreted in different ways. See S. K. Aiyangar, *Hindu Administrative Institutions in South India*, 1931, p. 18; K. A. Nilakanta Sastri, *The Pāṇḍyan Kingdom*, pp. 32-3; also Dikshitar, *Hindu Administrative Institutions*, pp. 161-2; *Studies in Tamil Literature and History*, p. 204.

[2] The allotment of the places was according to the prescription of the *Sāstra* which Aḍiyārkkunallār styles as *nūl*, from which he quotes the mode of arrangement on the stage. (See p. 118.)

[3] Placing the right foot in the first entrance of any new place or building is considered to be auspicious even today in India.

[4] For a similar expression see *Maṇi.*, canto vii, l. 45.

[5] For a similar order for playing on musical instruments see *Jivakacintāmaṇi*, st. 124 and 675, comm. See also *Iṛaiyaṉār Ahapporul*, *sūtra* 40, comm.

musical act, called *antarakkoṭṭu*, was over, the auspicious *pālaippaṇ* was sung without the slightest violence to its rigid measure.

150–53 The four parts[1] of the auspicious song were suitably introduced. Beginning with three *maṇḍilams* (or *ottus*) it ended with one *ottu* (*ēkatāḷam*); with this captivating *maṇḍilam* the *dēśi* dance came to an end.

154–64 Mādavi also danced the *vaḍuku* dance.[2] Then it appeared as if the five-beat-mode of each of the two styles of dancing, *dēśi* and *vaḍuku*, was concentrated in one style —so captivating was her dance. In her quick movement she looked like a golden creeper animated with life. Because her dance was perfect and scientifically correct,[3] the king, who protected the world, in due recognition, presented her with a green leaf-garland and one thousand and eight *kaḷañjus*[4] of gold, which was the customary present given to dancers who held the *talikkōl* and exhibited their talents for the first time.

164–75 Fawn-eyed Mādavi[5] handed over a garland to a hunchbacked woman, and asked her to stand out in the street where the rich citizens of the city passed to and fro,

[1] The names of these four are *ukkiram*, *turuvai*, *ābhōgam*, and *pirakalai*. *Sila.*, p. 75.

[2] In the *vaḍuku* style of dancing she began with *maṭṭattālam*, and ended with *ēkatālam* (single time-beat). *Sila.*, p. 76.

[3] *Nāṭṭiya-Naṉṉūl* is apparently a treatise dealing with *tāṇḍavam*, *nṛtyam*, and *nāṭyam*, something like the *Bharatanāṭyaśāstra* in Sanskrit, now being published in the Baroda Sanskrit Series.

[4] *Kaḷañju-poṉ* was an ancient coin of Tamil land. The term *kaḷañju* often occurs in Tamil inscriptions, and means sometimes a coin and sometimes gold bullion of the proper standard of weight and fineness. (See *An. Rep. Ep.*, 1912, p. 65 and op. cit., 1916, p. 116), 'In an early Pāṇḍya inscription (No. 90 of 1908) it occurs as the equivalent of the Sanskrit *Kṛṣṇakācha*, and Mr. H. W. Codrington of the Ceylon Civil Service informs me that in that island a coin of the *kaḷañju* weight was called *kāhapaṇa*. No. 197 of appendix B gives *kaḷañju* as the equivalent of *niṣka*.' Thus writes the epigraphist, op. cit., p. 106.

[5] From the expression *namkōḍi* in l. 166 it would be more appropriate if the words in ll. 164-6 were spoken by Mādavi's mother; but the commentators attribute them to Mādavi herself.

as if she was offering it[1] for sale, and to announce that 'this garland is worth a sum of 1008 *kaḷañjus* of very excellent gold. He who buys this garland becomes the husband of our creeperlike lady'. The garland representing the large lotus-eyed Mādavi was purchased by Kōvalaṉ, and, accompanied by the hunchback, he entered Mādavi's bridal chamber, and as he embraced her he was captivated so much by her charms that he forgot himself and did not like to part from her. In sooth, he forgot his own unsullied home and wife.

VEṆBĀ

With golden bangles, Mādavi of Pūmpuhār exhibited her skill on the dancing stage by word of mouth, in respect of numbers and letters, five *iyals*, four *paṇs*, and eleven kinds of *kūttus*, making her reputation spread on the earth.

[1] The garland was not worth 1008 *kaḷañjus*. But it was the symbol for Mādavi who was worth 1008 *kaḷañjus*, and it was announced that whosoever wanted to take her as his partner should be prepared to pay so much gold.

Canto IV

ANTIMĀLAIṢṢIRAPPUCCEYKĀDAI

OR

IN PRAISE OF THE EVENING

1–20 At the time when Mother Earth, enrobed by the waters of the deep, felt afflicted exclaiming, 'I do not see the mighty lord (the Sun) who sent out his rays all over the world and ruled it with his unequalled single disk! Nor is it known where is the (prince) Moon who illumines the wide sky with his cool rays.' And when her four faces (the four directions) turned pale, her flower-eyes moist, and her whole form covered with dew like the chieftain, who occupies, with the aid of rebellious subjects, the kingdom of powerful kings during their absence, to the grief of loyal tax-paying subjects, Evening (the alien chief) made his triumphant entry into fertile old Puhār, to the grief of faithful wives left alone by their husbands, and to the delight of disloyal women enjoying the company of their secret lovers. It was then that the Kōvalar[1] sent forth from their flutes the *mullai* songs, the buzzing bee sucked the honey from the *mullai* flowers, the soft-footed southern breeze warded off the six-footed bee (*kuṟumbu*)[2] which had forced his way into unopened buds,

[1] The term Kōvalar means Gōpālar or cowherds. They are a community belonging to the region of the *mullai*. The whole Tamil land was classified into five regions, namely *marudam* (river-bed), *kuṟiñji* (hill), *neydal* (littoral tracts), *pālai* (deserts), and *mullai* (forests).

[2] The six-footed bee is referred to by the term *kuṟumbu* as it acts like the Kuṟumbar, a term which stands for petty chieftains. The Kuṟumbar were a marauding tribe who suddenly fell on the enemy's cattle, and disturbed the peace and security of the land. In l. 24 of the same canto Evening is described as *kuṟumbu*, occurring as it does at the intervening time between the day and the night. (Cf. *Kalittogai*, st. 118, l. 8.) For the Kuṟumbar, see J. G. Frazer, *Totemism and Exogamy*, Vol. II, 1910, pp. 244 ff.

and wafted the fragrance into the open street, and maidens with glittering bangles lit their shining lamps.

(At that time), in his capacity being the lineal ancestor[1] 21–26
of the Pāṇḍyas, whose trait it was to turn back, in spite of their tender age, the invading enemy, the youthful crescent Moon appeared in the sky and drove away the annoying chieftain, Evening. Thus without losing his greatness, the silvery moon, the king of the stars, spread his milk-white brilliance all around.

Finding in her bedchamber, where the bed was strewn 27–34
with home-grown *mullai,* fragrant jasmine and many other flowers, that the clothing on her waist had slipped and the coral girdle enveloping it had consequently become displaced, Mādavi, who was in a wistful mood, betook herself to the open moonlit terrace, and gave her lover alternate moments of union (*kalavi*)[2] and lovers' quarrel (*pulavi*), compromising Kōvalaṉ then and there with a loving heart.

Besides Mādavi, there were others with lilylike eyes, 35–46
who were sleeping blissfully on the breasts of their lovers, fanned by the soft breeze after exhausting themselves in voluptuous enjoyment. But first they put out the fumes of incense made up by mixing the white *ayir*[3] of the western hills with the black *agar* of the eastern hills; they (still) wore the sandal-paste prepared by rubbing the sandalwood of the southern mountains[4] upon the sand-stone of the northern hills;[5] and they also wore green

[1] Tradition avers the Pāṇḍyas to be a branch of the ancient lunar race of kings. Compare this line with *Puṟam.*, st. 58, l. 8, where the term *pañcavar* occurs, more or less with the same attributes.

[2] The terms *kalavi* and *pulavi* are technical terms in Tamil love literature. See the *Tirukkuṟaḷ*, ch. 131 and 133.

[3] According to Aḍiyārkkunallār *ayir* is sugar-candy which was exported to India from the Yavana country. But *ayir* seems to be a fragrant substance white in colour.

[4] The Podiyil Hill noted for sandalwood (Sans., *candanācala*).

[5] The Tirupati Hills, the northern limit of Tamiḻaham; the term *vāṉkēḻvaṭṭam* occurs in the *Neḍunalvāḍai*, l. 51 and the *Aham.*, st. 340.

paṭalai garlands interspersed with segments of tender lotus stalk, the lotus flower, the blue flower, and the *kaḻunīr* in addition to pearl necklaces, which having slipped lay in mixed confusion on the flowery bed together with particles of fine powders.

47–57 But Kaṇṇaki[1] was sad at heart. Her anklet was no more on her charming feet; the girdle no longer graced her soft waist-cloth; her breasts were no more painted with vermilion paste: no jewel other than her scared *tāli* did she wear; no ear-rings were visible on her ears; no perspiration adorned her shining moon-like face; nor was there collyrium on her long fish-like eyes; no more was there the *tilaka* on her beaming forehead; her milk-white teeth were not revealed to Kōvalaṉ in a loving smile; nor was her dark hair softened by oil.

58–71 (Nor was Kaṇṇaki alone in her sorry plight.) Owing to their separation from their dear lords, other ladies who breathed heavily as bellows, abandoned the bedchamber[2] which they used during the hot season for that with narrow windows, which they used during the cold weather. They were sad that their breasts could not be decked with sandal-paste or with strings of pearls. They did not go near the bed of cool flowers plucked from flower-pots and watery fields. They could no longer repose on beds which were made of the soft down shed by the swan when it was pairing with its loving mate. These unhappy women, who once, unperturbed, in *ūḍal*[3] (lovers' quarrel) with their loving husbands rolled their eyes between the bridges of their noses and the tips of their ears, were now

According to some, the northern mountains may refer to the Himalayas. This is unconvincing as the Himalayas are not noted for sandstone. Even today visitors to Tirupati purchase stones on which sandal-paste is prepared.

[1] These ten lines describe the conduct of a chaste lady who is separated from her husband. In l. 50, the term *mangalavaṇi* is undoubtedly a reference to the *tāli* or the *māṅgalyasūtram*.

[2] Mention of five beds in the *Jīvakacintāmaṇi*, st. 838.

[3] *Ūḍal* is a term of much significance in Tamiḻ love literature. (See the *Tirukkuṟal*, ch. 133. Cf. *pulavi*.)

in despair. Their long eyes, red with weeping, dropped pearl-like tears because of their loneliness.

(At such a time) with the swan's soft tread for her 72–80
gentle gait, with the sweet-smelling and honey-hiding *āmbal* flower for her fragrance, with the blooming lotus for her rosy lips, with the black sand for her wavy hair, the ladylike[1] lake with the *nōtiṟam* melody of bard-bees opened her eyes, which were the fair *kuvaḷai* flowers, when the birds and fowls sent out from time to time their shrill and loud notes, as if they beat the drum and blew the conch, till the dawn expelled the darkness of the night from the city which resembled the expansive sea.

One would say that in these watches of the dark night 81–84
(*pakal*)[2] the fish-bannered prince (Cupid), going from place to place armed with his sugar-cane bow and flower-arrow, stood excellent guard over the city.

[1] The lake is compared to a lady. The blossoming *kuvaḷai* flowers in the lake are the lady's eyes which, as their petals open in the morning, represent the lady's awakening. The ancient custom was for members of a noble family to be roused by the singing of auspicious songs. In the allegory this is represented by the bees' humming round the lotuses.

[2] Note the peculiar use of the term *pakal* meaning midnight. Cf. *Maduraikkāñji*, l. 653; *Puṟam.*, st. 189, l. 3.

Canto V

INDIRAVIḶAVŪREḌUTTAKĀDAI

OR

THE CELEBRATION OF INDRA'S FESTIVAL

1–6 The Sun appeared over the top of the Udaya hill, removed the cover of darkness by spreading its shining rays to illumine the vast earth which erstwhile looked like a melancholy maiden, with the sea of waves for her robes, the hills for breasts, the large rivers for garlands and the clouds for flowing locks of hair.

7–23 The Sun shone over the open terraces,[1] over the warehouses near the harbours,[2] and over the turrets with air-holes[3] looking like the eyes of deer. In different places of Puhār the onlooker's attention was arrested by the sight of the abodes of Yavanas[4] whose prosperity was never on the wane. On the harbour were to be seen sailors come from distant lands,[5] but for all appearance they lived as one community. In the streets of the city hawkers went about with paints, bathing powders and cool pastes, flowers, incense and fragrant scents. In certain places weavers were seen dealing in fine fabrics made of silk, fur and cotton.[6] Whole streets were full of silks, corals, sandal and myrrh, besides a wealth of rare

[1] For a similar description of ll. 7-58, see *Maṇi.*, canto xxviii, ll. 29-68.

[2] This testifies to the existence of foreign trade on a large scale.

[3] It may be noted here that the lattice windows were a characteristic feature of ancient houses.

[4] Aḍiyārkkunallār interprets it as *mlēcchas.* To the ancient Hindus all foreigners were *mlēcchas.*

[5] Men of different nationalities engaged in maritime commercial ventures were seen in the city.

[6] Besides cotton and silk, it may be noted that the hair of the rat was used for weaving clothes. But rats have no hairs and therefore the reference cannot be to the hair of Indian rats. These weavers were known as Kārukas.

ornaments, perfect pearls, gems and gold, which were beyond reckoning.

There were also other streets where grain-dealers 24–39
lived who kept their grains in separate heaps.[1] Washermen, makers of muffins, wine-sellers, fishermen selling fish, dealers in white salt, those who sold betel leaves, those who dealt in scents, mutton-vendors, oil-mongers, meat-vendors, dealers in bronze, manufacturers of copper, carpenters, strong-armed blacksmiths, sculptors, potters, goldsmiths, jewellers, tailors, cobblers, skilled workers of all sorts who made fancy trinkets of pieces of cloth and cork, great musicians[2] who knew the whole technique of musical science[3] and could exhibit their faultless skill on flute and lute by sounding the seven notes; and finally the lower class of artists who excelled in several minor arts, had their respective localities. All these places in the city went by the name of *maruvūrppākkam*.

In another part of the city there were the king's street,[4] 40–58
the car street with flying flags, the bazaar street, the broad highway where highborn merchants lived on either side in the turreted houses, the Brahmana street,[5] the streets of physicians and astrologers[6] respectively, and of agricultural

[1] Generally the different varieties of grains were classified into eight kinds and sometimes into eighteen kinds. The eight varieties are paddy, grass, *varaku*, *tiṟai* (little millet), *śāmai* (common millet), *iṟungu* (great millet or black *cōḷam*), *tōrai* (paddy grown in the hilly tracts), and ragi.

[2] The term in the text is *perumpāṇ* as against the expression *śiṟupāṇ*. The first is a group of experts who could play with ease on superior instruments like the *pēriyāḷ*, and the latter are a group of minstrels who occupied a lower status, and who were skilled in playing smaller instruments like the *śēṟiyāḷ*. Belonging to these two groups, we have the *Perumpāṇāṟṟuppaḍai*, and the *Sirupāṇāṟṟuppaḍai*, two works under the category of the *Pattupāṭṭu*.

[3] This may be interpreted also 'who had inherited their skill from their forefathers'.

[4] See *Maṇi.*, canto iv, ll. 37-8. The *Rājamārga* of Sanskrit literature.

[5] It is interesting to see that the term *maṟaiyōr* is interpreted by the commentators as *pañcagrāmins*. In the light of the terms *bhūtagrāma* and *indriyagrāma* in Sanskrit literature, this term may refer to Brahmans who perform austerities by self-control.

[6] See *Maṇi.*, canto ii, l. 29.

communities, and the broad street having the residences of those who dexterously bored holes in gems and pearls and mounted them, and of those who polished the shells and the conches that were worn as ornaments. There were also separate quarters where dwelt *sūtas* and *māgadhas*,[1] religious dancers, astronomers,[2] mock-dancers, prostitutes, actresses,[3] maidens bearing flowers and betels, maid-servants,[4] bagpipe musicians, drummers of different sorts, buffoons and jesters.

In an extensive open space, on the outskirts of the city, were quarters occupied by cavalrymen with swift horses, elephant warriors, charioteers with lofty chariots and infantrymen with fearsome looks. This region was further celebrated by the presence of highly renowned great men. It went by the name of *paṭṭiṉappākkam*.

59–63 The central part of the city between the two divisions *maruvūrppākkam* and *paṭṭiṉappākkam*) was open and looked like the battlefield where the armies of two great monarchs could meet. Underneath the dense rows of trees were erected permanent booths and stalls. That was the market-place (*nāḷangāḍi*)[5] where the din and bustle of sellers and buyers could be heard throughout the day.

64–75 On the day on which the moon approached the *cittirai* star in the month of *cittirai* (i.e. on the full-moon day) the sacrifice of boiled grains, sweetened sesame balls, meat mixed with rice, flowers, incense, and toddy was offered by the elderly (*maṟava*) maidens, in fascinating dress, and as if devoid of shame at the altar in front of the guardian deity[6] who had arrived in obedience to the orders of the

[1] Cf. *Kauṭalīya Arthaśāstra*, Bk. X, ch. iii.

[2] *Maṇi.*; canto vii, l. 65.

[3] ibid., canto xx, l. 30. [4] ibid., canto xxiv, l. 19.

[5] The *nāḷangāḍi* is literally a day-market. It was situated in the central portion of the city, between the *maruvūrppākkam* and the *paṭṭiṉappākkam*, the two broad divisions of the city.

[6] For the work of the *Būta*, etc., see canto vi, ll. 7 ff. following, and the commentary thereon.

Lord of the Dēvas, to ward off the evil which might befall the victorious king (Mucukunda),[1] they then enjoyed themselves in the *tuṇangai*[2] and *kuravai* as if possessed with divinity and left the place with the loud prayer 'May the king of the land and all this vast kingdom not be troubled by hunger, disease or enmity but enjoy seasonal rains and prosperity'.

The valiant warriors residing in the suburbs (*maru-* 76–88
vūrppākkam) and the leaders of the army quartered in the city (*paṭṭinappākkam*), vied with one another in going first to the great altar to make the asseveration 'May all evil to our mighty king be warded off, and may you (the Būtam) stand firm on the side of those who propitiate you with offerings!' Stone-slingers, and different classes of soldiers who held shields stained with blood and human flesh, as well as lances, patted themselves on their shoulders, shouting exultingly, and cut off their dark-haired heads containing such fierce red eyes as seemed to burn those upon whom they looked, and willingly offered them upon the sacrificial altar (of the guardian deity) with the prayer that the conquering king might be ever victorious, when those headless trunks seemed to speak through the drums of untanned leather these words of thunder: 'We have given you our lives as a sacrifice: Accept them.'[3]

[1] For a different version of the story see the *Bhāgavata Purāṇa*. Mucukunda is one of the three sons of Māndhāta and Bindumatī. His brothers are Purukutsa and Ambariṣa (*Bhāga. Pur.*, Bk. IX, ch. 6, st. 38). Hearing that Kālayavana, or simply Yavana, was carrying destruction to the Dēvas, Mucukunda entered the cave, the residence of Yavana, and slew him, to the wonder of the Dēvas. Indra offered him a place of honour in heaven. But Mucukunda wanted to go on sleeping in that cave undisturbed for an unlimited period. Kṛṣṇa met him and blessed him as a *yōgin*, (ibid., Bk. X, ch. 51). He undertook penance in the Badari *āśrama*.

[2] The term *tuṇangai*, otherwise known as *śingi* (see *Divākaram.*, st. 9) is the dance in which the dancers rested their hands on their hips. In the *kuravai* they grasped each other's hands in a circle.

[3] The reference is to *talai-bali*, a very ancient custom prevalent in South India, bearing strong evidence to the early forms of Sakti worship. This is corroborated by the Pallava architecture. (See the interesting article, 'The Head offering to the Goddess in Pallava Architecture', of Dr. J. Ph. Vogel in the

89–98 Once Tirumāvaḷavan̲[1] felt that there was no foe on either side[2] fit to fight with him and thinking, in his thirst for war, that there might be foes in the north, he had an auspicious day[3] chosen for taking out his sword, umbrella[4] and war-drum,[5] and he prayed to his guardian deity that he might be lucky enough to find an enemy fit to encounter his broad shoulders, and advanced in that direction. Finding the great Himalayas, the residence of gods, as the barrier arresting his further progress, he retreated with pride after engraving his tiger-emblem on its rocky side.

99–110 On his return, the king of the great Vacciranāḍu[6] whose sway extended as far as the roaring sea (in the east), gave him a pearl canopy as tribute while the king of Magadha[7] famous for his sword-play, and his enemy a while ago, presented to him an audience-hall[8] (*paṭṭimaṇḍapam*). The king of Avanti gave him a friendly present of a tall and beautiful arch on the gateway. Though all these were made of gold and gems, their technique was not known to human artists even of exceptional skill; they were long ago given to the ancestors of these three monarchs by the

Bulletin of the School of Oriental Studies, London, Vol. VI, Pt. II, 1931.) See also the *Kalaimagaḷ*, Vol. I, pp. 416 ff., where Prof. K. A. Nilakanta Sastri translates the above contribution, and ibid., pp. 802 ff., where again Pandit M. Raghava Aiyangar re-examines it in the light of literature.

[1] Tirumāvaḷavan̲ is the name of Karikāl-Peruvaḷattān̲, who was actuated by imperialism and lust of conquest.

[2] Perhaps the Cēra and the Pāṇḍya kings. Cf. the closing lines of canto i, and the footnote.

[3] Cf. Vāṇāṭ-kōḍal, (*Pu. Por.*, *veṇbā* 'Vañji', st. 4).

[4] Cf. Kuṭaināṭ-kōḍal, ibid., st. 3.

[5] Muraśunāṭ-kōḍal, *Puṟam.*, st. 50 n.

[6] Vajranāḍu on the banks of the river Sōṇai (Son). Its king held the status of an *udāsīna* or neutral of the Arthaśāstra literature. We are not able to locate this country definitely. Perhaps it is the region where the tribe Vajjis of the *Jātakas* lived. This was on the northern shores of the Ganges opposite to Magadha (Tam., Magada). See S. B. L. Cowell, *Jātakas*, Vol. VI, p. 120.

[7] The king of Magadha was the *ari* or enemy.

[8] For *paṭṭimaṇḍapam*, see *Maṇi.*, canto i, ll. 60-1. The hall where learned men assembled and held discourse. (See *Tiruvācagam*, *paṭṭimaṇḍapam ēṟṟinai ēṟṟinai*, 'śatakam' 49.) Naccinārkkiniyar holds the view that it was more an assembly of Sanskrit pandits. See *Tolk.*, Porul., *sūtra* 490, comm.

divine Maya in return for some valuable service rendered to him. When they were all placed together, they formed an artistic *maṇḍapam* much praised by great men.

(In addition to this) there was the open space (*veḷḷiṭai-* 111–17
maṉṟam) where could be found many bundles of goods with marks indicative of the quantity,[1] weight and names of their new owners. Since there was neither gate nor lock nor watchman guarding them, thieves might sometimes be tempted to remove these bundles on their heads. And if they did so, the invisible deity guarding the place would make the thief go round and round the open plain, with the heavy burden on his head but would not permit him to pass away from there. The very thought of stealing anything made people quake with fear.[2]

Next, there was the place (*ilañjimaṉṟam*) with the 118–21
miraculous lake by bathing in and circumambulating which all hunchbacks and cripples, the dump, the deaf and lepers were cured of their infirmities and gained health and grace of form.

Then there was the open space where stood the tall 122–27
shining stone (*neḍumkalniṉṟamaṉṟam*), by the worship of and going round which were cured all those who had grown mad by being deceived (into consuming drugs), those who were suffering from palsy as a result of poison, those bitten by sharp-toothed venomous serpents and those who were possessed by devils with protruding eyes.

There was again the meeting-place of four roads 128–34
(*būtacatukkam*) where stood the Būta, proclaiming in a voice loud enough to be heard as far as four *kāvadams*[3] that he would bind with his rope and devour by thrashing

[1] The use of pictographic writing reminds us of South India's intercourse with Egypt on the one hand and the Indus Valley on the other.

[2] One of the references to superstitious belief of the times. See also ll. 133-7.

[3] The municipal limits of the city of Puhār seem to have been ten miles in circumference. The topographical description of ancient Puhār approximates to the modern city of Madras. A *kāvadam* or *kādam* refers to a distance of two and a half miles.

the wicked who assumed the garb of asceticism to cover their sins,[1] cunning wives who practised vice in secret, intriguing ministers, men who coveted other men's wives, and witnesses who gave false evidence, and tale-bearers.

134–38 Further there was the place (*pāvaimanṟam*) where stood the statue which would never open its mouth but would weep by shedding tears on every occasion when there was a deviation from the path of justice by the king, or when partiality was shown in his court of justice by wrong interpretation of the law.

139–40 Sacrifice was offered in all the five aforementioned places[2] held in veneration by men of wisdom who knew the real truth about them.

141–46 Then the auspicious drum was removed from the temple called Vaccirakkōṭṭam,[3] placed on the nape of the elephant adorned with the girdle, and conveyed to the temple where the young white elephant stood.[4] This was indicative of the beginning and the end of Indra's festival. After this the auspicious tall flag (bearing the ensign of the white elephant) which stood in the temple of the Kalpaka (*tarunilaikkōṭṭam*) tree was hoisted aloft in the sky.

147–56 On the verandas of the big mansions[5] were to be seen artistic planks set with emeralds and diamonds whereon stood coral pillars. At the entrance of these mansions

[1] Six kinds of heinous offences are mentioned here. It may be noted in passing that the *Kauṭalīya Arthaśāstra* prescribes heavy punishments in the case of pseudo-*sannyāsins*, false witnesses, adulterers, etc.

[2] As many as five *manṟams* are mentioned here.

[3] See *Mani*, canto i, ll. 27-8. (Sans., Vajrakōṣṭa.)

[4] The temple of the Airāvata, Indra's elephant.

[5] For a similar celebration of Indra's festival see *Vīramitrōdaya*, pp. 425-33; *Mhb.*, 'Ādi.', ch. 64. For the origin of the Indra cult in Rig Vēdic India, see A. C. Das, *Ṛig Vedic Culture*, 1925, pp. 56 ff. It would appear from the *Viṣṇu Purāṇa* (Pt. V, ch. 10), that the ancient cowherd communities celebrated Indra's festival, and this was discontinued from the time of Kṛṣṇa who wanted the Gōpas to take to the worship of cattle and mountains which alone afforded them food and occupation. A festival of Indra is referred to as being celebrated by King Sālavāhana and his subjects in the *Kālakācārya Kathā* (see W. Norman Brown's *The Story of Kālaka*, 1933, p. 83).

were suspended ornamental hangings having the shape of the *makara* fish from whose teeth (horns), carved with symbols representing auspicious things and adorned with *kimpuri*, hung strings of pearls in series. The streets were further beautified by golden pitchers filled with water, glittering *pālikai* vessels, lamps wrought in the shape of maidens,[1] golden flags, pure white feather fans, fragrant pastes and many other ornamentations.

There were assembled in these streets the five great 157–68
groups of the king's councillors (*aimperumkuḻu*)[2] and the eight great bodies of the king's retinue (*eṇpērāyam*),[3] princes of the blood royal, sons of the merchant aristocracy, fast riders on horseback, groups of elephant riders, and charioteers whose chariots were drawn by horses, for the glorification of their highly reputed ruler's sway over this wide world. One thousand and eight kings bore on their heads gold pots filled with cool and holy water rendered fragrant by floating pollen of flowers of the Kāvēri, taken from where it joins the sea, and performed the bathing ceremony of the Lord of Gods, to the delight of the earth and the admiration of heaven.

Joy prevailed everywhere on account of Indra's festi- 169–88
val in the temple of the great Lord who was never born (Śiva), in the temple of the six-faced red Lord (Subrahmaṇya), in the temple of Vāliyōn (Baladēva)[4] whose complexion was like the white conch-shell, in the temple of Neḍiyōṉ (Viṣṇu) of the dark colour, and in the temple of Indra of the victorious umbrella and the pearl garland.

[1] Cf. *Maṇi.*, canto i, l. 45.

[2] For *amperumkuḻu* see *Maṇi.*, canto i, l. 17; *Tolk.* 'Kiḷavi', *sūtra* 57; Naccinārkkiṉiyar's commentary: minister, *purōhita*, commander, ambassador, and spy.

[3] For a twofold interpretation of the term *eṇpērāyam*, see Dikshitar, *Studies in Tamil Literature and History*, pp. 204-5.

[4] The temple of Baladēva is mentioned, besides that of Indra. In later days these two cults have become extinct. See R. G. Bhandarkar's *Vaishnavism, Saivism*, pp. 3, 9, 11; also M. Raghava Aiyangar, *Āḷvārkālanilai*, p. 7. See also p. 50 *supra*.

On one side the Vēdic sacrifices,[1] as ordained by Brahmā, were faultlessly performed, and on another the festivals pertaining to the four classes of Dēvas[2] and the eighteen Gaṇas[3] and different other gods, were separately and correctly conducted. Inside the city were the Jaina temples and other Dharma institutions;[4] outside were Śrīkōil[5] and other sacred establishments. The Purāṇa reciters[6] also discharged their duties in another place. Elsewhere, the king's victorious chariot, with its banners flying, was taken out gracefully to annihilate the enemy-kings and others. In another place rose high immeasurable melodies produced by the flute, the drum, expert players on the *yāḻ* and the human voice of the Pāṇar.[7] Thus in that vast city, every lane and by-lane were alive with the sound of the drum by night and day.

189–203 Because she had not been separated from her lover, Mādavi, wearing beautifully serrated ear-rings, had not lost her charms. Mingled with the united fragrance of the *mādavi* flower,[8] the home-grown *mullai*, jasmine, the *mayilai* flower, the pot-grown blue-lotus, and the red

[1] This shows the popularity of the Vēdic sacrifices.

[2] The four classes are Vasus, Divākaras, Rudras and Maruts: all of them are Vēdic deities. In reality tradition speaks of thirty-three classes of Gods—the eight Vasus, twelve Ādityas (Divākara), eleven Rudras, and the two Maruts.

[3] One classification of the eighteen groups runs as follows: *apsaras* (?) *nāgas*, *siddhās*, *gandharvas*, *vidyādharas*, *piśācas*, *tarakas*, *bōga-būmiyar*, *kimpuruṣas*, *śēnas*, *asuras*, *butas*, *muṇis*, *dēvas*, *garuḍas*, *rākṣasas*, *yakṣas* and *cāranars*.

[4] This may refer to the Jaina or the Buddhist institutions or even to those of the orthodox religion. But the term *paḷḷi* shows that there was a school of dissenting sects, especially the Jaina.

[5] This is not necessarily a reference to the temple of Lakṣmī.

[6] The reading of the *Purāṇas* in the public places so as to be heard by all classes was a feature of ancient days. Cf. *Harṣacarita* where the *Vāyu Purāṇa* is said to have been read in public for the benefit of the masses.

[7] The Pāṇar were a class of minstrels and masters of music.

[8] This can also be interpreted thus: 'The red *mādavi* flower did not become the bud that people love, but grew into a beautifully bent root without losing its redness.'

kaḻunīr,[1] and pleased with love's delight, seeking sport in the pleasure garden made fragrant by the lovable flower-buds, entering into the fresh aroma of flowers in the ever-mirthful market-place[2] caressing the frankincense and the ever-wet sandal-paste, and continuously indulging in the joyous lovers' speech and laughter, the mountain breeze roamed about the city accompanied by the *iḷi*-sounding bee and by the mild rays of early summer, in the same way that Kōvalaṉ went about accompanied by minstrels singing the *kural* tune and by his city-companions skilled in love affairs.

One such companion spoke of his sweetheart: 'Has 204–7
the moon who roams in the beautiful sky become afraid of its enemy, the serpent Rāhu,[3] and left the sky to appear here in your disguise by carrying a heavy cloud on its head, parting with the little hare, and painting on its face the figures of two fishes (in the place of the two eyes) with the *kumiḻa* flower (the nose) between them?'

A second said: 'Does the flash of lightning nurtured 208–11
with great care by Cupid of the fish-flag (whose body was burnt by the spark of Śiva's third eye),[4] intend to come down here and regain it by drinking the cool nectar drops of the moon?'

A third said: 'Has the honeyed lotus, in the course of 212–17
searching for its companion (Lakṣmī), transformed itself into two dark *kuvaḷai* flowers, one on each side of the *kumiḻa* blossom? Or has it blossomed again into the red *ilavam* and into jasmine to proclaim that it is in this flourishing city that the goddess Lakṣmī[5] has entered so

[1] A categorical list of fragrant flowers which would increase sensuous desire.

[2] Here a full description of the *nāḷangāḍi* is furnished.

[3] Rāhu devouring the moon, says the legend, causes lunar eclipses, and devouring the sun, solar eclipses.

[4] The reference is to Śiva burning the God of Love. For a full description of the legend, see *Matsya Purāṇa*, ch. 154, 194 and 245.

[5] The term used in the text is *uḷvarikkōlam*. A classic example is that of the Pāṇḍavas in disguise in Virāṭanagara. See below, canto viii, l. 89, Aḍiyārkkunallār's comm.

that the monarch of the wide world may greatly prosper?'

218–23 Yet another said: 'Is the god of the devouring mouth (Yama), who destroys all and who, in fear of the righteous king, gave up the duty imposed on him and changed his male form for that of a girl, with a smiling countenance and covered with bashfulness, speaking words as soft as the notes of the pleasing *yāḻ*?'

224–34 With such frivolous talk the broad-shouldered lovers gained victory over their sweethearts, chaste as Arundati, who looked like a great army of the bodiless god (Cupid), and prevented them from running away from their presence by closely clasping them in voluptuous embrace and (thereby) smearing their chests all over with the sandal solution which adorned the breasts of these women. By thus giving them the pleasure of their union, they made their wives' lotus eyes lose the colour of the *kuvaḷai* and gain instead a reddish tinge (indicative of sleeplessness). The people of the city in a state of helplessness and tremor, spoke to themselves, 'If our great feast can do nothing to remove the redness from the eyes of our women-folk, is there any medicine at all that can cure this in the wide earth?'

235–40 It was then the middle day of the festival in honour of the King of Gods (Indra).[1] The dark left eye of Kaṇṇaki

[1] In the prehistoric days of Tamil India it appears that a certain Cōḻa monarch, by name Tuñjaiyileṟinda-toḍittōṭ-śembiyaṉ, introduced Indra's festival to be celebrated annually in his capital city Pūmpuhār. The duration of the festival was twenty-eight days. The festival continued to be celebrated by succeeding monarchs, as it came to be thought that by not celebrating it, the Catukkabūtam, engaged on the orders of Indra to check sin and sinners, would leave the city thus leading it to desolation and ruin. (See *Maṇi.*, canto i, 'Viḻāvaṟaikādai'.) Years rolled by and Neḍumuḍikkiḷḷi became the monarch. Once when he was spending some time in the royal park, a certain beautiful girl presented herself before him, and at his desire, lived with him as his wife. One day she suddenly disappeared, and when the King was aimlessly inquiring of passers-by, a certain Cāraṇa informed him that she was Pīlivaḷai, daughter of Vaḷaivāṇaṉ, King of the Nāganāḍu, and that she would return no more, but would send her son. The ship in which the son was sent foundered, and moved by great grief the King failed to celebrate

and the red right eye of Mādavi throbbed and were filled with tears of sorrow and of joy respectively like the *kaḻunīr* flower which shakes when the sweet pollen inside it emits honey and loses its external colour.

Indra's festival for the year. On this Maṇimēkalai the deity cursed that the city be swallowed by the sea. It so happened, and Aṟavana-Aḍigaḷ with his disciples left for Vañji (ibid, cantos xxiv-vi).

CANTO VI

KAḌALĀḌUKĀḌAI

OR

SEA BATHING

1–13 ONCE a Vidyādara hero celebrated, along with his lady-love of the long fish-like eyes, a feast in honour of the god of love in the extensive, fragrant and flowery grove in a Cēḍi[1] on the slopes of the silver-peaked Kailāsa.[2] He then realized that that was the day[3] when Indra's festival would commence in the flourishing city of Puhār (Campāpati) in South India, and he said to his wife, 'We shall go and witness the place where the great Būtam eats the sacrifice offered to it (in commemoration of its) having carried out Indra's orders to ward off the evil effects of the arrows aimed by hosts of swift-going Asuras against the terror-stricken but best of men, the victorious king Mucukunda,[4] while he was keeping watch, tiger-like over Indra's city.[5]

14–17 'We shall also see the five famous assembly-halls[6] of unrivalled architectural beauty, given by Indra in gratitude and refitted on the earth by the monarch's ancestor who once kept guard over Amarāvati.[7]

[1] The Cēḍi is the city of the Vidyādaras according to Jaina literature. Cf. *Jīvakacintāmaṇi*, p. 170, st. 546-(2).

[2] The Kailāsa Hills were the abode of the celestial Gaṇa, by name the Vidyādaras, among others. Cf. *Matsya Purāṇa*, ch. 154.

[3] The commentator says the same day next month.

[4] *Tirunduvēlaṉṉal* occurring in the text is a reference to Mucukunda, once the King of the Cōḻas.

[5] This city is known as Amarāvatī in Sanskrit literature.

[6] Five great *maṉṟams* are mentioned here.

[7] There is a Tamil tradition that the ancient Cōḻa monarch Mucukunda went to help Indra when Amarāvatī was besieged by the Asuras.

'(Agastya) finding that Nārada[1] did not play on the vīṇa properly, or appropriately, to the song of the dancing Urvaśī before the thousand-eyed Indra[2], or to the song of her accompanist (*tōriyamaḍandai*) who sang in the *vāram* which did not enrapture his ear, laid a curse, "Let the lute lose its charm, and let this dancer be born on the earth." In the line of that Urvaśī was born Mādavi with her hood like *alkul*. (In Puhār) we shall witness her dance. 18–27

'My dear coral-mouthed, slender-waisted girl, we shall there worship Indra, the lord of gods.' So saying, he started showing his lady-love the many-crested Himalayas,[3] the ever-flowing Ganges, the city of Ujjain,[4] the Vindhya forests, the Tirupati hills,[5] and the Kāvēri tracts overburdened with crops, and finally reached Puhār, enveloped by flowery groves. He showed her also the city, after performing the worship of Indra in the prescribed manner, and then witnessed the celebration of the enjoyable festival in that ancient and affluent town. 28–34

Said he then (to his fair companion): 'My dear, thou wilt hear the *dēvapāṇi*[6] in honour of Viṣṇu, the four songs in honour of the four *būtams* worshipped respectively by the four castes, and the song in honour of the Moon roaming in the sky for the benefit of all. Afterwards 35–43

[1] Nārada, the divine music master, and author of *Sīkṣa*, a musical treatise of the orthodox school. Because he did not play properly on the lute, the sage Agastya cursed his instrument.

[2] This is similar to the Sanskrit term *śahasrākṣa*.

[3] The geographical data are furnished. The Kailāsa Hills are on the Himalayan slopes. The way to Puhār lay through the Ganges, Ujjain, the Vindhyas, the Tirupati hills, and the Kāvēri tracts.

[4] Ujjain is an ancient city much celebrated in Sanskrit literature.

[5] Vēnkaṭam, or the Tirupati hills, is celebrated in ancient Tamil literature of the Sangam age. The Āḻvārs refer to it, and Pēyāḻvār speaks of it as Tirumalai Iyarpati (63 and 75). See also *Kamba-Rāmāyaṇa*, *Kiṣkinda*, 'Nadavitta Paṭalam', st. 26·8.

[6] *Dēvapāṇi* is not a celestial song but a song sung in honour of the God. *Dēvapāṇi* is of two kinds: *perumdēvapāṇi* and *sirudēvapāṇi*.

thou wilt see: The *koḍukoṭṭi*,[1] danced by Śiva, Umā keeping time on one side, on the burial-ground where Bārati (Kāḷi), danced with faultless rhythm and avoiding wrong time-measures, when the big fire-tipped arrow obeyed His command to burn the three cities (of the Asuras) at the request of the Dēvas;

44-51 'The *pāṇḍaranga*[2] dance which Śiva, in the form of Bārati,[3] displayed before the four-faced Brahmā standing in His chariot;

'The *alliyam*[4] dance performed by the dark-hued Viṣṇu (*añjaṉavaṇṇaṉ*) after disposing of the treacherous devices of Kamsā;[5]

'The *mallu* dance performed (by the same deity) after the destruction of the Asura (Bāṇa);[6]

'The *tuḍi* dance (of Subrahmaṇya) in the midst of the sea, which itself served as the dancing-hall, following the destruction of the demon Śūra[7] who hid himself there;

[1] *Koḍum-koṭṭi* is the original word according to Naccinārkkiṉiyar. See *Kali.*, 'Kaḍavuḷ'. For an actual description of the dance see canto xxviii, ll. 67-75. The translator has not been able to find parallels from the Sanskrit and other works corroborating all the eleven kinds of dancing mentioned here.

[2] *Pāṇḍaranga* is again a dance attributed to Siva.

[3] *Bārati-arangam*, the place where Bārati (Sarasvatī) or Bāravi danced.

[4] The *alliya* dance is said to be one among the ten dances engaged in by Kṛṣṇa.

[5] Kamsa, the uncle of Kṛṣṇa, wanted to kill the latter by means of a number of villainous guiles. One of them was to send an Asura follower of his in the guise of an elephant by name Kuvalayāpīḍa. Kṛṣṇa found it out, and killed him. See *Bhāga. Pur.*, Bk. X, ch. 43, st. 2-15. See also *Viṣ. Puṛ.*, Bk. V, ch. 20.

[6] Bāṇa was an Asura with a thousand arms. He was the son of Bali and Kōṭara. His capital was called Sōṇitapuram. He had a daughter Uṣā. Aniruddha, son of Pradyumna and grandson of Kṛṣṇa, carried her away. Hence Bāṇa had him imprisoned. Kṛṣṇa went to his grandson's rescue, and chopped off Bāṇa's thousand hands. See *Bhāga. Pur.*, Bk. X, ch. 62 and 63. Cf. *Cūḍāmaṇi*.

[7] This refers to the legend of the killing of the Asura Sūrapadma by Subrahmaṇya. Even today this festival is celebrated in all Siva temples in connexion with what is known as *Skandaśaṣṭi*, the sixth day in the dark-half of the month of Kārtikai. For details of the legend see *Kandapurāṇam*, § *Sūrapaṉmaṉvadai.* The reference is to the 'war-dance of triumph on the heaving wave-platform of the oceanic stage, to the accompaniment of the rattle of his drum (*tuḍi*)'.

'The *kuḍai*[1] (umbrella-dance) danced by (Subrahmaṇya) lowering the umbrella before the Asuras who gave up their arms in great distress ; 52–53

'The *kuḍam* (pot-dance)[2] exhibited by Viṣṇu (of the world-measuring stride) after walking through the streets of Bāṇāsura's extensive city ; 54–55

'The *pēḍi*[3] danced by Kāma (Cupid) who changed his male form to that of an hermaphrodite ; 56–57

'The *marakkāl* dance of Māyavaḷ (Durgā)[4] when She could not stand the wily deeds of the cruel Asuras ; 58–59

'The *pāvai* dance[5] of Lakṣmī when the Asuras clad in warlike attire ceased (from battle) ; 60–61

'And the *kaḍayam* dance[6] of lady Indrāṇī standing in the field on the northern gate (of Bāṇa's city). 62–63

'Thou wilt see, my dear, the above-named eleven 64–67

[1] It is not possible to trace this legend. To venture a conjecture, the reference is to the greatest victory of the baby Subrahmaṇya, six days old, over the great Tārakāsura and his satellites, a match for Viṣṇu, Indra and other Gods. See *Matsya Purāṇa*, ch. 160. It is said that Subrahmaṇya 'screened his face with a parasol, and played in exultant derision the *kuḍaikkūttu* or the umbrella-dance'. This is sometimes performed during temple processions when 'the God's umbrella-bearer cuts some capers with his unwieldy parasol ; but the *kāvaḍikkūttu* is a greater favourite in these days in Murugaṉ's worship and festivities'. *T. A. S.* Vol. II, p. 185. Cf. *Nighaṇṭu*, 14th ed., p. 179. For the sculptured figures representing the two varieties called the *kuḍaikkūttu* and the *kāvaḍikkūttu*, see the two Yāḷi panels flanking the entrance of the sanctum of the Adbhuta-Nārāyaṇa temple at Tirukkaḍaittannam (Chenganachery Taluk). *T.A.S.*, Vol. II, p. 187.

[2] This variety of dancing also has no counterpart in the Sanskrit *Nāṭya* treatises. 'Its origin has to be traced to the purely pastoral pursuits of its votaries, the shepherds, who eventually came to consider it as one of the three favourite dances of the God Viṣṇu in his special manifestation as Gōpāla, the Divine Shepherd.' The Vaiṣṇava Ālvārs refer to this (see *Periāḷvār Tirumoḷi*, *Nāccıyār Tirumoḷi*, etc.). It is popular even now in the *uriyaḍi* festival in commemoration of the sports of the baby Kṛṣṇa. The reference in the text is to the occasion of the defeat of Bāṇāsura in his capital of Sōṇitapura (Sōṇagaram). Cf. the account in the *Tiruvarangakkalambakam*.

[3] For the *pēḍi* dance, see *Maṇi.*, canto iii, l. 125.

[4] Durgā is otherwise known as Mahiṣāsuramardanī. See also canto xii, ll. 65-6.

[5] See *Maṇi.*, canto iii, ll. 116 f.

[6] It is rather difficult to identify this incident. The Tamil name for Indrāṇī is Ayirāni.

dances and the songs appropriate to them, acted and sung by the respective dancers with suitable garments and gestures, and in erect as well as bending postures, according to the established conventions.

68–71 'This is Mādavi, descended from the line of the great Mādavi mentioned by me when we were in the grove rich with the pollen of sweet flowers.' Thus said the highly distinguished Vidyādara entranced by the whole prospect.

72–75 Kōvalan̲, who was in the state of *ūḍal* (love-quarrel), was sorry to see the end of that Indra festival, which consisted of dancing in different kinds of attire, accompanied by the chiming of anklets, and which had been witnessed incognito by the denizens of Heaven.

76–98 To please him (so that his dejection might not gall him further), she (Mādavi) bathed her fragrant black hair, soft as flowers, till it shone, in the perfumed oil prepared by mixing up ten kinds of astringents, five spices, and thirty-two herbs soaked in water; she dried it in fuming incense, and perfumed the different plaits,[1] with the thick paste of the musk-deer. She adorned her little feet, reddened by dye, by wearing choice rings (*pīli*)[2] on her fair and slender toes, and on her ankles becoming ornaments known as *pariyakam*, *nūpuram*, *pāḍagam*, *śadangai*, and *ariyakam*.[3] She put ornaments on her rounded thighs. Over her waist was a girdle made of thirty-two strands of big pearls worn over a blue cloth embroidered with the figures of flowers. Round her upper arms she had armlets studded with pearls together with attractive bangles of precious stones (*kāmar-kanḍikai*). Round her soft-haired wrists were

[1] One of the many references to show that five plaits of hair were generally worn by Tamil ladies, especially when they were young.

[2] *Pīli* is in use even today, and it is considered inauspicious if it is not worn by a girl on her marriage.

[3] Here note the luxurious life led by the ancient Tamils. Some of the ornaments and finery are mentioned. These have been examined by S. Somasundara Desikar in a contribution to *Kalaimagal*, Vol. I, pp. 284-8.

beautiful bracelets (*cūḍagam*) in which was set the costliest gem in front with diamonds all round, gold bangles, bangles of nine gems (*pariyakam*), conch bangles, and bangles of coral. On to her tiny fingers, red as the *kāntal* flower, so as to hide them, she slipped a ring bent into the shape of an open-mouthed fish, and a highly brilliant and lustrous ring of gems, and a round ring glittering with rubies and brilliant diamonds.[1]

Her delicate and beautiful neck was adorned with 99–102
a chain necklace called *nuṇṭoṭar*, with a fine string of exquisite workmanship and with a garland. Added to these was a string of ornamental gems held by a clasp, which covered the small nape of her neck.[2]

A pair of ear-rings, in which emeralds alternated with 103–10
diamonds, glittered in her beautiful ears. In her dark tresses becoming head-ornaments such as *daivavutti* (also *śīdēvi*), *valampuri* (also *talaippālai*, sea-conch), *toyyaham* and *pullaham* were set.[3] She (Mādavi) gave Kōvalaṉ the happiness of union and of *ūḍal*, and stayed in her excellent nuptial chamber.

It was the full moon day in that ancient awe- 111–17
inspiring city. When she saw people in search of amusement hurrying to the beach, fragrant with the *tāḻai*, Mādavi became eager to follow them. At that time the swan uttered its cry from lotuses in the tanks; cocks sent out their clarion call betokening the approach of the dawn, Venus[4] shone on high, and darkness died away.

Kōvalaṉ wore sparkling jewels on his garlanded 118–127
chest, and like the prodigal cloud, mounted his mule,

[1] This and the following lines show the number and variety of jewels and clothes in vogue in those ancient days. Some of them have now gone out of use.

[2] *Piṉṟāli* is the term used by the commentators in this connexion.

[3] This is said to be a head ornament of two sections called *teṉpalli* and *vaḍapalli*.

[4] Tam., *veḷḷi*; Sans., *sukra*.

while the deer-eyed Mādavi got into her chariot (*vaiyam*).[1] They passed through the bazaar street beautified by towering mansions in which rich merchandise was stored in a million bundles. Here the beautiful lamps were glittering and some were decked with flowers. Maidens (*dāśiyar*) everywhere scattered flowers,[2] tender grass (*aṟugu*), and paddy, as being auspicious, and shone in their jewels. In this street[3] the Goddess Lakṣmī seemed to dwell, and on its two sides people were passing irregularly.

128–144 They then entered into the central highway of the city[4] rich with the wealth of sea-borne goods and reached the *cēri* regions on the seashore where the flags on high seemed to say: 'In these stretches of white sand can be seen different kinds of goods brought in ships by foreign merchants, who have left their native homes and settled here.' There were burning the lamps of those who sold dyes, sandals, flowers, scents, and all varieties of sweets, the lamps of dexterous goldsmiths, the lamps of those who, sitting in a row, sold *piṭṭu*, the black broad lamps placed on lamp-stands by the sellers of muffins, the lamps in front of the miscellaneous shops of girl-vendors, the lamps of fishmongers glimmering here and there, beacon-lights erected to guide ships on the seashore,[5] lamps taken out to sea by fishermen in their boats as they went a-fishing with

[1] This vehicle may be *kollāvaṇḍi*, a cart drawn by bullocks, or *kūḍārappaṇḍi*, a cart with a hooded top. The editor of the text notes in this connexion that in the Malaināḍu (p. 182), the vehicle is known as *kōlārvaṇḍi*. From this description of Kōvalaṉ riding a mule, and Mādavi a vehicle drawn by bullocks, we have to infer that these were used by persons of rank in the early centuries of the Christian era. The use of horses for vehicles had not come into practice.

[2] The habit of ladies both in the evening and early morning. Whether Iḷangō-Aḍigaḷ by the term *dāśiyar* means prostitutes, cannot be said.

[3] A description of the bazaar and other streets in Puhār before daybreak.

[4] This is *maruvūrppākkam* and the bazaar street was in *paṭṭiṉappākkam*.

[5] This bears testimony to the existence of lighthouses and a large volume of trade by sea.

nets, nightlong lights set up by foreigners[1] speaking different languages, and finally the lamps lit by the watchmen of (the warehouses containing) valuable merchandise.

The illumination of all these lights which were beyond 145–50
counting, was so great that the seashore[2] with its aloe hedges appeared more beautiful than the cultivated tracts with their fragrant lotus-ridges; even a small mustard-seed could be seen if it lay on the fine sands stretched out like fine flour.

Thither came creeper-like Mādavi with a group of her 151–4
playmates. There lay in repose ships which were filled with countless legions of hill-produce and sea-produce.[3]

In one place on the seaside were grouped together 155–6
princes and their retinue, as also merchant princes and their confidantes; there were again other groups of maidens skilled in dance and song, in curtained enclosures. Their multi-coloured clothes and many-sounding tongues[4] resembled the uproar inevitable on the festive occasion when king Karikāla,[5] whose great fame reached the celestial world, celebrated the first freshes in the Kāvēri, and came to be mingled with the unceasing tumult caused

[1] This testifies to the custom of lighting the streets. See *Perumpāṇā.*, ll. 349-51; *Mani.*, canto i, l. 16; *Puram.*, st. 60.

[2] Here follows a fine description of the beach in the evening.

[3] This again testifies to the rich sea-borne trade.

[4] See *Aham.*, st. 376.

[5] *Sila.*, canto vii, l. 4. This shows that some festivity was connected with the first freshes. It may be noted in passing that the Cōla king, Karikāla was the originator of the festival of the first freshes of the Kāvēri. This is quite in keeping with the statement of the *Paṭṭiṉappālai* that he was the founder of the capital Kāvēripaṭṭiṉam. Being Kāvirināḍaṉ or the Lord of the Kāvēri tracts, it is but natural that Karikāla was impelled by desire to institute a festival for the great service done by the river especially to the Cōḷadēśa. A modern relic of this ancient festival is what is known as the *padineṭṭāmperukku*, literally freshes on the 18th day of the month of Āḍi. It is a social function in which children, ladies and others take part. On the evening of that day, food of different kinds is taken to the riverside and after prayers to the river for its continual flow, the members of the family partake of the food. The children float old books, cadjan leaves, and sometimes manuscripts of rare books in the floods, and swim in the water and enjoy themselves in different ways.

by men and women of the four castes crowding on the narrow place where the great river Kāvēri joined the sea.

166–75 In the midst of that tumult the long-eyed Mādavi, soft as a flower, took the pleasure-giving tuneful-stringed lute from the hands of the fatigued Vasantamāla. There, on a white-legged couch with a canopy of picturesque paintings,[1] surrounded by a screen set on the newly-spread sands in the shade of a *puṉṉai* tree standing in the wide expanse enclosed by the flowering *kaidai* which swept away the foulness of the (fish-smelling) sea, Mādavi enjoyed the company of Kōvalaṉ.

[1] Further evidence of the art of painting in the Tamiḻnāḍu.

Canto VII

KĀṈALVARI

OR

THE SEASHORE SONG

Kaṭṭurai

AFTER worshipping with her hands Mādavi removed the 1
lute faultless in respect of *pattar*,[1] *kōḍu*,[2] *āṇi* and strings, from its fancy-coverings, its body adorned with flowers, which looked like a beauteous bride with her black eyes darkened with collyrium. And she began to produce its eight different sounds, *paṇṇal*, *parivaṭṭaṇai*, *āräidal*, *taivaral*, the majestic *śelavu*, *viḷaiyāṭṭu*, *kaiyūḻ*, and the sweet *kuṟumpōkku*, in order to satisfy herself as to their correctness. Her lustrous little fingers ornamented with ruby rings manipulating the different strings resembled a hive of humming-bees. Next she tested by ear the eight different tunes[3], *vārdal, vaḍittal, undal, uṟaḻdal,* the fair *uruṭṭal, teruṭṭal, aḷḷal,* and the beautiful *paṭṭaḍai*. Passing the instrument to Kōvalaṉ's outstretched hand, she said, 'It is not my object to command. Please let me know the *tāḷam*.' He too began playing odes to the Kāvēri and songs appropriate to the seashore (*kāṉalvari*)[4] to the great delight of Mādavi.

[1] The *Jīvakacintāmaṇi* styles these four faults as diseases of the vīṇa (st. 1720).

[2] Parimēlaḻagar speaks of these *iśai* as *pāṭaltoḻil* (duties), *Kuṟaḷ*, st. 573, and Naccinārkkiṉiyar on the *Jīvakacintāmaṇi* (st. 657) speaks of them as *kalaittoḻil*. What these eight terms mean are explained *in extenso* by Arumpadavuraiāśiriyar.

[3] See the commentary of Arumpadavuraiāśiriyar; also *Porunar*, l. 23, where four of these eight tunes are mentioned.

[4] *Kaḍaṟkāṉal-varippāṇi* is of two kinds: *daivamśuṭṭiya-varippāṭṭu* and *makkaḷaiśśuṭṭiya-varippāṭṭu*. Of these two the former consists of *kūṭaicceyyuḷ* and *vāracceyyuḷ*.

TO THE KĀVĒRI[1]

2 'Hail to thee, Kāvēri! Even if our Cōḷa king, whose garlanded parasol is as white as the moon, extends his righteous sceptre far and weds the Ganges,[2] thou wilt not sulk. I have learnt, O fish-eyed one, that not sulking, even though he weds the Ganges, is the supreme virtue of chaste ladies. Hail to thee, Kāvēri!

3 'If our king, whose garlanded umbrella is white and stable, extends his unbending sceptre far, weds Kaṉṉi (Kaṉyākumari), O Kāvēri! thou wilt not sulk. Hail to thee! I have learnt that not sulking, fish-eyed Kāvēri, even if he weds Kaṉyākumari,[3] is the mighty virtue of ever-chaste ladies. Live long, O Kāvēri!

4 'Hail to thee, Kāvēri! Thou walkedst (flowed) along, listening to the songs of the ploughmen,[4] the resonance of the sluices, the roar of the breaking waters, and the noise of the festive crowd celebrating thy freshes.[5] All this flow of thine, along with the din of merrymaking, is expressive of the prosperity of our king, who possesses soldiers with unbridled tongues. Hail to thee, Kāvēri!'

Again[6]

5 'How can we innocent people understand, sir, that

[1] Stanzas 2-4 go by the name of *āṟṟuvari*, literally an ode to a river.

[2] The implication is that the Cōḷa king's sway, as has been already said, extended up to the Ganges tracts in the north.

[3] The southern limit of the Cōḷa kingdom was Kaṉyākumari, the Cape Comorin of modern days.

[4] This points to the fertility of the soil and testifies to the irrigational works on the Kāvēri tracts. Cf. *Paṭṭiṉappālai*, ll. 277-91; also *A.S.S.I.*, Vol. IV, p. 204 ff. 'The Leyden Grant'.

[5] The first freshes of the year in the Kāvēri were the occasion of a carnival in which all classes of people from the king down to the peasant took a leading part. Tamil tradition is that Karikāla was the originator of this festival. See p. 129, *supra*.

[6] Stanzas 5-7 are a glowing description of the richness and simplicity of the city of Puhār. These words are spoken by the heroine's maid to her mistress's lover, who has come with a present in his hand. The theme (*tuṟai*) of these stanzas is said to be *varaivu-kaḍāyavai*. The idea is that the maid pretends to refuse presents and seems to insist on a regular marriage.

unrighteous men again and again show the sea-god[1] to our lady with long eyes like dark flowers, and make pious vows only to be broken. Our city is Puhār where the water-lily opens its blossoms at the sight of white conch bracelets and pearls, mistaking them for the moon and constellations of stars which spread their white rays.

'How can we know, sir, of those lovers, who approach 6
us on this beach from behind, with presents in their hands, and then turn out to be strangers expecting us to beg of them? Our home is Puhār where the bee is bewildered, unable to distinguish the (blue) eyes of maidens from two blue flowers blooming in the reflection of the moon (on the waters).

'Our city, sir, is Puhār where the sounding conch is 7
buffeted by the big dashing waves and is driven ashore and ruins our maidens' sand-castles.[2] These maidens, the flowers in whose hair are loosened and sway about, grow angry, and plucking the water-lilies from their garlands with tender fingers they throw them at the conch. Passers-by seeing these (flowers scattered on the ground) think they are observing eyes.'

Again

'To wipe out the appearance of the ploughed sands in 8
which the conches lay buried, the heavily-flowering *puṉṉai* had scattered its pollen-laden flowers on that sea-shore. The straight fish-shaped eyes in her full-moon face have caused love sickness incurable by medicine, but curable by the lady's soft and yellow-spotted breasts.[3]

'Pretending[4] to drive away the birds hovering around 9

[1] The sea-god described is Varuṇa. According to Sanskrit tradition he is the Lord of all waters, and figures prominently in the Vēdic pantheon.

[2] One of the pastimes of the girls in the littoral tracts.

[3] This stanza suggests that this is the only medicine for curing love-sickness. These words are spoken by the lover's companion who sees signs of love in the heroine. Cf. *infra* st. 45.

[4] This and the following stanza go by the name of *kāṉalvari*.

the foul-smelling dried fish on the beach, a maid holds in her hands fragrant jasmine from a young plant, with swarms of bees roaming about her. She is a goddess who dwells there in the sweet-smelling grove of flowers. Had I known of the existence of this goddess[1] there, I would not have come.

10 'In the open yard before fishermen's huts where their nets are dried, Death,[2] assuming the form of a maiden with long lance-like eyes, dwells on the foreshore where the waves beat the sands. There, with a wreath of flowers in her hand, she guards the fish dried for sale. Had I known that she was here, I would not have come at all.' (So said the lover.)

Again[3]

11 'Behold! This is the moon, this perfected picture of the face in which eyes have been painted like fish, brows like a bow and curls of hair like clouds in which Cupid's power is revealed. O tell me, has the moon left the wide sky in fear of the serpent (Rāhu)[4] and sought shelter in this little hamlet where fishermen dwell?

12 'Behold! Her eyes resembling a blood-stained lance[5] glance from side to side, to view the conch-shells cast on the shore. They are fierce Death. Has fierce Death assumed the form of a graceful young damsel, and come to live in this little village on the seashore?

[1] The goddess is the lady-love herself.

[2] For a description of Death in a maiden's guise, see *Tirukkuṟaḷ*, st. 1083, and *Kaḷittogai*, st. 56, l. 9.

[3] Stanzas 11-13 are put in the mouth of the lover who, on seeing his lady-love in front of him, rapturously breaks forth into descriptions of her.

[4] Rāhu is an evil planet like Kētu. Legend has it that Rāhu has only a head, while Kētu has only a body and possesses no face. Both are supposed to cause eclipses according to the mythical account transmitted by the *Purāṇas*.

[5] Red in the eyes of ladies is a sign of their youthful love. Hence the eye is compared to a blood-stained lance. The eye here stands for the person possessing such eyes.

'Behold! This is the goddess who drives away birds 13
from where the fish are spread to dry and who causes dire
sickness to those who gaze at her. Has that goddess
come to the cool seaside thick with hare-leaf (*aṭumbu*) in
the form of a damsel with five plaits of hair?'[1]

Again[2]

'The fragrant flowers of this grove, the fresh sweet 14
smell of these spreading sands, the faultless words of this damsel, her big youthful breasts, her face resembling the full moon, her bow-like curved brows, and her lightning waist that baffles the painter's brush;[3] it is these that have caused distress to me.

'This open seashore with its dashing billows, this stretch 15
of shining sand, these flowers that send forth their sweet scents, this pleasant thick grove, the fragrance-spreading tresses, this face like the moon, and this pair of carp-like eyes; all these have caused distress to me.

'This beach where shells are scattered in heaps, this 16
fine grove which charges the air with its fragrance, these flowers that scatter their soft petals, these haunts where she moves about alone, her young teeth which look like new-sprouting shoots (from the soil), her face that vies with the full moon, and her two youthful breasts; it is these that have caused distress to me.'

Again[4]

'Your elder brothers go out into the sea and live 17
by killing living things (fish); you, on the other hand, enter into my body and live by killing me. Pray do not lose your slender waist which is in danger of being

[1] Another reference to the hair being dressed in five plaits.

[2] Stanzas 14-16 are put into the mouth of the hero as addressing his comrade.

[3] Another reference to show that the art of painting had been developed to a large extent in the second century A.D.

[4] Stanzas 17-19 are the words of the hero addressing the heroine.

overwhelmed by the weight of your beauteous and well-moulded breasts.[1]

18 'Your father kills the living things (of the sea by catching them) in the cruel meshes of his net.[2] You, on the other hand, kill lives by catching them in the net of your long eyes. Pray do not lose your lightning-like waist, which is at the point of breaking, owing to the weight of your breasts decked with pearl-strings.

19 'By means of swift boats, your elder brothers kill lives (fish). You kill lives with your curved brows. Your fame consists in witnessing the distress you cause in others. Pray do not lose your slender waist which faints under the weight of your breasts!'[3]

Again[4]

20 'The red eyes of the damsel who holds the coral pestle in her hand and pounds the white pearls in the mortar,[5] the red eyes of her who pounds white pearls are not lilies, for, O, they are so cruel!

21 'The red eyes of the damsel who walks the walk of a swan in the shade of the *puṉṉai* where the waves dash against the foul-smelling shore, the red eyes of her who walks the walk of a swan are frightful; verily they are death, death!

22 'The red eyes of the damsel who holds honey-laden violets in her hand and scares away the birds that hover around the dried fish, the red eyes of her who scares away

[1] The term *miṭal* in the text means literally 'of abounding strength'.

[2] The eyes and the waist of the lady are compared respectively to the meshes of a net and to lightning.

[3] In these three stanzas 17-19 the hero makes a passionate appeal to the heroine to yield and to subject him to no more uncertainty.

[4] Stanzas 20-23 are put into the mouth of the hero's companion when he hears his words of passion.

[5] See below, canto xxix, 'Vaḷḷaippāṭṭu', l. 6. The coral pestle and the pearl powders seem to confirm that the city was noted for abundant pearls and coral.

the birds are not innocent darts; verily they are so cruel, cruel!'

Again

'O foolish swan! Do not go near her, do not go; your gait cannot rival hers. O foolish swan! do not go near her, do not go; your gait cannot rival hers. O foolish swan! do not approach her, who roams about stirring the waters of the sea as the waves fall one after another (on the shore), for your gait cannot rival hers. Do not go.' 23

The Narrative

At that time, Mādavi of the long beautiful eyes, who listened to the sea-song (of Kōvalan̲), feeling that his song was indicative of a change of attitude on his part, took the lute from him pretending that she was pleased though (really) sulking. Then she began to play, purposefully, an ode to the sea so fine that the goddess Earth[1] wondered at her skill; and all people were in ecstasy when they heard her sweet voice appropriately accompanying the notes of the lute. 24

TO THE KĀVĒRI[2]

'Hail to thee, Kāvēri! clothing thyself in a garb of fair flowers where bees cluster murmuring their songs, thou walkedst along with swaying steps, with carp-like dark eyes. All this walk of thine, with thy carp-like dark eyes, is, I know, due to thy husband's righteous sceptre which does not deviate from the right path.[3] Hail to thee, Kāvēri! 25

[1] A relic of the primitive concept of calling the Earth Mother and Goddess.

[2] Stanzas 25-27 go by the name of *āṟṟuvari* or a kind of ancient song to the river. Here the righteous rule of the Cōḻa king and the fertility of his kingdom are in evidence, the latter mostly due to the Kāvēri. Thus we find that the glorification of the Kāvēri is an important theme in all early Tamil poetry in general and of the *Silappadikāram* in particular.

[3] These are the primary duties of a righteous monarch. The Sanskrit term *pālanam* or *paripālanam* connotes the idea that protection of subjects is the chief duty of a king. See, for example, *Rāmāyaṇa*, Bk. II, ch. 106, st. 19.

26 'Hail to thee, Kāvēri! When thou movedst along and thy lovely garland swayed, the peacock strutted along the flowery grove, and the koel sent forth its mirthful notes; I have learnt that this walk, with thy lovely garland moving, is attributable to the might of thy husband's frightful lance. Hail to thee, Kāvēri!

27 'As a mother tends her babe so thou wilt not cease from everlasting help to the fertile country of him (our king) who is prosperous to the end of all time. This enduring help which thou renderest unceasingly is attributable to the grace of our king of the solar race, who, with his wheel of righteousness, confers protection on all.[1] Hail to thee, Kāvēri!'

TO PUHAR

28 'O sir, you come every day, like the God of love,[2] and ask us to receive pearls, which are no match for the bright teeth shining between the coral lips of our lady whose face is like the full moon. Our city is Puhār where the surging ocean, like a dealer, exchanges lustrous pearls for wreaths of flowers.

29 'Sir, these bracelets of the fair-armed ladies, the damsels of sturdy fishermen, make known (by becoming loose)[3] that they have been married in secret.[4] We are innocent. How can we understand all this? Our city is Puhār where the water-lily, with the murmuring bee inside, blossoms at the sight of the swan resting in the midst of the flower-laden branches of the long *puṉṉai*, imagining them to be the full moon and stars.

30 'How can we know, sir, in these regions where wine overcomes the consumer while the consumption cannot be

[1] This may also refer to the impartiality of the king.

[2] The theme of stanzas 28-30 is the glory of Puhār, the quondam capital of the Cōḻas.

[3] See in this connexion *Kaḷittogai*, 'Kuṟiñji', st. 17, ll. 8-11.

[4] It is a reference to the *kaḷavu* system of marriage. The term *marai* in the text is significant.

concealed, the fact that you cause sickness, incurable by any medicine, to ladies? Our city is Puhār where, when the waves destroy the houses of sand, sharp javelin-like eyes[1] in their full-moon faces shed tears of sorrow. Then gathering handfuls of sand we throw them against the waves imagining that the sea will be filled up.

Again

'Although he saw[2] the male crab with the female crab 31
and saw me also in this fair park thick with its clusters of flowers, the lord of the maritime tract, taking leave of his senses, deserted us of the five plaits. O girl with curly hair, I do not know his reason.

'Has[3] he taken with him his sympathy and his horse- 32
chariot, and gone without thinking of us? O fair-blossomed hare-leaf creepers! O swans! Let him abandon us. Yet shall we not forget him who has forgotten us.

'O *neydal* flower laden with honey like my weeping 33
eyes at the distressing nightfall, thou feelest no trouble but dost sleep. In thy dreams dost thou see my hard-hearted (lover) as he approaches this seaside?

'When he dashed along with the speed of birds in his 34
chariot drawn by horses, thou ruinedst the route wherever he went (his path), O clear waters of the sea. What can I do, O clear waters of the sea? Thou hast become at one with those who are spreading scandal around me here. What shall I do? Thou dost not know my woes.

'O waves! The ruts caused by the passing of the 35
strong, big chariot of my perfect lover were ruined.

[1] The idea here is that waves rise like sharp javelins as if to meet the moon in the sky and dash against the sporting-ground of these fisher-maids. Thinking foolishly that they could arrest the progress of the waters, they throw sand into the deep as if to fill up the sea.

[2] Stanza 31 describes the feelings of the heroine and shows her inability to gauge the love of her lord.

[3] Stanzas 32-36 represent the lament of the heroine at the neglect and indifference of her lover. She aimlessly addresses the hare-leaf, the *neydal* flower, the waves, the grove, and the swan.

O cool grove! O swan, sporting with thy mate! O wet shore! Will not you all tell my lover that (his deed) is not just?

36 'Bless you, O waves! You destroyed the ruts caused by the wheels of my perfect lover's strong, big chariot. You destroyed the ruts on the way. At the same time you pretended to be a friend of mine. Hail, you waves! You are no friend.'

Again[1]

37 'O lord of the sea, whose waves dash as far as the paddy fields, enrobed in beautiful corals and decked with excellent ornaments made of well-formed pearls! The fresh wounds caused in the *puṉṉai* park by the shafts of Cupid, who owns the flag of the *makara* fish, cover her body and make her unrecognizable; but if her mother sees her thus, what shall I do?

38 'O lord of the maritime tract, whose waves, smiling with their pearl-like teeth and opening their coral lips, spread over the courtyard where the fishermen's nets are (left for drying), what shall I do if her mother, seeing that this innocent damsel has changed her colour to that of the *pīra* flower that blossoms during winter, consults the deity[2] and finds out who did this cruel act?

39 'O lord of the maritime tract, whose waves move about to destroy the fishy smell of the beach and penetrate the cool grove spreading it with the fragrance of different fallen flowers,[3] my lady suffers mental anguish but the cause of her illness is not known. If this unknown disease

[1] Stanzas 37-39 have for their theme the *varaivu-kaḍāviyavai*. These are the words of the maid who is afraid of the discovery of signs of love in her mistress by the latter's mother. Anxious to see her wedded the maid thus addresses the lover.

[2] This points to the custom of consulting deities to rectify wrongs whenever trouble occurs.

[3] The reference is to old and withered flowers that have fallen down from the tree.

is detected by her mother who will be pained at it, what shall I do?'

Again[1]

'The evening darkness has spread everywhere. The 40
Day-maker (the sun) has disappeared. My eyes shed tears of sorrow from which it is impossible to recover. O fair one whose locks of hair are decked with open-petalled flowers! Is this maddening, fiery twilight, which loosens my bangles,[2] found in the country of the deserter?

'The sun has disappeared. Thick darkness has spread 41
everywhere. Collyrium-eyes, that look like opening flowers, shed tears of sorrow. O fair one whose face looks like the young moon! Is this maddening twilight, which comes vomiting the moon and devouring the sun,[3] found in that country to which he has gone?

'The birds have stopped singing. The Lord of the 42
Day has disappeared. These long eyes suffer from the pain of shedding unceasing tears. O fair one whose tresses contain blossoming flower-buds! Is this maddening twilight which attacks my life,[4] found in the country of the deserter?'

Again[5]

'Someone came to the *kaidai* fence through the swamps 43
(near the sea) and spoiled our sport. He who went away

[1] Stanzas 40-42 represent the distress of the heroine at eventide when she thinks of the country in which her lover has tarried. She addresses her maid.

[2] The idea is that maidens feel the separation of their lovers keenly when night sets in, so that their bodies grow thin and their bangles hang loose.

[3] The idea is that the sun has set and the moon has risen.

[4] The heroine considers evening her cruel enemy.

[5] Stanzas 43-45 are again the words of the maid to her lady. In Tamil love poetry the maid sometimes identifies herself so closely with the heroine that she speaks for the heroine. Here is an open declaration of her abiding faith in the lover who has deserted her, as she thinks, for the time being only. Alternatively these stanzas may be interpreted in another way. The first two lines of each of these three stanzas can be taken as the words of the maid and the next two lines as the words of the heroine in reply.

spoiling our sport, would not leave my love-stricken mind.

44 'Through the swamps, fenced by the park, close to the sea, someone came and stood before us saying "Make me pleased". He who stood before us saying "Make me pleased" could not be excluded from our deer-like glances.

45 'Seeing the swan playing with its mate, one stood looking on all yesterday. He, who stood looking on yesterday, would not leave (our minds) even as the gold-tinted moles[1] cannot leave our body.'

Also[2]

46 'Come not here, O crane! Come not near our park. Come not here, O crane, come not near our park; for you will not speak of my present love-sickness to my lord of the maritime tract. Come not, O crane! Do not approach our park.'

Also

47 Singing thus in the mode in which Kōvalaṉ had sung, the beautiful damsel (Mādavi) again exhibited with her rosy little fingers the charm of the *śevvaḻippālai*[3] in which the *kaikkalai*[4] was joined with *kural*. She sang in suitable strains a new melody-type (*paṇ*).

Again[5]

48 'O evening, during that charming *vilarippālai*[6] peculiar to the residents of the maritime tract, you made *iḷi*[7] blended

[1] 'Yellow spreading spots on the body of women, regarded as beautiful' —*Tamil Lexicon.*

[2] This address to the crane in stanza 46 represents the lament of the lovesick heroine.

[3] 'A secondary melody-type of the pālai class'—*Tamil Lexicon.*

[4] 'Poem in five *viruttam* verses of unreciprocated love'—ibid. This song shows that her love is one-sided and not reciprocated by the other party.

[5] The three stanzas 48-50 represent the passionate outburst of the heroine at the approach of the evening. Cf. stanzas 40-2 *supra.*

[6] *Vilari* is a descending musical scale.

[7] *Iḷi* is the *pañcamasvaram* and the sixth *kaikiḷai* is its inimical string. Instead of playing on the *iḷi* string the fingers automatically went to the enemy-string at that time, due to illusion of the mind.

with *kiḷai* (*kaikkiḷai*). O evening, even as you made *iḷi* join with *kiḷai*, you are able to take away my life. Please yourself. May you live long!

'O evening, you go to take away the life of people 49
who live dolefully seeking solace in the greatly comforting parting-words of their separated lovers. If you thus besiege them, O evening, you will be the invading king from outside besieging the fortress of the enemy-king.[1] Is it not so?

'O maddening twilight, you came with the setting of 50
the Lord of the Day, augmenting my distress, when the world began to close its eyes. If you are the maddening twilight, and if he be my wedded lord, the world has become impoverished indeed.[2] Bless thee, maddening twilight!'

Again[3]

'O god of the sea, we worship your lotus-feet. At 51
this cruel maddening, fiery twilight, our lover departed, without considering the effects of his vow made in this flowery park, with words removing all our mental pain. Please forgive his false vow.'

Hearing this, Kōvalaṉ said, 'I sang the *kāṉalvari*; but 52
she, the cunning one combining several deceitful lies, sang with her mind upon someone else.' Prompted by Fate which made the music of the lute its pretext,[4] he slowly withdrew his hands from the embrace of his full-moon faced lady-love, and said 'Since the day has come to

[1] The reference is to the *uḻijñaittiṇai* and the *nocciltiṇai*, and represents the monarch outside forcing an entry into the fortress and the defending king inside. (See *Tolk.* 'Porul.', sūtra 65.)

[2] She believes that everybody in the world must feel alike at nightfall.

[3] The lover has been separated for a long time. Knowing secretly that he had returned and was waiting for an opportunity to meet the heroine, the maid addresses the god of the sea so as to be heard by the lover.

[4] Here the author introduces the theory of *prārabdhakarmā*, that the effects of our actions in a previous birth have to run their course, do what we will.

a close, we shall make a move'. But she did not get up at once. After Kōvalan̲ had gone away with his retinue of servants, Mādavi rose up, and silencing the group of maids who were making a noise in the grove filled with the pollen of flowers, she betook herself home, getting into her carriage, with a sad heart, unaccompanied by her lover, and saying

'May the garlanded white parasol of Śembiyan̲ (Cōḻa king), who with his fiery sword and his elephant with an ornamental plate on its face, makes all the princes of this vast world bow their heads, bring under its shadow the entire Cakravāḷa[1] mountain !'

[1] A mythical range of mountains encircling the orb of the earth.

Canto VIII

VĒṈIṞKĀDAI

OR

THE ADVENT OF SUMMER

THE celebrated king Māraṇ (Cupid) with his delightful friend Spring held sway over the fertile Tamil country, bounded in the north by the Tirupati hills[1] sacred to Viṣṇu, and in the south by the Kumari sea,[2] having for its capitals high-towered Madura, Uṟandai[3] of great renown, awe-inspiring Vañji, and Puhār with its resounding waters. This approach of (Spring) was heralded by the ambassador, the South Wind, hailing from the fertile Podiyil hill sacred to the revered saint (Agastya). As if to announce the herald's message, 'Put on your garb, O ye regiments of the fish-bannered prince, befitting your respective ranks,' the cuckoo, living in a grove rich in creepers, acted as the young trumpeter of Cupid's army[4] and sounded his note. 1–13

Mādavi of the long flower-like eyes who had returned alone, after her love-quarrel with Kōvalaṇ at the pleasure-park filled with open buds on the seashore, betook herself to her summer-retreat in a lofty upper story reaching the sky. That beautifully adorned damsel decorated the 14–22

[1] The northern and southern limits of the Tamil country are furnished here. Once there was a river by name the Kumari, near the place which is now known as Cape Comorin. It has been swallowed by the sea. That the sea eroded into the interior as far as the river Pahruḷi is evident from this canto, ll. 18-20 and corroborated by the *Iraiyaṉār Ahapporuḷ*.

[2] The Kumari sea is compared to a young lady decked with bangles. It is to be noted here that the two capitals of the Coḷas are mentioned.

[3] The Cōḷa Perunaṟkiḷḷi was the king at this time at Uṟandai. Puhār was only the quondam capital.

[4] Māraṇ, the God of Love, had for his fourfold army the four capitals of the Tamil land, for his ally the Spring, for his ambassador the South Wind and as his royal herald, blowing the trumpet, the koel or cuckoo.

expanse of her breasts which were already smeared with *kunkumum*, with pearls of the southern sea and sandal-paste of the southern hills. These were the unexceptional tributes appropriate to the season[1] which she offered with her own hands.

23–26 Taking the spotless lute in her grasp she began to sing a sweet song and fell into a languor which she overcame by assuming the *padmāsanam* posture in the nine series of postures (*viruṭṭis*).[2]

27–35 With her right hand on the bend of the *vīṇa* in the attitude of the *padāhai* and with her left hand in that part of the instrument known as the *māḍagam*, she produced by the skill of her technique the notes *śempahai*, *ārppu*, *kūḍam*, and *adirvu*, avoiding discords.[3] She thus played the series of fourteen tunes in the traditional mode, beginning with *uḻai* and ending with *kaikkiḷai* carefully scrutinizing the respective notes of the strings known as *iṇai*,[4] *kiḷai*,[5] *pahai*[6] and *naṭpu*.[7] In this way she sang with judgement to the accompaniment of the *iḷi* string.

36–44 Later, in the same order, she sounded the fifth and the seventh strings beginning and ending with *uḻai*, and afterwards commencing and ending with *kural*. She tested her skill in the four modes of *ahanilai-marudam*,[8] *puṟanilai-marudam*, *maruhiyal-marudam*, and *peruhiyal-marudam*,[9] keeping an eye upon the three *śrutis* high, level and low and then began the *tiṟappaṉ* born of the above-mentioned tunes. Soon she who looked like a flower-creeper was

[1] This shows that different kinds of fragrant pastes were used by lovers according to the season.

[2] *Viruṭṭi* is also known by another term, *iruppu*, explained by Aḍiyārkkunallār from dramatic and other treatises. See *Perumkadai*, 'Narumadai', ll. 44-8.

[3] Cf. *Jīvakacintāmaṇi* st. 716-9, comm.

[4] The second string.

[5] The fifth string.

[6] The sixth and the third strings.

[7] The fourth string.

[8] This and the following two are supposed to have sixteen strings.

[9] This has thirty-two strings. The above are the four great classes of *paṇ* which is a melody-type.

overcome by languor when she set her mind to play the tune called *vēṉiṟpāṇi*.

She took up a garland formed by tying together *cam-* 45–55
paka, *mādavi*, *tamāla*, white jasmine, fragrant roots, and choice petals of the red lily intertwined with the white bent flowers of the ripe screw pine. On this she wrote, under the influence of Cupid who, single-handed, exercises his righteous sceptre over the vast world with his flower-arrows, and who is worshipped by the whole earth unexcepted, taking in her hand the long stalk of a flower and dipping it in the writing paste made of red lac and *agar*,[1] as follows :—

'He who has come to rule the world is the youthful 56–63
prince,[2] Spring, who brings together the lovers and their chosen ones. The moon who has risen with the love-anguish that shows itself in the evening, also is not faultless. Therefore whether they be lovers who had had union and departed and were delayed in coming back, or whether they be lovers who had deserted and forgotten their mates, that this moon should kill the lonely poor ones with his sharp darts of fragrant flowers should be no cause for surprise. Please understand this.'

Thus evidencing her excessive love wrote Mādavi, 64–73
sallow-complexioned and well acquainted with the sixty-four arts[3] when her sweet tongue expressed in musical *paṇ* and *tiṟam*, the tender tone of a lisping child. She then called aloud her maid Vasantamālā, on that pensive evening, and asked her to inform Kōvalaṉ of all that had been written on the flower-garland and to bring him to her. Receiving the garland, Vasantamālā of the lance-like long eyes went to Kōvalaṉ living in the quarter where grain was stored, and handed it over to him.

[1] It is interesting to note the nature of the writing materials used for love letters.

[2] The implication is that Spring being a youthful prince cannot rule fairly and well.

[3] Cf. Vātsyāyana's *Kāmasūtra* where the names of the sixty-four arts are given.

74–77 Then Kōvalaṉ refused to receive the message saying: 'The *kaṇkūḍuvari*[1] performed by the loving maiden having *tilaka* on her forehead, curls of hair adorned with flowers, small black eyebrows, *kuvaḷai*-like eyes casting love glances, *kumiḻ*-like nose, and *kovvai*-like lips,

78-83 'The *kāṇvari*[2] dance of the black long-eyed dancer, who moved backward and forward by coming and going, with a moon-like face which seemed to groan under the weight of rain-bearing clouds of hair, whose eyes frisked about like carps, and whose bewitching smile exposed pearl-white teeth from within her coral-coloured sweet lips,

84–89 'The dance of Disguise (*uḷvari*[3]), performed by the dancer whose piercing eyes were as sharp as a spear and who noticed the poverty of my heart after my separation from her owing to a lover's quarrel, and being lonely appeared at the approach of eventide in the guise of her maid cheered me up with words as sweet as those of the parrot, with steps as entrancing as those of a swan, and with grace as ravishing as that of the peacock,

90–93 'The minor dance *puṟavari*[4] which, drunk with passion, she, whose slender waist could bear no ornaments, danced, in front (of the house) to the tinkling of foot-ornaments and jingling waist-band (not embracing me) though she knew that I was pining for her,

94–101 'The dance of *kiḻarvari*[5] performed by her who had a beautiful forehead, garlanded locks of hair, forelocks adorned with petals, a string of pearls, and beauteous breasts causing distress to her waist and who appeared languid

[1] One of the eight *vari*; a kind of dancing or, more appropriately, gesture. It seems to have been a custom in ancient times for the dancing-girls to take to *vari* as distinguished from the *kuravai* in which housewives took the leading part. This literally means the first view of the heroine by the hero. See *Tamil Lexicon*, p. 184.

[2] Dance performed at frequent and repeated intervals.

[3] This was to disguise one's own form. An example of living incognito is that of the Pāṇḍavas in the city of Virāṭa king.

[4] Dance where the heroine coldly neglects her lover's company.

[5] 'Posture assumed by an offended lover or love, when an intermediary tries to conciliate'—*Tamil Lexicon*, p. 938.

with her sleek tresses devoid of all sheen after purposely misconstruing the message I sent to her through her maid-servant expressing my love for her,

'The *tērccivari*[1] performed by her when reflecting and 102–4
reflecting on her sufferings caused by my separation and by her unbearable love towards me, she expressed to my numerous relatives,

'The *kāṭcivari*[2] which she performed when she wore 105–6
the garland with bees buzzing on it and spoke about her distress to all onlookers,

'And the *eḍuttukkōḷvari*[3] which she danced one follow- 107–8
ing the other, seeing which, those upon whom she fell in a swoon comforted her after bringing her to her senses,

'All these dances, my dear girl bedecked with jewels, 109–10
are quite natural to her because she is only a dancing-girl.'

Thus when he refused to accept the garland sent by 111–18
the bejewelled Mādavi, with the message written on the white *tāḻai* flowers of the screw-pine, Vasantamālā was sorrow-stricken at heart and wasted no time in returning to tell her mistress adorned with a flower garland, what had happened. Mādavi of the long flower-like eyes, said in reply: 'Fair lady, if he does not come this night, we will see him at least tomorrow morning' and sat down with a heavy heart on the couch spread with flowers, sleepless.

VENBĀ

When[4] the Spring came and the red lotus opened its 1
petals, the tender leaves of the sweet mango tree hung down, and the beautiful *aśōka* blossomed. O, what mental suffering has to be endured by our lady of the good spear-like eyes!

[1] 'A dramatic action in which a person expresses in detail all his sufferings to his relatives'—*Tamil Lexicon*, p. 2060.

[2] 'Dance exhibiting sorrow and distress'—ibid, p. 848.

[3] 'Theatrical action of swooning in extreme anguish in order to be lifted up'—ibid., p. 515.

[4] Soliloqy of the hunch-backed Vasantamālā in taking the *ōla* (message) from her mistress.

2 When the cuckoo proclaimed 'O ye that quarrelled with your lovers,[1] it is the command of Cupid that you must love one another' (Vasantamālā remembered what she had said to Kōvalaṉ). 'O you who enjoyed her sweet words in the seaside park, enjoy now these sweet words written on tender flowers by her who has been embraced by the Spring.'

[1] This is what is known as *ūḍal*. See *Kaḷittogai*, st. 92, l. 61. It was a kind of 'love quarrel between the husband and wife, arising from jealousy, peculiar to the agricultural tracts, one of five *urripporuḷ*'.

Canto IX

KAṈĀTTIṞAMURAITTAKĀDAI

OR

THE TALE OF THE DREAM

In the evening when the sun disappeared, ladies with 1–4
creeper-like waists sprinkled[1] lustrous buds of *mullai* flowers, just blossoming, and paddy grains in their houses in the big city; they lit their jewelled lamps and attired themselves in a manner appropriate to the night.[2]

One day long ago, Mālati fed her co-wife's child with 5–15
milk; but the milk choked the child who hiccoughed and died. Being in a panic that her husband the Brahman and her co-wife would throw the blame upon her and would not accept the truth, Mālati took the dead child in her arms and went to the temple where stood the divine *kalpaka* tree (*amarartarukkōṭṭam*),[3] to the temple of the white elephant (*veḷyāṉaikkōṭṭam*),[4] to the temple of the beautiful white god (*veḷḷaināgarkōṭṭam*),[5] to the temple of the Sun who rises in the east (*uccikkiḻāṉkōṭṭam*), to the temple of the city-god (*ūrkkōṭṭam*),[6] to the temple of the spear-god (*vēṟkōṭṭam*),[7] to the temple of the Vajra (*vaccirakkōṭṭam*),[8] to the temple of the Deity who dwells outside the city

[1] Cf. *Neḍunalvāḍai*, ll. 39-44.

[2] It appears that ladies had two kinds of dresses: one for the day and the other for the night.

[3] *Kalpaka* was the divine tree in heaven, whose fragrance and flowers were enjoyed by Indrāṇī.

[4] This is the Airāvata temple, the Airāvata being the mount of Indra, the king of heaven.

[5] The temple of Balarāma.

[6] The reference is to the god enshrined at Kailāsa, that is, Siva.

[7] This is the temple of Muruga.

[8] Either it was a temple where Vajra specially was worshipped or it is a reference to Indra's shrine. Cf. *Maṇi.*, canto i, l. 27.

(Aiyaṉār) (*puṟampaṉaiyāṉvāḻkōṭṭam*),[1] to the temple of the Nigranthas (*niggantakkōṭṭam*),[2] and to the temple of the Moon (*nilākkōṭṭam*)[3] and besought all these gods thus: 'O ye gods! Relieve me of my great trouble.' Then she betook herself to the temple[4] of the famous Śāttaṉ learned in the *śāstra* called *pāṣaṇḍam* and besought his counsel.

16–25 At that time appeared before her one, a young creeper-like girl, as if mocking others by her beauty, who said, 'O faultless woman! God will not grant a boon to those who have not performed penance. This is not a false statement; it is a true saying: so hand to me this dead body.' Saying that, she forcibly snatched the corpse from the (poor) woman's hands and went in the darkness, when all slept, to the ground *śuḍukāṭṭukkōṭṭam*[5] where the goblin Iḍākiṉi who eats buried dead bodies, took the child's corpse and devoured it. Before her who cried out like a peacock at the visitation of thunder, appeared the God Śāttaṉ,[6] who comforted her with the following words: 'O mother! Do not weep in your distress. Look before you and behold the living child.'

25–28 To fulfil the promise, the God himself assumed the form of that child and lay in the grove which was the haunt

[1] Aḍiyārkkunallār identifies this with Sātavāhana's temple. See *Tolk.* 'Sey.' *sūtra* 118, comm. See also *Divākaram*, st. 12.

[2] This was a Jaina temple.

[3] Here is evidence of a separate temple dedicated to the Moon-god.

[4] This and the above few lines show that as many as eleven temples were found in the city belonging to different cults. They also show that the worship of Indra, of the Moon, of the Sun, and of Balarāma, which has now become practically extinct, was extant in the early centuries of the Christian era. In those days, it is also seen that the people worshipped at all temples including that of the Jaina and the *pāṣaṇḍa* (heretic gods). This demonstrates that there was no sectarian outlook in matters religious.

[5] The *śuḍukāṭṭukkōṭṭam* can be identified with *cakravāḷakkōṭṭam* mentioned in *Maṇi.*, canto vi. Though it is difficult to fix the date of the origin of the institution of cremation, it seems reasonable to suppose that it is as old as that of burial.

[6] Sāttaṉ can be identified with Sāsta now enshrined in the Sāsta temples which are generally found on the outskirts of villages. See article 'Aśōka's Religion' in *J.O.R.*, 1930, p. 278.

of cuckoos. The overjoyed Mālati took up this illusory child, clasped it to her bosom and (going home) handed it to its mother.

This divine Brahman child grew into a boy[1] and 29–32
acquired a profound knowledge of the sacred scriptures. Later, when his parents died, he settled all disputes among their relations, and performed all the religious obsequies due to them.[2] Afterwards he married a lady named Dēvandi and lived with her (for some time) saying 'May your flower-like eyes bear this (divine) sight.'

(One day) he appeared to her in his eternal form of 33–40
youth and then vanished asking her to go to his shrine. After he had gone with those inspiring words, Dēvandi, who was worshipping at his temple every day, gave out as a pretext[3] (for his absence) 'He has left me saying that he will visit all the sacred places. Please bring him back to me.'

Having come to know that the good lady Kaṇṇaki of 40–44
undiminished repute had cause for distress, and thinking of it with a sorrowful heart, Dēvandi worshipped the god for her sake with (offerings of) *aṛugu*, (*Aerua lanata*) and paddy, and went (to Kaṇṇaki), with the blessing 'May you get back your husband.'

But Kaṇṇaki replied, 'Though I may get him back, 45–54
my heart will still be pained; for I have had a dream.[4] It was thus. We went, hand in hand, to a great city. There some people belonging to the city said something which was unbearably unjust. Some crime was thrown upon Kōvalaṉ. It stung me like a scorpion-bite. Hearing it, I pleaded before the protecting king. The king as

[1] A *brahmacāri*.

[2] The *svadharma* of a Brahman *brahmacāri* and householder which is furnished here agrees with what is prescribed in the *Dharmaśāstras* and the *Dharmasūtras*. For the six duties incumbent on the householder see *Hindu Administrative Institutions*, pp. 188-9.

[3] To those who asked her why she was staying at the shrine, she used to answer thus.

[4] Note how the dream came true.

well as the city would witness a great calamity. I shall not say more because it was a bad dream. O lady with close-fitting bangles, if you listen to the evil deed done to me and the happy results[1] achieved by me and my husband, you will laugh (in derision).'

55–63 Dēvandi replied : 'O lady wearing golden bangles ! You have not been discarded by your husband. This trouble is due to your having failed to perform a vow in a former birth. If you wish to wipe off that evil, go to the spot where the Kāvēri meets the roaring sea. There is a park where the *neydal* opens its petals, and where two sacred tanks are dedicated to the Sun (*Śūryakuṇḍam*) and the Moon (*Sōmakuṇḍam*)[2] respectively. Those women who bathe in them and worship the God of love[3] enshrined there, will ever enjoy the company of their husbands in this world. Besides they will also attain Heaven (*Bōgabūmi*). We shall go there one day to bathe.'

64–71 But bejewelled Kaṇṇaki said in reply to the charming lady, 'That is not proper'[4] and sometime after this a young maidservant approached her and said, 'Our Kōvalaṉ has arrived at the gate. It looks as if he will protect us for a long time.' Kōvalaṉ went into the house and entering the bedchamber was stricken with grief at the sight of the pale Kaṇṇaki, his fair wife, and said, 'By consorting with a false woman who makes every false thing appear like truth, I have lost the rich store of my ancestral wealth. O, the poverty I have caused (to our house) makes me ashamed of myself.'

[1] The evil deed is the plucking off of one of her breasts. The happy results are the attainment of heaven.

[2] In a note Dr Swaminatha Aiyar seems to identify these with *Sōmatīrtham* and *Sūryatīrtham* in Tiruveṇkāḍu. The *Paṭṭiṉappālai* (*Pattuppāṭṭu*), l. 39, refers to these as *irukāmattiṉaiyēri*, the lakes which give one's desire.

[3] The reference is to a temple of Manmatha or the God of Love. Though festivals in his honour are still conducted, we have no separate temples to this deity. Cf. *Paṭṭiṉappālai*, l. 39, and *Jīvakacintāmaṇi*, st. 1598.

[4] This is in keeping with the sentiment of the *Kuṟaḷveṇbā*, st. 55, where it is stated that chaste ladies offer worship to no God but their husbands.

Comforting him with a fascinating smile on her brightening face, she replied, 'O, do not grieve! You yet have my anklets. Accept them.'[1] Then Kōvalaṉ retorted, 'O, my good girl, listen. I will use this anklet as my capital to recover all the jewels and all the wealth I have lost.[2] Rise up, O lady with the tresses decorated with choice flowers! Come with me to the city of Madura highly renowned for its tower.' Impelled by fate he decided to start before the heavy darkness of the night was dispelled by the sun. 72–79

VEṆBĀ

The dream dreamt by his wife made the words of the black and long-eyed Mādavi empty. Early, before the sun dispelled the darkness of night, (Kōvalaṉ and his wife) started, impelled by fate which had decreed their doom long ago.

[1] Kaṇṇaki spoke thinking that Kōvalaṉ wanted to take some more ornaments to the dancing-girl Mādavi.

[2] The author seems to infer from the life of Kōvlaṉ that the leading of an immoral life will result in the loss of all wealth and property.

Canto X

NĀḌUKĀṆKĀDAI

OR

THE SIGHT OF THE KINGDOM

1–4 On the last day on which the last watch of the night was dark,[1] when the eye of the sky (the sun) had not opened, and when the white moon that shone in the company of the stars had vanished, Kōvalan̲ and (Kaṇṇaki) started forth driven by their fate.

5–14 Having passed out of their tall outer gate with its very famous latched door[2] where the goat and the yak and the swan[3] with its soft down were roaming about in a sense of kinship, they circumambulated the temple sacred to Maṇivaṇṇan̲ (Viṣṇu) sleeping his all-perceiving sleep[4] on his beautiful serpent-couch. Going beyond it they left behind them the seven *vihāras*[5] made by Indra, where divinities moving in the sky explained treatises on *dharma*, which were the divine words of the Ar̲avōn̲ (the Buddha),[6]

[1] The Indra festival commenced on Saturday, *Citrāpaurṇami*, and continued for 28 days ending with Monday (Star *Anuṣam*) of the month of Vaikāśi and resulting in the *ūḍal* of Kōvalan̲ and Mādavi. The journey to Madura by Kōvalan̲ was begun the next Tuesday, when the star Keṭṭai was in the ascendant. (See Aḍiyārkkunallār's commentary.) This calculation is incorrect.

[2] The idea here is that when the gate was made, the latch formed an integral part of it. It means it was not separate from it.

[3] It would appear from the commentary that these domesticated animals were also artistically carved on the gateway. If so it bears evidence that wood carving was practised in the ancient Tamil land.

[4] *Yōganidra* of Viṣṇu. This demonstrates that Kōvalan̲ and Kaṇṇaki offered prayers to the Vaiṣṇava deity. Later it is said that they worshipped at the Jaina *śilātala*. This bears testimony to the fact that there was little difference between earlier Jainism and the orthodox religion.

[5] See canto xxvii, l. 92 *infra*. The literal meaning of the term *vihāra* is 'not constructed either by hand or by machinery'; it is a mind-born institution. See *Maṇi.*, canto xxvi, l. 55 and canto xxviii, l. 70.

[6] See *Maṇi.*, canto xxi, l. 48.

under the cool shade of the green *bōdi*[1] tree which had five lofty branches.

They then worshipped, and went round the highly shin- 15–25
ing *śilātala*,[2] jointly built by the Jaina householders for the benefit of the Cāraṇar[3] who would assemble, on festive days, such as the day of the first freshes (in the Kāvēri) and of the car-festival, under the entrancingly cool shade of the golden flowered *aśōka* tree, standing on a high platform where all the five termini sacred to the five great *yōgins* converged.[4] There gathered the men of penance who had abjured meat eating, and taken the vow of speaking the truth alone, and purified themselves of all sins, understanding the true path by restraining their senses.[5]

They then passed beyond the entrance-gate (of the 26–31
city), which looked like a long river with its source in a hill, and reached the outer wall which enclosed a lake and a grove (*ilavandikai*)[6] lined by beautiful trees thickly covered with several sorts of flowers, which were offered along with lovely Spring and the Hill-breeze as a tribute to the (Cōḻa) king by the bodiless God (Kāma).

Proceeding further still, they crossed the broad road ren- 32–45
dered cool by the low branches of trees on either side which led to a bathing place on the *Kāvēri*, and going westwards they penetrated to the distance of a *kādam* into the flowery grove on the northern bank of the river celebrated for its freshes, until they reached the residence of the saint Kavundi (*Kavundippaḻḻi*) which was a grove of

[1] *Mābōdi* is a tree with five branches. *Maṇi.*, canto xxx, l. 10. *Bōdimūlam* (*mahābōdi*) is the *aśvattha* tree under which Gautama Buddha saw the great light.

[2] It was made of *candrakānta* or moonstone.

[3] The Jaina Cāraṇar are under reference. They visited Puhār on certain festival days. The tree sacred to them was the *aśōka*.

[4] These *yōgis* are commonly known as Pañcaparamēṣṭins. They are Arhat, Siddha, Ācārya, Upāḍhyāya and Sādhu.

[5] The practice of the Sāvakas is referred to.

[6] *Ilavandikai* was the king's park in which was a lake. Cf *nirāḻimaṇḍapam* used nowadays in connexion with temple festivals. See canto xxv, l. 4, *infra;* also *Maṇi.*, canto iii, ll. 45-6.

flowering trees. There the slender-waisted (Kaṉṉaki) felt fatigued. Her feet were sore (with walking). Breathing hard, she of the fragrant tresses asked in a lisping voice, displaying her sharp-edged teeth, 'Which is the ancient city of Madura?' Kōvalaṉ smiled a smile of hidden grief and said, 'Girl of the fragrant five-plaited hair, it is over thirty leagues[1] from our extensive city. It is very near.' Then he visited with his sweet-voiced wife the venerable Kavundi who lived there,[2] and both prostrated themselves before her.

46–49 The saint looked at them and said 'You have attractive features, noble lineage and highly commendable conduct. You appear to be faultlessly observing *dharma* as laid down in the sacred Jaina scriptures.[3] Why is it that you have left your home and come so far in great distress?'

50–63 Kōvalaṉ replied: 'There is not much to say in reply to what you ask, O great saint! I am only eager to go to the ancient city of Madura to make a fortune.' The saint answered, 'If that is so, these tender feet (Kaṉṉaki's) cannot stand the sharp and rough gravel. This fair lady is not fit to go through the jungle. But who knows? Though the journey is not fit for you, you will not abandon it even if I ask you to do so.[4] Since I am very anxious to visit flawless Madura in the good Tamil country of the south, there to worship Aṟivaṉ by listening to the *dharma* preached by the sinless saints, who have, by their purity, got rid of all their *adharma,* I shall also go with you. Let us go!' Thereupon Kōvalaṉ worshipped the venerable Kavundi with lifted palms and replied 'O saint, if you

[1] The distance from Uṟaiyūr to Madura is 30 *kādams.* Feeling that Kaṉṉaki was already wearied, Kōvalaṉ did not tell her outright that it was 30 *kādams,* but said it was six times five leagues, so that she would not be alarmed at the long distance!

[2] This is referred to as a portion of the Śri-kōil where he lived with the revered Kavundi. It may be noted that the two forms Kāvundi and Kavundi occur in the text.

[3] Kavundi was a Jain and so she speaks with a partiality to the *dharma* of that religion.

[4] The implication here is, 'Who knows what Fate has in store for you?'

so favour us, I shall be relieved of my anxiety about this girl with shoulder-bangles.'

Kavundi continued : 64–75

'See, O Kōvalaṉ! There are various kinds of troubles to be met in our way (to Madura).[1] Listen : If we decide to go through shady places covered with cool flowers with this tender lady who cannot endure the scorching sun, we may, perchance, encounter the dire distress which comes to people who do not avoid the deep and deceitful pits caused by the men who dug out the edible *vaḻḻi* roots growing underground, and covered over with the faded flowers from the grove of *campaka* trees. If they cautiously avoid these fallen flowers and walk on, they will knock their heads against fully ripe jack-fruits. If then they go into the luxuriant gardens where the turmeric and ginger plants are grown, they will unwittingly tread upon the hard seeds of jack-fruits lying hidden.

'O loving husband of the lady with carp-like long eyes, 76–81
if we decide to go along the fields,[2] this damsel will be frightened by the otters, who drive away the quarrelling carps in ponds fragrant with flowers, and seize in their mouths the long-backed *vāḻai* fish when they are leaping across the tank where the *malangu* live.[3]

'Again, the honey-filled hives built (by bees) on sugar- 82–85
canes, will have been dismantled (by the wind) filling the drinking-water of the tank encircled by sugar-canes with honey[4] and bees. It is possible that our lady, in a fit of delusion will take the water in her joined palms and drink it (along with the bees) to quench her insufferable thirst.

'Again those who pluck out the weeds will have scat- 86–89
tered the water-lily on the ridges in which multi-tinted

[1] The forest-route is described as containing snares and pitfalls. The chief produce was jack-fruit; turmeric and ginger also grew there.

[2] The second route through the agricultural tracts is suggested. Here were cultivated fields interspersed by ponds.

[3] A fish whose head resembled that of a snake.

[4] The statement suggests that honey was food forbidden to Jains.

beetles[1] will be lying in a stupor after having drunk the honey of the flowers. As you walk along, your feet may unconsciously tread on them.

90–93 'If you decide to walk along the bunds of canals where waters splash you will tread upon multi-spotted crabs and snails, and cause unbearable pain to them.[2]

94–97 'There is no other route anywhere except through fields and groves. O friend with a tuft of curly hair! Know these signs and avoid such dangers as you go along in the company of this fair lady.'

98–101 Thus saying, the venerable Kavundi took up her sacred begging-bowl and her netted bag suspended from her shoulders.[3] Holding a peacock's feathers in her hand and praying that the *pañcamantra*[4] might be their guide on the way, Kavundi, unrivalled in the practice of virute, accompanied the other two in their journey.

102–11 Though Saturn gets angry,[5] though the (fiery) comet[6] is visible, though Venus of the bright rays travels towards the south (of the sky),[7] no harm is rendered to the Kāvēri which has its source in the wind-swept heights of the Coorg hills where, to the accompaniment of raging thunder, the seasonal clouds pregnant with rain pour down their blessings; the Kāvēri which dashes along with such diverse hill produce to meet the advancing tide of the wealth-bearing sea.[8] But finding her movement arrested by the barrier

[1] Here is the preaching of *ahımsā* or non-injury carried to its utmost limit.

[2] Further emphasis on observing the principle of *ahımsā*, the cardinal doctrine of the Jains, though it largely figures in the orthodox religion of the Hindus.

[3] The begging-bowl (*kaṭıṇai*), the uṛi, and peacocks' feathers are the outfit of the Jaina ascetic. See *Nālaḍiyār*, 'Ekai', l. 9; *Mani.*, canto vi, l. 93.

[4] The *pañcamantra*: a, si, ā, u, sā. The Jains style this *pañcanamaskāram*. These symbols represent Arhat, Siddha, Ācārya, Upādhyāya, and Sādhu, the first letters of the *Pañcaparamēṣṭins*. Its counterpart in orthodox religion is *pañcākṣara*, *namaśivāya*.

[5] Evidence of the author's knowledge of astronomical science. Saturn grows angry when he lodges himself in Ṛṣabha, Mīna, and Simha.

[6] The *Dhūmakētu* of Sanskrit literature.

[7] These signs are supposed to forebode evil by causing drought.

[8] Conch, coral, pearls, etc., are the products of the sea.

—the anicut with its doorway—she noisily leaps beyond it in the sportive mood natural to her first freshes. No sound other than this can be heard. We can hear there neither the sound of the bucket,[1] nor of the water-lift; neither the usually loud *pecottah*, nor the palm-leaf basket used in irrigation.

In the beautiful forest of lotuses appearing out of ponds 112–19
in regions surrounded by paddy-fields and sugar-cane could be heard, just as in a battle-field[2] where two monarchs fight, different kinds of sounds produced by the water-fowl,[3] the loud-voiced crane, the red-footed swan, the green-footed heron, wild fowl, the water crow (black heron), fishes, creeping insects, birds and big herons.

Wallowing in the mire, in regions left unploughed, 120–26
black buffaloes would come out with their unwashed hair and their red eyes, and rub their itching backs upon the straw granary when it gets loose and releases the grain stocked within amidst the sheaves of paddy whose rice-corn hangs down like fly whisks[4] made of the fur of the *kavari* yak. In those places brawny-armed labourers and cultivators would assemble making a motley of sound.

There was also the sound of (rural) songs[5] sung to (new) 127–31
tunes by low-caste women in their drunken moods[6] while they looked through their fish-like large eyes and uttered indecent words standing in playful postures and, threw mud upon each other, covering up their broad, bangled shoulders and breasts with mud, having removed the (faded) fragrant flowers from their hair and replaced them with paddy-shoots.

[1] It is interesting to see here the different methods of irrigating fields. Cf. *Kaut. Artha.*, Bk. II, chap. 'Sītādhyakṣa'. See also *Maduraikkāñji*, ll. 89-93. Most of these methods still survive in rural areas.

[2] The confused noise of the battle-field is compared to the different kinds of sounds made by a number of water-birds.

[3] Here is a categorical list of water-birds.

[4] Fly whisks were generally made of the fur of the yak.

[5] A description of typical rural life.

[6] Low-caste women were addicted to drinking. They decked themselves with paddy-shoots in their hair.

132–35 There was also the sound of the benedictory songs (*ērmangalam*) sung reverently by ploughmen[1] standing by their ploughshares and seeming to break open the ground which they decorated with garlands made of paddy-stalks, luxuriant *aṟugu*, and water-lilies.

136–39 There was also heard the *muhavai* song[2] sung (by the field-labourers) when they drove cattle over the reaped paddy sheaves to thresh the corn; and the cheering applause[3] of those who heard the round-shaped tabor smeared with mud played by proud minstrels who used to produce clear music by their *kiṇai*.[4]

140–41 Having heard these sounds in regular succession along the banks of the great rivers, the travellers grew glad in their hearts and did not feel the fatigue of the journey.

142–47 As they passed along, with success due to the prowess of the reigning Cōḻa who owned the chariot with the tiger-flag, they saw everywhere the sacrificial smoke, raised by Brahmans in the *agniśāla* of their tall houses[5] which closely resembled fog-covered hills, capable of impregnating even the rain-bearing clouds.[6]

148–55 Going further, they saw ancient and prosperous villages of cultivators,[7] the sons of Dame Kāvēri and her expansive waters, who were responsible for the support of the needy and their dependants, and for the victory of the

[1] This refers to the simplicity and sincerity of the ploughmen at their work and points to the dignity of field labour. They knew the advantages of deep ploughing.

[2] A kind of song sung by field-labourers on the threshing-floor of paddy fields. Cf. *Puṟam.*, st. 371.

[3] This is what is called *kaḷuvaḻivalttu*. According to the *Tolkāppiyam* it is *erkkalavaḻi* (the song of the plough) different from *pōrkkaḷavaḻi* (a war-song). Cf. *Puṟa.*, *Veṇbāmālai*, 'Vāhaippaḍalam', st. 32.

[4] One of the many rural amusements. They were minstrels who sang the praises of Veḷāḷas to the accompaniment of the *kiṇai* drum.

[5] A description of the Brahman residences.

[6] Conclusive proof of the fire rite being practised on an extensive scale by Brahmans in the early Christian era in the Tamil land. It implies the acceptance of the theory that sacrifices cause rain, which finds a parallel in the *Bhagavat Gītā* (ch. v), where it is said *'Yajñad bhavati Parjanyah'*.

[7] Different types of villages were encountered.

monarch.[1] They also saw rustic parts interspersed by villages where the rising fumes of the ovens, in which the sugar-cane[2] juice was being boiled, spread far and wide over heaps of stored corn which appeared like dark clouds resting on mountains. They did not travel more than one *kādam* each day.

After several days' journey, they reached Śrīrangam,[3] 156–64
where the river (the Kāvēri) was hidden by the city. Nearby was the habitation of the Dēvas—a spot filled with the fragrance of different independent flowers in the middle of groves of trees fenced by the bent bamboo. There appeared one Cāraṇa[4] who was well known for his great skill in expounding the rules of *dharma*, given to the world by the pre-eminent Perumakaṉ,[5] and who was returning from the glittering bright *silātala* of the *paṭṭiṉap-pākkam* of Puhār which had been jointly erected by the high-minded householders (*aiyar*)[6] and where he was in the habit of sitting.

Kavundi who had recognized the approach of this 165–69
Cāraṇa, fell prostrate with her companions at his feet saying: 'May all our past sins perish.' Though the Cāraṇa who had a knowledge of the past, present and future[7] knew the reason for their coming there, he did not feel afflicted being a hero who had completely put aside attachment and anger.

[1] The author realized that agriculture is the mainstay of the king and kingdom.

[2] The manufacture of sugar and jaggery from sugar-cane was a common industry in the rural parts of ancient Tamil India.

[3] Śrīrangam, now two miles from the town of Trichinopoly.

[4] In a note Dr Swaminatha Aiyar identifies these Cāraṇar with Samaṇa sages of whom there were eight classes. See *Cūḍāmaṇi*, p. 36.

[5] Perumakaṉ is an epithet for Arhat in the context. The threefold eminence is related to three *adiśayams* which are natural, *karmaic* and providential.

[6] The term *aiyar* used here is significant. It seems to be used in connexion with people who evoked regard from the masses. Undoubtedly it comes from the term *ārya*, which has in our opinion no ethnic connotation as scholars would make us believe.

[7] *Avatijñānam* according to Arumpadavuraiyāśiriyar.

170–75 He then spoke as follows: 'O Kavundi of great and abundant distinction! You know how inexorable are the laws of destiny.[1] They do not cease (from action) even if ordered to cease. Nor can its wholesome effect be wiped away. They are like the sprouts shooting forth from sown seeds. Like the lighted lamp that is extinguished in an open plain when the high winds blow, is life in a body.

176–91 'The All-Knowing, the incarnation of *dharma*, He who has transcended all limits of understanding, the great Friend, the great Victor (Jiṉēndra),[2] the Accomplisher,[3] the Great Person (Bhagavaṉ), the foundation of all *dharma*, the Lord, the All-Righteous, the Inner Essence (of the Āgama), the Pure, the Ancient-One, the All-Wise, the Vanquisher of Wrath, the Dēva, the Blissful Lord,[4] the Supreme Being, the Possessor of all virtues, the Light that illumines the world above, the great Truth, the All-Humble, the great Cāraṇa,[5] the Root Cause of all, the *yōgin,*[6] the great One, the great Illumination, the Dweller in everything,[7] the great Guru, the Embodiment of Nature, Our great God, the One of undiminishing fame, the great King of virtues,[8] the All-Prosperous,[9] the great God,[10] the Self-born,[11] the four-faced,[12] the Bestower of the *angas*,[13] the *Arhat*, the peace-bestowing Saint, the

[1] Cf. *Nālaḍiyār*—the whole of 'Paḻaviṉai', esp. st. 4.

[2] They are *jñāṉāvāraṇīyam*, *darišanāvāranīyam*, *vēdanīyam*, *mōhanīyam*, *āyūṣyam*, *nāmam*, *gōtram*, and *antarāyam*. See Aḍiyārkkunallār's gloss.

[3] Also *Kṛtakṛtya* (Sans.) The term in the text is *sidda*.

[4] The one who gives liberation to all. It should be noted that the term *mōkṣa* is given as *śivagati*, literally the attainment of the Śaiva world.

[5] He who could move about at his will.

[6] The master of the eight mystic powers.

[7] Cf. *Maṇi.*, canto v, l. 71.

[8] Also the possessor of all virtues.

[9] Śankara.

[10] Iśa.

[11] Svāyambhuva.

[12] Caturmukha.

[13] It may be the *anga* portion of the Vēdic texts. As applied to the Jains it is *anga-āgama.*

One God, the Possessor of eight qualities,[1] the indivisible old Substance, the Dweller in the Heaven, the foremost of the Vēdas,[2] and the shining Light that dispels ignorance. None can escape the prison[3] of this body unless he obtains the illumination of the revealed Vēda proclaimed by Him who has the various (above-mentioned) names.'

Hearing these truthful words of the Cāraṇa, Kavundi, 192–213
pre-eminent in penance, joined her hands on her head, and said: 'My ears will not open themselves to hear anything other than the words of wisdom revealed by Him who vanquished the Three (Desire, Anger and Delusion). My tongue will not say anything other than the 1008 names[4] of the victor of Kāma. My eyes will not see, though they seem to see, anything other than the pair of feet of Him who overcame the Five (senses).[5] My useless body will not touch the earth except before the holy body of Him[6] who has taken upon himself virtue out of His grace. My two hands will not join together to reverence any one other than the Knower who expounds *dharma* to *Arhats*. My crown will not suffer any flower to be placed on it except the flower-like feet of Him who walked upon flowers.[7] My mind will not permit me to learn by heart anything other than the sacred words uttered by the God of interminable bliss.'

Hearing with approval these words of praise from her, the Cāraṇa arose from the *śilāvaṭṭam* and rising to a

[1] These are *anantajñānam, anantadarśanam, anantavīryam, anantasukham, nirnāmam, nirgōtram, nirāyuṣyam* and *aliyāviyalpu.* See Arumpadavuraiyāśiriyar. For the term *eṇkuṇattāṉ,* see *Kuṟaḷ,* and commentary of Parimēlaḻagar.

[2] The three *āgamas*, Angāgama, Pūrvāgama, and Bahuśrutiāgama, are supposed to be the Vēdas of the Jains.

[3] The term used is *podiyaṟai,* literally the 'underground chamber with no opening'. In *Maṇi.*, cantos iii, l. 95; xxiii, l.60; iv, l. 105, it is named *puḻukkaṟai.*

[4] What is called the Sahasranāmas of the Lord. Cf. *Mani.*, canto v, ll. 77-9.

[5] A *Jitēndriya* according to the Sanskritists.

[6] The idea is that she will not prostrate herself before anybody except God.

[7] Cf. *Kuṟaḷ* where the expression *malarmiśai ēkiṉāṉ* occurs. We have not been able to trace any legend of the God walking on flowers.

height of two spans, blessed Kavundi saying, 'May thy birth-causing bondage cease!'[1] and as he went away along a path in the sky, they worshipped him saying, 'May our bondage cease.'

214–18 After having stepped into a boat at the landing-place of the great river Kāvēri where rain-bearing clouds rested on the flowery groves, the couple and the great saint crossed over to the peerless temples on the southern bank where they rested for a while in a flowery grove full of fallen flowers.

219–28 Just then a trifler passed by their side in that grove filled with fragrance, prating useless love-talk to a newly-found sweetheart.[2] Desiring to know who the couple (Kōvalaṉ and Kaṇṇaki) were, who looked like Kāma and Rati, they approached (Kavundi) and said: 'O Saint whose body has been famished by going without food on all fast days,[3] who are these people who have come with you?' Kavundi replied: 'They are my children. They are human beings.[4] Do not approach them.[5] They are tired on account of their journey.' The newcomers asked in return, 'O wise one, who has known all the *śāstras*, have you ever heard the children of the same parents becoming husband and wife?'

229–44 Kaṇṇaki closed her ears when she heard these sarcastic words and shuddered in the presence of her husband. Kavundi imprecated on them a curse of an extraordinary penance: 'Since these two seem to insult my dear one, fair as a flower garland, they shall become old jackals in the thorny forest.' Because this curse was uttered by one who had done penance, Kōvalaṉ and his wife of the fragrant tresses, soon heard the long howl of the jackals

[1] *Saṃsārapāśa-bandham.*

[2] Cf. *Kuṟaḷ*, 1311; *Maṇi.*, canto x, l. 22.

[3] See *Maṇi.*, canto xviii, l. 122; *Jīvakacintāmaṇi*, l. 1547.

[4] The statement implies that they were not Kāma and Rati as supposed by them.

[5] Implying 'go your own way'.

(into which the lovers had been transformed) and trembled. They said, 'Though those who deviate from the path of virtue speak unjust words, still should it not be attributed to their ignorance?[1] O Saint, please state when these men who have blundered in your presence will be released from this curse.' The saint replied: 'Those who have descended into a lower order of birth due to lack of knowledge will wander in trouble for twelve months in the forest-belt outside the Uṟaiyūr fortress-wall; they may afterwards regain their original forms.'

After their release from the curse had been pronounced, 245–49
Saint Kavundi, Kōvalaṉ and Kaṇṇaki went to the place *vāraṇam* (Uṟaiyūr) so-called because once in that place a fowl, having feathers on its body, had vanquished in war an elephant (*vāraṇa*) whose ears were as broad as a winnowing fan.[2]

[1] Cf. *Kuṟaḷ*, st. 127.
[2] Cf. *Kaḷittogai*, st. 42; *Maṇi.*, canto xxix, l. 121.

Katturai

Thus ends the Puhār section describing the descendence of the Cōḷa line which, among the three crowned kings,[1] shone with their strong arms glittering with bracelets. It speaks of the monarch's virtue, valour[2] and high deeds of renown;[3] of the fame of the ancient city of Puhār; of the greatness of festival;[4] of the visit of Dēvas;[5] of his subjects who were perpetually happy;[6] of the abundance of their food;[7] of the unparalleled glory of their faultless, divine Kāvēri,[8] of the unfailing first freshes due to seasonal rains; of their courts,[9] dances,[10] ballads and minstrelsies;[11] of their dramatic representations of *bārata-virutti*,[12] of erotic compositions relating to *aintiṇai*, and other analogous compositions;[13] of the tunes of their musical instruments (*yāḻ*) of the fourteen *śakōṭams*;[14] of the *iḍanilaippālai*;[15] of their songs the *tārattākkam*[16] and the four *pans;* of the noises of the city-chariot;[17] and of the lustrous *pāṇi*;[18] all these and many more redounding to the unique glory of the king.

VEṆBĀ

Like the sun that rises in the morning and the moon that appears in the evening, may far-famed Puhār which forms the garland of the sea-girt earth, live for ever.[19]

[1] The Cēra, the Cōḷa, and the Pāṇḍya, the principal kings of the Tamil land.

[2] v, ll 97-8.

[3] ibid. vi, l. 14.

[4] ibid. v.

[5] ibid.; also vi, ll. 72-73.

[6] x, ll. 149-50.

[7] ibid. ll. 123-4.

[8] ibid. ll. 102-109; vii, ll. 2-5; ll. 25-7.

[9] iii, ll. 99 and 106.

[10] iii, l. 16.

[11] viii, ll. 74-108.

[12] vi, ll. 39-63.

[13] vi, ll. 17-23.

[14] iii, l. 88.

[15] iii, l. 70.

[16] viii, ll. 35 and 44.

[17] v, ll. 38-40.

[18] iii, l. 135 and x, l. 131.

[19] The idea is 'let Puhār last as long as the sun and moon endure'.

BOOK II

MADURAIKKĀṆḌAM

Canto XI

KĀḌUKĀṆKĀDAI

OR

THE SIGHT OF THE FOREST

UNDERNEATH the thick shade of the *aśōka* tree with 1–8
its hanging flowers, the woman ascetic (Kavundi) worshipped the first God Aṟivaṉ,[1] more radiant than the rising sun, under three umbrellas arranged like three moons placed one above the other, and graciously spoke the good and wise words uttered by the Cāraṇar, to all the sages of the *kandaṉpaḷḷi*,[2] in the extensive grove adjoining Arangam.[3]

After spending that day at their residence and wishing 9–14
to go in a southerly direction, Kavundi, Kōvalaṉ and Kaṇṇaki left Vāraṇam (Uṟaiyūr) before day-break, and when the sun began to illumine the eastern sky, they reached a beautiful *maṇḍapam* situated in the midst of a grove of young trees in a fertile spot containing a tank.

There they met a venerable Brahmana who praised the 15–31
Pāṇḍyan of unblemished repute thus: 'May our great king live for ever, protecting this world from æon to æon! Long live the Teṉṉavaṉ, the ruler of the southern region, who added to it[4] the Ganges and the Himalayan regions in

[1] The Nāyaṉār enshrined in the temple at Uṟaiyūr. This was a Jain temple. The expression *ādiyiṟōṟṟam* may mean 'the god with no beginning or end' or 'a very ancient god'.

[2] This may refer to Uṟaiyūr *Kandaṉpaḷḷi*, the sacred hall of the Nirgranthas. Or it may refer to a shrine sacred to Kandaṉ or Subrahmaṇya.

[3] Śrīrangam was then known as Arangam and later as Tiruvarangam. It is situated two miles from Trichinopoly.

[4] This is a reference to the Pāṇḍyan invasion of North India, thus corroborating the tradition that the three prominent kings of the south went on a conquering mission as far as the Himalayas. In the south itself the Pāṇḍyan wrested Muttūrkkūṟṟam from the Cōḷa and Kuṇḍūrkkūṟṟam from the Cēra (see Aḍiyārkkunallār's commentary).

the north, who once showed his prowess to the other kings by standing on the shore of the sea and throwing his spear upon the fierce waters which, in a spirit of revenge, consumed the river Pahṟuḷi[1] and the Kumari with their adjoining groups of hills.

'Long live he who wore on his shining breast the bright garland of Indra, adding glory to the lunar race! Long live our king who, when thunder-clouds withheld abundant showers, smote the bracelet[2] set in the crown of Indra, and imprisoned the clouds, so that there might be great prosperity from an unfailing harvest of crops.'

32–34 Thereupon Kōvalaṉ asked, 'Where is your native home? What brings you here?'

The Brahmana of undiminishing distinction replied as follows:

35–56 'I am a native of Mānkāḍu[3] in the region of Kuḍamalai (the western hills). I came to satisfy my heart's desire, to see with my own eyes the glory of Viṣṇu, whom many worship with prayer as He reposes with Lakṣmī in His breast, on the couch of the thousand-hooded Serpent, in the temple in Turutti[4] jutting out on the widening waves of the Kāvēri, even as the blue clouds repose supine on the slopes of the lofty golden mountain (Mēru). (I also came to see) the beauty of the

[1] See *Puṟam.*, st. 9. A river Parali seems to exist even now (see *The Travancore State Manual*, Vol. I, p. 240 n.). Here is a legendary description of the sea eroding the land. Kumarikkōḍu may refer to the river or to the hills of Kumari. It is better to take it as a reference to the river, since a river of that name is mentioned in the *Brahmāṇḍa Purāṇa*.

This legend and the following are attributed to Ugra Pāṇḍyan, in the *Tiruviḷaiyāḍal Purāṇam*. The king is said to have stemmed the tide of the sea by throwing his spear on the rising waves. (See *Kadalśuvaṟa vēlerinda Tiruviḷaiyāḍal*, No. 21, pp. 80-1, 2nd ed., by Dr. Swaminatha Aiyar.)

[2] ibid., *Indiraṉ muḍimēl vaḷaieṟinda paṭalam*. The reference is to king Ugra Pāṇḍyan.

[3] Also known as Māngāl.

[4] The term *turutti* denotes an islet in general. To venture a conjecture the place under reference may be Srīrangam lying between the Kāvēri and the Coleroon.

red-eyed Lord, holding in His beautiful lotus-hands the discus which is death to His enemies, and also the milk-white conch; (to see Him) wearing a garland of tender flowers on His breast, and draped in golden flowers; and dwelling on the topmost crest of the tall and lofty hill named Vēnkaṭam,[1] with innumerable waterfalls, standing like a cloud in its natural hue, adorned with a rainbow and attired with lightning, in the midst of a place both sides of which are illumined by the spreading rays of the sun and the moon.

'Since I saw to the delight of my eyes, the glory and the greatness of the Pāṇḍyan kingdom,[2] I stayed here blessing the king. This is the reason of my coming here.'

Having heard this from the Brahmana who had 57-59
performed the Vēdic sacrifices, Kōvalaṉ said, 'O first among Brahmanas! Pray tell us the best route to Madura.'

The Brahmana replied: 'You have come with your 60-67
lady in the season when jungle and mountain tracts have given up their natural appearance and taken the form of a desert, losing their smooth surfaces, thus causing deep distress, since King Sun, along with his minister Spring, by reason of his fierce heat, has diminished his essential quality and lost his beneficence, like a great kingdom whose monarch has deviated from the path of right policy under the influence of an unrighteous councillor.[3]

[1] The modern Tirupati Hill. See canto vi, l. 30 above. It is still famous for the number of its waterfalls.

[2] It is worth noting that the poet stresses the glory of the Pāṇḍyan through the mouth of a Brahmana who does not belong to his kingdom. The greatness of the kingdom is to be contrasted with the injustice meted out to Kōvalaṉ later by the king, and the consequent bending of the rod of justice. It must be noted also that the age-long righteous sceptre only bent and did not break. For did not Kaṇṇaki herself claim to be the king's daughter and inform us of his innocence? (See 'Vāḻttukkādai', xxix, p. 577.)

[3] Here the author of the epic wants to convey to the reader, by comparison and contrast, the impressions of unrighteous rule and the consequent prevalence of anarchy in the land.

68–73 'If, in this long journey, you "swim" across rocks, hillocks (*porai*),[1] illusory places and the bunds of lakes full of water, and reach Koḍumbai[2] by the bund of a great lake, you will come to a spot which looks like the devouring trident[3] wielded by the God whose tuft is adorned with a crescent.

74–86 'If you decide to take the route lying to the right and pass by the *kadamba* tree with outspread branches, the dried *ōmai* tree, the *vāhai* with its cloven stem, the withered bamboo, the equally withered *maral* dark with fissures, jungles where thirsty deer roam about vainly in search of water, and the haunts of the Eiyṉar,[4] you will come across the celebrated Śiṟumalai[5] of the Pāṇḍyan covered on all sides with plants of wild rice, ripe sugar-cane, full-grown millets, *ragi* that grows on rich soil, garlic, saffron, beautiful *kavalai* creepers, plantains, arecas, coconuts growing in bunches, mangoes and jack tree. Keep that hill on your right and reach Madura.

87–103 'If you do not take that route, but choose the route to the left, you will hear winged beetles singing the tune of *śevvaḻi*,[6] in the low-lying fields, in glades with cool flowers, and in jungles, primarily desert regions. Passing these

[1] Also known as *pottaimalai*.

[2] Koḍumbāḷūr containing a tank Neḍunkuḷam. It was the capital from which the Vēḷir line of kings ruled. The present town Koḍumbāḷūr in Pudukkottai State contains a large number of inscriptions forming excellent historical material for reconstructing the history of the Vēḷir line. One of the inscriptions supplies the genealogy of this ruling family. Thus the Koḍumbai of the *Silappadikāram* played an important part in the early and medieval history of South India. According to the *Periyapurāṇam*, Iḍangaḻi Nāyaṉār, one of the sixty-three Saiva saints, had Koḍumbāḷūr for his capital. (See *Chronological List of Inscriptions of the Pudukkottai State*, 1929, Nos. 14, 33, 82, etc.; *An. Rep. Ep.*, 1907-8, paras. 87-9.)

[3] This indicates that from that spot branched off three routes as explained in the text below.

[4] See Dikshitar's article 'Eiyṉar' in *Sentamil*, Vol. XXXI, No. 1, for other details.

[5] Literally, the little hill. This hill exists today bearing the same name and is noted for its sweet plantains.

[6] *Sevvaḻi* is a primary melody-type of the Mullai region. Cf. *Puṟam.*, st. 144.

you reach Tirumālkuṉṟam,[1] that opens into a cave which removes all delusion, and leads to the miraculous three ponds, greatly praised by the gods, and called the sacred Śaravaṇam,[2] Bava-kāraṇi and Iṭṭaśiddi,[3] ever renowned. If you bathe in the sacred Śaravaṇam, you will gain knowledge of the book attributed to the king of the gods (*Aindra-Vyākaraṇam*);[4] if you bathe in the Bava-kāraṇi, you will learn the deeds of your past which led to your present birth; if, on the other hand, you bathe in the Iṭṭaśiddi pond, you will gain all that you wish for.

'If you choose to enter that cave, worship then the great Lord on that very lofty hill, meditating on His lotus-feet and going thrice round the hill; there, on the broad banks of the Śilambāṟu[5] cutting its way through the soil, will appear at the flower-strewn base of the blossoming *kōngu* tree, a nymph[6] fair as a golden creeper, as 104–111

[1] Tirumālkuṉram (literally, the hill sacred to Viṣṇu) is the name of a hill near Madura, known as Irumśōlai and Tiṟumālirumśōlai, sung of by most of the Āḻvārs. See also *Paripāḍal*, st. 15. According to this authority this place was noted for the worship of Vāsudēva and Balarāma. It is not clear when the cult of Balarāma became extinct here or in the Tamil land generally. Today this shrine is known as the Aḻagarmalai. It seems that Aḻagar may be a representation of the form of Balarāma, and not necessarily of Kṛṣṇa. Sundararājan is the Sanskrit rendering of the term Aḻagar.

[2] This and the two following are the names of tanks, what we now call *Puṣkaraṇi*, to bathe in which was supposed to purify. The Sanskrit *Purāṇas* are full of such lakes noted for their miraculous properties.

[3] Sanskrit Iṣṭasiddhi.

[4] A grammatical treatise by name *Viṇṇavarkōmāṉ Viḻunūl* attributed to Indra. The reference in the *Silappadikāram* is possibly to the *Aindra-Vyākaraṇam*, the oldest school of Sanskrit grammarians, known to and quoted by Pāṇini and others. It is mentioned in Buddhist Canonical works like the *Avadānaśataka* (C. Lassen, *I. A. K.*, Vol. II, 2nd ed., p. 477); cf. Tārānātha's *History of Indian Buddhism* (Schiefner's trans., p. 54). That this grammar was known to Tolkāppiyaṉār is evident from the preface to the *Tolkāppiyam*. On this subject there is an excellent monograph by A. C. Burnell entitled *On the School of Sanskrit Grammarians*, 1875.

[5] Also known as the Nūpura-Gaṅgā. We have, similarly, Ākāśa-Gaṅgā, Pātāla-Gaṅgā, etc.

[6] The reference is to a Yakṣiṇī. From the *Rāmāyaṇa* of Vālmīki we are led to infer that the Yakṣas were one of the South Indian tribes contemporaneous with the epoch of Rāvaṇa and Vāli. The Yakṣas were the ruling tribe in Ceylon in the fifth century B.C. when Vijaya landed there. But they had

striking as lightning with cloud-like locks of dark hair,
12–133 and wth serrated bracelets on her shoulders, saying: "Tell me what constitutes the happiness of this birth,[1] the happiness of the next[2] and also eternal happiness[3] which results neither in birth nor rebirth. I live on this mountain and my name is Varōttamā. To them who answer these questions I am bound in service. So, good people, if you give the right answer, I shall open the door (leading to this cave). On opening the door several passages with entrances will be revealed, and beyond them a gateway with double doors. Beyond that, a creeper-like lady resembling a picture[4] will again appear before you asking, 'What is eternal bliss?'[5] If you reply, you will obtain one of three desired things.[6] But if you are not able to answer, I shall not harm you. You can go on your long journey; I shall help you."

'If people answer her questions she will show them the three ponds mentioned above, and retire. If you bathe therein, desirous and uttering any one of these things, meditating upon and uttering with equal reverence the two great Vēdic mantras of five letters[7] and eight

practically become extinct by the commencement of the Christian era though a few lingered here and there in forest regions. See Dikshitar's paper 'South India in the Rāmāyaṇa' in the *Proceedings of the Seventh Oriental Conference*, 1933, p. 243 ff.

[1] *Poruḷ* (Sans., *artha*) or wealth is said to constitute one's happiness in this birth. The idea is that a man of no wealth will always feel miserable. See the *Mānavadharmaśāstra*, ch. 2, st. 224: Cāṇakya *Rāja Nīti Sāstra*, canto iv, st. 21: also, *Tirukkōvai*, st. 332.

[2] Good and righteous deeds on earth contribute to happiness after death. The fruits of actions in this birth are judged and rewarded only in the next birth. This is, in other words, the theory of pre-ordained fate.

[3] Salvation or freedom from the bondage of samsāra or worldly life is said to be the highest of the Puruṣārthas. Cf. *Kuraḷveṇbā*, 233; *Puṟam.*, st. 50. See also Dikshitar, *Hindu Administrative Institutions*, p. 37.

[4] The word *vaṭṭikai* in the text means a picture or portrait.

[5] *Mōkṣa* is the term for this in Sanskrit literature.

[6] The reference is to *muppāl* or *trivarga* of Sanskrit literature.

[7] The significance of the *Pañcākṣara* mantra *Namaśivāya* is brought out here. Constant meditation on it is said to rid one of all ills. Even today many orthodox Hindus are initiated by their *gurus* and continue meditating on this great mantra sacred to Śiva.

letters[1] you will achieve results which cannot be realized even by the hardest of penances.

'If you do not desire these benefits, meditate on the 134–140
lotus-feet of the Lord standing on that hill. If you so meditate, there will appear His lofty Eagle standard. By its mere sight and by meditation on His lotus-feet there will be no more rebirth. Rejoicing in that thought go to Madura of traditional glory. Such is the sight worth seeing in that cave.

'If you reject these routes, there is the straight path 141–149
that lies midway between them with pleasant villages and groves and several jungles therein. Beyond these dwells a terrific deity who appears to travellers, not causing fear but treating them with civility and causing no harm. If you escape this, the path to Madura will of itself be known to you. So depart and I shall go (to sacred places) to worship the feet of the Lord who measured the whole universe.'[2]

After listening to the Brahmana's account of the routes, 150–164
the saint Kavundi made a categorical reply: 'O Brahmana versed in the four Vēdas and engaged in doing good! We have no wish to go to the cave. The literature given by Indra, who lives longer than the Dēvas, can be found in our holy scriptures.[3] If you wish to know of deeds done in the past, do you not look for them in the present birth? Is there anything that cannot be gained by those who lead a life of truthfulness and non-injury?[4] Go your way seeking the feet of the God sacred to you. We go

[1] This is the *Aṣṭākṣara* '*Ōm namōnārāyaṇāya*'. This statement is significant in as much as it proves that the spirit of sectarianism was still non-existent. For, while the *Pañcākṣara* is sacred to Siva, the *Aṣṭākṣara* is sacred to Nārāyaṇa or Viṣṇu. It is said that the two mantras must be uttered with equal reverence. Belief in the efficacy of such mantras is still current.

[2] The reference is to the Trivikrama Avatār of Viṣṇu.

[3] The *Aindra-Vyākaraṇam*, according to tradition, belongs to the *Paramāgamas* of the Jains.

[4] The chief Jaina doctrines. Here we may note Kavundi's reply to the Brahmana who quoted his scriptures. In meeting all his three points she seems to imply that the Jaina scriptures contain these and more.

the way suited to us.' After speaking words befitting the occasion to that Brahmana, she spent that day in a resting-place along with Kōvalaṉ who never swerved from his principles.

165–191 Then they resumed their journey. One day, the sage Kavundi and the lady of the long dark eyes rested themselves on the way owing to fatigue. From that place frequented (by people), an adjoining pathway branched off, which Kōvalaṉ took and reached a lake and stood on its great bank to slake his thirst. Then the forest-deity[1] passion-lorn and hoping that he might fall in love with her, appeared before him in the form of Vasantamālā. Like a trembling creeper she fell at his feet and shed false tears saying, 'Mādavi told me, "I am not guilty of what I wrote on the fragrant garland. You must have told Kōvalaṉ some falsehood, which made him harsh towards me." Saying this, she fell in a faint overcome by grief, but (recovering) said, "The worst of all careers is that of a courtesan, shunned like a disease by pious and learned men who avert their faces, and by people who can distinguish right from wrong."[2] In this way she burst into tears which dropped like pearls from her cool eyes, and with her hands she wrenched her string of lustrous white pearls and scattered them. Forsaken by her, and hearing the news from travellers on their way from the ancient city of Madura, I have come in great distress along with a caravan.[3] Generous man, what relief can you give me?'

192–200 Having been apprised by the distinguished Brahmana that in that dreadful forest there was a luring deity,

[1] Belief in forest-deities was very usual. They were supposed to assume any form. For instance, the deity that appeared before Kōvalaṉ assumed the guise of Vasantamālā, the maid in attendance on the courtesan Mādavi.

[2] See *Maṇi.*, canto xxiv, l. 79. The author ridicules the life of the courtesan by making Mādavi herself condemn it. According to him any decent and self-respecting man looks upon a prostitute as the embodiment of disease.

[3] The word *śātta* (Sans, *sārtha*) is a reference to the caravan trade carried on in those days between one part of the country and the other by groups of merchants.

Kōvalaṉ decided to employ the mantra to disillusion himself about the identity of that lady. The mantra he uttered was the mantra[1] sacred to the goddess riding on the deer,[2] so that the deity went away confessing,[3] 'I that deluded you am a spirit of the forest. Pray do not tell of this misdeed of mine to your wife, lovely as a peacock, or to the holy sage, but go your way.'

Carrying water in a lotus-leaf[4] to the weary women 201–216
he relieved them of their distressing thirst. Finding that it was not possible to proceed farther in that desert-region as the rays of the sun ascending the heavens increased in heat, Kōvalaṉ, Kaṇṇaki of the curved ear-rings, and the saint, came upon a flowery grove of the *kurava*, *kadamba*, *kōngu* and *vēngai*, closely intertwined with one another. There they entered the shrine of Aiyai-kumari[5] who dwells in heaven, whose eye was in Her forehead and who was worshipped by the gods. From those hardy bowmen whose lands were unvisited by rains, and whose bows were therefore their ploughs, and who deprived passers-by of their belongings, she expected sacrificial offerings in return for Her blessing them with victory when, as if guided by Yama, they invaded the neighbouring territory with their cruel bows.

[1] Another instance of faith and belief in the efficacy of mantras.

[2] This goddess is known by other names such as Antari, Śakti, or Aiykalaippāvai. Kōvalaṉ shows here that he was a Śakti-upāsaka, or a devout worshipper of the goddess as Śakti. For a history of the cult see R. G. Bhandarkar, op. cit., pp. 142-6.

[3] Here is the deity's confession of guilt. She could not withstand the efficacy of a Vēdic mantra.

[4] This shows that Kōvalaṉ and Kaṇṇaki did not even take a drinking vessel with them.

[5] The deity worshipped by the Vaḍuvar or the Maṟavar. She is known by different names. Cf. *Matsya Purāṇa*, chap. 154, st. 73-83, where the Creator addresses Vibhāvarī the night-deity. In the *Harivaṁśa* there is a hymn to Āpya (Durgā) in which she is represented as the goddess of Śabaras, Pulindas, Barbaras, and other wild tribes, and as fond of wine and flesh. See R. G. Bhandarkar, op cit., p. 143. Aiyaikōṭṭam was the name of the temple where Koṟṟavai or the Goddess of Victory was enshrined. She is known as Kāḷi or Mahākāḷi in Sanskrit literature, and we thus see a marvellous blending of two ancient cultures, evolving what is known as the Śakti cult.

Canto XII

VEṬṬUVAVARI

OR

THE HUNTERS' SONG

1–5 The sun continued to spread his cruel, fierce rays and made it impossible (for the travellers) to go on their journey. She of the fragrant locks of hair (Kaṇṇaki) breathed hard, and her tender feet were red with blisters: so they rested in an unfrequented place in the temple of Aiyai.[1]

6–11 Later, Śāliṉi,[2] born in the family of the Maṟavar who ever had bows in their hands, began her dance with appropriate gestures and became possessed with divinity, her hair standing on end, and her hands raised aloft; she continued to dance moving from one place to another to the wonderment of the foresters, in the *maṉṟam*, the common eating-place[3] of the Eiyṉar[4] situated in the midst of the village, encircled by a thorny fence. She then proclaimed aloud their unfulfilled vows thus:

12–19 'The cattle-herds of the towns of your enemies are flourishing: the common places (*maṉṟam*) of the strong-bowed Eiyṉar are lying empty: the Eiyṉar of the Maṟavar tribe have become meek like persons observing *dharma*,

[1] From the earliest times Aiyai or Koṟṟavai has been the favourite deity of hunters in South India. The goddess was worshipped as the Goddess of Victory. Her temple was located in a *maṉṟam* in the middle of the village. A *maṉṟam* was a common meeting-place for village folk, answering to the public hall of a town today.

[2] A woman possessed with divinity. Generally, an old lady of the family of hunters who considered herself inspired and spoke out as if she were herself a goddess.

[3] This points to the custom among the Maṟavar of eating from a common table.

[4] The expression in the text for this is *ūr-naḍu-maṉṟam*. This implies that there were other *maṉṟams* also.

and no more rob the wealth of passers-by. Unless you render[1] what is due to the goddess riding on the stag,[2] She will not send victory to attend your bows, O ye that live by robbery![3] If you desire to live merrily drinking toddy, render your dues.'

From among the ancient family of the Eiyṉar, who 20–50
preferred offering their own heads in sacrifice to cremation[4] (after dying a natural death), a virgin[5] was chosen to represent the goddess. Her short hair was dressed in the form of a *jaṭa* (the coiffure of Śiva), and ornamented with a small silver snake and a crescent-like semicircular tooth from wild hog which had destroyed tender plants in well-guarded fields. Her *tāli* was a necklace made of white teeth plucked from a strong-limbed tiger,[6] and her girdle was a cleaned tiger-skin with mingled spots

[1] The Maṟavar generally made a vow to their goddess just before an expedition to celebrate their hoped-for victory by a sacrificial offering.

[2] *Kalittogai*, st. 39, ll. 12-14.

[3] The Maravar were addicted to drinking toddy, and their only occupation was highway robbery.

[4] It is remarkable to note that the method of disposal of the dead among this primitive tribe was cremation and not burial. It has been assumed by certain scholars that burial was a custom of the pre-Aryan tribes, and cremation was a later introduction. This statement of Iḷangō-Aḍigaḷ, who lived nearly one thousand eight hundred years before our time, is entitled to respect, and judged by this, it seems that both cremation and burial were as much the institutions of the Aryans as of the pre-Aryans. Both have been prevalent from prehistoric times, and it is impossible to decide which institution is the older.

[5] Here we are introduced to the actual method of worship in vogue among these primitive tribes. It was usual to select a virgin from among their community and make her appear like the goddess installed in the shrine. This virgin was taken in procession to the temple of their guardian-deity and worshipped in front of the shrine, where the goddess was said to appear and approve what the damsel spoke. The commentator Aḍiyārkkunallār is not clear here. He seems to take the virgin to be the idol enshrined in the temple itself. This cannot be accepted in the light of ll. 72-3 where it is expressly stated that the Kumari in the shrine blessed the Kumari of the Eiyṉar.

[6] The Eiyṉar decked their goddess with ornaments and clothes peculiar to their *mores*. For instance, a tiger-skin and an elephant-skin formed the clothing of their goddess. Similarly the teeth of the tiger formed her garland. From the description given it is to be understood that their virgin goddess becomes later on the consort of the God Siva and assumes all His paraphernalia.

and stripes on its outer surface. The bow in her hand was of heart-wood. She was mounted upon a stag with twisted horns. The Eiyṉar ladies, who feted her with offerings of dolls, parrots, wild fowls of soft feathers, blue peacocks, balls (*pandu*) and *kaḻanku*, followed her carrying paints, powders, cool and fragrant pastes, boiled grains, sweets of gingili seeds, rice with meat, flowers, frankincense, and fragrant scents, when she was taken before the shrine of Aṇangu who accepts sacrificial offerings in return for victory. This was accompanied by the beating of the drum used during highway robbery, and the blowing of the trumpet, generally heard when looting, the horn and the pipe, and the ringing of the loud bell, simultaneously. There she worshipped Her with the stag for Her mount, and became inspired. Pointing to Kaṇṇaki, of the fragrant locks of hair, standing with weary little feet by the side of her husband, she spake as follows :[1] 'This is the lady of the Kongunāḍu, the mistress of the Kuḍamalai (the western hills), the queen of the south Tamil country, and the sprout of her (Kaṇṇaki's) prior penance; she is *tirumāmaṇi* (literally, the bright jewel) far-famed as the peerless gem of the world.'[2]

51–53 At this Kaṇṇaki smiled a derisive smile and stood modestly behind the broad back of her dear husband thinking that this soothsayer spoke in ignorance.

54–64 Just then, She who wore the moon in Her coiffure, who had an unwinking eye in Her forehead, coral lips,

[1] The inspired Sāliṉi could read the future and therefore foretold what Kaṇṇaki was to become. Neither Kaṇṇaki nor her party realized the inmplications of these statements and Kaṇṇaki showed that she had no faith in such reports.

[2] A note may be made of the significant terms *orumāmaṇi*, and *tirumāmaṇi* attributed to Kaṇṇaki by the inspired Sāliṉi. It is not possible to get at the implications of these terms, but it is a remarkable coincidence that the *Naṟṟiṇai*, another Sangam classic, refers to the incident of Kaṇṇaki's casting off one of her breasts and uses the expression *tirumāmaṇi*. Perhaps it was the title given to Kaṇṇaki after she was installed as the Goddess of Chastity. This reference is enough to show that the *Naṟṟiṇai* belongs to the post-*Silappadikāram* epoch.

white teeth, a throat darkened by poison,[1] who had the serpent Vāsuki of unquenchable ire for Her girdle, and mount Mēru for Her shoulder-bangles, whose breasts were enclosed within a bodice resembling a serpent's venomous teeth, and who wore elephant hide for Her upper garment and a lion's (tiger's?) skin for Her petticoat, (appeared), with a trident in Her bangled hands. Her left foot was adorned with *śilambu* and the right with a victorious anklet. Skilled in sword-fighting, the Lady who stood on the head of the double-bodied broad-shouldered Asura,[2] the goddess worshipped by many, Kumari, Kavuri (Sans., Gaurī),[3] Śamari (Sans., Samhārī or the slayer), the holder of the trident, She whose hue is blue, the younger sister of Viṣṇu[4] the giver of victory, the holder of the cruel axe, Durgā,[5] Lakṣmī, Sarasvatī,[6] the image adorned with rare gems, the ever-youthful Kumari whom Viṣṇu and Brahmā came to worship, declared the form and attire of the divinity-possessed Kumari quite god-like.

URAIPPĀṬṬUMAṬAI

(The glory of the courtyard)

In front of the sacrificial altar of the Goddess who sits by the side of the three-eyed God, the *nāgam* and the

[1] Sans., *Nīlakaṇṭhī.*

[2] The deity is named Mahiṣāsuramardanī. The Story of the Dēvī who destroyed the demon in the shape of a buffalo is found in almost all the *Purāṇas*.

[3] For an interpretation of the term Gauri, see Dikshitar's article 'Umāgauri' in the *Kalaimagal*, Vol. III, p. 227 ff.

[4] According to literary tradition, as embodied in legends, Durgā is the sister of Viṣṇu. According to the *Harivamśa* the Dēvī was born to Yaśodā, and when she was dashed against a stone, she attained heaven. Hence she is said to be a sister of Vāsudēva—Kṛṣṇa.

[5] Durgā described as Siva-Sakti.

[6] It is remarkable to find a total absence of sectarianism in the *Silappadikāram*. Kumari is addressed as Durgā who rode a stag, as Lakṣmī (Paimdoṭippāvai) and as Sarasvatī (the deity sacred to learning), the respective consorts of the Hindu triad, Siva, Viṣṇu and Brahmā.

[7] These three stanzas are addressed to the glory of the courtyard of the shrine dedicated to Aiyai. It was adorned by a grove of trees bearing flowers of different hues and fragrance.

sweet *narandai* flowered luxuriantly; everywhere the *āccā* tree and the sandal rose high: also the *śe* tree and the mango were thick with foliage.

In front of the shrine of Her who wears the crescent in Her coiffure, the *vēngai* tree shed its golden flowers: numerous were the branches of the excellent *ilava* (cotton) tree. The *punga* let fall its white petals.

In front of the shrine of the younger sister of Viṣṇu, blossomed the *kadamba* tree, the *pādiri*, *puṉṉai*, odorous *kuravu*, and *kōngu*; and on their branches swarms of bees hummed as if playing upon the *yāḻ*.

Again,[1]

(The Kuṟava girl said) 'O, how wonderful is the penance of this damsel of golden ornaments who stands here assuming the form and adornment of the Goddess of Victory! The only family worthy of mention is that of the hunter-archers,[2] in which this damsel of golden bangles was born.

'O, how wonderful is the penance of this damsel with a waist like the hood of a cobra,[3] who now stands adorned with the decoration of Aiyai! The only family worthy of mention is that family of the Eiyṉar who used to shoot their arrows, in which she was born.

'O, how wonderful is the penance of this damsel of lovely bangles who stands with the trappings of Her who rides fast upon the stag! The only family worthy of

[1] The editor of the text informs us that, according to some manuscripts, this and the following two stanzas are in the praise of Sāliṉi engaged in dancing.

[2] We get further light on the customs and manners of the Maṟavar. They were great hunters and archers. If we compare their mode of living with the elaborate and luxurious life said to have been led both by town folk and village folk in other parts of the book, we have only to infer that persistence is writ large in the cultural development of the ancient Tamils. Their primitive occupations have been continued down to historical times.

[3] The word *algul* which occurs frequently in Tamil classics is very difficult to translate. It seems to stand for that part of the abdomen below the navel.

mention is that family of the Eiyṉar with bamboo bows, in which this damsel of lovely bangles was born.'

Again,

'How is it that you, who receive the worship of all gods and stand undaunted as the sprouting wisdom in the Vēda of all Vēdas, once stood upon the dark head of the wild buffalo, clad in a tiger's skin and covering yourself with an elephant's skin?

'How is it that you who stand as the shining light spreading its rays over the lotus-heart of Hari, Hara and Brahmā, also stood upon the stag with the dark-twisted horns, after slaying Mahiṣāsura, holding your sword in your bangled hands?

'How is it that you who stand praised by the Vēdas as the consort of Him who has an eye in His forehead and the Ganges in His coiffure, stood upon a fierce red-eyed lion,[1] holding a conch and discus in your lotus-hands?'

There,[2]

With a garland made of the *koṉṟai* flower and with a shoulder-garment of basil leaves, this damsel in the form of Kumari, began dancing to the delight of the Dēvas, and to the distress of the Asuras.

Again,

Sword in hand, and to the repeated tinkling of her metal-filled anklet, her bracelet, and her waist-band all of

[1] The lion is the steed of Durgā. Legend has it that Vibhāvarī, the Goddess of Night, entered into Umā's body at the order of the Creator. After Umā's marriage with Siva, Vibhāvarī was ordered to leave Umā's body and reside in the Vindhya hills. Here the Dēvī was given a lion to ride. See *Matsya Purāṇa*, ch. 157. Treatises on architecture in Sanskrit and the evidence of sculpture testify that the lion was invariably the steed of this goddess as was the stag also. It is but natural that a daughter of the Great Mountain thick with forests, should have the stag or the lion as her favourite animal.

[2] What follows is the dance of victory by Durgā.

gold, our Goddess danced the *marakkāl*[1] to vanquish the deceitful Asuras who also bore swords. If She, sword in hand, could perform that dance on the *marakkāl* to vanquish the deceitful Asuras, who also bore swords, the gods would praise Her of the hue of *kāya*, and shower flowers on Her with their hands.

At the time when an unrivalled and fierce warrior of a small village sets out to seize the enemy's cattle,[2] and is desirous of wearing the *veṭci* garland,[3] he invokes the aid of the Goddess who slays with Her shining sword. O if he should desire to wear the *veṭci* garland and invoke the aid of Her who slays with the bright sword, the king-crow[4] of the forest will send forth its ominous note in the enemy's village.

When the female vendor of toddy[5] refuses to serve the angry Maṟavaṉ he will draw his bow, and observing the good omen of birds, start out in search of the enemy's cattle. And at the time when he goes out in search of the enemy's cattle, observing the omen of birds, the Goddess of Victory will raise Her lion-standard and march in front of his bow.[6]

[1] Arumpadavuraiyāśiriyar explains thus: 'When the Asuras sent illusory reptiles and scorpions over Her, Durgā with wooden legs danced with a spear in Her hand.' This is called the *marakkāl* dance of Durgā.

[2] *Karandai* is a theme for recovering a herd of cattle captured by the enemy and is regarded as a declaration of war. *Karandaiyar* are those warriors who rescue the cattle seized by the enemy. See *Tamil Lexicon*, p. 743. Here we have to note that cattle-lifting was one of the causes of ancient Tamil warfare.

[3] Cf. *Pura. veṇbāmālai*, 'Veṭci', st. 3, where cattle-lifting is under reference. The *veṭci* garland was a symbolical representation of success over an enemy.

[4] The crying of the king-crow is a bad omen. This points to the custom of foretelling future events from the actions of birds. It may be remembered that in ancient Rome there was an augur—a religious official who foretold future events by omens taken from the actions of birds. Such superstitious beliefs were common in the ancient world.

[5] The implication is that the Eiyṉar has failed to pay his old dues owing to poverty, because of slackness in his profession which consisted of looting his neighbours' cattle.

[6] The flag of *aḷi* is appropriate to the goddess whose steed was a lion.

Again,

'O young maid with lovely teeth, behold! The great herds of cattle, which your elders brought by capture in former times, have filled the courtyards of the blacksmiths,[1] drummers, and celebrated bards who play on the *yāḻ*.

'O girl with white teeth, behold! The herds of cattle, captured by your elders to the distress of their defenders, have filled the courtyards of the women who sell toddy, of the expert forest spy, and of the soothsayers who interpret bird omens.

'O girl with eyes smeared with collyrium and like *kāya* flowers, behold! The big herds of cattle. seized by your elders causing distress to the enemy's villages, have filled the courtyards of the grey-moustached Eiyṉar of unsympathetic speech, and of their old women.'

TURAIPPĀṬṬUMAḌAI[2]

Again,[3]

'We have worshipped your two feet that graciously relieve the suffering of the Dēvas and the Muṉis who roam in company of the sun. Now accept this blood,[4] by cutting our necks, as the price of the victory you confer upon the brave and strong Eiyṉar.

[1] See *Puṟam.*, st. 312. Distribution of the captured property was made among blacksmiths, spies, soothsayers, toddy-sellers, bards and drummers. Special mention may be made of the use of spies by the Eiynar

Turaippāṭṭu is a verse which illustrates minor themes in *Aham.* and *Puṟam.*

[3] This and the following two stanzas are styled *avippali* by the commentator. Here is an allusion to the tradition that sages like the Vālakhilyas go with the sun as he moves. See *Puṟam.*, st. 43, and *Tirumurugā.*, l. 107 and the commentary thereon. See *Matsya Purāṇa*, ch. 126, st. 28-45; *Brahmāṇḍa Purāṇa*, ch. 23. It is said that as many as seven *gaṇas* including gods and sages followed the sun in his course. The other five are the Nāgas, Yakṣas, Gandharvas, Apsaras, and Rākṣasas.

[4] Also *Kurutippali*: see Aḍiyārkkunallār's gloss.

The idea of a human sacrifice belongs to the primitive neolithic peoples, and it would not be far from the truth to consider these hunters to be the descendants of early neolithic inhabitants of South India. See also F. J. Richards's article 'Sidelights on the Dravidian Problem' in the *Q.J.M.S.*, Vol. VI, pp. 156-201.

'We have worshipped the lotus-feet of you who are like a blue gem, and who are worshipped by the gods along with their crowned king. Accept the flesh and blood offered to you as the price of the great victory you confer upon the Eiyṉar, in their seizure of herds of cattle.

'O Kumari! Accept the blood of sacrifice[1] at your altar in fulfilment of the oath made, touching your feet, by the tiger-like Eiyṉar, who sally forth in the dead of night, with *tuḍi*, the small *paṟai*, and the pipe, sounding as if to pierce the sky.'

THE OFFERING OF SACRIFICE[2]

'O Śankari, Antari, Nīli, who wear in your coiffures the red-eyed serpent along with the crescent! Accept this sacrifice from the Eiyṉar with strong bows and arrows, and in answer to our prayer grant that travellers[3] may come oftener that (by robbing them) we may increase our riches.

'O you, who blessed the Dēvas, who had to face death in spite of having drunk nectar! O you, who are immortal even though you drank the poison which can be drunk by no one, eat this offering made by us, the heartless Eiyṉar, who enter neighbouring villages when all are sleeping, and sound our *tuḍis* before we plunder them.

'O you, who blessed all by kicking the rolling wheel sent in disguise by your uncle (Kamsā)[4] and walked through the *maruda* tree,[5] accept this offering given as

[1] It is evident that the time of sacrifice and worship by these hunters was the dead of night, when the whole world was sleeping.

[2] The following three stanzas describe the actual offering of sacrifice.

[3] These hunters pray for the prosperity of travellers because they are one source of their livelihood.

[4] For a version of this legend see the *Bhāgavata Purāṇa*, Bk. X, ch. 7, st. 6-7. Kamsā sent an Asura in the form of a rolling wheel which the baby Kṛṣṇa kicked, and broke to pieces.

[5] ibid, ch. 10, st. 23 ff. The reference is to two Gandharvas who became two *arjuna* trees by the curse of Nārada. Kṛṣṇa, being a mischievous baby, was one day tied to a mortar by his mother. With that he ran between the two trees, making them prostrate on the earth. This relieved both the

your due, by us the ungrateful Eiyṉar, who know nothing but how to rob people of their wealth and cause[1] unhappiness.'

Again,

May the Pāṇḍyan greedy for victory, and the Lord of the lofty, fertile Podiyil hill where dwells the sage next in rank to Brahmā[2] who gave us the Vēdas, wear the *veṭci* flower in his crown leading to the ruin of his enemy's camp and of the defence of their cattle.

Gandharvas from the curse of the sage. The *Viṣṇu Purāṇa,* Bk. V, ch. 6, st. 12-17, gives a slightly different version of this incident as also of the breaking of the wheel by Kṛṣṇa.

[1] Cf. *Kalittogai,* st. 15, where this very line occurs as if one is a copy of the other.

[2] Agastya was born after Brahmā according to Aḍiyārkkunallār. But the *Arumpadavurai* says that he was born after Mahēśvara. Nacciṉārkkiṉiyar is unable to accept this view. See *Maduraikkāñji,* ll. 40-2, commentary. See also *Matsya Purāṇa,* (ch. 61, st. 17 f.), where he is said to have been born from a pitcher and as a brother of Vasiṣṭha.

Canto XIII

PUṞAÑCĒRIIṞUTTAKĀDAI

OR

THE SUBURBS OF MADURA

1–14 After the departure of Śālini, the female religious dancer, Kōvalan paid his respects to the feet of the first among saints (Kavundi) and said:

'This girl cannot stand the scorching rays of the sun: and her tender feet can no more endure the gravel of this barren region. As this is the kingdom of the Pāṇḍyan of the righteous sceptre,[1] whose fame has spread far in all directions, the fierce bear will not hunt the terrible ant-hill,[2] the striped tiger will not be at enmity with the deer; the reptile, the malignant spirit, the crocodile in search of its prey, and thunder will cause no distress to friends. Instead of travelling by daylight, we can cross this forest by night in the light of the moon who protects many living beings.[3] We will suffer no harm.'

The saint accepted the sugggestion with approval.

15–29 Before these travellers, who awaited the departure of the cruel sun like the subjects of a tyrannical king,[4] appeared the ancestor of the Pāṇḍyas,[5] the moon, with

[1] The poet ironically makes Kōvalan refer to the righteous sceptre of the Pāṇḍyan when he first enters the city of Madura where, later, injustice is done to him.

[2] Notice the author's correct knowledge of the habits of animals. It is said that the bear eats from the *puttu*. The implication here is that even wild animals behaved righteously in the Pāṇḍyan kingdom.

[3] The days were so hot that night travelling was preferred.

[4] Cf. *Perumkadai*, Bk. LII, canto i, l. 81; also *Perumpāṇārṟuppaḍai*, ll. 42-3. The subjects of a cruel king look forward anxiously to the departure of their monarch.

[5] Tradition attributes the Pāṇḍyan dynasty to a branch of the lunar race. See *Sila.*, canto iv, l. 22. Recent investigations have not thrown much light on the origin of this ancient dynasty, which is certainly more ancient than the visit of Megasthenes to India. Ktesias refers to a people called Pandore

his retinue of stars, spreading his milk-white rays, when Mother Earth heaved a deep sigh and fell asleep after expressing pity (on Kaṇṇaki) in the words :

'Dear girl, up to this time thou hast not suffered either the starlike necklace or the sandal-paste to adorn thy young breasts ; thou hast not permitted thy locks of hair to be dressed with the flower-dust-laden lily linked up in a chain with other flowers ; thou hast not allowed thy body, soft as a tender shoot, to be decorated with garlands, made from the fresh petals of many a flower. Art thou now attracted by the south wind, born in the Malaya hills, nourished in Madura and ever on the tongues of poets, blowing over thee, and by the spring moon shedding his milk-white rays copiously upon thee?'

Kōvalaṉ said to his wife, fatigued by the journey : 30–33
'This night,'[1] the tiger will cross our path, the owl will screech, the bear will make a thundering sound ; but walk fearlessly on.' He placed her fair arms shining with bangles to rest upon his shoulders.

Then they passed through the forest listening to the 34–37
righteous words of all-knowing[2] and venerable Kavundi, till a wild fowl, dwelling in a thicket of bamboos which had been scorched by the hot sun, announced the approach of dawn.

(At that time) they reached a village inhabited by 38–52
Brahmanas,[3] who wore the sacred thread but who were

while Clitarchus and Megasthenes call them Mandi (Pāndai?). See *Ancient India* by J. N. McCrindle, Frag. XXX. In the present state of our knowledge the theory of an indigenous origin of the dynasty lacks much force and can be said to be inconclusive. See *Studies in Tamil Literature and History*, p. 179, for their probable origin.

[1] According to Aḍiyārkkunallār, this day was the last day of the month of *Āṇi* (June-July).

[2] She was well read in works of *dharma*. Evidently Sanskrit learning had come to stay in the Tamil land much earlier than is generally supposed.

[3] A community of Brahmanas, but coming low in the social hierarchy. They are said to be *ambaṇavar* who took to the profession of acting and dancing. As they did not pursue their *svadharma* society regarded them as socially inferior. The position which the Brahmana held in society in the age of the Sangam classics is clear. There was the Vēdic Brahmana engaged in

given to music and dancing, having fallen from the Vēdic life.[1] Kōvalan̲ lodged the holy saint and his loving wife in a harmless place; and crossing a fence of thorns, he passed along a great road in search of water for his morning ablutions. (On his way) he recalled the journey in that forest alongside his wife and sighed heavily like a bellows. His grief burnt within him. Even his form looked altered, and clouded the vision of Kauśikan̲,[2] who, without recognizing him, addressed the green-leaved *kuṟukkatti* in whose shade he was standing: 'O *mādavi*[3] plant, with all thy flowers fallen down, unable to bear the heat of summer, thou seemest to be distressed, even like the flower-like Mādavi of long eyes who has fallen into deep affliction unable to bear Kōvalan̲'s separation from her.'

53–78 Kōvalan̲ who was listening to these words of the Brahmana Kauśikan̲ asked, 'What is it you are saying?' The young Kauśikan̲ went up to him and exclaimed: 'There need be no more anxiety: I have found him.' He then narrated all that had happened in Puhār, as follows: his (Kōvalan̲'s) wealthy father and pious mother are like

reading and teaching the Vēdas and also in performing Vēdic sacrifices. He evoked respect from every one. There was the *laukika* Brahmana who strayed from the prescribed path and took to professions other than those enjoined by the law of the land. In the *Ahanānūṟu* (st. 24) we have the expression *vēḷappārppān̲* meaning Brahmana engaged in making bangles. Among the *laukikas* come the *ambaṇavar* also. The term *ūrpārppān̲* in *South Indian Inscriptions* is another reference to the *laukika* members of the Brahmana community. This only shows that in addition to the Vēdic Brahmanas there also existed Brahmanas who took to worldly professions, and to whom society did not give the same status as that enjoyed by Vēdic Brahmanas.

[1] Cf. *Kuṟaḷveṇbā*, 133-4.

[2] The commentator interprets Kōśikan̲ as Bandikōśikan̲. It may also be Bandakauśikan̲. Apparently this Brahmana belonged to the well-known *Kauśika gōtra*. The suffix *mān̲i* in l. 56 shows that he was a bachelor and still in the first stage of life (*āśrama*). Both terms Kōśikan̲ and Kauśikan̲ are used.

[3] *Kuṟukkatti* is the *mādavi* plant, and the reference to *paśalai* or green leaves shows that the season was summer. The *mādavi* plant is compared to the courtesan Mādavi. The distress to the plant is caused by the departure of spring, and to the courtesan by the departure of Kōvalan̲.

a serpent that has lost its priceless jewel; his near relations have drowned themselves in an ocean of sorrow like bodies deprived of their souls; his servants have departed to different regions determined to find him out and bring him (Kōvalaṉ) back; the very city of Puhār of ancient fame has gone mad—like Ayōdhyā[1] at the separation of the great hero (Rāma) who (left it and) penetrated the thick jungles saying, 'To me the kingdom is nothing, but my father's command is everything';—Mādavi who heard (the news) from Vasantamālā's lips, lost her colour and turned green, and fell in a swoon upon the decorated bed in the bedchamber in the middle part of her tall mansion. Kauśikaṉ then continued: 'Much moved by her extreme agony I went to console her,[2] when that sorrow-stricken lady said: "I prostrate myself before your feet; kindly see that I suffer no more." She then wrote out a message with her tender hands and gave it to me saying, "Please hand this sealed palm-leaf[3] to him who is as dear to me as the jewel of my own eye".' He, the performer of Vēdic sacrifices, concluded by saying that he went to several places aimlessly with that message.

He said all this in good faith, and placed in Kōvalaṉ's 79–92
hands the leaf, given him by the grief-stricken creeper-like Mādavi, with the flowerbuds in her hair. The seal reminded him of the fragrance of her tresses which she had dressed with perfumed oil during his stay with her,

[1] The capital of Daśaratha, king of Ayōdhyā, presented a deserted appearance at the news of Rāma's entering the forest under the orders of his father. (See *Rāmāyaṇa*, 'Ayōdhyā', ch. 48.) This shows that the epic tradition of the *Rāmāyaṇa* had become popular in the Tamil land in the early centuries of the Christian era.

[2] It was the Brahmana Kauśikaṉ who brought Mādavi's message to Kōvalaṉ. In those days it seems to have been a custom for Brahmanas to have free entry into the women's apartments, and give succour to them whenever they needed aid. Also Brahmanas were sent on errands either for the state or on private business.

[3] The message was written on a palm-leaf. It was sealed before it was handed over. It is known as *candirakam*, with an *ōla* envelope to an *ōla* letter, shaped in the form of a ring. (See *Tamil Lexicon*, p. 1268.) That the sealing of letters was common is also evident.

and he was therefore loath to break it open. But as he opened the palm-leaf, he read these words :[1]

'My Lord, I fall prostrate before your feet. Kindly forgive my indiscreet words. What is my mistake which made you leave (our city) during the night with your wife of noble birth, even without the knowledge of your parents? My mind suffers in ignorance. Please relieve me. O great and true one of exquisite wisdom, may you bless me!'

93-101 When he had read these words he felt, 'She is not in the wrong; I alone am to blame', and gave Kauśikaṉ back (the message) as if to explain his departure, saying 'The contents of this sealed letter are quite fit to be seen by my faultless parents. I bow at their lotus-feet. O young Kauśikaṉ, show it to them so that they may cease to be anxious about me and be free from their agony. Please go.'

102-114 Afterwards he went back to the place where the holy, righteous Kavundi was staying with his faultless and chaste wife, and there he joined the company of bards who were singing (in praise of) Durgā's valorous dance. He took up the *śengōṭṭi yāḻ*[2] and sounding the *śentiṟam*,[3] he fastened up *tantirikaram* and *tivavu*,[4] joined properly *paṟṟu* with the existing *oṟṟuṟuppu*,[5] tied up the strings starting from *uḻai* and ending with *kaikkiḷai*, tested carefully with his ear the *āśāṉṟiṟam*[6] of *pāṭaṟpāṇi*[7] sacred to Durgā, at

[1] This is Mādavi's message. The implication is that she had done nothing to cause his final departure or separation from her. Even if she had committed a fault, she suggests that it was no greater than his own mistake in leaving his residence and city without the permission and knowledge of his aged parents. Her letter was so convincing that Kōvalaṉ thought it fit to redirect it to his parents to keep them informed of his situation.

[2] One of the four kinds of *yāl* (see Intro., p. 61).

[3] *Śentiṟam* constituted of *paṇ* (*śampūraṇam*), *paṇṇiyaṟriram* (*śāḍavam*), *tiram* (*auḍavam*) and *tiṟattiṟam* (*caturttam*). See Aḍiyārkkunallār's gloss, p. 349.

[4] Two of the six limbs of the *śengōṭṭi yāl*.

[5] *Oṟṟu* was a limb of the *śengōṭṭi yāḻ* and *oṟṟuṟuppu* is probably a fret.

[6] Four kinds of *āśāṉ*: *Gāndāram*, *Sikaṇḍi*, *Daśākari*, and *Śuddagāndāram*.

[7] Here was a mixing up of *paṇ* and *tiṟam*. See above, canto vii, st. 24.

three places (*tāṉam*) according to well recognized conventions;[1] and after playing the *pāṭaṟpāṇi* with those *pāṇar*, he asked them the distance from there to Madura (Kūḍal).

They replied: 'Do you not feel here the south wind 115–134
blowing from Madura? It is mingled with the divinely fragrant, thin soft mixture made up of the black *akil* paste, the odorous *kunkumam* flower, civet, the excellent sandal-paste, and the paste made from the musk of deer. On its way it rests for a while in the newly-opened flower-buds of the pollen-laden water-lily, maidenly *campakam*, *mādavi* petals, jasmine (*mallikai*), and home-grown *mullai*. It then mixes with the smoke rising from kitchens, the smoke of the broad bazaar where numbers of cooks fry cakes in pans, the fragrant fumes rising from terraces where live men and women, the smoke of sacrificial offerings, and various other sweet fumes. It finally issues with innumerable and indistinguishable odours from the palace of the conquering Pāṇḍyan wearing (Indra's) garland[2] on his broad chest, and fills all places with its oppressive perfume. This is much unlike the south wind coming from the Podiyil hills, which is often praised by the unfaltering tongues of (Śangam) poets.[3] Therefore that prosperous city is not very far from here. Though you go alone, none will obstruct you.'[4]

Afterwards Kōvalaṉ and Kaṇṇaki began their journey 135–150
by night, as previously, in company with the lady of great penance. On their way they heard the thundering sounds of the morning drum,[5] beaten with great eclat in the great

[1] This clearly demonstrates that Kōvalaṉ was a master-musician and was equal to experts in his knowledge of playing the lute.

[2] For the tradition of the Pāṇḍyan wearing Indra's garland see above, canto xi, ll. 24-5.

[3] The reference here is to Śangam poets who have sung the glories of the Podiyil in many a song. This establishes the antiquity of the Śangam as an institution regarded so even in the days of the *Silappadikāram*.

[4] This indicates the hospitality offered to aliens in ancient Madura.

[5] Drums were usually beaten in the morning both in the temple and at the palace.

temple of Śiva and other gods, and in the celebrated palace of the far-famed king; (they further heard) the chanting according to established rules by Brahmanas who knew the four Vēdas,[1] and the speech of penance-performers engaged in instruction. (They also heard) the usual daily sound of the *mulavu* in honour of the king's sword-warriors[2] who would not return from the field without victory, the uproar of war-elephants captured in battle, the screams of wild elephants captured in the forests, the neighing of horses standing in line, the beat of the *kiṇai* drums[3] at daybreak by dancing minstrels, and other tumultuous noises arising from Madura, all of which rivalled the roaring of the dark sea. These noises seemed to welcome the travellers and made them forget all their miseries.

151–173 The divine damsel, by name Vaigai, who is ever on the tongues of the poets, celebrated by them for her right conduct in offering protection to the world, and who belongs to the Pāṇḍyas, resembled a flawless noble[4] maiden with robes of different flowers[5] fallen from the date-palm, *vakulam*, red cotton tree, *vēngai*, white *kaḍambam*, *nāgam*, *tilakam*, *marudam*, jasmine, pear tree, the tall *campakam*, and *pāṭalam*; with her banks the zone of her broad *algul*, studded with *kuruku*, golden jasmine, *muśuṇḍai* with thick creeper, blossoming wild jasmine (*atiral*), the white

[1] Vēdic chanting was usually heard everywhere in the mornings. Is it a reference to the chanting of *Sattram-Yajur-Āraṇam?*

[2] This may be a reference to a festival of arms. The playing on *mulavu* is said to be a daily function and is generally in honour of soldiers who fought to the end without retreating from the field of battle.

[3] *Kiṇainilai* is the theme of the song in praise of a Veḷḷāḷa chief to the accompaniment of a *kiṇai* drum. It was generally performed by dancing minstrels called *kiṇaipporunar*.

[4] The term *poyya* applied to the river means it was everflowing. And these waters prevented alien kings from entering the Pāṇḍyan capital. It was a kind of *nadidurga* or river-fortress.

[5] The river Vaigai is described as a lady, wearing flower-robes, her banks representing her girdle, islets her breasts, *mullais* her teeth, carps her eyes, and the flowing water her wavy hair.

kūtāḷam, *kuḍaśam*, *vediram*, luxuriant *pakanṟai* creepers, *piḍavam* and Arabian jasmine closely intermingled; flowery islets—being accumulations of sand, facing one against the other, and richly covered by many flower trees growing thickly on their sides—her young and beautiful breasts; the red flowery tree shedding its flowers on her banks, her red mouth, and the *mullais* brought by the current, her lovely teeth; the carps that frisked along, hiding and revealing themselves alternately, her long eyes; the flowing water, never without odorous flowers, her tresses.[1]

She (the Vaigai) covered herself with the holy robes of sweet flowers and restrained the flow of tears that filled her eyes[2] as if she knew the trouble in store for youthful Kaṇṇaki.

Kaṇṇaki and Kōvalaṉ who had followed a foot-path 174–180
through the forest (reached the river and) praised it extravagantly saying,[3] 'O this is no stream of waters, but a stream of flowers.' They avoided the great thronged landing-stages where all the different boats were moored, some shaped like horses, some like elephants and others like lions.[4] Instead, they crossed over the river on a raft, accompanied by the saint, to a fragrant grove full of beauteous flowers on the southern bank.

They regarded it as an act of great merit to circum- 181–190
ambulate the city, the dwelling-place of gods, and they went round the moat enveloped by the indestructible forest

[1] *Aral* may mean thin black sand, or flowing water. Both are generally compared to the curls of ladies' hair.

[2] Here the Vaigai is compared to a lady sympathizing with Kaṇṇaki's future.

[3] The river Vaigai was worshipped by the three travellers as the divine stream. Cf. Sītā worshipping the Ganges and other rivers when she was leaving for the *Daṇḍaka* forest.

[4] Rafts of logs were also not uncommon. Evidently boat-building as an industry was in existence.

of defence.[1] At that time, the dark water-lily, *āmbal*, and the lotus, as if they understood for certain the unparalleled trouble in store for Kaṇṇaki and her husband, seemed to quake with grief (represented) by the waving of their stems[2] and their eyes filled with tears, while the bees that rested (in them) seemed to produce a mounring note in a spirit of sympathy. Lofty flags that[3] were set upon the outer wall of the fortress in commemoration of victory over enemies, seemed to say by a deprecating wave of hands 'Do not come (into the city)'.

191–196 The travellers passed through fertile paddy fields filled with birds and groves and entered the suburbs of the ancient city-fortress,[4] inhabited by none other than the men practising *dharma*, with residential quarters intersected by streams of fresh floods, lakes of expansive waters, fruit-bearing coconuts, plantain trees, areca palms, and bamboo sheds[5] for supplying water.

[1] A forest which served as a defence surrounded the moat encircling the city fortress.

[2] Their shaking is caused by the wind waving their stems, and the tears are drops of honey.

[3] The capture of the flags of the enemy was a sign of victory. After capture they were usually fixed on the outer wall of the fortress. The flag waving its hands means that the wind blew against it and thus seemed to urge the travellers to go back.

[4] The suburbs near the forest wall (*puṟañcēri*) were the residential quarters of the penance-performers, ascetics and other *sādhus*.

[5] This shows that rest-houses were erected at important places for travellers and the chief material used for such buildings was bamboo. Cf. Aśōka's inscriptions where this emperor is said to have built rest-houses on the roads.

Canto XIV

ŪRKĀṆKĀDAI

OR

SEEING THE CITY

To the singing of birds in the suburban groves, in the 1–14
tracts of shining water, and in the paddy fields bent with the weight of crops, the sun, an object of worship by the whole world, made the lotus in the lake open its petals, and awoke to the morning half-light the inhabitants of lofty Madura of the Pāṇḍyan who held the sword that made his enemy's heads tremble. At that time the thunder of the morning drum rose high accompanied by the blowing of the white conch from the temples[1] of Śiva with the forehead eye, of Viṣṇu with the Garuḍa standard, of Baladēva with the plough, and of Subrahmaṇya with the cock-flag, and from the residences[2] of those proclaiming *dharma*,[3] as well as from the palace of the victorious king.[4]

Kōvalaṉ went to make obeisance with his hands to 15–24
the saint Kavundi and said :[5] 'O saint distinguished for great penance, as one who has strayed from the righteous path, I am in the abject condition of seeing this girl, tender as a flower, suffer great pain by wandering through unknown lands. Until I return after informing the

[1] Cf. *Maṇi.*, canto v, l. 54.

[2] The terms used in the text to denote a temple are *kōil, niyamam, nakaram, kōṭṭam* and *paḷḷi*. The last term, *paḷḷi*, is invariably used in connexion with Jaina temples.

[3] Cf. *Maṇi.*, canto i, ll. 54-5. For an explanation of the term *aratturai* see *Kuraḷveṇbā* 41, *et seq.* The *tuṟai* of *tuṟavaram* constitutes *carya, kriya, yōga* and *jñānam*: the means of attaining *yōga* are eightfold. (See *Tolk.*, 'Puratt.', *sūtra* 20 and the commentary of Naccinārkkiniyar thereon.)

[4] The *tuṟai* of *maram* is sevenfold: *veṭci, karandai, vañji, kāñji, nocci, uḻiñai*, and *tumbai*. See *Pura.*, *veṇbāmālai*. The reference here is to seven kinds of conquest. Cf. *Studies in Tamil Literature and History*, pp. 239-42.

[5] A confession by Kōvalaṉ of his guilt.

princely merchants[1] of this ancient city about my situation, this lady of mine will be under your protection.[2] Have you any objection to that, O holy saint?'

25–34 To this Kavundi replied: 'Because your good deeds in past births are exhausted, you and your lady-love now experience unequalled distress. Though virtuous men proclaim eloquently with the drumstick of their tongues on the drum of their mouths, "Avoid the path of unrighteousness; if not, it will lead to bitter reaction," still those who are by nature bad will not take this precept to heart. But when an evil deed brings its own reaction, they become maddened excessively by misery born of ignorance. On the other hand wise and learned people will not grieve when the unavoidable reaction of past *karma* shows itself.

35–49 'The suffering at parting from one's love, the suffering leading to the union of lovers, and the suffering caused by the formless god (Cupid) visit only those who enjoy the love of curly-headed maidens, and not sages who lead a life of celibacy. Many in the world have fallen into dire distress by regarding women and food as objects of pleasure, and seeing this, sages have relinquished the desire for both. Not only now but many times in the past man has been entrapped by the wiles of a love based on desire and endless suffering. Do you not know that he[3] who went with his wife (into the forest) on the command of his father (Daśaratha) and suffered great agony at her (subsequent) separation, was the father of Him who revealed the Vēdas?[4] Is it not a long-remembered fact?

[1] Literally, Vaiśyas next in rank to the Kṣatriya caste.

[2] Here Kōvalaṉ seems to imply that Kaṇṇaki was already under the protection of Kavundi and was to continue so.

[3] Another statement to demonstrate that the *Rāmāyaṇa* was well known in South India at this time.

[4] This refers to the legend that when Viṣṇu was engaged in *yōganidrā* Brahmā the Creator came out of his navel. Hence Brahmā was the son of Viṣṇu and was the giver of the Vēdas.

'He (Naḷa) lost his kingdom in a gambling court[1] and penetrated the deep forest in company with his tender wife.[2] Neither was he devoid of love for her, nor was she a woman of bad and low nature. Was not Fate hard that he went away in the dead of night leaving her in the wild jungle?[3] Can you say that any accused her (Damayantī) of any fault? You are not like them, for have you not enjoyed union with your pretty wife? Do not grieve: but go to the king's city, Madura, and return when you have found a suitable (dwelling) place.' 50–61

Kōvalan̠ then went through a street above a narrow passage (*śuranga*)[4] constructed to admit groups of elephants with their long trunks, leading from the moat with its vast expanse of sparkling waters, encircled by a well-guarded defence forest.[5] Unsuspected by the ranks of the best Yavana swordsmen[6] who guarded it, he next entered the forest-gate, where flags waved in the westerly breeze, and saw the interior (of the city) glittering like the opened jewel-box of thousand-eyed Indra. 62–70

In the streets[7] he saw courtesans, lost to all shame and chastity, accompanying their rich lovers to the pleasure garden with its tall *maruda* trees[8] on the banks of the 70–75

[1] *Vallāḍāyam* (Sans., *dyūtam*).

[2] The reference is to the story of Naḷa and Damayantī, which is the theme of the *Naiṣadha Kāvya*.

[3] Naḷa left Damayantī in the forest in a half naked condition in the dead of night (*Mhb.*, 'Vana Parvan', ch. 62). This also shows that the story of the *Mahābhārata* was popular in the Tamil land (see 'Naḷōpākhyāna-parvan' for the full story).

[4] It may be remembered that this word *śuranga* is important as determining the authenticity of the *Arthaśāstra*. See *The Mauryan Polity*, pp. 16-17.

[5] *Iḷai* is the defensive wall of a fortress and *miḷai* is the forest zone encircling the moat surrounding a citadel.

Aḍiyārkkunallār speaks of them as Turks. It may possibly be a reference to Greeks. But to the natives of ancient India all foreigners were Yavanas. They were employed by Tamil kings for military service.

[7] A description of the interior of the city. The rest of the canto shows Kōvalan̠ going through the principal streets.

[8] It would appear that there was a special place which went by the name of *tirumarudanturai*. The *Kalittogai* also makes a reference to it. These references show that that place was a public park. See *Maduraikkāñji*, l. 356.

swelling Vaigai, and on white sand dunes. He also saw them engaged in water-sports, in boats with high cabins and in canoes, swimming and holding on to the rafts.[1]

76–82 He saw, besides, in a grove of the ancient city which appeared like a golden creeper, courtesans gracefully placing cool fragrant *mullais*, water-lilies, and *neydals* with open petals in their hair which was already dressed with long wreaths of white flowers, jasmine, *viriyal*, and the pollen of the cool red lily, and fastened with pearls from the great harbour of Koṛkai.[2] (They were further seen) anointing their bodies with luxurious sandal-paste from the southern Malaya hills.

83–96 At nightfall he saw maidens on their flower-strewn beds in the moonlit terraces where their lovers banished their fatigue (by recalling their experiences in the different seasons of the year).[3] (During the rainy season, they said,) when the king of the clouds appeared with the north wind, decorated the noisy city of Madura in red (*cevvaṇi*),[4] and showed to her (Madura) the king of Gods (Indra) who had clipped the wings of mountains with his

[1] Boats and rafts of different descriptions were used to cross the rivers. The names given are *nīrmāḍam*, *nāvāi*, and *puṇai*. Some of them were covered and some open. The *puṇai* was an open raft. People either swam holding on to it or they sat on it and crossed.

[2] Korkai was one of the great ports of that time. It was noted for excellent pearl-fisheries. See *Maduraikkāñji*, ll. 134 and 144. Probably Ptolemy's Kolkhoi was Koṛkai (McCrindle, op. cit., p. 57 ff.). The site of this town is now about five miles inland, where a new emporium arose. This was the Kayal of Marco Polo who visited it in the thirteenth century. (See *Travels of Marco Polo*, ed. by Sir Henry Yule, Vol. II., pp. 372-3.) There is a clear reference to the pearls and to the port in the *Kauṭalīya Arthaśāstra*.

[3] The poet describes the life led by men and women in the city during the six different seasons of the year—the rainy season, the cold season, the season of early dew, the season of late dew, spring and summer. These are known in Sanskrit as Varṣaṛtu, Siśiṛtu, Hēmantaṛtu, Saratṛtu, Vasantam, and Grīṣmam. When Kōvalaṉ entered the city it was the middle of summer.

[4] *Cevvaṇi* is a term of much importance in *Ahapporuḷ*. If during his wife's menstrual period the hero spent his time with a courtesan, the custom was for the confidante to appear before him dressed entirely in red. The hero then returned home. Perhaps Iḷaṅgō took Madura to be the confidante, Indra to be the hero, and the women of Madura to be the heroines.

thunderbolt,[1] they (the ladies of the city) wore in their waists scarlet silk with flower-work thereon, adorned their tresses (already dressed with flower-buds) with wild olive, adorning them further with the fragrant and fresh-blown *kuṟiñji* and red *tāḷi* flowers which grew on the slopes of the Śirumalai hills. (They then) painted their breasts with red sandal-paste, and further beautified them with garlands of coral, and garlands of the curved petals of red *śengōḍu* flowers.

During the cold season modest damsels and their 97–101
lovers, who had painted their chests with fragrant pastes, seated themselves in front of the censer charged with the wood of incense trees, and closed the lattice windows[2] (of their apartments) in mansions seeming to reach the sky, built by expert architects.[3]

During the season of early dew, ladies sat with their 102–105
lovers on the moonlit terraces of their big houses, to receive the warmth of the rising sun, who appeared with his expanding rays on the southern horizon dispelling the white clouds.

(The lovers continued to talk, asking) where is the 106–112
king (the season) of late dew in the month Panguni, who would witness the festival of the Bow sacred to hard-hearted Cupid (Neḍuvēḷ)[4] in the Pāṇḍyan city and enter

[1] This legend is well known in Sanskrit literature. Tradition has it that mountains once had wings and consequently flew from one place to another. Then Indra had their wings clipped. Some of them in fear hid themselves in the deep waters of the ocean. See the *Rāmāyaṇa*, ' Sundara ', ch. I.

[2] These were windows peculiar to those days. See *Studies in Tamil Literature and History*, pp. 263-4. It is of absorbing interest to note similar institutions in the Indus Valley during the chalcolithic period. In the *Annual Report, 1928-9* of the Archæological Survey of India, the remark is made that no windows have been discovered in the Mohenjo-daro buildings excavated. 'In all probability there were only simple ventilation holes just beneath the ceilings of the rooms.'—*Report*, p. 69.

[3] Arumpadavuraiyāśiriyār refers to a treatise on architecture entitled *Mayamatam*.

[4] *Vilviḻa* is the festival in honour of the God of Love. Neḍuvēḷ, literally, means 'The Great Vēḷ' or one who kindles eternal desire. The festival is generally held in the month of Panguni in the season of late dew. In the Tamil land the festival is still celebrated in that month. See *Kuṟuntogai*, st. 31.

with the east wind and with a fleet of high, broad ships, carrying different kinds of incense, silks, sandals, scents, and camphor brought as tribute, from Toṇḍi?[1]

113–117 Moreover, where else can we see the king of spring, who unites joyful lovers in the Pāṇḍyan city, bringing with him the south wind from the Podiyil hills of Tennavaṉ, giving *mādavi* creepers luxuriant growth and filling groves and jungles with fragrant flowers?

118–119 In this way creeper-like ladies rested with their husbands recalling the different seasons.

120–145 (Continuing, they said) on the last day when the king of spring reigning over Madura considered removing to other places, the continuously hot sun and the westerly breeze, entered (the city) and scorched the entire jungle and hilly tracts, making herds of elephants and their young ones tremble; wealthy maidens (wearing golden bangles) completely loyal to the king, embraced him anew and received from him as presents covered carts, palanquins, sleeping-couches with jewelled legs, physical happiness in the pleasure-gardens,[2] *kauri* fans of yaks' tails, golden betel-boxes, and sharp swords. These maidens drank sweet wine from pure golden goblets held by their maid-servants and became inebriated. When trying to drive away with their fragrant flower-garlands striped bees[3] (that had settled on them), they hit places where the bees were

[1] This Toṇḍi must have been a great port, belonging to the Cōḷa, or more probably the Pāṇḍyan kingdom. This must not be confused with Toṇḍi, another port in the dominion of the Cēras. See *Puṟam.*, st. 17 and 48. The tribute offered by the chief of Toṇḍi in ships was *akil*, silks, garlands, scents, and camphor. Most of these came from the Archipelago islands in the east. For detailed comments on these articles see the gloss of Aḍiyārk-kunallār. The *Silappadikāram* says that ships entered with *koṇḍal* or the east wind. If it is a reference to Cēra Toṇḍi, *koṇḍal* would not have been mentioned. Perhaps this Toṇḍi can be identified with a place of the same name in the present Ramnad district.

[2] Tam., *uyyāṉam*; Sans., *udyāna*. This refers to the king's concubines to whom he occasionally made presents, such as those mentioned.

[3] The women drank so much that their eyes became reddened and deceived the bees into thinking that they were not eyes but honey-laden flowers.

not. In smiling they showed their pearl-like teeth through their red lips and sang words of praise which they had not sung during their separation (*pulavi*); but when they began the eight modes of singing,[1] their tongues failed and provoked only laughter in their hearers. The extremities of their long carplike eyes, red like the opened buds of a bright *śengaḻunīr* flower, bespoke their anger, while perspiration gathered on their tiny foreheads, bearing the *tilaka*, and their murderous bow-like eye-brows curved downwards, all of which was longingly observed by men of noble families. In this way these women afforded amusement to the ruler of the earth.

(After passing this street) Kōvalaṉ went through the highway with its double row of[2] beautiful mansions which crowned kings frequented secretly. These were the residences of courtesans who had never been punished with the carrying of burnt tiles,[3] and of dancers who knew the technique of the two musical conventions, *vēttiyal* and *poduviyal*,[4] and had perfect knowledge of the four[5] characteristics (of dancing),[6] songs, time-beats, the music of bagpipes accompanied by musical instruments made of leather used in the dancing theatre. They also knew of the much renowned *talaikkōl* and of the sweet and seven- 146–167

[1] *Kaṭṭurai* constitutes eight kinds of song if the reading is எட்டுக்கு. But the reading எக்கும் may be conveniently substituted. It would then mean that they tried to speak but their words stuck in their throats.

[2] The double rows are probably *śirudaṉam* (residences of the middle classes) and *perudaṉam* (residences of the wealthy classes).

[3] This may mean that they were living in lofty houses built of burnt bricks and tiles. Another meaning (adopted here) is that the courtesans were free from the punishment of bearing tiles. The custom was to inflict this punishment on anybody who swerved from the prescribed conventions. The damsel had to walk round the city in procession bearing seven tiles on her head. To this disgrace the courtesans of Madura were not subjected.

[4] Both these are known as *Vaśaikkūttu*. See *Maṇi.*, canto ii, l. 18. While *vēttiyal* was intended for royalty, *poduviyal* was a popular performance (see *Arumpadavurai*).

[5] The *paṇ* was fourfold, *pālai, kuriñji, marudam* and *śevvali*.

[6] *Vari* is of seven kinds. It may also refer to the seven strings beginning with *kural*.

fold strains, and were accompanied by the *tōriyamaḍandai*[1] who sang the *vāram*, by the girl who sang the opening song and by the girl who sang the middle song and who acted in four different entertaining ways, and (when singing) reached the eighth (note) for which she was rewarded every day with gifts ranging from one to 1008 *kaḻañjus* of gold.

Caught in the eye-nets of these goddess-like damsels (*aṇanku*),[2] even religious men, take leave of their disciplined senses, while young people dallying carnally with girls like bees sucking honey from flower after flower, and new initiates to the revelries of Cupid, will not leave those mansions, without listening to the girls' songs, and to the parrot-like talk of the women skilled in the sixty-four arts.[3]

168–179 Kōvalaṉ then saw in the bazaar,[1] covered carts and other vehicles,[5] ornamented chariots, coats of mail, attractive goads, gloves used in warfare, efficacious medicines, curved bludgeons, white furry fans, pig-faced shields, leather shields, shields with a picture of the forest on them, machines fitted with spears,[6] workers in copper, bronze-workers, newly-made ropes, garland-makers, saws made of steel, instruments for ivory cutting, burning incense (*pukai*),[7] pastes, and flower-work, which were so rich and innumerable that they even evoked the envy of monarchs.

[1] The *tōriyamaḍandai* was an aged dancing girl who sung the *vāram* to the accompaniment of a dance by a young girl. She was assisted by two more girls, the *talaippāṭṭukkūtti* initiating the song, and the *iḍaippāṭṭukkūtti* helping in the middle by singing.

[2] *Aṇanku* corresponds here to the *Mōhinī* of Sanskrit Literature.

[3] The sixty-four arts are elaborately given in the *Kāmasūtra* of Vātsyāyana.

[4] What we call *kaḍangu* streets in modern Indian cities. These are shops of wholesale dealers. Four such are mentioned.

[5] It may be noted that these vehicles were all drawn by bullocks.

[6] A number of instruments of war are mentioned here as being sold in open bazaars. The instruments for ivory cutting, flower-work, the decorative arts, etc., show the high state of culture reached in the early centuries of the Christian era.

[7] *Pukai* stands for all the varieties of burning incense used at that ancient time.

Kōvalaṉ next passed through the wealthy street un- 180–200
penetrated by enemies, full of groups of dealers in superior diamonds[1] which were free from such defects as crows' feet, spots, holes and lines, which had no natural deficiencies observable by experts of trained acuteness, and which reflected the colours of the four castes.[2] Emeralds of green brilliance free from black spots and defects of line and curve; the *māṇikkam* variety known as *padumam*, *nīlam*, *bindu*, and *spaṭikam*, all of which were free from recognized defects; the *puṣparāga* set with gold resembling a cat's eye; the beautiful sardonyx (*gōmēdaga*) with the faultless brilliance of the sun; the blue gem with crystallized darkness; the double-coloured *vaidūrya*;[3] the good gems of five different kinds born from a common source[4] and glimmering like the setting sun, as well as heaps of white pearls (*candrāguru*), pink-lustred pearls (*angāraka*)[5] and pearls of the finest quality (*āṇimuttu*),[6] all of which sparkled without any blemish caused by wind or sand, stone or water. There were also well-formed corals completely free from flaws in their inner cavities, without stones in their interspaces, and untwisted.[7]

The excellent streets of the goldsmiths were next seen 201–204
with flags[8] enabling the gold-dealers to avoid confusion as

[1] Experts in the art of cutting gems. The nine kinds of precious stones are mentioned. Aḍiyārkkunallār furnishes interesting details as regards their superiority and fineness as well as of the defects of each one of them. The commentator's study is scientific and deserves close scrutiny.

[2] The colours of four castes, white, red, green and black are distinguished in the diamonds.

[3] The interpretation of *Arumpadavurai* is followed in ll. 189-90. What this *Aśiriyār* interprets as *gōmēdaga*, Aḍiyārkkunallār interprets as *Vaidūrya*, and vice versa.

[4] The common source of some of the gems was crystal quartz.

[5] It is interesting to note that some of the pearls are named after the planets, *sōma*, *guru*, and *angāraka*.

[6] Aḍiyārkkunallār interprets ll. 195-6 as follows: 'Pearls of the round sort, their natural colour white (*veḷḷi*) and pink (*angāraka*).'

[7] The defects and merits of corals are furnished here. One defect is that during the course of its growth, stones entered into the interspaces. Such corals were considered inferior.

[8] Four kinds of gold were offered for sale and in front of each shop hung a flag—the signpost indicative of the kind of gold available within.

to the kind of gold available in each shop variously called *jātarūpa*, *kiḷiccirai* (parrot's wings), *āḍakam* and *jāmbūnadam*.

205–218 He then went through the street of cloth merchants, where several kinds of bundles were piled up, each of a hundred cloths woven of cotton thread, hair, or silk thread ;[1] the street of corn-chandlers where merchants were seen going about here and there with balances, measuring-vessels known as *parai*, and grain-measures (*ambaṇam*),[2] filled with sacks[3] of grain and black pepper irrespective of the seasons ; the four different streets occupied by the men of the four castes ;[4] the intersection of three streets ;[5] the termini of four streets ;[6] the streets of petty shops ; *maṉṟams* ; lanes and broad streets ; and finally went beyond the ramparts (of the city) through the shade of an arbour[7] of clustering green leaves, impervious to the fierce rays of the sun blazing in the sky. Seeing thus the great city of the protecting (Pāṇḍyan) king, Kōvalaṉ was highly pleased.

[1] Clothes were made from cotton, rat's hair, silk thread, see *Jīvakacintāmaṇi*, st. 2686.

[2] For *ambaṇavaḷavai*, see *Padiṟṟu.*, p. 66, 2nd. ed. It was a grain-measure equal to the modern *marakkāl*. *Parai* was another measuring-vessel in use.

[3] The word grain, according to the commentator, stands for sixteen kinds of grains grouped in bags in the streets. One of them was pepper.

[4] There were caste streets as distinguished from other streets of the city, where lived artisans and other classes pursuing different arts and crafts.

[5] The term used generally is *candi*, sometimes, *muccandi*.

[6] The *śatukkam* was also known as *nāṟcandi*.

[7] According to the commentator, the shade of the numerous flags and festoons offered shelter to the passer-by. But this does not seem quite appropriate, since Kōvalaṉ went outside the rampart from the interior of the city.

Canto XV

AḌAIKKALAKKĀDAI

OR

THE HAVEN

Having seen the ancient and great city of Madura dis- 1–8
tinguished for the highly righteous sceptre, the coolness
of the (royal) umbrella, and the prowess of the spear of
the Kauriyar[1] who dutifully turned the wheel of law under
the merciful guidance of a bountiful providence,[2] and never
deserted by its law-abiding citizens,[3] Kōvalaṉ went outside
the gates of the fortress, into the grove wherein dwelt
monks engaged in imparting *dharma*.

And while he was narrating to the sage Kavundi the 9–20
undiminishing prosperity of Madura and the prowess of
the Pāṇḍyan king, Māḍalaṉ of Talaiccengāṉam,[4] the first
amongst Brahmanas, well versed in the four Vēdas,

[1] Among the titles given to the Pāṇḍya, one is Kauriyar. The two terms Pāṇḍyan and Kauriyar which occur in Sangam literature strongly suggest that they are derived from Pāṇḍu and Kuru. We know of the Pāṇḍavas and Kauravas as foster-brothers fighting the great war recounted in the *Mahābhārata*, at ancient Kurukṣētra. Both belonged to one and the same stock. Apparently a branch of this stock was established in the extreme south of India and became prominent among South Indian dynasties. But there is evidence suggesting an indigenous origin to this dynasty as the present writer has ventured to conjecture in a footnote in his *Studies in Tamil Literature and History*, p. 179. The subject requires further examination and scrutiny.

[2] It means there was no hunger, disease, theft or trouble from neighbours (see canto v, sl. 72).

[3] The idea is that the king was such a just monarch that the people of the city never thought of leaving it for a foreign land. It may be noted in passing that it was a custom in ancient India for the people to forsake their kings if they conducted themselves unrighteously, by deserting their capital for that of other and more just kings. See the *Kauṭalīya Arthaśāstra*, Bk. XIII, § 1. This seems to have been an effective weapon on the part of the subjects to make the king conduct himself justly and truly towards them.

[4] Talaiccengāṉam is Talaiccengāḍu, a village of the ancient Cōḷa kingdom, perhaps identical with the village now bearing that name about six miles south-west of Kāvērippaṭṭiṉam. It is a sacred place mentioned in the *Tēvāram*.

appeared at their residence in the grove surrounded by a shallow moat. He had come there to obtain relief from the fatigue of his journey while returning to his own family, after circumambulating the hill[1] sacred to the great sage, and bathing in the bathing ghat of the Kumari.

To him Kōvalaṉ prostrated himself, while the Brahmana skilled in speech,[2] on being addressed, replied as follows:

21–39 'When Mādavi, tender as the young mango-leaf, after winning the king's gift[3] for dancing, gave birth to a tender babe and passed through the period of pollution,[4] you responded to the sweet words appropriate to the occasion of the older dancers who desired that the daughter should be given a fitting name, by saying. "An ancestor of mine[5] was once shipwrecked in the dead of night in the great sea of mighty waves; but because he had performed several good deeds, he kept himself afloat by swimming for some days.[6] Then appeared before him the deity of the sea[7]

[1] Podiyil, sacred to the sage Agastya. For the Agastya tradition in the South and Greater India, the reader's attention is drawn to Dikshitar's *Some Aspects of the Vāyu Purāṇa* (Madras University, 1933), in the section entitled 'Agastya and Greater India'. See also K. A. Nilakanta Sastri's 'Agastya', in *Tijdschrift Van Ind.*, Vol LXXVI, No. 4.

[2] This special attribute given by the poet to Mādalaṉ shows that the latter was famous for his oratorical powers.

[3] The Cōḷa king under reference who had given Mādavi a special gift for dancing is identified by the commentator Aḍiyārkkunallār as Karikāla. But the latest researches point to a somewhat different conclusion. (See P. T. S. Iyengar's *History of the Tamils*, pp. 372 ff. ; K. A. Nilakanta Sastri's *Studies in Cōḷa History and Administration*, pp. 19 ff.; M. Raghava Aiyangar's *Cēran Seṅguṭṭuvan*, 3rd ed., pp. 101 ff.; and K. N. Sivaraja Pillai's *The Chronology of the Early Tamils*, pp. 88 ff.)

[4] Evidently the observance of rules regarding pollution during the period of confinement was an ancient Tamil practice.

[5] Cf. *Maṇi.*, canto vii, ll. 33-8; canto xxix, l. 19. See Dikshitar's paper 'Buddhism in Tamil Literature' in *Buddhist Studies* (Calcutta), edited by B. C. Law, p. 679, for a fuller version of the story.

[6] 'Some days' may be taken to be 'seven days' in the light of the text in the *Maṇimēkalai*, canto xxix, l. 16.

[7] This story has a parallel in the Buddhist Jātaka stories. See E. B. Cowell, *Jātakas,* Vol. IV, pp. 9-13; Vol. VI, Nos. 442 and 539, p. 22.

saying, ' I live here under orders from Indra. I have come before you. Be not afraid; my name is Maṇimēkalai.[1] The fruits of your great charity are not lost. Surmount the great ocean of your suffering'; and thus she saved him from his distress by bringing him back to the shore. As she is my family deity, let her name be given to this baby." Then a thousand courtesans with jewelled girdles blessed the child with the name Maṇimēkalai.[2]

'On that day when you sat with that happy lady 40–53
Mādavi, and showered gifts of gold with your beautiful hands, a Brahmana, with bent body, having attained the very limits of knowledge and good conduct,[3] came feebly along with the aid of a stick in order to receive gifts. Seeing him in the clutches of a fast and furious elephant which had thrown its mahout and was rushing in all directions to the loud noise of the drum,[4] O merciful hero, you stepped forth instantly with a cry, and after rescuing that man of high birth, you released yourself from its curved hollow trunk and remaining between the white tusks, stood on its nape like a Vidyādhara on a dark hill, and curbed the still furious beast.

'On another occasion, a Brahmana left for the north 54–75
abandoning his wife who had caused the death of a young mungoose.[5] When she followed him, the Brahmana said: "It is not proper for me to eat food served by your hands.

[1] Maṇimēkalai, the guardian deity of the sea, was the family deity of Kōvalaṉ.

[2] The ceremony of naming a child, still current in India as *nāmakaraṇam*, was one of the many *samskāras* specially incumbent on the twice-born classes. We know from literature that Kōvalaṉ was a Vaiśya and hence belonged to the class of the twice-born.

[3] The *śiṣṭa* according to Sanskrit didactic literature.

[4] It seems to have been a peculiar ancient custom in Tamil India that when an elephant became *must* and went rampaging through the streets, a drum was sounded so as to be heard throughout the city warning citizens of the mad elephant's movements. This kept people within doors lest they should fall victims to the beast.

[5] For this folk-tale see the *Pañcatantra*. See also Dikshitar's paper on 'Folklore and the Migration of Legends' in the *Annals of the Bhandarkar Research Institute*, 1934, pp. 212-19.

You give this note containing a Sanskrit verse[1] to people leading a virtuous life." With this the Brahmana lady went through the bazaars where the tall mansions of the wealthy merchants were, and showed the note from house to house proclaiming, "O, will no one relieve me of my sins and enjoy the fruits of so doing?" At once you called to her and asked "What is your trouble and what is this (note)?" The lady narrated to you the great distrees she was in, and said, "Take this leaf on which has been written the verse, and by giving me money absolve me from my great sin." You replied to her, "Do not fret, do not be afraid. I shall relieve you of your difficulty"; and in order that her sinful deed might be atoned for, you made gifts in accordance with the instituted rules,[2] and relieved that lady of her worry. O wealthy man of imperishable riches! Then you made her husband, who had left for the forest, (come back and) live with her in the right path (of household life) by giving them copious wealth out of your limitless riches.

76–90 'On still another occasion, a chaste lady was falsely accused. A man who went to her husband and gave false evidence was seized by the cruel noose of a

[1] The *śloka* quoted by Aḍiyārkkunallār is from the *Pañcatantra*, Bk. V, Tale 1, and is as follows:

Aparīkṣya na kartavyam kartavyam suparīkṣitam |
Paścāt bhavati santāpō brāhmaṇī nakulam yathā ||

The context shows that the story occurred in Puhār during the lifetime of Kōvalaṉ. But as it finds mention in an earlier text like *Tantrākhyāyika*, an earlier recension of the *Pañcatantra*, this raises a great chronological difficulty. One way out of this tangle is to consider it a later interpolation. Whether or not the story be true, it bears testimony to the fact that Kōvalaṉ possessed a sound knowledge of Sanskrit. Apparently the note was a cadjan leaf on which had been written the verse by the Brahmana.

[2] Belief in expiatory rites shows that the influence of the *Dharmasūtras* and *Dharmaśāstras* had gained ground in the Tamil land. This indicates the charitable nature of Kōvalaṉ, and also that Kōvalaṉ's wealth was limitless. In this connexion the term *uṟuporul* is interesting. According to the *Kuṟaḷ-veṇbā 756*, it is the unclaimed property that went to fill the coffers of the king. But Kōvalaṉ could not have unclaimed property. Hence it is correct to accept Tolkāppiyaṉār's interpretation of 'much' or 'copious'.

Būtam, who devoured such offenders.[1] Seeing the deep sorrow of the mother of that erring man, you at once entered the knots of that noose and said to the gracious and good Būtam, "Take away my life and yield him his". Without agreeing, it said, "There is no prescription to accept a good life in the place of a bad life, lest I should lose thereby the enjoyment of the next world. Please give up the idea." When the Būtam had devoured him in your presence, O best among householders, you accompanied that lady, grief-stricken at heart, and like a close relative, prevented for several years the exhaustion of hunger which would have overtaken his family[2] and all its cognate branches.

'I know all the good things you have done in this 91–94
birth,[3] but owing to your deeds in the past birth, O Gōpāla[4] of ripe knowledge, you have fallen into indescribable suffering along with your gem-like young wife who is like Lakṣmī herself.'

To this Kōvalaṉ replied, 'Half awake in the middle of 95–106
the dark night I dreamt thus :[5] "Through a low person in this city, well defended by the righteous monarch, this

[1] This points to the prevalent practice of punishing false witnesses with death. Cf. *Kuṟuntogai*, st. 184. It is interesting to note that the *Kauṭalīya Arthaśāstra* rules to that effect. But the method of meting out this punishment is rather strange. There was the Būtam whose function it was to punish with death all who committed heinous offences. It would not accept a good life for a bad one. In fact the Būtam had no power to do so. See also canto v, ll. 128 and 134.

[2] *Dāyādins* of Sanskrit literature. This also demonstrates the existence of the joint-family system in the Tamil land, and how there was a vast family of dependents on a single earning member, and how after his death, wealthy neighbours volunteered to give succour.

[3] Cf. *Kuṟaḷveṇbā*, 169, and the commentary of Parimēlaḻagar.

[4] Gōpāla seems to be the Sanskrit variant to the Tamil name Kōvalaṉ.

[5] Dr Swaminatha Aiyar refers to the treatise entitled *Kaṉāنūl*, discovered and published for the first time in *Sentamil*, Vol. I, Pt. III, and subsequently published as a booklet by Vidvan R. Raghava Aiyangar. A parallel may be drawn from the *Rāmāyaṇa*, 'Ayōdhya', ch. 59, where Bharata dreams a fearful dream during the night of Daśaratha's death, the latter riding in a southerly direction, in a chariot yoked with asses. Cf. *Kaṉāṉūl*, st. 2, 4, 10 and 15; *Puṟam.*, st. 41; *Kuṟaḷveṇbā*, 247.

girl with the five plaits of fragrant hair suffered great agony; stripped of my robes by some stranger I mounted a horned buffalo. Later in the company of this handsome lady of the charmingly curled hair, I attained the great status[1] of those who have renounced attachment. I also saw Mādavi yielding her daughter Maṇimēkalai to a Buddhist saint of great glory,[2] thereby making the god of love fling his flower dart on the barren ground and sob helpless.''

'I anticipate some imminent trouble.'

107–114 Then the Vēdic Brahmana and the saint Kavundi together observed: 'As this place outside the city[3] is not fit to be lived in except by righteous monks, leave here for the interior of the vast city, to the residences of Vaiśyas[4] who will receive you because of your past reputation. Leave this place before sunset and enter the city of Madura with its tall mansions.'

115–124 Just then, Mādari, an old woman of the cowherd caste, who was returning after making the usual offering of milk to the flower-eyed yakkiṇi,[5] enshrined outside the city gates in the quarters of monks practising *dharma*, saw and prostrated herself before the saint Kavundi who then thought within herself: 'The life of cowherds who

[1] He obtained salvation which was generally secured only by men of detachment from mundane things. This means that the bondage of birth and death ceased to exist for him.

[2] See *Maṇi.*, canto ii, ll. 73-4, etc.

[3] *Puṟacciṟai* are the quarters outside the gates of the city, being the residences of those who dedicate themselves to a life of holiness and detachment and consequently householders are unfit to live in them.

[4] Vaiśyas are said to be next in rank to the Kṣatriyas.

[5] Yakṣi-dēvatā. Dr Swaminatha Aiyar in a note informs us that in the Jaina books, every one of the twenty-four *Tīrthankaras* was served by a Yakka and Yakkiṇi. This name is current as Iśakki in places round about Cape Comorin. Aḍiyārkkunallār interprets it as *āriyāṅgaṉai*, and on the authority of the *Tiruviḷaiyāḍal Purāṇam*, st. 63, l. 17, *āriyāṅgaṉai* is one who takes to asceticism during the life-time of her husband. Her shrine was situated outside the city proper (*puṟacciṟai*). But we know from history and legends as testified to by the *Rāmāyaṇa* and *Mahāvamśa* that the Yakṣas were one of the early ruling tribes in ancient South India and Ceylon, and died out some time before the commencement of the Christian era.

protect cows and offer what they yield is not harmful.[1] This aged lady is without fault and is, besides, virtuous and merciful. It is not therefore wrong to lodge Kaṇṇaki with Mādari.'

She then addressed Mādari thus: 'Listen! If mer- 125–148
chants of this city hear the name of this lady's father-in-law,[2] they will welcome him (her husband) as a guest, as if they had received a rare fortune, and take him and this lady of the beaming-eyes to their well-guarded home[3] along with them. Till she goes to the houses of those very rich people, accept her, O cowherdess, as a refugee. Give this auspicious girl an excellent bath, decorate her long red eyes with black collyrium, adorn her soft tresses with choice flowers, deck her in pure clothes and as becomes worthy people, remain as her maid, protectress and mother. Accept her. Mother Earth had no compassion[4] on the tender tread of this creeper-like girl, who came with me. Oblivious of her own suffering this celebrated lady, although fainting from thirst in the scorching sun, felt more keenly the suffering of her husband. We (Kavundi) have not seen any shining deity other than this goddess who has taken the vow of chastity necessary to devoted housewives. Do you not know the truth of the good saying that in a land where chaste women live, rains will not fail,[5] prosperity will not decrease, and the great monarch's victory will not diminish?

'Listen again. Though what is given for safe- 149–160
keeping by men of penance be small,[6] it is bound to

[1] This testifies to the simple and god-fearing life led by members of the community of cowherds.

[2] This shows that Māśāttuvāṉ's name was well known to the merchants of Madura. It would appear that he was a princely merchant.

[3] This points to the fact that the houses of wealthy merchants were under watch and ward, and this is not surprising considering the stories of expert thieves given in the classic itself.

[4] In simple language it means that she was footsore. And yet in spite of this she felt for her husband's distress and not her own.

[5] Cf. *Kuraḷveṇbā*, 55.

[6] For a definition of penance, see *Jīvakacintāmaṇi*, st. 1547.

yield many fruitful results. Before the Cāraṇar preaching *dharma* from the shining slab of stone, erected by Sāvakas,[1] beneath the unchanging shade of the flowery *aśōka*, in the town adjoining the Kāvēri[2] region, stood a Dēva of great power, with beauteous form, resplendent like Indra's bow, adorned with garlands of flowers and gems, wearing gold ornaments, fit to be worshipped by the many invisible gods, but with one of his hands resembling that of a monkey with black fingers.

161–162 'All the Sāvakas worshipped the Cāraṇar and wanted to know the reason for the appearance of this Dēva, when the god spoke as follows :

163–173 "Once there was a merchant called Eṭṭi-Sāyalaṉ.[3] In his house many would gather who observed fasting. One day the chief lady of the house reverentially received the foremost among the monks. At the same time a small monkey from the village silently entered the house and worshipped the feet of the great divine. Impelled by hunger, it ate the leavings of the food and water consumed by the ascetic, and gazed on him. The wise person of steadfast mind became glad at heart and addressed the lady of the house, saying, 'Regard this monkey as one of your own sons.'

174–191 "The lady agreed to the wise words of the saint. When the loving monkey died, the lady gave away the property set apart[4] for it, to the assembled Cāraṇar and prayed that it might be absolved from all its sins.[5] Hence it was born as the only son of Uttaragautta[6] at Vāraṇāsi

[1] The Sāvakas were Jaina householders who heard with reverence occasional preachings of *dharma* from the Cāraṇar, a class of divinities accepted by Hindu tradition.

[2] *Kāvirippūmpākkattuppaṭṭiṇam* : cf. *Maṇi.*, canto xxv, l. 16.

[3] A title given to merchant-princes by the king. Cf. *Maṇi.*, canto iv, l. 58; *Perumkadai*, Bk. I, ch. 40, l. 116.

[4] In accordance with the advice given by the monk to regard it as one of her sons, the lady treated it as such, set apart a portion of the family property to the monkey, and on its death, distributed that wealth in charity.

[5] The idea is that it may not be born hereafter as an animal.

[6] Uttaragautta was the ruling king of Benares.

in the middle country.[1] This son who was celebrated for his beauty, wealth and great wisdom, and noted for his great gifts died in his thirty-second year. Later he attained the form of a Dēvakumāra and has come here with the monkey's hand on one of his arms, as if to announce to all the Śāvakas, "Please note that all my wealth and enjoyments were the outcome of the gifts of her who protected me with grace. Though in my previous birth a monkey, this change of form is due to the gifts of Śāyalaṉ's wife."

'The pious men of that city who heard these good and 192-199
wise words of the Cāraṇar and regarded them as God's very words, men of penance in that region, the Śāvakas leading the life of virtuous householders, the Eṭṭi and his wife who gave away gifts (*dāna*)—all of them went to the last world of unending bliss.

'Now that you have heard this account, accompany this lady (Kaṇṇaki) with the flower-decked hair, without wasting any more time.'

When Kavundi said this, Mādari became glad at heart. 200-206
She praised the saint and took leave of her at the time when the sun was setting. Beside wise Kaṇṇaki, with beautiful, tender breasts, with shoulders resembling the bent-bamboo, and with sprouting white teeth she passed along, hearing cows bellow aloud in search of their calves. They soon found themselves in the midst of cowherds bearing on their shoulders, lambs, axes and poles with *uṟi*,[2] and cowherdesses with shining bracelets.

[1] Benares in the Madhyadēśa. The geographical limits of ancient Madhyadēśa have hardly been settled satisfactorily. Madhyadēśa is frequently mentioned in Vēdic and epic literature as well as in Buddhist literature. Manu makes Prayāg the eastern boundary of the region and by this he seems to exclude the region of Kāśi from the Madhyadēśa. But Kāśi is a part of it according to the authority of the *Kāvyamīmāmsā*. This agrees also with the statement in the *Śilappadikāram*.

[2] A brief description of cowherds and their womenfolk returning home after nightfall.

207–216 The cowherdess Mādari entered her house with her refugee, after passing through the gateway—with the daily flag flying thereon[1]—of the fortress walls encircled by a forest of defence and a moat, surmounted by a mechanical bow with self-projecting (arrows),[2] a clutching machine[3] with its black claws, slings, shooting stones, boiling oils, cauldrons for smelting copper, furnaces for smelting iron, baskets of stones (for throwing), hooks,[4] chains,[5] traps shaped like *āndalai* birds,[6] iron arms,[7] sharp poles,[8] bundles of arrows and of nails, fearful beams, needles to be thrust into the fingers (of enemies), the kingfisher machine which would pluck out the eyes (of the enemy), pig-shaped implements,[9] bamboo-like machines,[10] heavy weighted bolts,[11] wooden bars thrust across the entrance, clubs, missiles, lances, and many more such things.[12]

[1] The flag celebrating daily victory. The interpretation is appropriate in the light of the *Maduraikkāñji*, l. 368.

[2] Lines 207-16 have been quoted by the celebrated commentator Parimēlaḻagar in commenting on the *Kuraḷveṇbā* 743. Here is a detailed description of defences in the fortification.

[3] The machine would clutch, like a monkey, those who touched it.

[4] Hooks were to pull up people scaling fortress walls.

[5] Chains were used for strangling.

[6] Traps which would fly like the bird *āndalai* and peck forcibly at the crown of the head. This bird is said to possess a manlike head. (See *Kalinga.*, 'Kōil', l. 16.)

[7] Iron rods for throwing enemies into the moat if they attempted to cross it.

[8] These were poles with pointed heads upon which the enemy was transfixed and pulled downwards so as to rend his body into two halves.

[9] These were of iron whose spikes would tear out the bowels of an enemy.

[10] These were fastened with iron rods to beat enemies with.

[11] The mechanism by which these bolts would drop suddenly on the heads of persons who attempted to open the doorways.

[12] This suggests that the abovementioned devices did not exhaust the defences of the fort.

CANTO XVI

KOLAIKKAḶAKKĀDAI

OR

THE PLACE OF EXECUTION

THE cowherdess (Mādari) who delightedly took the 1–7
precious damsel (Kaṇṇaki) under her protection, left her to the other cowherdesses with excellent bangles, in a secure cottage,[1] beautified with red mud, which had a cool courtyard in front, separated from the hedge-encircled residential quarters[2] of the cowherds who sold buttermilk.

After giving her a refreshing bath, Mādari addressed 8–17
her in words of praise thus: 'O you, who have come here with beauty unadorned, as if to destroy the made-up beauty[3] of Madura ladies decorated with costly and glittering jewels of gold, take my daughter Aiyai, as your personal attendant. I shall keep watch over you, O girl with the fragrant locks of hair, as keenly as I would over gold.[4] O lady, live here with me.' She continued: 'The lady of great penance (Kavundi) has cured[5] you of the fatigue of your journey and brought you to a faultless place; have you any more anxiety for your husband?'[6]

[1] Apparently it was the guest-house of the cowherd community. The courtyard in front perhaps resembled those invariably found in front of the houses recently excavated in the Indus valley.

[2] A description of the residential quarters of the cowherds, their architecture and outward appearance. The simple life of these people is portrayed. Cf. *Perumpāṇā.*, l. 163; *Kalittogai*, st. 104; *Aham.*, st. 394.

[3] A contrast between the natural beauty of Kaṇṇaki and the made-up beauty of Madura women.

[4] The importance and value of gold are emphasized elsewhere also (see *Ācāra*, st. 99).

[5] Spiritual cure is implied.

[6] The word for husband in the text is *makaṉ*, a rare use of the term in this sense. See *Maṇi.*, canto xxi, l. 29.

18–28 Turning to her maidens she said: 'Since this lord (Kōvalan̲) observes the vows of the Śāvakas,[1] get ready without delay the good vessels needed by Kaṇṇaki to cook the daily meal with the aid of her husband's sister.'[2] At this the cowherdesses offered unused cooking-vessels as befitting wealthy people and some almost ripe, round jack-fruits that never flower,[3] white-striped cucumbers, green pomegranates, mangoes, sweet plantains, rice of the first quality, and milk from their own cows,[4] saying: 'Lady of the round bracelets, please receive these.'

29–39 When Kaṇṇaki had cut the different green vegetables with a curved knife, her tender fingers became reddened, her face perspired, her superb eyes became bloodshot; and she turned aside from the smoking oven. Then with the aid of the fire of straw lit by Aiyai, Kaṇṇaki cooked to the best of her ability for her husband. When that lord had seated himself on a small mat dexterously made from the white leaves of the palmyra tree by a trained maid,[5] with her flower-like hands she sprinkled water from an earthen-pot over the feet of her lord.[6]

40–53 Then as if to remove the unconsciousness of Mother

[1] Aḍiyārkkunallār makes Kōvalan̲ a Jain and interprets the passage in the light of the Jaina custom of not eating after nightfall. It may be a reference to the daily meal.

[2] The reference is to Aiyai whom Kaṇṇaki treats as though she were Kōvalan̲'s sister.

[3] *Kōḷippākal* is still eaten in Madura.

[4] This list of the food of the *Āyar* community indicates their standard of living. The inference is that they were vegetarians.

[5] These are some of the Vaiśya practices and conventions before taking food. Cf. *Tolk.*, 'Marap.', *sūtra* 85. The earth is cleaned by sprinkling it with water so that the surface may be even and will not injure the leaf on which the meal is served. The plantain-leaf, then, as today, served this purpose. It may be noted that the *āsana* or seat was made not of wood but of grass.

[6] It was then a practice, as is still observed among certain communities, to wash the feet before going to meals. Here it is not clear whether Kaṇṇaki removed the water from Kōvalan̲'s feet consequent on his washing, or whether she poured water on his feet and then sprinkled it on her face as an act of purification. Relics of these practices still linger in this country.

Earth, she sprinkled water on the ground and making it smooth with her palms, spread a tender plantain leaf and said : 'Here is food, O Lord ! Please eat.' When everything prescribed for those born in the Vaiśya caste had been performed as well as possible,[1] Aiyai and her mother looked at them with pleased eyes and said : 'Is this lord who eats good food Kṛṣṇa[2] with the colour of the newly-opened *kāya* flower, nursed by Aśōdai[3] in the village of cowherds? Is this lady with many shoulder-bracelets the brightest lamp (Piṉṉai) of our community, who gave succour to the Lord of the blue gem, on the banks of the river Yamunā?[4] Our eyes are not (keen) enough to see this splendid sight.'

To great Kōvalaṉ who was sitting fully satisfied 54–70
after his meal, were offered tender betel leaves and nuts[5] by (Kaṇṇaki) of the black tresses. He said to her : 'Come' and clasping her, continued : 'Doubting whether these tender feet of thine would have strength enough to walk over the tracts covered with gravel and stone, and taking pity on us for having crossed these painful deserts, how miserable will our aged parents[6] feel? Is this (our

[1] 'As well as possible' is used by the poet advisedly. It implies that Kōvalaṉ could not attend to all his daily religious duties as thoroughly and punctually in a foreign place as he could in his own home.

[2] Kōvalaṉ and Kaṇṇaki are compared to Kṛṣṇa and Nappiṉṉai, the cowherdess whom Kṛṣṇa took in wedlock. Here is a hard fact proving the antiquity of the Kṛṣṇa cult, well known in the early centuries of the Christian era.

[3] Yaśōdā (Tamil, Aśōdai) is the wife of Nanda and foster-mother of Kṛṣṇa, the family god of cowherds. (See *Bhāga. Pur.*, Bk. X, ch. 9, st.,14-20.)

[4] The Yamunā is the river where Kṛṣṇa sported with the cowherdesses. This is a reference to the aquatics (*jalakrīḍa*) indulged in by Kṛṣṇa in the course of his *rāsakrīḍa* (ibid., ch. 30-34) : see also *Viṣṇu Purāṇa*, Bk. V, ch. 13.

[5] Note the reference to the use of betels and nuts after food. The reader may profitably compare this with ll. 240-3 of canto xxviii of the *Maṇimēkalai*, where Maṇimēkalai entertains Aṟavaṇaḍigaḷ to dinner. This proves that even Bhikṣus took betels, a custom forbidden by Hindu law; also that camphor took the place of *chuṇām*. Cf. *Jātakas*, Vol. I, pp. 132 and 152. See also *Tolk.*, 'Etai', *sūtra* 36, commentary by Iḷampūraṇar.

[6] The expression *yemmudukuravar* in this line means 'our parents' and consequently the reference is to the parents of both Kaṇṇaki and Kōvalaṉ.

present condition) illusion? Is it due to cruel fate?[1] My mind is so confused that I know nothing. O is there hope for one who has wasted his days in the company of useless men and debauchees, among groups of scandal-mongers indulging in boisterous laughter, ever hankering after sinful deeds, neglecting the good words spoken by wise men? I have not been dutiful to my aged parents. I have also disgraced thee who art young in years, but old in wisdom. I never thought that I was doing wrong. Even though I asked thee not to leave our great city for this place,[2] thou camest with me. What a thing thou didst!

71–83 Kaṇṇaki rejoined: 'Though I could not give charity to observers of *dharma*,[3] or honour Brahmanas, receive saints and ascetics, or entertain guests as befits our great family, I hid from your revered mother and your highly reputed and honourable father, much esteemed by the king, my sorrow at not having you before me; but they knew it and were full of affection for me and spoke loving words. In spite of my pretended smile, my emaciated body made them know my inner anxiety at which they were highly grieved. Though you deviated from the right path, because I kept to the path of rectitude, I volunteered to come along with you.'

84–93 Kōvalaṉ said: 'O thou who hast given up they parents and relations, menial servants, nurse-maids[4] and female-attendants, and taken as thy great aids modesty, credulity,

[1] Cf. *Kuraḷveṇbā* 1311.

[2] The reference is to Puhār and Madura.

[3] The duties of a true householder are given. Cf. *Kuṛaḷ*, ch. 8. Parimēlaḻagar quotes ll. 71-3 in his commentary. It may be noted in passing that these duties correspond to the injunctions of Hindu law. Chaste women could not give charity in the absence of their husbands.

[4] *Aṭiyōr-pāṅku*. Five are distinguished: one who plays with a child, one who feeds it, one who lulls it to sleep, one who teaches it to speak, and its foster-mother. See *Jīvakacintāmaṇi*, st. 363 and commentary.

good conduct, and chastity,[1] hast rid me of my troubles by accompanying me.

'O purest gold, creeper, girl with fragrant curls of hair!

'O embodiment of modesty, light of the vast world!

'O tender offshoot of chastity, storehouse of virtues!

'I shall go with one of the anklets that adorn thy beautiful feet and return after exchanging it for money. Till then do not lose heart.'

Closely embracing his lady-love of the long black eyes, 94–104
feeling much for her being lonely and without relations, and restraining the tears rising in his eyes because of his mental anxiety, he left the home of the cowherds and wearily walked along the street, without knowing —because his caste men were not aware of it— that the humped bull[2] coming in front of him indicated a bad omen, passed beyond the *tāterumaṉṟam*; then passing through the streets of courtesans, he reached the bazaar.
There he saw a goldsmith who with a coat on, was walk- 105–112
ing at some distance,[3] pincers in hand, followed by a hundred goldsmiths famous for their delicate workmanship and exquisite handiwork in jewellery;[4] and thinking within himself that this must be the state goldsmith[5] of the much-celebrated Pāṇḍyan, Kōvalaṉ asked him, 'Can you please estimate the price of an ornament for an ankle, suitable for the queen of the protecting king?'

[1] These four attributes took the place of parents, maidservants, companions and associates. The *Pingalandai Nighaṇṭu* speaks of *nārguṇam* as four masculine qualities and four feminine qualities.

[2] Superstition of the *Āyar* in observing bad and good omens. What was a superstition for one community was not for another. Vaiśyas did not consider a humped bull coming in front a bad omen, but cowherds did.

[3] Arumpadavuraiāśiriyar remarks, that being a member of a low caste, he kept himself at a respectable distance from the members of higher castes. But the expression may be interpreted as referring to the particular gait of the goldsmith which distinguished him from others of his class.

[4] *Kaṇṇūlviṉaiñar* and *nuṇviṉaikkollar* are interpreted by Aḍiyārkkunallār as skilled in 'melting gold' and 'making beautiful jewels'.

[5] The office of state goldsmith was an institution in ancient India. See *Kaut. Artha.*, Bk. II, § 13.

113-124 The goldsmith who resembled Yama's messenger replied (as if) reverentially, 'Though I am ignorant about that,[1] I can make crowns and other ornaments required by kings.' Thereupon Kōvalaṉ opened the bundle which contained the invaluable anklet. The goldsmith, a habitual liar, minutely examined the workmanship of the artistic anklet, embossed with shining gold and containing inside the best rubies and diamonds carved with serried depressions, and said, 'This anklet can be demanded by none other than the great queen (Kōpperundēvi). I shall go now and inform the victorious king about this. Till I return, please stay here near my little hut.'

125-130 Then Kōvalaṉ went to the *dēvakōṭṭam*[2] near that lowly man's house, and when he had entered a small chamber, the hard-hearted thief (goldsmith) said to himself, 'Before the fact of my having stolen the anklet is publicly known,[3] I will accuse this stranger from another land of the theft to the king', and walked on (to the palace).

131-138 There the great queen imagining that the king's heart had been won by the graceful appearance of the Madura dancing-girls who sang different songs, and displayed the wealth of their instrumental music in their dances, hid her jealousy in a love-quarrel, and feigning a headache left him. When his ministers and councillors[4] went away, the king repaired to the great queen's chamber attended by female servants with long glowing eyes.

139-147 The goldsmith who saw the king at the last entrance of the guarded gateway prostrated himself before him, and praising him in several ways, said: 'The thief who used

[1] Note the dishonesty of the goldsmith, and the price he pays for it in the end.

[2] *Dēvakōṭṭam* may refer to a small shrine erected in front of the goldsmith's shop.

[3] From this it would appear that the goldsmith had very recently robbed the queen of her anklet, and this fact was not yet known to the public.

[4] The term used in the text is *mantiraššuṟṟam*.

neither crow-bar nor auger,[1] but relied on the strength of sleep-giving incantations to put to sleep the watchmen at the gate before stealing the palace anklet,[2] is now staying in my lowly little hut hiding himself from the watchmen of this bustling city.'

Because that was the moment of the ripening of past 148–153
karmā, the wearer of the garland of margosa[3] flowers (the king) without any inquiry, sent for the city watchmen and ordered: 'Now, if you find the foot-ornament of my consort resembling the flower-garland in the possession of an expert thief, kill him,[4] and bring the anklet here.'

At this command of the king, the villainous goldsmith, 154–163
glad at heart, said to himself, 'I have achieved what I wished,' and approaching Kōvalaṉ, whose cruel fate had enmeshed him in its close net, said (pointing to the men), 'These have come here to see the anklet at the bidding of the king, possessor of the victorious army'. This false goldsmith convincingly explained to them all the things relating to the workmanship of the anklet. But the valiant (executioners) observed: 'The appearance and features of this man do not show him to be deserving of execution.'[5]

The wily goldsmith smiled scornfully at them, and set 164–173
forth his reasons:[6] '*Mantra*, *daiva*, drugs, omen, trickery, place, time and instrument are the eight aids employed by low persons pursuing the ignoble profession of thieves. If you are deceived by this man's drugs, you will expose

[1] Crowbars and boring sticks were some of the instruments of robbers. Note also the belief in incantations.

[2] *Kōil* is a technical term for the palace.

[3] The Pāṇḍyan king wore a margosa garland.

[4] This is a case of punishment without judicial trial, contrary to the accepted practice. This was resorted to by the king in order to reconcile his queen.

[5] The first impression of the executioners was that Kōvalaṉ was innocent.

[6] The eight aids employed by a thief. Dr Swaminatha Aiyar shows in a footnote that *kaḷavunūl* (the science of theft) was the *stēyaśāstra* attributed to Karṇīsuta, the teacher of Kaca.

yourselves to the great wrath of our renowned king. If thieves utter a *mantra* and meditate upon it, they can become invisible like the sons of gods.[1]

174–182 'If they perform the feat of making gods appear before them, they can show in their hands the stolen objects and yet walk safely away. By stupefying us with their drugs they can make us sit still in the same place. Unless a good omen presents itself they do not steal, however valuable a thing, even if it easily falls into their hands. If they resort to magic,[2] they can deprive even Indra of the garland on his breast.

183–189 'If they decide upon the place whence they will to steal a particular object, who could discover them at that place? If they decide upon the time and get possession of the object, even the gods could not deprive them of it. If they steal valuables by employing their tools, who, in this wide world, could find them out? To them, there is neither day nor night. If you would listen to the science of theft,[3] there is no end to it.

190–201 'Once, a certain thief stayed at the palace gate like an ambassador (all the day) and when it grew dark, disguised as a woman, he entered without any hesitation, in the shadow cast by the lamp, and in an instant removed the garland of diamonds sparkling like the sun's rays[4] from the Crown Prince.[5] The awakened (prince) found it

[1] The term in the text *Indirakumarar*, literally means sons of Indra. Aḍiyārkkunallār interprets *Indirar* as *dēvar*. Therefore the expression may mean sons of gods. The commentator points to another interpretation: *Antarakumarar*.

[2] *Tantira-karaṇam*, in the text refers to one of the eight aids mentioned in the work. According to the *Arumpadavurai*, it is a reference to *Karavaṭa-śāstram* itself.

[3] The reference here is certainly to *Karavaṭanūl* (*Karaviṭam*) or *Karvaṭa* by Mūladēva. Can it be a reference to the *Kharapaṭṭa* of Kauṭalya? See T. Ganapati Sastri's edition of the *Arthaśāstra*, Vol. II, p. 156, ll. 5-6; also J. J. Meyer, *Das Altındische Buch*, p. 953.

[4] The implication is that the brilliance of the diamonds was such that they served as the light with which the thief was able to remove them.

[5] The reigning Pāṇḍyan king was Neḍuñjeḻiyaṉ. His younger brother's garland was stolen by a skilled thief.

missing from his shoulders and drew his sword from its sheath, which the thief clasped and warded off all the blows with it. Tired of this, the prince attempted a hand-to-hand fight, but the thief, expert in his science, escaped after making the prince attack a jewelled pillar. If anyone of you has seen him, show him to us. Is there any on this earth who is equal to this thief?'

Among those who heard this murderous goldsmith, a young executioner with a lance in his hands spoke: 'Once on a dark night in the middle of the rainy season, when all the village was deep in sleep there appeared a thief,[1] with a chisel used for splitting the earth, clothed in blue robes, desirous of jewels, fierce like a tiger. I unsheathed my sword, but he plucked it from my hands and could not afterwards be seen anywhere. Rare indeed are the deeds of thieves. Failure to carry out the king's orders will cause trouble to us. O men of martial valour, say what is to be done.' 202–211

At this, an unlettered person, in a fit of drunkenness, hurled his well-polished sword from his hand (upon Kōvalaṉ), cutting him across. The blood that gushed forth from the wound spread over Mother Earth, who felt extreme agony. Vanquished by his pre-destined fate, Kōvalaṉ fell, causing the Pāṇḍyan sceptre to become crooked. 212–217

NĒRISAI VEṆBĀ

Because of the injustice done to Kaṇṇaki's husband, the never-crooked sceptre of the Pāṇḍyan, became crooked,—a result of pre-ordained fate. Good and bad actions yield their results unfailingly. Therefore always perform righteous deeds.

[1] See *Maduraikkāñji*, ll. 639-42. Another instance of a thief and thieving is furnished.

Canto XVII

ĀCCIYARKURAVAI

OR

THE DANCE OF THE COWHERDESSES

1—10 'The morning drum will soon be heard in the palace of the Pāṇḍyan, famous for his garlanded white umbrella. He is acknowledged ruler of the whole earth by all the kings of Jambūdvīpa, with its cool groves, and even by the Cōḷa and Cēra who have carved their Tiger[1] and Bow[2] marks side by side with the Fish[3] carved by the Pāṇḍyan himself on the Himalayan crests. It is our turn to supply ghee,' said the elderly lady (Mādari)[4] calling to her daughter Aiyai, who came out with the churning stick and rope.

URAIPPĀṬṬUMAḌAI

Then she said:

'Alas! The milk in the pot has not curdled. The beautiful eyes of the big humped bulls are full of tears; some calamity is happening.

'The fragrant butter in the *uṟi*[5] does not melt. The lambs do not frisk about; some calamity is happening.

[1] The emblem of the Cōḷa monarch.

[2] The ensign of the Cēra.

[3] The emblem of the Pāṇḍya monarch. This shows that all the three Tamil kings led Himalayan expeditions.

[4] The cowherds evidently supplied the palace with ghee by turn. A similar custom is referred to in the *Viṣṇu Purāṇa*, Bk. V, ch 15, st. 22. It appears that Kamsā, king of Mathurā, was supplied with milk and ghee by the cowherds of the Vraja or Gōkula. In sending Akrūra to fetch Kṛṣṇa and his brother Rāma, Kamsā asked Akrūra to tell the cowherds to speed up the supply of milk and ghee to the palace.

[5] A pot suspended in a network of rope or iron.

'Herds of cows with their four-nippled udders are shuddering and bellowing in fear; the big bells (tied to their necks) fall down. O! Some calamity is happening.'[1]

THAT WHICH IS PROGNOSTICATIVE (KARUPPAM)

The milk in the pot not curdling, the beautiful eyes of the humped bulls being filled with tears, the butter in the *uṟi* not melting, the lambs lying without frisking, and the big bells falling down to the earth—all these signs portend some coming evil. Looking at her daughter she (Mādari) said: 'Do not feel perturbed. To alleviate the grief of our cattle, we shall dance the *kuravai*,[2] in the presence of Kaṇṇaki, that jewel among the damsels of the earth. Among the many boyhood games[3] played by Māyavaṉ and his elder brother Balarāma in the *erumaṉṟam* of the *Āyar-pāḍi*,[4] the *kuravai* was one. It was played by Māyavaṉ with Piṉṉai of the long lance-like eyes.

[1] The evil portents which point to an impending calamity according to the belief of the cowherds.

[2] After enumerating again the evil portents, the cowherdess told her daughter the remedy to avert the impending calamity. The remedy was *kuravai* (*rāsakrīḍa*) the origin of which is traced back to Lord Kṛṣṇa and his spouse Nappiṉṉai. In commenting on the term *rāsa* occurring in *Viṣṇu Purāṇa*, (Bk. V, ch. 13, pp. 33[illegible]-5), H. H. Wilson, the translator, notes the following. 'The *rāsa* dance is a dance in which men and women hold each other's hands and go round in a circle, singing airs varying in melody and tune.' According to Bharata the number of persons should not exceed sixty-four. There is a reference to the *rāsamaṇḍala* in the *Brahmavaivartta Purāṇa* where Rādhā is accompanied by thirty-six Gōpis, each of the latter being attended by many inferior personages. In the *Brahmavaivartta* the *maṇḍala* is not a ring of dancers but a circle of definite space within which Kṛṣṇa, Rādhā, and the Gōpis diverted themselves.

[3] Here is a distinct reference to a number of dramatic performances by the boy Kṛṣṇa with Balarāma and Nappiṉṉai. The *kuravai* was one such performance. The term *nāṭakam* cannot be taken in its absolute sense as a dramatic composition.

[4] *Āyar-pāḍi* = the quarters of the cowherds; *Gōkulam* is perhaps its Sanskrit equivalent. *Erumaṉṟam* or *Tāterumaṉṟam* is the public place of the *Āyar*. It was an open courtyard with a raised platform.

REHEARSAL (KOḶU)[1]

1. 'This sweet lady with the garland of flowers loves him who can jump upon the black bull undaunted by its rage,' she said, pointing to a certain damsel.

2. 'The shoulders of this girl with golden bracelets become the possession of him, who can suppress the bull with red spots[2] on its forehead.

3. 'This girl with her beautiful hair decked with jasmine flowers is the recognized bride for him who can mount that strong young bull.

4. 'The shoulders of this creeper-like damsel will be owned by him who can crush the bull with the small white spots.

5. 'The soft breasts of this creeper-like girl are the possession of him who can overcome the bull with the golden spots.

6. 'This damsel with her beauteous hair decked with *koṉṟai* flowers, becomes the wife of him who can mount that victorious young bull.

7. 'This girl resembling burgeoning flowers will be of right his, who can control the milk-white bull.'

[1] It was a custom in the cowherd community for young girls, until they were married, to select their own bulls from the common stall, and to tend them. The bulls would then be let loose, and whichever young cowherd could successfully bring the beast under control in an open contest, was deemed the proper life-partner for the girl. Apparently it was one of the ancient wedding customs among the *Āyar*. This custom also can be traced to their family deity Kṛṣṇa, who, tradition affirms, curbed the fury of seven bulls coloured black, white, and brown, and married the girls who were tending them. The Āḻvārs, who flourished several centuries after the composition of the *Silappadikāram*, also attribute this incident to Kṛṣṇa. (See Dikshitar's article on 'Kṛṣṇa in Tamil Literature' in *Indian Culture*, Vol. IV, No. 3, Calcutta, 1937.) One can see a remnant of this institution surviving today in the form of mimic shows on the *Māṭṭu-Pongal* day following *Pongal* festival every year, in the middle of January. Selected bulls are let loose in the villages with new towels and other things tied to their necks or horns. Many people of all castes come from neighbouring villages and take part in the contest to bring the animal under control. But now it has lost all connexion with marriage.

[2] Cf. *Kalittogai*, 'Mullai', ch. 4, st. 65 in this connexion. The expression used is *neṟṟiccivalai*.

STRINGENDO (EḌUTTUKKAṬṬU)[1]

(Then the elderly Mādari proceeded to allocate their places in the dance) saying to her daughter that these seven young damsels had selected seven bulls from the cattle stall and nourished them.

She made them stand in the traditional order (according to the arrangement of the seven strings in the *yāḻ*) and gave them names appropriate to their acting.[2] Beginning from the western end, the regular places (of these girls) were *kural*, *tuttam*, *kaikkiḷai*, *uḻai*, *iḷi*, *viḷari* and *tāram*. These are the names which were given by the fragrant haired lady (Mādari).

She (who stood at the place) of the *kural* was named Māyavaṉ. She (who stood at the place) of *iḷi* was called (by the name of) the victorious Balarāma. She (who stood at the place) of *tuttam* represented the cowherdess Piṉṉai. The others were named in the order described above.[3]

Piṉṉai and *tāram* were then joined to Māyavaṉ; *uḻai* and *viḷari* joined the white Balarāma. *Kaikkiḷai* stood to the left of Piṉṉai. The good *viḷari* stood to the right of *tāram* (*muttai*, also *mundai*).

Among them,

She who garlanded Māyavaṉ with the luxurious *tulasi* garland, would perform the faultless *kuravai* dance. Is Piṉṉai of bangled arms so beautiful that He who had won

[1] The seven girls selected for the *kuravai* dance were those who tended bulls in their cattle-stalls for the sake of getting suitable husbands. The song sung stated who was for whom. In this particular performance the seven maidens represented the seven strings of the *yāḻ* in their order and were named after each respective string.

[2] This is called *vaṭṭappālai*. For a detailed description see Abraham Pandithar's *Karuṇāmṛtasāgaram*.

[3] *Kaikkiḷai, uḻai, viḷari,* and *tāram*. High and low pitched strings are called *tāra* and *mandara*. See *Viṣṇu Purāṇa*, Bk. V, ch.13, st. 6.

great reputation by measuring the universe, would not look at Lakṣmī dwelling in his own breast? Ha! Ha!

So said Mādari (in great glee).

THE DANCE (KŪTTUḶPAḌUTAL)

They then[1] stood evenly in the form of a circle, and clasping their fingers in the *karkaṭaka* pose,[2] began the dance in that posture. In the beginning the girl representing the *kural* looked at her neighbour the *tuttam* and said, 'We shall sing with the sweet *paṉ* called *mullai*, in honour of Him who broke the *kurunda*[3] tree in an extensive upland (of the Gōkula).'

Thus saying, (the damsel representing) the *kural* began to sing in a low tone, (the damsel representing) the *iḷi* to sing in a level tone, and (the damsel representing) the *tuttam* to sing in a high tone. The low singer representing *viḷari* in her low pitch followed the tone of her ally representing the *tuttam*.

THE SONG (PĀṬṬU)

1. O friend! If Māyavaṉ (Lord Kṛṣṇa), who used a calf as a stick to knock down (*vila*) fruits,[4] comes here among our cattle, shall we not hear Him playing on his fine *koṉṟai* flute?[5]

2. O friend! If Māyavaṉ, who churned the ocean with a serpent as his rope, comes here among our cattle, shall we not hear Him playing on his fine *āmbal* flute?

[1] What follows is a description of the actual dance.

[2] The *karkaṭaka* pose was made by each dancer bending her middle finger and ring finger in front, and joining the other two with the respective two fingers of the maid next to her, and so on, the big finger being excepted. In that posture each pair of clasped hands resembled a crab (*karkaṭa*).

[3] The *kurunda* tree is a species of wild lime (*Atalantia*). This was one of the heroic exploits attributed to Kṛṣṇa. It is said that a demon stood in the form of a tree to deceive and kill Kṛṣṇa. This was perceived by the god who killed the demon by uprooting the tree.

[4] *Bālakrīḍa* of Kṛṣṇa, Cf. *Bhāga. Pur.*, Bk. X, ch. 18, st. 12-15.

[5] *Koṉṟai*, *āmbal* and *mullai* are referred to. Five kinds of flutes are said to have been in existence.

3. O friend! If Māyavaṉ, who broke the *kurunda* tree[1] in our extensive uplands comes during the day among our cattle, shall we not hear him playing on his fine *mullai* flute?

We shall sing of the charming beauty of Piṉṉai as she danced with her husband on the banks of the Yamunā.[2]

1. 'How can we describe the form of Him who hid the clothes of the slender-waisted lady[3] whose figure was bent to the point of breaking? Or how can we describe the face of the handsome lady who was (visibly) touched by the regretful look of Him who hid her clothes?[4]

2. 'How can we describe the perfection of her who stole the heart of her husband, who deceived all in the water-sports of the Yamunā? How can we describe the form of Him who stole away the charm and the bangles of her, who had captivated him?

3. 'How can we describe the face of the lady who hid it in her hands when she lost her clothes and bangles? Or how can we describe the beauty of him who was pained by the distress of her who hid her face in her hands?'

SONGS WITH THE SINGLE TĀḶAM OR TIME-BEAT (OṈṞAṈ-PAKUTI)

With fragrant flower-buds in her locks of hair, Piṉṉai, has, to her left, the sea-coloured god who hid the sun with his discus;[5] and to her right, his elder brother whose body is white like the moon. Among her (Piṉṉai's)

[1] Cf. the *Bhāga. Pur.*, Bk. X, ch. 30-34.

[2] Tamil, *Toḷuṉai.*

[3] The poet makes out that Kṛṣṇa hid the clothes of Piṉṉai but felt sorry when he noticed a change of colour in her face. Noticing his feeling for her, Piṉṉai also was troubled.

[4] The plain meaning is that the great dissembler Kṛṣṇa deceived all the world; but Piṉṉai deceived him by stealing his heart. The term *niṟai* may mean either beauty or chastity.

[5] The reference is to the legend of Kṛṣṇa having hid the sun with His discus.

choristers is the Vēdic bard Nārada[1] who keeps correct time to her strains by playing upon the first string.

Our Piṉṉai, with the nape of her neck bent, stood on the right of Māyavaṉ bright as the neck of a peacock, and on the left of his elder brother whose body was white as a flower-stalk. He who plays upon the first string, beating time to her strain, is Nārada, the foremost chorister.

IN PRAISE OF THE DANCERS (ĀḌUNARPPUKAḶDAL)

O splendid was the *kuravai* dance praised by Aśōdai and danced in the *tāterumaṉṟam* by Māyavaṉ,[2] his elder brother, and Piṉṉai of the striped bracelet, which disarranged the flower wreaths on the curly heads of the young cowherdesses, who with measured tread were beating time[3] with their bangled hands.

'O friends!'

Mādari said. 'All of us shall sing the song of *uḷvari* and praise the god, riding upon the Grauḍa bird. Let us praise him!'

THE SONG OF *UḶVARI* (UḶVARIVĀḶTTU)

1. On the breast of the Pāṇḍyan king[4] can be seen a garland painted with Podiyil sandal-paste,[5] a string

[1] During the dance of Kṛṣṇa and Balarāma it is said that sage Nārada, the first *vīṇa* master of the world, was beating time. He was a Vēdic bard in the sense that a *Sikṣā* is attributed to him. There is now extant the *Nārada-Sikṣā*, a treatise on Vēdic music (published in the Benares Chaukhamba Sanskrit Series). The idea is that the girl who represented Nārada, followed Piṉṉai in her song and dance.

[2] Māyavaṉ can be translated literally as the Great Dissembler.

[3] The plain meaning runs thus: 'To the movement of the feet of the principal figures Kṛṣṇa, Balarāma and Piṇṇai, the cowherdesses beat time during the dance. By so doing these maidens became wearied in the performance, but not the chief dancers.'

[4] Note that the poet, who was a Cēra prince, gives prominence to the Pāṇḍya and Cōḷa and relegates his own king to third place, demonstrating that he is impartial in his treatment of the subject. The place of honour given to the Pāṇḍyan may also be due to the fact that the poet is now dealing with the 'Maduraikkāṇḍam'.

[5] This means that sandal-paste was painted on his breast to look like a garland.

garland of pearls, and a jewelled garland of the king of gods.

It is said that he who wears the garland of the king of gods[1] is He who tended the cattle in the Gōkulam (adjoining) the flourishing Dvārakā,[2] and rent asunder the *kurunda* tree[3].

2. King Vaḷavaṉ (the Cōḷa)[4] the ruler of fortified Puhār carved the Tiger on the golden crests of the Himalayas and ruled the earth.

It is said that king Vaḷavaṉ, the ruler of fortified Puhār, holds a golden discus[5] as a weapon of war.

3. The Cēra, king of kings, and the ruler of flourishing Vañji, crossed the ocean and destroyed the never-ageing *kaḍamba* tree.[6]

It is said of this Cēra, king of kings, and ruler of flourishing Vañji,[7] that he is Viṣṇu himself who swung His hill-like shoulders and churned the ocean.[8]

[1] For the legend see *Tiruviḷaiyāḍal Purāṇam*, §44.

[2] Dvārakā was the capital of the ancient Yādava kingdom, over which Kṛṣṇa ruled. It may be noted that Mathurā was originally the capital, and it was under Kṛṣṇa's guidance that the transference of the capital was effected. See *Viṣṇu Purāṇa*, Bk. V, ch. 23.

[3] This and the following two stanzas represent the three kings as Viṣṇu and thus attribute divinity to the ruling chieftains. The divine power of kings was accepted as a matter of course in ancient India.

[4] The reference seems to be to the famous Karikāla. See Introduction, p. 22.

[5] Viṣṇu is said to wield a discus as a weapon of war. The usual weapons attributed to him are *śankha, cakra* and *gadā*.

[6] From *Aham.*, st. 199, we see that Naṉṉaṉ was the head of the Kaḍamba clan and being powerful took possession of some Cēra territory and Nārmuḍiccēral had to discomfit him and take back the lost possessions. It also transpires that chiefs who held island kingdoms thought that they were unassailable. One such was the kingdom of the Kaḍambas. It would appear that Senguṭṭuvaṉ inflicted a crushing defeat on them and earned the title *kaḍal-piṟakōṭṭiya* (see *Padiṟṟ.*, *padikam* 4 and 5).

[7] The Cēra capital, identified with Karuvūr. *Contra* K. G. Sesha Aiyar, in the *J. I. H.*, Vol. XII, pp. 184-214, 1933. See also his *Cera Kings of the Sangam Period* (1937), ch. 5.

[8] For this legend see *Bhāga. Pur.*, Bk. VIII, ch. 5, st. 11 ff.

MUNNILAIPPARAVAL

OR

DIRECT PRAISE

1. O sea-hued god! Once, in days gone by, you churned the bowels of the sea,[1] using the northern mountain[2] for your churning stick and Vāsuki[3] for your rope. O Lord with the lotus in your navel,[4] your hands which once did churn were fastened with the churning rope of Aśōdai.[5] Is that your *māyā*?[6] O, deceptive indeed is your work!

2. O wearer of the luxurious *tulasi* garland! When the host of the Dēvas praised you reverentially as the One Supreme Being,[7] you, who could never know hunger, ate up the whole universe. Your mouth which swallowed thus (the whole universe), ate by stealth the butter from the pot in the *uṟi*.[8] Is it your *māyā*? Deceptive indeed is your work!

3. O Tirumāl! When the assembled host of Dēvas worshipped and praised you, you overstepped the three worlds[9] with your two lotus feet, to drive away darkness.[10] O Narasimha! Destroyer of enemies![11] Yet

[1] *Bhaga. Pur.*, Bk. X, ch. 9, st. 14-20.

[2] Mandaragiri. This finds mention in all *Purāṇas*.

[3] Vāsuki is the great serpent which was used as the rope in the mythical churning of the ocean.

[4] Sanskrit, Padmanābha.

[5] Yaśōdā fastened baby Kṛṣṇa with the rope as a punishment for stealing butter from other houses. (See *Viṣṇu Purāṇa.*, Bk V., ch. 6.)

[6] *Māyā* is a subtle word that means deception or illusion. It is a term of much philosophical significance.

[7] Aḍiyārkkunallār conjectures that it may be a reference to the god accepted by the followers of all the six systems of philosophy.

[8] See for this legend the *Bhāga. Pur.*, Bk. VIII, ch. 29-31.

[9] The reference is to the Trivikrama *avatār* of Viṣṇu. See *Bhāga. Pur.*, Bk. VIII, ch. 20-21. A huge figure representing the incarnation is found in the Ulakaḷandaperumāḷ-koil, Conjeevaram.

[10] In other words 'spreading divine light everywhere'.

[11] Narasimha, as an incarnation of Viṣṇu, half-man and half-lion, to kill the demon Hiraṇyakaśipu.

those feet of yours which thus overstepped, went as the messengers of the five Pāṇḍavas.[1] Is this your *māyā*? Deceptive indeed is your work!

PAṬARKKAIPPARAVAL

OR

INDIRECT PRAISE

1. Vain are the ears which do not hear the glory of the doughty champion, who measured the three worlds with His two feet and yet found them too small; who penetrated with His younger brother[2] into the wild jungle to the reddening of His lotus-feet; who pulled down in battle the *Sō* fortress,[3] and deprived ancient Lankā of its protection.[4] Vain are the ears which do not hear[5] the glory of Tirumāl.

2. Vain are the eyes which do not see the dark-hued Lord, the great God, the Māyavaṉ (Dissembler), the God in the blossomed lotus of whose navel appeared all the great worlds, and who has red eyes, red feet, red hands, and red lips.[6] Vain are the eyes of those who while looking (upon the Lord) must wink.[7]

3. Vain is the tongue that will not praise Him who triumphed over the deceit of the foolish schemer Kamsā,[8]

[1] See *Mhb.*, '*Udyōga*', ch. 90-91.

[2] Rāma's conquest of Ceylon with his brother. See the *Rāmāyaṇa*.

[3] The *Sō* fortress or the Sōṇapura of Bāṇa was pulled down and its inmates put to death. This interpretation cannot fit in here. *Sō* may mean the great and wonderful fortress and *Sō araṇ* is an attribute of the citadel of Lankā.

[4] Rāma's conquest of Ceylon with his brother. See the *Rāmāyaṇa*, 'Yuddha'.

[5] This is the *Harikathāśravaṇam* so much stressed in the *Bhāga. Pur.*

[6] His form was dark except for his eyes, feet, hands, and lips which were reddish.

[7] Winking eyes are the eyes of ordinary mortals. Thus this sight can be enjoyed only by gods whose eyes are said not to wink.

[8] For the many villainous deeds of Kamsā, see the *Bhāga. Pur.*, Bk. X, ch. 36; also the *Viṣṇu Purāṇa*, Bk. V, ch. 20.

and who went as the messenger of the five Pāṇḍavas to the Hundred (Kauravas), praised (by the Dēvas) in all four directions, to the accompaniment of Vēdic chanting.[1] Vain is the tongue which does not say 'Nārāyaṇa'.

'May the deity celebrated in the *kuravai* dance in which we were now engaged alleviate the distress which has befallen our cattle! May the drumstick of the drum of our Pāṇḍyan with the shoulder-ornaments, who broke the crown of Indra,[2] whose weapon is the victorious thunder, strike terror among his enemies and every day proclaim his victory!'

[1] He was himself a Vēda Puruṣa and hence the Vēdas in mortal form followed Him.

[2] See the *Tiruviḷaiyāḍalpurāṇam*, § 44. It must be noted that the poet attributes the heroic exploits of an ancestor of the Pāṇḍyan king to the ruling monarch. The idea is that he belongs to a distinguished line of kings.

Canto XVIII

TUṈBAMĀLAI

OR

THE GARLAND OF SORROW

There the elderly cowherdess of dynamic charm[1] went to 1–7
bathe and to worship with flowers, incense, sandal-paste, and garlands, Neḍumāl[2] on the bank of the deep Vaigai. Towards the close of the *kuravai* dance someone[3] who had heard a cry in the city came back in haste.

She said nothing; but stood without opening her 8–10
mouth to Kaṇṇaki, who said:

'O! friend, speak, speak out. 11–15

'I do not see my husband. My mind is in a flutter. The air expelled from my lungs surpasses the air (driven into the fire) from bellows. If the air expelled from my lungs surpasses the air from bellows, will you not tell me what is being said in the city?[4] Long live you, friend!

'Even during daytime a fit of shivering[5] takes hold of 16–19
me. Not seeing my beloved, my heart is restless with grief. As my mind is restless with grief at not seeing my beloved, tell me what it is that people said. Bless you, my friend.

[1] The expression in the text is *āḍiya śāyalāḷ*. While the *Arumpadavurai* sees in *śāyalāḷ* a reference to Aiyai, Aḍiyārkkunallār interprets it as some other lady. Both do not seem to fit.

[2] Śrī Iruntavaḷamuḍaiyār or Antaravāṉattemperumāṉ. The offerings to the god consisted of flowers, sandal-paste, etc. In India the end of the most important festivals and rituals was marked by a sacred bath, the *avabhṛtasnānam* of Sanskrit literature. See *Sentamiḻ*, Vol. VIII, p. 183 f.

[3] This may refer to Aiyai or any other lady. It is here taken as a reference to Aiyai, from the fact that Kaṇṇaki addresses her as friend and companion later on. From this we have to infer that only Aiyai's mother Mādari went to the river and the temple there, while Aiyai remained at home. Or, Mādari who went to the river, heard the news and returned post-haste.

[4] *Etilār* is the term for people of the same neighbourhood.

[5] Generated by extreme fear.

20–24 'I seek your aid, friend! I do not see my lord returning. I scent some danger; my mind faints. As my mind faints at something hidden from me, I pray you, my friend, tell me, what it is that they (*eñcalār*)[1] said (in the city).

25–28 She replied:

'O! Saying that he was the thief who silently stole the glittering anklet from the palace, the king's residence—that he was the thief who silently stole—the men who wore jingling anklets executed him.'

29–33 Hearing this, Kaṇṇaki sprang up in rage and then fell down on the earth, as if the rising moon had fallen with the clouds on the wide earth.[2] She wept making her red eyes redder. She cried out, 'O! Where are you, my dear husband? Ah! Ah!', and fell down in a swoon.

(Recovering, she again continued to rave)

34–37 'Like the distressed women who keep difficult vows after their loving husbands have been burnt in fire,[3] am I to perish in misery, because I have lost my loving husband through the fault of the king censured by his subjects?

38–41 'Like the distressed women who, after losing their husbands who had worn fragrant garlands on their broad chests, go in despair to many places of pilgrimage[4] and bathe therein, am I to perish in anguish, O foolish goddess

[1] *Eñcalār* is the term for 'others', 'strangers'. The citizens of this place were strangers to Kaṇṇaki who had only arrived that day.

[2] The moon is compared to Kaṇṇaki's face and the clouds to locks of her hair.

[3] It transpires from this that cremation and not burial was customary and that widows led a life of fasting and arduous penance. They cared no more for their mortal bodies.

[4] Even today Hindu widows go on pilgrimages after the decease of their husbands to bathe in the waters of holy rivers and pools in order to obtain final salvation. Bathing in *tīrthas* and fasting are generally practised by women after the death of their husbands. It may be noted that the practice of suttee was not the rule but only the exception. We may call attention here to a statement of the *Maṇimēkalai*, canto ii, ll. 42-50, where three classes of women are distinguished.

of Dharma,[1] through the fault of the king wielding the sceptre of injustice?

'Like the afflicted women, who are ever plunged into 42–45
hard vows of widowhood after their beloved husbands have fallen a prey to the funeral fire, am I to pine away in grief, losing fame in this life also, through the wrong committed by the Pāṇḍyan, whose sceptre swerved from the righteous path?

'O! Look at me. 46–53

'Hear my words,[2] O all you good damsels of the cowherd community who have gathered here, and have with foresight, engaged yourselves in the *kuravai*![3] Hear my words! Hear, all of you cowherd girls!

'O, Lord of the hot rays![4] You who are a witness for all the deeds of this seagirt world, speak! Is my husband a thief?'

Then was heard a voice from the welkin: 'He is not a thief, O, lady of carp-like eyes! This city will be consumed by blazing flames.'

1 According to Arumpadavuraiyāśiriyar, the term *aṟam* stands here for the deity of righteousness or the Goddess of Dharma. Kaṇṇaki addresses the deity as a foolish Goddess for She was a witness of the king's injustice towards her innocent husband. This suggests the belief that Fate is more powerful than Gods, and its laws cannot be transgressed.

2 ll. 47-53 are quoted by Naccinārkkiniyar in commenting on *Tolk.*, 'Ceyyul'., *sūtra* 149.

3 Kaṇṇaki pays a tribute to the cowherdesses who anticipated a calamity and danced the *kuravai* to avert it.

4 The reference is to the Sun-god. Kaṇṇaki who had already addressed the *Dharmadēvatā* now appealed to the Sun. According to tradition the Sun is supposed to be the unfailing witness of all acts and deeds. She demanded from the Sun-god an answer to her question: 'Is my husband a thief?' The Sun immediately replied. 'No'. In ancient times the sun cult was universal. Greece and Rome took to the worship of the sun, and Plato in the *Republic* idealizes the Sun as 'the author of all light and life in the material world'. A great part of the oldest Vēdic rituals are permeated with the worship of the sun implicitly as well as explicitly. There was also the Mithraism of ancient Persia.

CANTO XIX

ŪRŚŪḶVARI

OR

THE TALK OF THE TOWN

1–8 So said the Sun. She of the sparkling armlets wasted no more time. Taking in her hands the remaining anklet she lamented: 'O women of chastity who live in this city ruled by the unjust king! Listen to this.

'I have suffered incomparable distress this evening. That which should not occur, has occurred to me. How can I endure it? See this injustice.

'Is my husband a thief? They[1] killed him, unwilling to pay the price[2] of my anklet. What injustice!

'Shall I ever see (again) my beloved husband in the company of you all, O women of great chastity? See this injustice!

9–14 'If I shall see my loving husband, shall I hear him utter the longed-for words, that he was not in the wrong? See this injustice!

'If I do not hear him say that he was not in the wrong, condemn me by saying that I did unjust things.[3] Listen to this!'

[1] According to Aḍiyārkkunallār the use of the verb in the plural shows that the responsibility for the deed did not merely rest with the king but with his ministers also. If this interpretation has any value, it bears testimony to the fact that the king could not and did not act on his own initiative but consulted and took the previous advice of his cabinet. It is not clear whether in this particular case the advice was taken. It can be presumed, however, that no such consultation was held.

[2] The implication here is that her anklet was so valuable that the king could not pay the full price for it and hence wanted to deprive her husband of it by killing him. To that extent the king alone was the thief according to Kaṇṇaki.

[3] She vows that she will make her dead husband rise up and say that he was in the right and the king was in the wrong. This is in keeping with the prescription of the *Kuṛaḷ* that chaste ladies could do and undo anything. See *Sila.* (Tamil ed.), pp. 245, 315, 555.

All the residents of the flourishing city of Madura 15–18
beheld the afflicted woman and were moved by her suffering agonies. In bewilderment they exclaimed: 'Since irremediable wrong has been done to this woman,[1] the unbending[2] and righteous sceptre of the king has been bent. What is (the meaning of) this?

'Lost is the glory of Teṉṉavaṉ, the king of kings 19–20
(Pāṇḍya), possessor of the moonlike umbrella and the spear.[3] What is (the meaning of) this?

'The sheltering umbrella of the victorious king that 21–22
had cooled the earth now generates heat. What is (the meaning of) this?

'A new, great goddess has now come before us bearing 23–26
in her hand an anklet of pure gold. What is (the meaning of) this?

'This afflicted woman, weeping from her beautiful, red, and collyrium-stained eyes, looks as one possessed of divinity. What is (the meaning of) it?'

Saying such things, the people of Madura sympathized 27–30
with her and comforted her by raising their accusing voices. Among those who caused the tumult, some showed (to Kaṇṇaki) the body of her (murdered) husband. She, the golden creeper, saw him; but her he could not see.

At that moment the red-rayed sun withdrew his fiery 31–34
rays and hid himself in the great mountain, causing the vast world to be enveloped in darkness.[4] In the brief twilight of that evening the flowery creeper-like Kaṇṇaki

[1] The sympathy of the women of Madura goes out to Kaṇṇaki. They condemn the king's action, and seem to endow her with divinity.

[2] This is an important statement as it suggests that the Pāṇḍyaṉ rule was tainted with unrighteousness for the first time. Here we may recall the words of the Brahmana Kauśikaṉ at the commencement of canto xiii in which he paid a glowing tribute to the Pāṇḍyan rule.

[3] The umbrella and the spear were symbols of grace and prowess respectively (see *Perumpāṇ.*, l. 422).

[4] The poet wants to impress upon us the idea that that sight was so horrible that even the sun shut his eyes. In other words 'the sun set and night came'.

lamented aloud and the whole city reverberated with her cry. She who in the morning had received from her embracing husband the flower-wreath worn by him and decked her tresses with it, saw him that evening in a pool of blood gushing from his wounds. But he did not see her in an agony of grief. She then mourned for him in sorrow and wrath :[1]

39–42 'O! Seeing me in deep affliction and without a word of consolation, is it fit that your body, fair as the fairest gold, should lie here in the dust? Will not people say that it was my inevitable fate[2] that made the righteous king act thus wrongly in ignorance?

42–46 'Is it just that, in this elusive twilight with none to aid me, your garlanded beautiful breast should lie on the bare ground, before me who pine in lonely grief? Will not people say that it was my pre-ordained fate which made the Pāṇḍyan commit a wrong, that the whole world proclaimed unjust?

47–50 'Is it right that you should be lying here in the dust with blood gushing from your gaping wounds, in front of me, the unfortunate one, whose eyes are brimming with unceasing tears? Though his subjects accuse the Pāṇḍyan who committed the crime, will not good people say that it is the result of my past actions?

51–53 'Are there women[3] here, are there women? Are there women who can endure such injustice done to their wedded husbands? Are there such women?

54–56 'Are there good people? Are there good people here? Are there good people who nurture and fend for children born of them? Are there good people here?

[1] Kaṇṇaki wants the people to accuse her and not the king for her misfortune.

[2] The poet repeats in a number of places his belief in past *karmā* and its results.

[3] According to Kaṇṇaki such injustice could not be perpetrated where good women, good men and gods live. In brief, she regards it as a god-forsaken place.

'Is there a god? Is there a god? Is there a god in 57–59
this Kūḍal whose king's sharp sword killed an innocent?
Is there a god?'

While she lamented in this manner, and embraced the 60–67
breast of her husband, where (once) the goddess of wealth had resided, he stood up exclaiming: 'O the full moon face has faded!' and wiped away her tears with his hands.[1]

The fair lady fell to the ground, sobbing and wailing, and clasped the feet of her revered husband with both her bangled hands. Then he arose and discarded his mortal form and departed surrounded by a host of gods, saying as he went: 'O, my dear, stay; stay here.'

She cried out then: 'Is this illusion? What else is 68–75
it? Is it a spirit that has deceived me? Where shall I go and find the truth of this? Else I will not seek for my husband till my furious wrath is appeased. I will meet the cruel king (*tīvēndaṉ*) and ask him for an explanation of his action.' So saying she arose. As she stood up, she recollected her terrible dream, and her long carp-like eyes were overflowing with tears. She stood up and remembered it.[2] Wiping away her tears she went to the front gate of the king's palace.

[1] This means that the wounded Kōvalaṉ lay in a state of unconsciousness for a long time, and smitten by a flash of consciousness, he rose up to look at her changed face for the last time, and removed her tears. He died with his last words, 'Stay here!' It is for students of psychology to explain this state of the mind of a dying man. But the poet puts it in such a way that we are moved to tears.

[2] This apparently refers to the dream which Kaṇṇaki dreamt and recounted to Dēvandi, before setting out for Madura (see canto ix, ll. 45-54).

CANTO XX

VAḶAKKURAIKĀDAI[1]

OR

THE DEMAND FOR JUSTICE

1–7 AT that time (the queen narrates her dream):[2]

'Alas! I saw, I saw (in my dream) the sceptre fall and the umbrella. The bell[3] at the palace-gate shook itself and tinkled as it quaked.

'Alas! I also saw, I saw the eight cardinal points agitated: and darkness swallowed the sun. Alas! I also saw, I saw an iridescent rainbow in the night;[4] a meteor glowing with heat fell by day. Alas!'

THAT WHICH IS PROGNOSTICATIVE

8–12 'The righteous sceptre and the white umbrella falling upside down to the hard ground; the bell at the gate of our victorious king's palace quivering and making the mind shiver with fear; the rainbow appearing in the night, the meteor falling by day; the eight cardinal points in a state of agitation; all these indicate some impending calamity. I shall inform the king of it.'

13–23 Followed then by maids decorated with sparkling and radiant jewels, some of them bearing her looking-glass and others her ornaments, and surrounded by many hunch-backs, dwarfs, mutes and other menials, some carrying new clothes, some carrying silks, some carrying betel-

[1] There is no commentary of Aḍiyārkkunallār available for this and the succeeding ten cantos.

[2] The queen who was fast asleep, woke up and recalled her dream indicative of evil portents to the State.

[3] *Kaḍaimaṇi* or the bell of justice, also called *ārāyiccimaṇi* in Tamil literature. See *Kamba-Rāmayaṇa*, 'Bāla'.

[4] A rainbow seen in the night is considered a sign of impending calamity. Or is it a reference to a comet?

boxes, some carrying paints, some carrying pastes, some carrying the musk of deer, some carrying garlands, some carrying wreaths, some carrying feather-fans, and others carrying incense. Several ladies with fragrant flowers in their hair sang praises thus: 'Long live the great queen of the Pāṇḍyan (Perundēvi)[1] protecting the vast world', and followed again by her companions and bodyguards making obeisance, and speaking in praise of her, the great queen (Kōpperundēvi) approached king Teṉṉavaṉ in whose bosom Lakṣmī ever dwells, and communicated her evil dream to him who was sitting on the lion-throne.

Just then was heard a cry: 'O, you gate-keeper![2] O, 24–29
gate-keeper! O, you gate-keeper of him who has lost his wisdom, and whose virtueless heart deviated from the path of kingly justice,[3] go tell (the king) that one who bears an anklet from a pair of tinkling anklets, and who has lost her husband, waits at the gate. O, tell him that.'

At this the gate-keeper approached the king, saying: 30–33
'Long live our lord of Koṟkai;[4] long live the lord of the southern mountain; long live Śeḻiyaṉ;[5] long live Teṉṉavaṉ; long live Pañcavaṉ, unstigmatized by calumny!

'Someone waits at the gate. She is not the deity 34–44
Koṟṟavai, the goddess of victory,[6] holding in her hand the victorious spear, and standing upon the nape of the buffalo with an unceasing gush of blood from its fresh wound. Nor is she Aṇangu (Bhadrakāḷī),[7] youngest sister of the

[1] The *Arumpadavurai* calls the queen *tambirāṭṭi*. The editor draws our attention to the fact that even today in the Malaināḍu the king and the queen go by the technical terms *tambirān* and *tambirāṭṭi*.

[2] The doorkeeper addressed by Kaṇṇaki was an official of the royal household, the *dauvārika* of Sanskrit literature.

[3] The term used in the text is *iṟaimuṟai* (Sanskrit, *rājanīti*).

[4] The quondam capital of the Pāṇḍyan kingdom.

[5] Śeḻiyaṉ, like Teṉṉavaṉ is another Pāṇḍyan title. Pañcavaṉ is yet another title.

[6] Mahiṣāsuramardanī.

[7] Piṭāri (also Cāmuṇḍī) one of the seven *lōkamātas*. (Also known as *mahā-māyā*.) The names of these mother-goddesses are mentioned in the *Purāṇas*. The *Purāṇas* also speak of the fourteen daughters of Dakṣa

seven virgins, who made Śiva dance; nor even is she the Kāḷi of the forest,[1] which is the residence of ghosts and goblins; nor again is she the goddess that tore up the mighty chest of Dāruka.[2] She appears to be filled with resentment. She seems to swell with rage. She has lost her husband; she has in her hand an anklet of gold, and she waits at the gate.'[3]

45-47 The king said: 'Let her come: bring her here!' Then the gate-keeper brought her and showed to her the monarch and she went near the ruling king, who said:

'O lady with the tear-stained face, who art thou, my young lady? What has brought thee hither before us?'

50-63 She replied:

'Inconsiderate king! I have something to say. I am a native of much celebrated Puhār, one of whose kings of untarnished glory once allayed the suffering of a dove[4]

married to the progenitor Kaśyapa, as *lōkamātas*. It is also said that Cāmuṇḍī was responsible for making Siva dance. This dance was, perhaps, *ūrdhvatāṇḍavam* which tradition records in the shrine of Tiruvālangāḍu, near Madras.

[1] It is to be noted that Kāḷī is different from Bhadrakāḷī.

[2] The Goddess who killed the *asura* Dāruka. This mighty *asura* engaged in austere penance for which he was blessed by Brahmā and told that he would not be killed by a Dēva, *asura*, man or any other creature or weapon either in the day or night. He was lording over the whole universe, and the chief gods attacked him in vain. Angry at his behaviour, a Kāḷī came out of Siva's third eye, and she was sent against Dāruka. But even she could not equal him as he had the knowledge of a secret mantra which he and his wife alone knew. Umā went in the guise of a Brahmana lady to his wife and offered to pray for her husband's life with her and thus learned the mantra. Then in the evening Kāḷī challenged him again and killed him. This Kāḷī is is said to be Bhadrakāḷī whose cult is now prevalent in Malabar. The Malabar legends *Kāḷikarpam* and *Badrōtpatti* furnish details of this story. Cf. the article entitled 'A Note on Kali or Bhagavati cult of Kerala', by C. Achyuta Menon in S. K. Aiyangar's *Commemoration Volume* (1936), pp. 234-39.

[3] The gate-keeper's first impression of Kaṇṇaki is that she looked like Mahiṣāsuramardanī, Cāmuṇḍī, or Kāḷī.

[4] The story of Sibi. Cf. *Puram.*, st. 37, 39 etc. *Kuṟalveṇbā* 72, Parimēlaḷagar, comment. The original story is contained in the epic *Mahābhārata*. Sibi was a monarch of the solar race and renowned for his kindness to animals. Once a dove fell into his lap and asked him to protect it from the pursuit of a hawk. The hawk demanded of the king either the dove or flesh from his

to the wonderment of gods, and another sacrificed at his chariot-wheel his dear and only son[1], grieved at the sight of a cow whose eyes were filled with pearl-like tears and who rang the bell at the palace-gate (for justice). From that city, Kōvalan̲, the son of the merchant Māśāttuvan̲, belonging to a reputed and exalted family of faultless name, driven by fate, entered your city, O king with tinkling anklets, to earn his livelihood, when he was murdered by you while out to sell my anklet. I am his wife. My name is Kaṇṇaki.'

The king replied: 'Divine lady, it is not injustice to 64–65
put a thief to death. Know that it is kingly justice.'[2]

The lustrous lady retorted:

'O Lord of Koṛkai, you have fallen from your righteous 66–81
course! My golden anklet contains gems inside.'

'O lady,' said the king, 'what you said now is well said. Our anklet contains pearls inside. Give it here.' It was given and placed before him. Kaṇṇaki then broke open her beautiful anklet, and a gem flew into the king's face. When he saw that gem, the king, with his umbrella falling and his sceptre faltering, said: 'Am I a ruler—I who have listened to the words of a goldsmith? It is I who am the thief. The protection of the subjects of the southern kingdom has failed in my hands for the first time. Let me[3] depart from this life.' Speaking thus the king fell down in a swoon, and his great queen collapsed and shuddered saying: 'It is impossible for woman

body equal to its weight. The king offered to give his flesh and cut it from his thigh and from other parts of his body. The weight proved unequal to that of the dove. He therefore offered his whole body to be weighed and thereby saved the poor dove from being killed.

[1] Man̲unītikaṇḍa Cōḻan̲. Cf. *paḻamoḻi*, st. 93; *Kuṟaḷveṇbā* 547, Parimēlaḻagar, comment. He had his son crushed under the wheels of a chariot, because his own vehicle had accidentally run over a calf, for which its mother, the cow, pleaded for justice by approaching the palace and ringing the bell of justice with its horns. (See Dikshitar, *Studies in Tamil Literature*, p. 191.)

[2] Rājanīti, also Daṇḍanīti.

[3] The king's sense of justice led to his extreme repentance and final collapse.

to replace the loss of a husband.'[1] Worshipping both his feet, she fell down.[2] Poor woman!

VEṆBĀ

1. The saying of several assembly-men, that *dharma* will become the god of Death to those who do sinful deeds, is not wrong. O queen of the conquering king who did an unjust and cruel deed! I have indeed committed a great sin.[3] See what I shall do.

2. Seeing me and terrified at me, the sinner with tears flowing from my red eyes, with the matchless anklet in my hand, with a body which seemed bereft of life, and with my dark forest-like tresses of hair, the Lord of Kūḍal became a corpse.[4]

3. The moment the Lord of Vaigai saw the dust on her (Kaṇṇaki's) body, her dark hair hanging loose, her tears, and the matchless anklet in her hand he was overwhelmed.[5] And the moment his ears received the words of the lady he gave up his life.

[1] People who lose their parents may be consoled, but not women who lose their husbands. The idea is that husbands are their very lives; without them women are dead to the world. Any relative can be substituted, but not a husband. The poet puts these words into the mouth of the queen when the king collapsed, but their significance is increased by their being addressed to Kaṇṇaki. This can be fitly compared with the statement in the *Rāmayāṇa* where Vālmīki puts into the mouth of Rāma a statement to the effect that wives and relatives can be found in every country but no country can give one one's own brother. The verse runs as follows.

देशे देशे कलत्राणि देशे देशे च बान्धवाः ।
तं तु देशं न पश्यामि यत्र भ्राता सहोदरः ॥

[2] The queen fell down unconscious, but not dead.

[3] The caption veṇbā marked above this stanza seems out of place for these words are spoken by Kaṇṇaki to the queen who fell down in extreme sorrow.

[4] Again Kaṇṇaki's utterance.

[5] It is doubtful in the light of the expression அக்காரிகை whether the third stanza of the veṇbā contains Kaṇṇaki's words. It seems to be the statement of the author, for Kaṇṇaki cannot speak of herself as அக்காரிகை.

CANTO XXI

VAÑJIṈAMĀLAI

OR

THE GREAT WRATH

(THE SEVEN WOMEN OF CHASTITY)

KAṆṆAKI spoke thus to the Pāṇḍyan queen: 1–4

'O, Dēvi of the great king! I am one pursued by cruel fate. Though by nature I am ignorant yet you will see that he who did harm to another in the forenoon will find himself harmed in the afternoon.'[1]

At midday a lady[2] with abundant locks of hair called 5–6
upon the *vaṉṉi* tree and the kitchen[3] to bear evidence to her chastity.

When a woman with a wide, striped *alkul* was told by 7–10
her companions that her husband was a figure of sand upon the banks of Poṉṉi (Kāvēri), she remained[4] there without returning home even when the waves encircled her without ruining her husband's image.

The daughter of the celebrated king Karikāla[5] followed 10–14

[1] See *Kuṟaḷveṇbā* 319; *Perunkadal*, st. 56. l. 239.

[2] Kaṇṇaki narrates the legends of seven women of Puhār who had won a name for their exemplary chastity.

[3] This tradition is still current in Tiruppuṟampayam and Tirumaru-kal. The Lord enshrined at the former place goes by the name of Sākṣīnātha. See Dr Swaminatha Aiyar's note. A similar legend is recorded in what is known as *Sāṉṟalaitta Tiruviḷaiyāḍal* (st. 62) where the *vaṉṉi* tree, the God Siva and a well are cited as witnesses.

[4] The moment the woman, who was apparently a widow, heard from her companions that the sandy figure was that of her husband, she did not return home but stood firm in that place lest the figure should be destroyed by floods. Even today it is a custom among some classes for the chaste wife to go to the river bank, make an image of her husband in sand and after making offerings to it, to cast off the clothes she was wearing and to put on new ones.

[5] See *Kuṟuntogai*, st. 31; *Aham.*, st. 45, 76, etc. The name of Karikāla's daughter was Ādimandi, also Mandi, (*Aham.*); *Tolk. Ahattiṇai*, sūtra 54

the floods which carried away her husband, Vañjikkōn,[1] calling aloud: 'O, my lover with hill-like shoulders!' Then the sea itself came and presented her husband before her. She, the golden creeper, returned embracing him.

15–17 There was the lady (in the form of a stone) who remained in the park by the seashore looking at the approaching vessels. After the return of her husband, she cast off her form of stone.[2]

18–19 There was another lady with lancelike eyes who, when her co-wife's child had accidentally fallen into a well, dropped her child also into it and thus saved both the children.[3]

20–23 Seeing a stranger staring at her with lascivious eyes, a lady changed her full-moon face into that of a monkey. When her departed husband returned, that flower-soft lady, with pure gems on her *alkul* gave up her monkey-face.[4]

24–34 Last there was the lady, beautiful as a golden image, who overheard her mother speaking thus to her (the girl's) father: 'Without paying heed to the wise saying of the learned,[5] that a woman's wisdom is fraught with folly, in the course of our play, I told my maid servant, "If I give birth to a daughter, and if you, O, maid of lustrous

Naccinārkkiniyar's gloss. She seems to be younger than Auvvaiyār, the great Sangam poetess. This shows that not only Tamil princes but princesses also were poets. Tamil women were highly learned.

[1] Also Āṭṭanatti or merely Atti. The incident referred to took place at Kaḻār on the banks of the Kāvēri. See Dr Swaminatha Aiyar's detailed note (*Sila.* Tamil ed., p. 488).

[2] The fourth lady turned herself into a stone when her husband went overseas, but assumed her original form on his return. Though not a parallel, the Ahalyā legend in the *Rāmāyaṇa* of Vālmīkī affords a comparison Ahalyā, once turned into a stone, assumed her original form at the touch of Rāma.

[3] The fifth lady dropped her own child into the well after her co-wife's child, when in her custody, had fallen into it. Then she started a hue and cry and with the help of her neighbours saved both children. She thus hoped to be above reproach.

[4] Assuming forms at will shows the force and power at the back of chastity, the virtue of virtues.

[5] Cf. *Iṛai*, sūtra 23.

armlets, give birth to a son, he will be my daughter's husband." She has borne this in mind, and now demands their wedlock. I hear this with pain, my mind is much exercised. How unfortunate I am!' At this, she who looked like a golden image (even before the proposal from her parents) dressed herself in a new silken robe, tied up the tresses of her hair, approaching the son (of the maid) prostrated herself before him, and bore his feet on her head![1]

'I was born in that city (Puhār) in which such great 35–38
women of fragrant tresses[2] were born. If these things happened truly, and if I am also a chaste lady, I shall not allow this city to flourish but will destroy it along with its sovereign. You will see the truth of this.'

(After speaking thus) she left that place and cried 39–42
out: 'O, men and women of Madura of the four temples (*māḍam*)![3] O, gods in the heavens! and O, ye saints! Listen to me. I curse this capital of him who did wrong to my beloved husband. I am not to blame.'

Then she twisted off her left breast with her hand, and 43–52
going round the city of Madura thrice making this vow, in deep anguish, she threw that beautiful breast whirling into the fragrant street. 'Before this illustrious lady who had made this vow, appeared the god of fire, with flames, in the form of a Brahmana, blue in hue, his tuft like the red sky, and with milk-white teeth, saying: 'O, chaste lady![4]

[1] Having overheard the promise made by her mother to her maid-servant—before her birth—to give her to that maid's son, she volunteered to marry him when the time came.

[2] See *Paṭṭiṉattupiḷḷaiyār Purāṇam* for a slightly changed version of the tale of seven women (Pūmpuhār Śarukkam).

[3] The four are named Tiruvālavāi, Tirunaḷḷāṟu, Tirumuḍangai, Tirunaḍuvūr. According to Naccinārkkhiṉiyar, *Kali.*, st. 92, the four are Kaṉṉi, Kariyamāl, Kāḷi and Ālavāi. See *Sila.* (Tamil ed.), p. 490. It would appear that the name Kūḍal was derived from these four temples of which a description is given in Sambandar's *Tēvāram*.

[4] A description of the god of fire as he appeared before Kaṇṇaki. On the Agni cult there is an interesting contribution by Dr J. P. H. Vogel in *Ind. Ant.*, December 1933.

As I long ago received the order that I should destroy this city by fire on the day on which you would be cruelly wronged, who can escape death here?'[1]

53-57 The wrathful Kaṇṇaki then ordered : 'Spare[2] Brahmanas, the righteous[3], cows, chaste women, the aged and children, but go towards unrighteous people.' And the city of Kūḍal, belonging to the king of the mighty chariot,[4] was enveloped by fumes and flames.

VEṆBA[5]

When the glorious Pāṇḍyan, his maidens, palaces, army with its shining bows, and elephants, were consumed by the fire of chastity, the immortal gods of that unfortunate city went out of sight because of their great purity.

[1] This means that Agni asked Kaṇṇaki who should be spared.

[2] This shows that the slaughter of innocents was not countenanced at any stage or in any manner. It is interesting that Brahmanas were exempted, surely having evoked respect for their learning and character. These must have been the Śrōtriyas often mentioned in Sanskrit epics and law-books. See Dikshitar, *Hindu Administrative Institutions*, pp. 187-9.

[3] This shows that members of other castes who were wedded to *svadharma* were also spared.

[4] The Pāṇḍyan was noted for his chariot force.

[5] This veṇbā, says the editor of the text, is not found in certain manuscripts.

CANTO XXII

AḺARPAṬUKĀDAI

OR

THE CONFLAGRATION

(IN Madura) the burning mouth of the messenger god 1–15
(Agni)[1] opened itself. The guardian deities[2] closed their doors.[3] In order to prove to Mother Earth that his rule was righteous, Śeḻiyaṉ, the warrior king of kings, gave up his very life on account of the dishonour caused by his bent sceptre.[4] Not knowing that the king was dead on his throne[5] along with his queen of untarnished chastity, the *purōhita*,[6] the astrologer, the Brahmana judges, the financier (Kāvidi),[7] and the learned ministers, attended by the

[1] The god Agni is ministering to the wants of the Dēvas. Hence the epithet Dēvadūta in Vēdic literature. The rationale of all religious offerings to Agni is that he takes them to the respective gods and *pitṛs* to whom such *havis* were intended.

[2] Among the guardian deities of the city are mentioned the four caste-būtams:—the Brahmana-būtam, the Kṣatriya-būtam, the Vaiśya-būtam and the Vēḷāṇ-būtam. This proves that the social polity Varṇāśramadharma had come to this part of India at a much earlier period. It may be noted that different colours—white, red, brown and black—are assigned to these respective [illegible] showing that once the division of communities was according to colour.

[3] 'That they closed their doors' means 'that they gave up their legitimate function of defending the four gates of the city walls'.

[4] The poet skilfully weaves beautiful ideas into the text. When the straight sceptre hung its head, it seemed to give a message to the king's mind that unless he sacrificed himself it would not come back to its original pristine straightness of justice. The rapid march of ideas—the rod of justice bending, the king dying, and the rod attaining its original form—is all vividly described.

[5] *Araiśukaṭṭil* is the term used in the text for the throne.

[6] The executive officers of the king are mentioned. The *purōhita* is mentioned first showing the high dignity which was attached to his office. For the place of the *purōhita*, in the scheme of ancient Indian polity, see Dikshitar, *Hindu Admin. Institutions*, ch. iii, sec. 2.

[7] Kāvidi is perhaps the technical term for the Superintendent of Finance. For different meanings of the expression see the *Tamil Lexicon*, p. 903.

palace-servants, and maid-attendants, stood speechless like a group in a painted picture.[1] (At that time) the elephant-riders,[2] cavalrymen, charioteers, and the Maṟava[3] soldiers with terrible swords, were bewildered by the fire at the victorious gate of the king's palace, and were permitted to leave.

16–36 The presiding deity of the Ādibūtam,[4] [whose body shedding its cool and lustrous rays like a cluster of pearls, was white as the moon, wore a brilliant pearl necklace along with other ornaments, and had on his shining tuft a wreath of white lotus, *aruhai*, *nandi* and other flowers. He was robed in the purest white, thin silk, not yet dry, and his breast was painted with paste made from the unblossomed *vaṭṭihai*, the bright dust of *vaṇṇikai* (sandal) and *kōṭṭam*. He consumed heartily the sacrificial smoke, caused by the pouring of honey, milk and jaggery (into the fire),[5] and moved in the forenoon from the bathing ghats and the temple of the gods, to halls of Vēdic chanting.[6] He would stand on his feet at midday and go to his home in the afternoon, holding in his hands an unfolded umbrella, a staff, a water-bowl, a fire-stick,[7] and inseparable *kuśa* grass, with the Vēdas on his tongue and his sacred thread on his breast] without deviating from the established procedure, would kindle

[1] This is an indication of the flourishing state of painting in the early centuries of the Christian era.

[2] The traditional fourfold forces are given. The fourfold army had come to stay in the Tamil land.

[3] The term Maṟava may mean a hardy warrior.

[4] A full description of the Vēdic Brahmana and his outfit. The Brahmanabūtam was an ideal example for the members of that community to copy and follow. The description is told twice in certain particulars. Lines 16-33 are not found in certain manuscripts and from the redundant nature of the description, they can be taken as interpolations.

[5] The *havis* offerings consisted of honey, milk, curds, and ghee.

[6] These are evidently *pāṭaśālas*, the institutions in modern times, for teaching the Vēdas.

[7] The fire-stick is a twig of the sacred fig tree, called *samit* in Sanskrit literature.

the three fires[1] with the sacrificial utensils as ordained by Brahmā.

Next was the great deity of the Kṣatriya-būtam,[2] 37–61
[whose body was the colour of the red rays of the sun, and who wore among jewels set with spotless gems, other ornaments like the diadem (worn by a king). He decked his tuft with a wreath of *campaka, karuviḷai,* red *kūdāḷam* and cool and sweet water-plants, *jāti* and other flowers. He wore garlands strung with choice flowers and other ornamentations. He had rings on all ten fingers of his hands,[3] and his broad breast was of *kumkumam* colour. He wore around his waist a soft brilliant-red silk, and he consumed the hot preparation of *śāli* rice brought to him in a gold vessel, besides other agreeable sweetmeats]. His body had the sparkling brilliance of coral, and he ruled the sea-girt world, holding in his hands the *muraśu*, white umbrella, feather-fan, tall flag,[4] the famous *ankuśa*, a steel spear and a binding rope of steel. He drove away countless kings of great fame, and capturing the whole earth,[5] he ruled righteously, punishing evil-doers, and protected the world like Neḍiyōṉ himself with great and growing fame.

Then came the great deity of the illustrious Vaiśya- 62–88

[1] The three fires are the *gārhapatya*, *āhavanīya* and *dakṣiṇāgni*, worshipped by *Agnihōtrins,* a practice that continues today in Tamil districts.

[2] The outfit of the Kṣatriya-būtam. Lines 37-50 also are interpolations giving a description more or less as is found in the lines following. To wear a tuft was the accepted custom of the day for all communities.

[3] The term *añjumakaṉ* is vague but has been interpreted as meaning 'one having rings on all five fingers.' No light is forthcoming from the commentary. The line may be interpreted as 'he who wore rings on his fingers emitting rays of light' (*añju*).

[4] The chief characteristics (*lakṣaṇa*) and deeds of the Pāṇḍyan have been attributed to the Kṣatriya-būtam.

[5] Reference here is perhaps to Kṛṣṇa helping the Pāṇḍava Arjuna against his enemy Duryōdhana. The *Arumpadavurai* interprets *āḷvōṉ* as Arjuna in l. 52 and *maṉṉar* as Duryōdhana and others in l. 56.

būtam[1] with his body the lustrous colour of pure gold, wearing every ornament except the diadem worn by celebrated monarchs of the strong spear, catering for the vast world as befits a member of the merchant community and bearing in his hands the ploughshare and the balance. [His cloth was of the much praised golden colour. In his tuft was a wreath linked together with flowers of *veṭci*, *tāḻai*, honey-laden *āmbal*, *śēḍal*, *neydal*, *pūḻai* and *marudam*. On his lightning-like breast was sandal paste of a brilliant colour shining like burnished gold. He would give and accept food well mixed with gram, peas, *dhal*, black gram, and several other green grains. It was he who enjoyed his meal before noon with water in his hand and frequented granaries where paddy was stored, fields full of birds, merchants' shops and shady *kāñci* trees.

Holding the plough, the weighing balance needed in bazaars, the *tāl*[2] of enveloping brilliance, and the *yāḻ*, he would favour (people) with abundance of produce and entertain guests. He would also sell to those who needed them rare articles brought from mountains and seas.][3] He assumed the form of a chieftain pursuing the harmless agricultural life[4] and resembled Śiva wearing a young crescent in his resplendent coiffure.

89–102 There also appeared the chief of the (Vēḷāḷa) Vēḷāṇbūtams,[5] who received sacrificial offerings in noisy Madura,

[1] The outfit of the Vaiśya-būtam is furnished. The ploughshare and the balance are the symbols of the duties of Vaiśyas and represent the *bhūvaiśyaṉ* and *dhaṉavaiśyaṉ* into which the whole community was divided. The Vaiśyas could give gifts and receive gifts in their turn. Lines 67-84 also are interpolations and repeat more or less the same description of the būtam.

[2] *Tāl* is another vague term and has been taken to mean 'lampstand'.

[3] This shows that the Vaiśyas had sea-borne trade as well as caravan-trade.

[4] The Vaiśya chief was the lord of the agricultural tracts. He is likened to Śiva.

[5] The outfit of the Vēḷāṇ-būtam. Lines 89-96 are interpolations being a repetition of the būtam's description.

(who was the colour of the *karuviḷai* flower with decorative ornaments of gold and silver, who wore lustrous *kaḻakam*, whose broad breast was painted with the dried paste of fragrant *ahil*, who wore in his tuft a wreath of flowers grown on the branches of trees, creepers, water-plants and others, who held a plough[1] made by expert blacksmiths, and who had attained praiseworthy prestige), whose body was like a cleaned sapphire, who had a dress made of the bright *kaḻakam*, and who had the technique needed for dancing and was versed in the different modes of singing.[2]

(These four būtams) said : 'Since we know beforehand 103–108
that this city is to be consumed by fire on the day on which the king's justice fails, and since we know that this is just, it is proper that we should go away from here.' All these four guardian deities deserted their respective quarters even before the heroic woman plucked off her breast.

Then the street of grain-dealers, the car street decora- 109–111
ted with festoons, and the four streets occupied respectively by men of the four castes, began to be agitated as on the day when the Kāṇḍāvaṉam[3] blazed forth [set on fire by the reliant (Arjuna) of the powerful monkey-standard].[4]

The flames did not go near the residences of the right- 112–118
eous though they blazed among the dwellings of the unrighteous. Unaffected by the fire, cows and calves reached the broad streets of the pious cowherds.[5] Strong

[1] The plough was common to the Vēḷāḷa and the Vaiśya. The latter had the balance as well.

[2] It transpires that the Vēḷāḷas had their own rural amusements of singing and dancing so as to relieve the monotony of their agricultural occupation.

[3] The reference is to the burning of the Kāṇḍāvaṉam. For a description of it, see the *Mahābhārata*.

[4] This flag signified the leadership of Arjuna. It may be noted that l. 111 is not found in certain manuscripts.

[5] Followers of *dharma* as well as the animal kingdom were left untouched by fire. Similarly chaste women and innocent children were spared. It was by no means a slaughter of innocents.

and fierce male elephants and herds of female elephants and fleet steeds ran away outside the city walls.

119–127 (In that city) there were women[1] lying unconscious in their soft, smooth widespread beds under the spell of love and wine in the company of their husbands. Their beauteous young breasts were painted with unguents, their eyes were darkened with collyrium and their hair was adorned with wreaths of fragrant, honey-laden, gaping buds filling the air with perfume. From these alighted pollen on to their breasts painted with *kumkumam* and decorated with pearl necklaces.

128–132 Other women, with yellow spotted *alkuls* and fragrant tresses, whose lisping children with rosy mouths and toddling gait came in the company of grey-haired women, awoke from sleep on cotton mattresses.

133–137 The matrons who unfailingly attended to household duties and entertained guests, rejoiced greatly. They worshipped and praised the fire-god, whose flames rose high, saying: 'Losing her husband, whose chest shone with a beautiful garland, this lady won her victory with her anklet. Is this war waged by her breast unjust?[2] Not so.'

138–146 In the far-famed street of the songstresses,[3] trained in the sixty-four arts,[4] where could be heard the reverberations of the *mṛdangam,* the sweet subdued flute, and the vibration of the singing *yāḻ* produced by variations in tone, the dancing-girls who lost their theatre, burst out: 'Where does this woman come from? Whose daughter

[1] Two kinds of household women are distinguished. The women described in ll. 119-27 are those who have not yet given birth to children. The women described in ll. 128-32 are those who have children. Besides these there were old women, as the reference to grey hairs indicates.

[2] Here is a justification by the chaste women of Madura of the action of Kaṇṇaki and of her curse. It is said that they prostrated themselves before the blazing fire as an act of religious duty.

[3] Here is a reference to the public theatre of the city which was consumed by the conflagration.

[4] See above, p. 206, n. 3.

is she? Wonder it is that one single woman who had lost her husband, could vanquish the inconsiderate king with her anklet, and finally set fire to this city.'

Seeing the great city had lost its evening festivals,[1] 147–157
the chanting of the Vēdas (*āraṇam*), the kindling of sacrificial fires, the worship of gods, the lighting of domestic lamps, the healthful repose of nightfall, and the resounding notes of the *muraśam*, and because it was unable to bear the thrust of the blazing flame, the goddess Madurāpati appeared before the sorely oppressed heroic wife, who, pained at heart by the decease of her beloved husband, heaved a deep sigh (which shook her frame), and roamed aimlessly through the streets and lanes[2] in a state of agitation, partly struggling hard to walk and partly bewildered and unconscious.

VEṆBĀ

The goddess known as Madurāpati[3] came before her who had wrung off her fierce young breast, and whose victory[4] equalled that of the Goddess of Wealth,[5] the Goddess of Learning,[6] and the great Goddess[7] who killed and stood upon the demon Mahiṣāsura.

[1] *Sībali* offered usually at evening. Other features were Vēdic chanting and prayers to sacrificial fires and at temples.

[2] The term used for lanes is *kavalai*.

[3] Madurāpati was the family-deity of the Pāṇḍyan king. Every reigning Hindu king, ancient or modern, has his own *kuladēvatā*. In the *Raghuvamśā* Kāḷidāsa says that after Rāma's death the family-deity of Ayōdhyā appeared at midnight to Kuśa, son and successor. Today Padmanābhasvāmi is the family deity of Travancore kings, and Cāmuṇḍī of Mysore Rajas.

[4] Kaṇṇaki's signal victory over the Madura king was tantamount to all the victories of the three goddesses put together.

[5] Lakṣmī.

[6] Sarasvatī.

[7] Umā in the form of Mahiṣāsuramardanī.

CANTO XXIII

KAṬṬURAIKĀDAI

OR

THE EXPLANATION

1–20 WITH her head decorated with a crescent and her matted locks, *kuvaḷai*-like eyes, white radiant face, coral-mouth revealing her teeth, with the left half of her body dark blue, and the right half golden, with a golden lotus in her left hand, and a glittering and terrifying sword in her right, with a victorious *kaḻal* on her right leg, and a matchless jingling anklet on her left, Madurāpati,[1] the family deity of the chief—who ruled the cool harbour of Koṟkai[2] and Kumari port, whose northern limit was the golden Himalayas[3] and who was lord of Podiyil—unwilling to face the graceful but sorrow-stricken woman, the heroic wife who, highly perturbed, had plucked out one of her breasts, went behind her[4] and said: 'Blessed lady! Canst thou listen to my complaint?' Whereupon, the woman

[1] A description of the form of the presiding deity of the city of Madura. This is in agreement with the idea in Sanskrit legends that every great capital of ancient times had its own guardian deity who was in charge of the city. We hear in the *Rāmāyaṇa* of the presiding deity of Lankā, appearing before Hanumān, the monkey ambassador of Sugrīva.

[2] Koṟkai and Kumari were the ports of the Pāṇḍyas. Here the poet refers to the Pāṇḍyan as chief of the maritime tracts while in the next line he describes him as chief of the hill tribes. This is one way of extolling his name and fame.

[3] This does not necessarily mean that the Pāṇḍyan kingdom extended on the north as far as the Himalayas. It demonstrates however that the prowess of Pāṇḍyan arms had been felt by the ruling princes of northern India whose northern limit was the Himālayas. This is in keeping with the statement of Āriyappaṭaikaḍanda Neḍuñjeḻiyaṉ occurring in the *kaṭṭurai* towards the end of 'Maduraikkāṇḍam'. A short poem is ascribed to him (*Puṟam.*, st. 183).

The poet graphically describes how the Goddess of Madura approached the Lady of Chastity, giving us the impression that she thought herself inferior to Kaṇṇaki. She therefore appeared from behind and made an appeal to her to give a patient hearing to her words.

with the grief-stricken face, turned to her right and asked: 'Who art thou following me from behind? Art thou aware of my deep pain?'

Madurāpati replied: 'Yes, I am aware of thy great 21–30
suffering, O faultless lady! I am the tutelary deity of the vast city of Kūḍal. I wish to speak a word. I am much concerned at the fate of thy husband. Lady of golden bracelets, listen. O listen to a word of mine, noble lady! Wilt thou not pay heed, O friend, to the lamentable disease causing anguish to my mind? Hear, my dear, the fruits of our kings' deeds in their previous births.[1] Listen also to the account of your husband's past deeds resulting in this present misery.

'My ears have heard only the sound of Vēdic chanting[2] 31–40
but have never heard the sound of the bell (clamouring for justice).[3] Except for the slander of kings who pay their tributes by prostrating themselves before our monarch, his sceptre has never incurred the displeasure of his subjects.[4] Moreover though fair-faced girls cast shy looks towards him forcing the passion of his powerful heart beyond the control of his intellect[5], as the young elephant runs wild uncontrolled by a trained rider, yet this is no stain to kings born in this noble family associated with high morals.

[1] The theory of belief in past *karmā* is once again stressed.

[2] The deafening chanting of the Vēdic Brahmanas in every corner of the city. Cf. *Maduraikkāñji*, l. 656.

[3] The bell of justice, also called *ārāiccimaṇi*. Tradition affirms that every palace had such a bell in front of it, for the use of people and even animals whenever injustice was done to them by the State, so as to bring it to the king's notice. The Goddess of Madura says that she had never heard the sound of that bell, implying that there had never been a breach of justice in the State to her knowledge, and that this was the first time that injustice had been done.

[4] Protection of his subjects is the supreme duty of the king. This is also the prescription of all *nīti* treatises in Sanskrit. (See also *Puṟam.*, st. 72. Cf. l. 34 with ll. 76-7 of 'Vaḻakkuraikādai', canto xx.)

[5] The weakness of the Pāṇḍyan who lacked control over his senses is brought out, but this was never attended by injustice of any sort.

41–54 'Hast thou not heard that a Pāṇḍyan king, whose hand had broken the golden crown and the glittering bracelets of the king of gods wielding the thunderbolt, knocked one day at the door-less house[1] of Kīrandai, whose life was valueless (to others), and overheard his (Kīrandai's) wife telling her husband : "You departed for a distant place, and left me in this *maṉṟam* saying that no fence was stronger than the protection of our monarch. Has that fence ceased to protect us today?" Instantly the king closed his ears, as if pierced by a red-hot smoking nail. He quaked with fear as his heart burnt within him, and he cut off his hand[2] in order to maintain a righteous sceptre without any slur. There is, therefore, no blot on those born in this royal family. Hear, again, the truth of the matter.

55–70 'When a king of this dynasty, a wielder of the polished spear, who had richly fed (the combatants in the Mahābhārata war) had secured peace, he held a great durbar.[3] An able Brahmana, Parāśara, who belonged to the good and fertile kingdom of the Lord of highly reputed Puhār wielding a righteous sceptre and a triumphant sword—one of whose kings weighed (his flesh) to save a dove,[4] and another awarded justice to a cow[5]—and who had heard of the peerless munificence of the Cēra of the curved lance,

[1] This statement agrees with that noted by Megasthenes in his *Indika* that there were no thieves in the land and that the people slept with their doors open.

[2] Cf. *Sila.*, padikam; also *Paḻamoḻi*, st. 102. The commentators on the *Tolkāppiyam* refer to this incident.

[3] This may also refer to an assembly of State when there was an army review including a feast in honour of the army. This practice is evident from the *Kalingattupparaṇi*, and the technical term for this is *nāḷōlakkam* and here it is termed *perunāḷirukkai*. Hence it may be a reference to the Pāṇḍyan king. There are others who find here a reference to a certain Cēra king Udiyaṉcēral (see below, 'Ūśalvari', st. 29; also *Puṟam.*, st. 2, *Aham.*, st. 233). Several references go to strengthen the tradition that a Cēra took an active part in the Mahābhārata war.

[4] This reference is to Sibi; see above, p. 248, n. 4.

[5] This reference is to Manunītikaṇḍa Cōḻaṉ; see above, p. 249, n. 1.

by offering the heavens[1] to a Tamil Brahmana poet, said to himself: "I shall see this Cēra of great valour and long lance." He then passed through jungles and country
places and towns leaving behind him the tall Malaya hills.[2] 71–84
There, by the force of his dialectical skill,[3] which he had acquired in the traditional manner, from the twice-born Brahmana—who with the thought of achieving oneness with the infinite[4] kindled the threefold fires[5] as ordained in the four Vēdas and performed the five great sacrifices[6] and the six great duties[7]—he defeated his rivals and earned the title of *pārpaṉavāhai.*[8] As he was returning home with great and valuable gifts, he reached the village of Tangāl[9] of the righteous Pāṇḍyan and of *dharmaic* Brahmanas. In this village, on a platform beneath a Bōdi tree,[10] luxuriant with green leaves, the tired man stayed awhile with

[1] Pālaigautamaṉār. Cf. *Padiṟṟu*, Third Ten, colophon. The Cēra is Palyāṉaicelkeḻukuṭṭuvaṉ, younger brother of Imayavarambaṉ. The legend goes that Gautamaṉār, a Brahmana and a Tamil poet, performed ten sacrifices (*yajñas*) and in the course of the tenth, the Brahmana and his lady disappeared by going to heaven. In its accomplishment Keḻukuṭṭuvaṉ helped him (see below, canto xxviii, ll. 137-8; also *Aham.*, st. 233).

[2] The Malaya hills are the Podiyil of Tamil literature.

[3] An expert in the science of *tarka.*

[4] Desirous of *mōkṣa* or salvation so as to be liberated from the trammels of *samsāra.*

[5] *Gārhapatya, āhavanīya* and *dakṣiṇāgni.*

[6] *Pañcamahāyajña,* or *pañcayajña* as it is called. It is incumbent on the members of the twice-born classes to perform these every day.

[7] The six duties are learning and teaching, performing sacrifices and having sacrifices performed, giving and receiving gifts. See *Hindu Administrative Institutions*, p. 188.

[8] It is a theme which describes the greatness a learned Brahmana attained through the performance of sacrifices. (See *Puṟa.*, *Veṇbāmālai*, 'Vāhai.', st. 9.) But here it is the conferment of a distinction by a king on one who comes out successfully in debates with equally learned men. The reference is to the branch of a tree worn to indicate literary powers.

[9] Identified with Tiruttangāl near Śivakāsi railway station. The Brahmanas of this village are termed Pañcagrāmikaḷ by the commentator. Apparently they were one among the many local Brahmana communities.

[10] The reference is to the sacred *aśvattha* tree which was also the Buddhist Bōdi tree. Cf. *Rāmā.*, Bk. II, ch. lxviii, st. 17 where *Bōdhibhavana* is mentioned.

his staff,[1] water-bowl, white umbrella, fire-stick, a small bundle of articles and slippers, and said: "Long live the victor whose protecting white umbrella assures his certain success. Long live the protector who uprooted the *kaḍambu*[2] from the sea! Long live the king who engraved his bow on the Himalayas! Long live the Poṟaiyaṉ[3], possessor of the beautiful and cool Porunai! Long live King Māndaraṉ-Cēral!"[4]

85–98 'Surrounded by a group of playful youths, some with curly hair and some with tufts and some with lisping mouths and coral lips, toddling some distance from their homes, he addressed them: "Young Brahmana boys, if you can recite the Vēda after me, you may go away taking this little bundle of jewels."[5] Then the son of the famous Brahmana Vārttikaṉ, by name Ālamarśelvaṉ (Daksiṇāmūrti) whose rose lips still retained the fragrance of his mother's milk, in the presence of his playmates, with prattling tongue and great inward pleasure, recited the Vēda, faultlessly observing the correct rhythm. The elderly man was exceedingly pleased with young Dakkiṇaṉ and presented him with a sacred thread of pearls and bright jewels, as well as with bangles and ear-rings before he departed for his native place.

99–122 'But the sentinels (of the locality) jealous of Vārttikaṉ because his child had been beautified and decorated with fine ornaments, accused him saying: "This Brahmana has

[1] The impedimenta of an orthodox Brahmana. *Kuṇḍikai* may answer to what we call *jāri* still used by orthodox Brahmanas. *Kāṭṭam* (*kāṣṭha*) are twigs of the sacred pipal used for *havis* in the fire.

[2] See below, canto xxviii, ll. 135-6.

[3] Poraiyaṉ was a title of the Cēra kings.

[4] Perhaps another name of Palyāṉaicelkeḻukuṭṭuvaṉ. He was a contemporary ruler and chief of Kuṭṭanāḍu while Senguṭṭuvaṉ was reigning in Vañji.

[5] The Brahmana's love for the Vēda and his magnanimity in giving away valuable jewels to a child reciting it according to established practice show how unselfish were the learned Brahmanas of those golden days.

misappropriated treasure-trove[1] which belongs legitimately to the king." They then threw him into prison. Kārttikai, the wife of Vārttikaṉ, grew frantic. She wept in grief. She threw herself on to the ground rolling and fulminating. Seeing this, the goddess Durgā of untarnished glory refused to open the door of her temple for the conduct of daily worship. When the king of the mighty spear heard that the massive door remained shut and would not open, he was confounded, and inquired: "Has any injustice been done?[2] Come and tell me if you have heard of any failure in the discharge of our duties to the Goddess of Victory." Then his young messengers made obeisance to the protecting king and informed him of the case of Vārttikaṉ. "This is not fair", burst forth the king in anger and addressed Vārttikaṉ: "It is your duty to forgive me. My righteous rule still has life, though, owing to the ignorance of my men, it has deviated from the ordained path." The king granted[3] him Tangāl with its paddy fields watered by tanks, and Vayalūr of immeasurable yield, and prostrated himself[4] on the ground before Vārttikaṉ the husband of Kārttikai, and in part appeased the unappeasable wrath of the latter.

'Then the door (of the shrine) of the Goddess who 123–125
rode upon the stag, opened so loudly as to be heard throughout the long and broad streets of mountain-like mansions of that ancient city.

[1] All treasure-trove went of right to the king and misappropriation was severely punished.

[2] This shows the religious mind of the king and his fear of the obloquy of wielding an unrighteous sceptre.

[3] Both Tangāl and the adjoining village of Vayalūr were granted as a *brahmadēya* village by the king in order to appease the wrath of the Brahmana and his lady.

[4] Literally: 'showed his chest to the damsel of this vast world.' The commentator says that so far the king had not prostrated himself and hence the earth was raging with heat. But, now, that heat subsided a little. However the term *avaḷ* may refer to Kārttikai and may mean her rage (which at the miscarriage of justice to her husband would not fully subside) subsided a little.

126–131 'At that time, the triumphant king issued the following proclamation by beating a drum placed upon the back of an elephant which was sent throughout the city :[1] "Release all prisoners from the prison. Remit all taxes from those who owe them. Let all who find unclaimed things and discover treasure-trove enjoy them."

132–137 'Listen how even such a king committed this act of injustice. There was a prediction that, in the month of Āḍi, on the *tithi* of Aṣṭamī, in the dark fortnight, on a Friday,[2] with *Kārttikai* and *Baraṇi* (in the ascendent),[3] a great fire would envelop renowned Madura to the ruin of its king. (That has come to pass now.)

138–151 'Hear again, O lady of glittering bangles! The kings of mighty spears, Vasu and Kumara, who ruled in an exemplary manner with their armies, over the good kingdom of Kalinga encircled by a thick grove, at Śingapuram[4] with its fair and fertile fields, and at Kapilapuram with its bamboo forests, became enemies, being agnates, though born in an ancient family of undying prosperity. And to a distance of six *kāvadams*[5] all round, owing to their war, none could penetrate that region. Then a merchant, Śangamaṉ by name, ambitious to increase his wealth, came with his wife, like people escaping unnoticed, bearing a great bundle on his head and began to dispose of his valuable wares in a bazaar of Śingapuram of undiminished glory.

[1] A general amnesty and remission of taxes; even treasure-trove became the property of the finder. The state relinquished its rights voluntarily. What affected a certain individual became a general law. Cf. *Kuṟaḷveṇbā*, 172.

[2] The mention of the weekday (Friday) has made some scholars draw the conclusion that the epic *Silappadikāram* must be a later composition on the ground that weekdays were unknown to India until the fourth century A.D. But this is arguing from one unknown to another unknown.

[3] *Alalśērkuṭṭam* is *Kārttikai* and *Baraṇi* (see *Puram.*, st. 229).

[4] Simhapuram and Kapilapuram were cities of the ancient kingdom of Kalinga. Vasu and Kumara, agnates, ruled over them. See Intro., p. 34.

[5] The battlefield extended to a distance of six *kādams* all round.

'O lady of gold bangles! Your husband, Kōvalan̲, 152–169
in his previous birth was called Barata,[1] and being in the service of this valorous monarch, had in disgust given up the vow (of non-killing).[2] He mistook (Śangaman̲) for a spy,[3] captured him, brought him to the presence of the king of the conquering spear and beheaded him. Nīli, the wife of the murdered Śangaman̲, finding that she had no resting-place, wandered about the streets and courtyards, and created a commotion proclaiming: "O king, is this your justice? O Vaiśyas, is this justice? O commoners, is this justice? O residents of this place, is this right?" She raved thus for fourteen days, and exhilarated by the thought that that was a sacred day she ascended a cliff in order to rejoin her murdered husband in heaven, and fell down cursing[4] thus:

"He who has inflicted this injury upon us shall be overtaken by the same fate."

'That unerring curse has now descended upon thee.[5]

'This is my explanation. Please listen. When 170–178
actions in a past birth by those devoid of goodness yield their results, no (amount of) penance can stop them. O lady of abundant tresses of hair, after fourteen days[6] thou shalt see thy wedded lover in the form of a celestial being, but never more in his earthly form.' When she had finished explaining these things in the proper manner to the lady of chastity, the Goddess of Madura liberated the city from the conflagration.

[1] *Sans.*, Bharata.

[2] *Ahimsā* or non-injury to any living creature.

[3] This shows that the spy system was widely prevalent. For a study of this institution see the *Kauṭalīya Arthaśāstra*.

[4] Nīli's curse and its effect upon Kōvalan̲ in this birth. See *Maṇi.*, 'Vañjimānagarpukkakādai', ll. 5-34, for this curse.

[5] No amount of *dharma* in the present birth can stop the laws of pre-ordained fate. The actions of a previous birth yield their fruit in the next birth and, according to one theory, for several continued births if they be of a heinous nature.

[6] See *Sila.*, *padikam*, ll. 50-3.

179–193 Kaṇṇaki then said: 'I will not sit nor shall I stand till I see the husband of my heart'; and she broke her gold bangles at the temple of Koṟṟavai,[1] and once again cried: 'I entered this city with my husband by the eastern gate. Alas! I am now going out alone through the western gate.' Unconscious of day or night, she went helpless along one side of the flooded Vaigai. Dejected and sad, little thinking whether she was descending into a pit or ascending a cliff, she climbed step by step up the hill sacred to Neḍuvēḷ,[2] the bearer of the long fiery lance, which tore out the bowels of the sea,[3] cut out the heart of the mountain,[4] and vanquished Asuras; and there, under the shade of a flowery *vēṅgai* grove, she pined saying: 'Alas, I am a great sinner.'

194–200 When fourteen days had thus passed, the king of gods,[5] who with celestials regarded that day as fit for worship, praised the great name of this famous woman, showered unfading flowers upon her and revered her. In a divine chariot at the side of Kōvalaṉ, murdered in the king's city, Kaṇṇaki with the forest-like hair went up to heaven.

[1] Breaking the bangles was a custom in vogue in ancient times. Immediately after her husband's death, the wife broke her bangles, this being the first sign of her widowhood. Kaṇṇaki did this before the Durgā temple. It is interesting that this custom still prevails among certain communities in Southern India.

[2] Arumpadavuraiāśiriyar identifies this with Tiruccengōḍu, which is not probable. Personal inquiry about any local tradition of a Kaṇṇaki temple there proved fruitless. This hill must therefore be one which was at a distance of fourteen days' walk from Madura to the west. To venture a conjecture it may be the Palni range containing a sacred shrine of Subrahmanya.

[3] A reference to the vanquishing by the war-god of the *Asura* hiding in the sea. This tradition still exists in association with the Subrahmaṇya shrine at Tirruccendur in Tinnevelly district. The story runs that after vanquishing the *Asura*, Subrahmaṇya departed for Tirupparankuṉṟam in Madura district where he married Dēvayānī, the daughter of Indra.

[4] This refers to the piercing of the Krauñca hill.

[5] It is said that Indra in person took her to Heaven—a rare honour reserved only for women of chastity.

VEṆBĀ

Because it is a fact that gods will worship her who worships not God but worships her husband,[1] Kaṇṇaki, that jewel among the women of the earth, became a goddess and the guest of the ladies of heaven.

EPILOGUE

Thus ends the Maduraikkāṇḍam which describes the virtues, victories, and heroism of the dynasty of the Pāṇḍyas, who held the distinguished spear in their hands among the dynasties of the three crowned monarchs. It also describes the great glory attached to their ancient and famous capital, the richness of their festivals, the approach of the gods to the city, the unfailing happiness of the village communities, the abundance of their rich foodstuffs, the fertility yielded by the great Vaigai river, the never-failing fresh showers supplied by the rain-bearing clouds, the two *viruttis* called *ārapaṭi*[2] and *śāttuvadi*,[3] and the songs and dances in which these were exhibited. These and many other things, illustrative of the unmatched rule of righteousness of the Pāṇḍyan Neḍuñjeḻiyaṉ,[4] who van-

[1] Cf. *Kuṟaḷveṇbā*, 55.

[2] *Ārapaṭi* (*Ārabhaṭi*)—'a kind of drama having for its topic the acquisition of wealth and centering round the achievements of great warriors as heroes, one of tho four *nāṭakaviruttis*' (*Tamil Lexicon*, p. 242). See also *Slia.*, canto iii, l. 13, comment.

[3] *Sāttuvadi* (*sātvati*)—'a variety of dramatic composition which has a semi-divine being for hero and treats of vihue, one of the four *nāṭakaviruttis*' (ibid., p. 1362).

[4] This Pāṇḍyan king who was a contemporary of Cēraṉ Seṅguṭṭuvaṉ is called Araiśu-kaṭṭiliṟuñjiya Pāṇḍya-Neḍuñjeḻiyaṉ. We have other kings whose names were prefixed by Pāṇḍyan Ilavantikaippaḷḷituñjiya Naṉmāṟaṉ, Pāṇḍyan Cittiramaṭattutuñjiya Naṉmāraṉ, etc. The term 'tuñjiya' in these contexts means, simply, 'dead'. In order to distinguish the one name from the other it was probably then a tradition to prefix to each king's name the place where he died. It is said that the Sāmudiri dynasty ruling at Calicut continues this custom of naming themselves. See *Puṟanāṉūṟu*, p. 581 n.

quished the army of the northern Aryas, and established peace in the southern Tamil country, and who again slept eternal sleep seated on the throne with his queen of faultless chastity, are described.

BOOK III

VAÑJIKKĀṆḌAM

CANTO XXIV

KUṈṞAKKURAVAI

OR

THE DANCE OF THE HILL-MAIDENS

URAIPPĀṬṬUMAḌAI

THE hill-maidens spoke thus: 'We came to the hillside to scare away little birds and drive off parrots, to sport in the waterfalls and plunge into springs;[1] and while wandering about with no other concern, we saw a lady and asked her: "O lady, who lookest like Vaḷḷi, who art thou that standest in the shade of the fragrant mountain tree, *vēngai,* after losing thy breast and breaking our hearts?" (Kaṇṇaki) coolly replied: "I am she whose cruel destiny it was to lose her husband on that evil day when ever-joyous Madura and its king were fated to be ruined." Hearing this, the hill-maidens were struck with awe and worshipped her with their bangled hands uplifted, and the gods showered flowers like copious rain.' 1–9

The maidens continued: 'In our presence and in that of other hillfolk she was taken to Heaven by the gods with her husband. There is no deity like her for our community, O people of small hamlets![2] O people of small hamlets! Let us acclaim this lady as our Goddess, O people of small hamlets! Under the cool shade of the *vēngai* whose odorous flower-buds (grow) on the slopes of the hill with enchanting waterfalls, acclaim this deity, O people 10–22

[1] Here we are introduced to the daily life of the hill-men and women. They were devotees of Murugaṉ, the god of the *kuṟiñji* region. Vaḷḷi is the consort of this god.

[2] Siṟukuḍi as opposed to Perumkuḍi. This indicates that their residences were simple in character.

of small hamlets! Play upon the *toṇḍakam*,[1] beat the little drum, blow the horn, and ring the noisy bell, sing the *kuṟiñji*,[2] offer spicy incense, perform the sacrifice of flowers, and erect the surrounding wall with its door, hymn songs of praise and scatter flowers—all in honour of this lady who has lost one of her breasts—so that the great hill may, without diminution, flourish in plenty.'[3]

KOḶUCCOL

Then began the song. (The maid said to the lady) :[4]

'Dear girl of beautiful ornaments! You will not see anything there, (come and) see what is here. The mountain-stream comes bubbling along, as beautiful as Indra's bow, mixed with the black powder of *añjaṉa*, the yellow powder of *aritāra* and the red powder of *sindura* (vermilion). We shall go and bathe in it. Let us bathe, friend; let us bathe.

'Though the lord of the hill who enjoyed us has departed from us, saying "Give up your fears", shall we bathe in the stream that comes from the hill surrounded by a misty grove? We find no reason, do we, to be displeased at the fresh floods which come after embracing the rocks of his mountain?[5] O, it is only with the fresh stream which

[1] A kind of musical instrument now gone out of use. This and the mention of similar instruments like the drum, the horn and the bell show that music formed an essential part of prayer.

[2] A song appropriate to the hilly region. It may be noted that the ancient Tamils developed peculiar modes of music according to the geographical environment of the whole Tamil land. There was *pālai* music, *neydal* music, *marudam* music, and so on.

[3] Kaṇṇaki was first adopted as a deity by the hill-maidens, and then by the important kings of South India. A shrine was built for her.

[4] The words of the maid to the heroine. When the hill-maidens began bathing in the waterfalls, their thoughts turned towards their lovers who were at that time separated from them.

[5] The lord of the mountain is the hero. The poet hints that the stream (a lady) embraces this mountain of which their hero is the lord. But the maiden says that they need not be jealous of this action on the part of the stream.

comes after embracing the hillock that we shall play : with whom else should we play, dear friend?

'We can see no single reason to vex our hearts at the new floods which come after sporting with the gold of the hill, do we? O, it is only with the fresh floods that come after sporting with the gold of (our lord's) hill we shall frolic : with whom else should we frolic, dear friend?

'We do not see anything that should vex our hearts, do we?—at this new stream which brings the flower-buds of his mountain? O, it is only with this new stream which brings his mountain flower-buds that we shall play. With whom else should we play, O my friend?'

PAṬṬUMAḌAI

'O girl of sweet words! We have been sporting, diving deep into pure water till our collyrium-eyes became red, praying to (Subrahmaṇya)[1] the wielder of the strong deadly spear, and engaging ourselves in *kuravai* (dance). Come along, friend, let us sing.

'O! This is indeed the spear wielded by the deity who never deserts the highly renowned Cendil,[2] Cengōḍu,[3] the white hill (Veṇkuṇṛam)[4] and Ērakam[5]—the white, shining, leaf-shaped spear, which put an end to (the Asura)

[1] After bathing to the accompaniment of singing and dancing, these girls prayed to their god Murugaṉ that they might be married.

[2] The identification of Cendil with Svāmimalai, by the annotator, seems to be wrong in the light of Erakam being called Svāmimalai by Aruṇagiri-svāmigaḷ. Naccinārkkiṉiyar in his commentary ('Murugu', st. 189) perhaps followed the *Arumpadavurai*. Cendil is Tiruccendūr, the famous Subrahmaṇya shrine in Tinnevelly district.

[3] Seven miles from Sankaridroog railway station, and twenty-two miles from Nāmakal, Salem District. The place is also noted for an Ardhanārīś-vara temple containing a shrine of Viṣṇu in the same compound. (See Dikshitar, *The Matsya Purāṇa*, p. 71.)

[4] The identification of this shrine is not yet established.

[5] Erakam is Svāmimalai, seven miles from Kumbakonam railway station in Tanjore District, situated on the northern bank of the Kāvēri. The god enshrined goes by the name of Svāminātha.

Śūra (in the form of a) mango-tree,[1] in olden days, by chasing him into the sea surrounding the earth.

'O! This is indeed the spear held aloft by the matchless deity with six faces[2] and twelve arms; this is the shining spear wherewith (the God) riding the peacock (*piṇimukam*)[3] and celebrated by the king of the celestials, vanquished the Asura enemies and destroyed their greatness.

'O! This is indeed the spear decorating the lovely hands of him who was suckled by six mothers in the lotus-bed of the Śaravaṇai pool (Śaravaṇappūmpaḷḷi);[4] this is the long spear that destroyed the Krauñca mountain, after cleaving the breast of the Asura who had that hill for his residence.'[5]

PĀṬṬUMAḌAI[6]

'O good girl with bracelets! I am moved to laughter. To cure me of the (love) sickness caused by the owner of the cool hill on which pepper grows,[7] my mother who is not aware of the idle talk in the village (*alar*) thinks that (the spirit of) Kaḍamban[8] (Murugan) has manifested itself in me, and has sent for the Vēlan's[9] (exorcist) *veṟiyāḍal*,[10] intending to abjure it.

[1] The present village of Maṇappāḍu, about eight miles from Tiruccendūr, is supposed to be another form of the original name Māpāḍu, and is connected by tradition with the Asura Sūra.

[2] Ṣaṇmukham of Sanskrit literature.

[3] *Piṇimukam* may also refer to an elephant (see *Paripāḍal*, st. 5). The reference is to a *dēvāsurayuddha* ending in the victory of Indra, the king of Heaven.

[4] Cf. *Tirumurugāṟṟu*, ll. 253-5. This is a favourite legend found in every *Mahāpurāṇa*, dealing with the birth of this war-god.

[5] Cf. *Maṇi.*, canto v, l. 13.

[6] These also are the words of the heroine to her maid, evidently after prayer to their favourite deity.

[7] The chief produce of the hill consisted of cane and pepper.

[8] One of the Tamil names for Subrahmaṇya.

[9] Another Tamil name of the same deity.

[10] It is a kind of dance performed to cure a man possessed of an evil spirit. The Vēlan invokes the aid of Subrahmaṇya and is possessed by the God's spirit and thus exorcises the bad spirit out of the victim.

'O good girl with the lovely bangles! This again provokes my laughter! If the exorcist who is appointed to deliver me from love-sickness caused by the lord of these mountains, comes, that exorcist is a fool. If Murugaṉ will manifest Himself then He will be a greater fool, even though He destroyed the Krauñca mountain.

'O good girl with the serrated bracelets! This also provokes laughter in me. If the exorcist appointed to remove the love-sickness caused by the chieftain of the hill of exceeding fragrance, comes, that exorcist is a fool. If the son of Śiva, seated under the banyan tree[1] manifests Himself then He will be a greater fool.

'O good girl with the choice ornaments! This further provokes my laughter. To expel my severe sickness caused by the embrace of the lord of this mountain, if the exorcist comes, he is a fool indeed. And if my deity who wears the garland of *kaḍappam*,[2] and the wintry blossoms, manifests Himself, He is much more a fool than the exorcist appointed to drive away my sickness.'

PĀṬṬUMAḌAI[3]

(The maid replied):

'The son of the god seated under the banyan tree (Śiva) will come (riding) his peacock with his consort to the courtyard where the appointed exorcist will perform the *veriyāḍal*.[4] When he comes, we shall ask his blessing on our marriage with the lord of this great mountain.[5]

'O son of the god of Kailāsa hill![6] We worship Your feet that look like red *aśoka* flowers, and also the youth-

[1] Cf. *Kalittogai*, st. 81-3, *Maṇi.*, canto iii, l. 144. The Dakṣiṇāmūrti form of Siva is alluded to.

[2] This flower blossoms during the rainy season.

[3] Now follows the reply of the maid to the heroine. Invariably we notice the plural form used by the maid in all love-themes in Tamil literature. The idea underlying this is that the maid identifies herself with the heroine.

[4] Cf. *Puṟam.*, st. 22.

[5] The reference is to the *gāndharva* form of marriage.

[6] Legend has it that the abode of Siva is Kailāsa, the divine hill, and hence Siva is known as Kailāsavāsi.

ful daughter of the mountain folk, who has a crescent-like forehead of the peacock's hue. We beseech you to give us the hero in (a form of) marriage other than that sanctioned by Brahmā.[1]

'We worship your two feet, O son of the daughter of the mountain (Pārvatī)[2], with Vaḷḷi of the crescent-forehead, the youthful daughter of the Kuṟavas[3] dwelling in this our ancient mountain. O great god! Make our hero marry so that it may be known unto many.

'She is a Kuṟava lady. She is of our community. With her we worship your two feet, you of the six faces! May he, who touched your two holy feet and promised to wed me, be blessed with a good marriage, and be rid of a disapproved union.'[4]

PAṬṬUMAḌAI

'When we were singing thus, the lord of our mountain wearing a gorgeous garland, overheard us with sympathy keeping himself hidden.[5] Before he would depart, I went up to him, touched his revered feet with my hands and stood praying to him. Long live you, friend, and listen to what I said (to him).

[1] The reference here is to the *prājāpatya* form of marriage, which shows that all the eight forms of marriage prescribed by Hindu law-codes were by this time known to the Tamil land.

[2] For the legend see the *Matsya Purāṇa*. Umā is the daughter of Himavān and Mēnā.

[3] The Kuṟavas are a primitive tribe living among hills and mountains from prehistoric times. They still linger in small numbers leading the lives of nomads.

[4] Here we see that the hero and heroine had already had a clandestine union of which there was idle talk among the villagers. There was fear on the part of the maid that if her parents came to know of it, she would be taken to task. We seem to read in these stanzas the disadvantages of *kaḷaviyal* and the benefits of *kaṟpiyal*. See *Nālaḍiyār*, st. 86.

[5] What follows is the narration by the maid of what had happened when she was making the above remarks. The maid noticed that the hero was overhearing their conversation, and finding him slip away, she ran to him and requested him to marry the heroine in public. She noticed signs of sympathy on his part and opined that the proposed marriage would soon take place.

'You came to this village wearing a *kaḍamba* garland and wielding a spear, for the sake of our damsel. But you have neither six faces nor a magnificent peacock; nor have you the Kuṟava girl (Vaḷḷi). Nor do you possess the Lord's well-knit shoulders. The people of these small hamlets will not recognize you as the god who is the wearer of the *kaḍamba* garland. Verily, they are ignorant folk.'

PAṬṬUMAḌAI

'Thus then, having heard what I told him of the idle talk in our village, he became sad at heart, but quietly went away. It is likely that the lord of this mountain country will (soon) marry you.

'We shall sing an appropriate song in honour of the chaste lady who is worshipped by many, who was shown her husband by groups of several Dēvas and who destroyed the glory of ancient Madura with her breast.

'We shall sing; come, live you long, friend; we shall sing.

'We shall sing; come, live you long, friend; we shall sing.

'We shall sing in praise of her who burnt the city of Kūḍal of the tall mansions when its righteous rule vanished. When we sing in praise of her who burnt (Madura), we shall (also) pray for the hand of the lord of these mountains in an honourable wedding.'[1]

With sympathy the chaste ladies praise and worship the pretty lady (Kaṇṇaki) in this fertile field of ours. Even after the Dēvas had with extolment restored this pretty lady (Kaṇṇaki) to her husband, they did not cease magnifying her greatness.

[1] In anticipation of the early consummation of marriage the maid advised the heroine to worship the new deity, the Lady of Chastity, and be blessed by her, in the belief that Her blessing would not be in vain.

'Praised and worshipped by the Dēvas of the celestial regions, the lady who stood under the sweet-smelling *vēngai* of the forest—she who stood in the shade of the *vēngai* of the forest—attained her abode along with her husband in Heaven from which she will not be sent back. If we sing in praise of her who will not be sent back from Heaven,[1] this village will also be granted a similar boon.[2]

'O, our village is blessed with a great boon! It is blessed with a great boon. This village which is to witness the marriage of our lady of gold bangles with her husband, is blessed.

'In this way, while we were singing the song of praise for boons received, witnessing our *kuravai* dance[3] and our *koṇḍunilai*[4] song, our lover would come to this very place by His blessing and enjoy the drink (of heroes). May he, the chief of the western country (Kuḍagu)[5] who carved the bow-emblem on the Himalayas and ruled the Kolli[6] (in the south) live many days in happiness!'

[1] She has attained, in philosophical language, *nirvāṇa*.

[2] The implication is that the blessing of the Lady of Chastity would not only benefit a particular individual but the whole community.

[3] This canto shows that *kuravai* was of different kinds of which at least two are mentioned in the *Silappadikāram*. That which was perfomed by the women of the cowherds was in honour of Viṣṇu, and that by the hill-maidens in honour of Murugaṉ. We notice differences in their technique.

[4] *Koṇḍunilai* is a kind of *ceyyuḷ* or song sung apparently to the accompaniment of *the kuravai* dance. This is evident from the *Kalittogai*, st. 39, and the commentary thereon.

[5] The term *kuḍavar-kō* is important, and stands for the king of the western region of the Tamil land. It is worth noting that the ancient poets divided the whole Tamil land into three regions—west, east and south. At the head of the eastern region was the Cōḷa, the *Kuṇavar-kō*, and of the south was the Pāṇḍya, the *Teṉṉavar-kō*. (See *Padiṟṟu*., st. 55 for the use of the term *kuḍavar-kō*.)

[6] The Sangam classics refer to Kolli in their addresses to the Cēra (see, for example, *Puṟanāṉūṟu*, st. 22; *Ahanānūṟu*., st. 209; *Padiṟṟu*., st. 73). From this we can deduce that the Kollimalai formed an important portion of the ancient Cēra kingdom.

CANTO XXV

KĀṬCIKKĀDAI

OR

THE DECISION TO MARCH NORTH

WHEN the prince of the powerful sword, the son of 1–7
the Cēra,[1] who, to the astonishment of the Dēvas, destroyed the *kaḍambu* fenced in by the deep sea, and who carved his bow-emblem on the Himalayas, stayed happily in his silver-white palace beside the (artificial) fountain, with his consort Iḷangō-Vēṇmāḷ,[2] he expressed a desire to go and see the mountain, whose groves were surrounded by clouds, and the music of whose waterfalls resembled an ever-sounding tabor.

Thereupon he left the neighbourhood of Vañji accom- 8–16
panied by a large retinue of women spread over an extensive route so that he appeared like Indra of the mighty spear, who desirous of sporting with the divine damsels dwelling in the grove, rich in the wealth of its flowers, mounted his great elephant (Airāvata)[3] and spread his retinue over a distance of one hundred and forty *yōjanas*, in a region of golden-flowered trees, wide stretching river-banks, islets set in sparkling waters, groves edged with young trees, play-houses and assembly halls.

[1] *Aham.*, st. 127, 347. The reference is to Cēralātaṉ. See *padikam*. Cf. *Aham.*, st. 396. The Cēra line is mythically traced to Heaven.

[2] Seṅguṭṭuvaṉ's queen. It would appear that she belonged to the line of Vēḷir who reigned in later days from Koḍumbālūr in the Pudukottai State. (See *Pudukkottai Inscriptions*. Also *Ep. Rep.*, No. 315 of 1903, and 1908, pp. 87-9.) Similar names Irukkuvēḷ, Irungōvēḷ and Iḷangōvēḷ are found in the inscriptions. The Koḍumbālūr line is a branch of the ancient Vēḷir dynasty that was flourishing in the days of the Śangam epoch (see M. Raghava Aiyangar, *Cēraṉ-Seṅguṭṭuvaṉ*, p. 24, and *Cēravēndar dāyavaḻakku*, pp. 35-6).

[3] Indra's elephant,

17–23 With his suite he reached the bank spread with fine sand dunes from the Pēriyār river,[1] which falls from the great mountain and appears like a garland on the breast of Viṣṇu. Its flowing waters were covered with fully blossomed *kongu, vēngai, koṉṟai* in overhanging clusters, as well as with *nākam, tilakam,* and fragrant *āram,* around which swarms of bees and beetles were murmuring their sweet songs. Here he stayed at ease.

24–32 Everywhere could be heard the songs of the hill-women accompanying the dances proper to each region, the music of the priest[2] (Vēlaṉpāṇi) in honour of the victorious God of the red lance, the *vaḷḷai* song sung to the pounding of the grain, the shrill shouting of the guards in the *tiṉai*-fields, the clamour of the Kuṟavar as they broke open honey-combs, the heavy drum-beat of waterfalls, the trumpeting of elephants attacking tigers, the loud high-pitched voices of the watchmen (*śēṉōṉ*) in their lofts, the noises of mahouts as they trapped elephants in the *kheda*, besides the clangour of his promenading army.

33–55 Then there appeared before him the hill-folk like vanquished kings,[3] laden with tribute, awaiting his audience in the court at floурshing Vañji, rich in rare articles. They came carrying on their heads such presents[4] as : the white tusks of elephants, loads of *ahil*, whisks of deer-hair, pots of honey, chips of sandalwood, lumps of red *sindura*, loads of *añjana* and beautiful *aritāra*,

[1] This is *Poṉṉāṉi* (Sanskrit, *Pūrṇavāhinī*) which takes its source in the Anaimalai Hills. See Pandit R. Raghava Aiyangar's *Vañjimānagar*, p. 54.

[2] Here are depicted the customs and the habits of the hill people. Their priest was named Vēlaṉ. They trapped elephants and gathered honey. In addition to ordinary watchmen it appears that there were guard-stations, made by erecting huts in the thick branches of lofty trees where men were stationed to raise a hue and cry whenever they anticipated danger from wild animals or their enemies.

[3] This demonstrates that there were a number of tributary kings to the Cēra, who was the *de facto* overlord of the Tamil country. It appears that the tributes were generally paid in kind. Cf. *Perumkadai,* Bk. I, ch. lviii, ll. 83-99.

[4] Here we are furnished with a list of fauna and flora of the mountain.

cardamom stalks, pepper stalks, *kūvainūṟu* (arrowroot flour), luxuriant *kavalai*, ripe coconuts, delicious mangoes, garlands of green leaves (*paccilai*), jack-fruits, garlic, sugarcane, flowery creepers, rich bunches of areca-nuts from luxuriant palms, bunches of the big variety of sweet plantains, *āḷi* cubs, lion cubs, tiger cubs, young rutting elephants, young monkeys, bear cubs, *varuḍai* deer that roam the hillsides, fawns of the timid deer, fawns of the musk deer, harmless little mongooses, peacocks with beautiful feathers, *nāvi* kittens (civet cats), wild hens, and parrots with their honeyed words.

They said: 'We have been your slaves for seven 56–63
generations. Long live your prowess! Under the forest *vēngai* tree a lady with a breast plucked out, suffered unequalled distress; but celebrated by celestials she ascended to Heaven. The celestials praised her. We do not know which is her native place, and whose daughter she is. But we know that she came to your country. May your line last for several hundred years!'

Thereat the great Tamil scholar Śāttaṉ,[1] who had 64–86
been witnessing with wonder and joy (all that was happening), addressed the king, the delight of the world and the wielder of the long spear, thus: 'Listen, O great and powerful king! I shall tell you what happened to the lady of lustrous bangles, and to her dear husband, as a result of an ill-fated anklet. I will also tell you how that beautiful woman took her anklet and pleaded before the king of powerful troops, and also how the great and ancient city of Madura was razed by the rising flames from the undeveloped breast of that great lady of chastity, who threw her fair anklet before the queen and left her in wrath

[1] Śittalai Śāttaṉār, the author of the epic *Maṇimēkalai*. Here is unquestionable internal evidence that Sāttaṉār and Iḷangō-Aḍigaḷ were contemporaries, and that both the *Maṇimēkalai* and the *Silappadikāram* are not romances but are historical documents portraying contemporary political and social life in the Tamil land. Sāttaṉ was an eye-witness to what happened in Madura.

declaiming thus: "O lady of the five-plaited hair! Know this: 'The Pāṇḍyan king, who sat on the lion-throne wearing Lakṣmī in his breast, fainted and died, unable to resolve the perplexity of the lady of flower-wreaths.'" Without waiting to hear Kaṇṇaki's heroic words in full but not uneasy in mind although unable to support her great sorrow, the noble queen touched his flowery feet and fell dead, saying: "Let me go the way my lord has gone"—as if her soul sought the departed one.

87–92 'As if it were her intention to point out to you, and to tell you, O mighty king, the nature of the injustice perpetrated by the powerful Pāṇḍyan, (Kaṇṇaki) came to your kingdom, not (wishing) to return alone to her own native place. O king, may your rule of great fame prosper from æon to æon!'[1]

93–104 When he heard of the cruel deed of the king of the Pāṇḍyan country, the Cēra, the king of kings, was anguished and said: 'Before these words, which well deserve condemnation from any monarch of our status, reached our ears, it is good that the Pāṇḍyan laid down his life. For it is the departing soul of the king that has straightened the righteous sceptre,[2] which was bent by this irresistible act of destiny.

'If rains fail, great havoc is caused (to the country). If living beings suffer unrighteousness, widespread fear is caused. Paying due regard to the welfare of his subjects, and wary of tyrannical rule, a protecting king[3] born of a noble line occupies a position which is but suffering and is not to be sought after.'

[1] Cf. *Maduraikkāñji*, l. 194.

[2] In simple words: hitherto the sceptre had been straight, but an unjust act made it bend. The king's voluntary death, however, removed the stigma attached to it and made it once more a righteous sceptre.

[3] The responsibilities of a king are emphasized here by the author. These lines follow the Sanskrit law-codes where the king is ordained to discharge his duties without any regard to rights. The ancient kings did their duty first and then claimed their right. Even an autocratic ruler like Rāvaṇa followed *svadharma*. (*Rāmāyaṇa*, 'Yud'., ch. lxiii.)

The king spoke thus gracefully to the learned poet 105–109
who had graphically narrated the tale of woe, and said to his queen: 'One chaste lady lost her life in peace when her husband died. The other in wrath came to our kingdom. Of these two, O fascinating lady, speak, who is better?'

When the monarch said this, the great queen replied:[1] 110–114
'Let the (Pāṇḍyan) queen whose soul departed before she experienced the agony of surviving her husband, enjoy the great bliss of Heaven! And let this Goddess of Chastity who has come to our extensive country be duly honoured.'

The king with the garlanded white umbrella, approved 115–121
these words and turned towards his learned councillors when they said: 'Either from the Podiyil hills of immortal renown, or from the great Himalayas where the bow-emblem has been carved, a stone should be brought to fashion her image. Both are equally sacred because one is washed by the floods of the Kāvēri and the other by the holy Ganges.'

The monarch replied: 'It is no matter for felicitation 122–140
if kings born in my family of great swords and high valour, be satisfied merely with picking up a stone from the Podiyil hills and cleansing it in the waters of the ancient Kāvēri.[2] If the king of the high mountains (Himalayas), where live the twice-born[3] Brahmanas[4] distinguishable by their matted locks of hair, undried garments, three-stringed sacred threads on their chests, and the strength of their three sacrificial fires, does not give us the stone needed to carve an image of the great Lady of Chastity, then we,

[1] This shows that the queen also took part in the deliberations of the State. We know from the *Rāmāyaṇa* that Maṇḍōdarī went to Rāvaṇa's court after the death of Prahasta, and dissuaded him by several arguments from fighting Rāmā. (See Dikshitar, *Hindu Administrative Institutions*, p. 160.)

[2] This proves beyond doubt that a part of the Kāvēri region belonged to the Cēra Kingdom. It may be noted that the Kāvēri which is seven miles from Vañjikkaruvūr is as much the Cēra river as it is the Cōḷa.

[3] *Dvijas* of Sanskrit literature.

[4] Some of the habits and customs of Brahmanas are mentioned here.

wearing our *vañji* garland from the south, shall demonstrate to those who have survived those already dead, the instability (*kāñci*)[1] of infamous lives which do not pursue the ordained path, the bridal *kāñci*[2] indicative of the giving in marriage of the ever-youthful girl (Umā) born in the ancient family to the moon-crested Dēva (Śiva), and the great *kāñci*,[3] to the opposing northern (king). We shall deprive him (the Himalayas) of his high crown, resplendent like the moon, and shining with a victory-giving garland of *mandāra* flowers strung together with full-blown *vēngai* blossoms. We shall look to all this.'

141–149 With these words, he adorned his elephant-soldiers with *vañji* garlands, celebrating the auspicious day when the umbrella was taken out (*kuṭainilaivañji*),[4] the glorious success of the Cēra (*koṟṟavañji*),[5] the high distinction of earning the perpetual title the *mahārājya*,[6] the great and glorious *vañji* (*peruvañji*)[7] victory, and the unmatched fame achieved by the supply of large quantities of food (*perumcōṟṟuvañji*)[8] and lastly, the triumphant *vaḷḷai* of everlasting glory (*koṟṟavaḷḷai*).[9] He made his war-attired

[1] This is *kāñci-t-tiṇai*, a major theme describing a warrior defending his position, wearing a garland of *kāñci* flowers. (See *Tolk.*, 'Puṟat', *sūtra* 24).

[2] *Makaṭpār Kāñci.* See *Puṟa.*, *veṇbāmālai* iv, st. 24.

[3] *Etirūṉrutal* is 'to take a firm stand for making an attack' (*Tamil Lexicon* p. 525). Cf. *Pingalandai* 'Vaḍkar'—*etirūṉral kāñci.*

[4] 'Theme of a king sending the royal umbrella in advance in an auspicious hour before he actually sets out on an expedition' (*Puṟa.*, *veṇbāmālai* iii, st. 3). See also *Tamil Lexicon.*

[5] 'Theme extolling a king who destroyed his foes with his sword' (*Puṟa.*, *veṇbāmālai* iii, st. 7).

[6] *Mārāyavañji* is a theme indicating the status of overlordship after vanquishing the enemy. See *Tolk.*, 'Puṟat', *sūtra* 8, comm. by Iḷampūraṇar: cf. *Puṟa.*, *veṇbāmālai* iii, st. 11).

[7] *Peruvañji* is yet another theme (*Puṟa.*, *veṇbāmālai* iii, st. 22) treating of setting fire to the enemy's country.

[8] *Perumcōṟṟuvañji* is what the *Tolkāppiyam* styles *perumcōṟṟunilai*; 'Porul', 63. (See also *Puṟa.*, *veṇbāmālai* iii, st. 23.) It is a theme treating of a king feasting his soldiers sumptuously on the eve of a battle.

[9] *Koṟṟavaḷḷai* is 'a theme indirectly describing the prowess of a king by regretting that the enemy's country will be destroyed' (*Tamil Lexicon,* p. 1167). See *Puṟa.*, *veṇbāmālai* iii, st. 7: also *Tolk.*, 'Puṟat', *sūtra* 8.

army wear garlands of unbroken palmyra leaves, and exhorted them saying: 'Outside the golden city of unflowering Vañji[1], we shall wear the *vañji* garlands[2] so that they may keep company with our fierce swords.'

Villavaṉ Kōdai (his minister), then addressed the 150–159
king: 'May your righteous rule last many years! You fought against your equals who surrendered their tiger-flag and fish-flag on the bloody battlefield of Konkaṇ.[3] This (incident) has reached the ears of elephants stationed in the eight directions.[4] My eyes will never forget the sight of your advancing elephant in the midst of Tamil hosts which destroyed the joint forces of Konkaṇar, Kalingar, the cruel Ḳarunāṭar, Bangalar,[5] Gangar, Kaṭṭiyar[6] famous for their innumerable spears, and the northern Aryas.

'Nor can we forget the valour you displayed single- 160–164
handed, when having made your mother bathe in the full and rising floods of the mighty Ganges,[7] you waged such a terrific war against a thousand Aryas, that the cruel God of Death stood aghast.

[1] Cf. *Puṟam.*, st. 100: also st. 22 and st. 27.

[2] Here is a pun on the word *vañji*. The city is ever young and can never become old on account of the monarch's prowess.

[3] The Cēra defeated the Pāṇḍya and the Cōḷa monarchs and became the overlord of the Tamil country.

[4] *Diggajas* of Sanskrit mythology.

[5] The enemy kings of the Cēra king. The Bangalar are probably the people of Bengal. The Gangar may be the early Gangas.

[6] The Kaṭṭis seemed to have occupied the region, south of *Vaḍugarbūmi*. They are frequently mentioned in the *Ahanāṉūṟu* (st. 44 and st. 226) and also in *Kuṟuntogai*, st. 11.

[7] This shows that Śenguṭṭuvaṉ had already been to North India once and shown his prowess. From a vague reference in the *Puṟanāṉūṟu* (st. 62 and 63) that when Śenguṭṭuvaṉ's father and others fell slain in battle their women also committed *sati*, it is argued that this expedition of Śenguṭṭuvaṉ was to secure a stone on which to carve an image of his mother. Against this theory must be set the fact that (1) there is no implicit reference to the *sati* of Śenguṭṭuvaṉ's mother, (2) that there is no reference, explicit or implied, of a stone for an image, and (3) that according to Arumpadavurai-āśiriyar it means that she was taken on a pilgrimage for a sacred bath.

165–172 'If you now propose to extend the Tamil sway over the entire region fenced in by the roaring sea, there will be none in the whole world who can stop you from doing it. So send a message to the following effect: "The object with which our king goes to the Himalayas is to bring a stone on which to carve the image of a deity." Seal it with your clay seal[1] bearing the designs of the strong bow, the fish and the tiger, emblems of the Tamil country, and send it to all the kings of the north.'

Thereupon Aḻumbilvēḷ[2] replied:

173–177 'The spies of all countries situated in the cool shade of the *nāval* tree (i.e. *Jambūdvīpa* or India) never leave the borders of our protecting (capital) Vañji.[3] Will not these spies send information to their respective kings famous for elephants with ornamental trappings? So, it will be enough if we proclaim (your expedition) by tom-tom in our own city.'

178–194 The king of the troops irresistible in battle (Śenguṭṭuvaṉ) agreed. When he reached the glorious unfadable city of Vañji, rich with tribute obtained from expeditions against enemies, it was proclaimed throughout that magnificent city by the beat of a drum carried on the nape of the strong elephant of state.[4]

'Long live our gracious king! May he protect the world from age to age. Because our guardian monarch marches forth to procure a stone from the great Himalayas inscribed with the bow-emblem, all ye who are kings of

[1] Note the use of the clay seal for letters of administrative importance. It is of interest that similar seals have been discovered among the recent prehistoric finds in the Indus valley.

[2] Aḻumbilvēḷ was apparently a Vēḷir chieftain of a small area called Aḻumbil. In this sense the word occurs in Sangam works like the *Ahanāṉūṟu*, st. 44 and *Maduraikkāñji*, ll. 344-5.

[3] This proves the extensive nature of the spy system explained in the *Kauṭalīya Arthaśāstra* and the *Tirukkuṟaḷ*.

[4] A feature of *dharma-yuddha*, (the *dharma-vijaya* of the *Arthaśāstra* and of Aśōkan inscriptions). This was to inform everyone concerned beforehand.

the northern countries, come forth to meet him with tributes. Save yourselves, by remembering (before it is too late) the heroic exploit of our monarch who overthrew the *kaḍambu* of the sea,[1] and his equally heroic deed of carving the bow-emblem on the Himalayan slopes.[2] If you will not listen, abandon your wives and lead the lives of anchorites. Long live the army,[3] precious as his own face to the king who wears victorious anklets.'

[1] See above, canto xxiii, ll. 81-2.

[2] There is a special reference to Śeṅguṭṭuvaṉ's planting the emblem of the bow on the Himalayas in the *Śirupāṇāṟṟuppaḍai*, ll. 47-50.

[3] The term *sēnāmukham* is a Sanskrit expression and means generally a division of an army. In military literature it may also mean a division of the army consisting of three elephants, three chariots, nine horsemen and fifteen footmen.

Canto XXVI

KĀLKŌṬKĀDAI

OR

BRINGING THE STONE

1–18 After the tom-tom[1] had been sounded, the king mounted his ancestral lion-throne when the *purōhita*,[2] the chief astrologer, the celebrated ministers, and army commanders gathered together and blessed him: 'Long live our king of kings.' They requested him to indicate to them the royal intention (to march) in the (northern) direction. The Cēra of the white umbrella, which rose higher than that of all the rival kings of great armies, declared publicly thus: 'If the remarks of the kings of the north, who lead insecure lives, communicated to me by saints residing in the Himalayas, when they came here, are to be passed over in silence, that will cause humiliation to kings such as ourselves. So, if my unfailing sword does not successfully help me to make the northern kings carry on their crowned heads the stone on which the deity's image is to be carved, and if I fail to strike terror into the hearts of my enemy-kings who are ardently war-like and who wear glittering anklets, may I become the wielder of a sceptre striking terror in the subjects of my own fertile regions.'

19–24 The *āśāṉ* then said: 'O mighty conqueror in battle! These remarks apply only to kings (the Cōḷa and the Pāṇḍya) wearing garlands of *ār* and margosa flowers, and

[1] See below, canto xxix, 'Uraippāṭṭumaḍai'.

[2] The *purōhita* was an important limb of the State and was a member of the ministry. This reminds us of the status he occupied in the *Arthaśāstra* polity, where it is said that the arms of the Kṣatriya aided by the science of the Brahmana attain success. The technical term is *āśāṉ* (Sans., Ācārya). (*Ar. Śās.* Bk. I, ch.3.)

beautiful jewelled crowns. O Imayavaramba! Is there any monarch who dares to defy your wrath?[1] They meant no insult to you; so curb your anger.'

At this the astrologer versed in the five *kēḷvis*,[2] who 25–31
knew the effects of the planets in each of the twelve signs of the zodiac,[3] rose up and said: 'Powerful king! Long live your valour! The time is now auspicious for making the rulers of this vast earth prostrate themselves before your beautiful lotus-feet. Prepare to start out in that direction which you intend to follow.'

When the monarch of unfailing success heard this, he 32–42
ordered that his sword and umbrella should be taken northward. Then to the accompaniment of cheers from the *Porunar*,[4] the war drum made a deafening noise, so as to cause Ādiśēṣa, bearer of the weighty earth, to bend down his head.[5] Jewelled lamps dispelled the darkness of the night; and (lifting up) their ranks of closely flying banners, the striking-force, the five great assemblies and the eight great groups, the *purōhita* in the service of the king rich in fierce horses and elephants, financiers, upholders of *dharma*, and executive officers, all spoke (with one voice): 'Long live the ruler of the whole earth.'[6]

[1] Cf. *Kuṟaḷveṇbā* 773.

[2] *Titi*, *Vāram*, *Nakṣattiram*, *Yōgam* and *Karaṇam*. Also *Naṭpu* (ally), *Āṭci* (success), *Uccam* (leading to glory), *Pakai* (enemy), and *Nīcam* (leading to dishonour).

[3] This shows the development of astronomy in the Tamil land and the blind faith of the people in the effects of the movements of planets on individuals and the State. *Mauttikaṉ* (Sans., *Mauhūrtika*) is the technical term for the astrologer.

[4] Bards who encouraged and cheered an army. That such a system was in vogue, even with regard to Aryan warfare, is testified to by the dramatist Bhāsa and the statesman Kauṭalya. Here it was the *purōhita* who instilled enthusiasm into the minds of the soldiers. (See *Hindu Administrative Institutions*, p. 294.)

[5] The reference is to the legend of the serpent Ādiśēṣa bearing the heavy weight of the earth.

[6] The blessings of the officers of the State on the eve of the march of the army.

43–49 His sword of increasing martial repute and garlanded white umbrella were then placed on the nape of the great elephant[1] accustomed to swallowing large balls of rice, and taken outside to their appointed places near the fortified walls.[2] Then the monarch who was distinguished by a garland of palmyra leaves intertwined with perfect *vañji* flowers, entered his assembly hall, and entertained to a grand feast[3] the leaders of the great troops who were clamorous and eager for vigorous warfare.

50–57 The sovereign lord of the sharp sword, decorated his crown of gems with *vañji* blossoms from the unflowering Vañji when the morning drum sounded at the gate, announcing the time for other kings of the earth[4] to pay their tributes. With the victorious *vañji*-wreath were worn the sandals of the great God in whose form the whole universe manifests itself (Śiva), and who wears the crescent in His long, dark matted hair; and having laid the head that bowed to none (else) at His holy shrine,[5] he circumambulated it. The sweet fumes from the sacrificial fires[6] offered by the Vēdic Brahmanas deprived his garland of its lustrous colour. He then mounted the nape of his proud war-elephant.

58–67 There appeared before him some persons bearing the

[1] Paṭṭavarttaṇam was the name of the State elephant.

[2] Preliminaries on the eve of the march of the army. Belief in an auspicious hour was universal and the *parasthānam* and prayers show the prevalence of superstitious ideas.

[3] It is to be noted that the feast was given in the night. See, for an explanation of the term *perumcōru,* canto xxv, l. 144. and n. 6.

[4] A reference to the time for meeting subordinate chieftains.

[5] This shows that Senguṭṭuvaṇ was a follower of the orthodox religion which consisted in the worship of Śiva and Viṣṇu, without any sectarian bias. The temple under reference must have been the Paśupati-Kōil of the present Karūr.

[6] Here is a clear reference to the religion followed by the Cēra monarch. It was the *Vaidika* religion, an important feature of which was the fire-rite. This shows that the Brahmanas of those days were largely engaged in performing Vēdic sacrifices, and were *agnihōtrins* and hence Dīkṣitars in the real sense of the term,

prasādam of the Lord (Viṣṇu) who slumbers[1] in a (yogic) trance at Āḍakamāḍam[2] and addressed him with benedictory words : 'May success attend on Kuṭṭuvaṉ,[3] the lord of the west!' Since the king had already placed on his crown of gems the beautiful sandals of the Lord whose matted hair bears the Gaṅgā, he received this *prasādam* and carried it on his fair, bejewelled shoulders.

As he thus gloriously set forth, the dancing-girls 68–73
who had gathered in the different theatres appeared with clasped arms and said : 'O conquering monarch! May you under the shadow of your white umbrella on your elephant with its forehead decked with *vāhai, tumbai* and *pōndai*, present so delightful a sight as to cause our lustrous bangles to become loosened.'[4]

On the one side Māgada poets,[5] Vaitāḷikas and Sūtas 74–77
praised his success in the field of battle; on the other, elephant warriors, cavalry captains and soldiers with shining swords,[6] celebrated the might of the royal sword.

[1] This refers to the *yōganidrā* of Viṣṇu as mentioned in the Purāṇas.

[2] The identification of Āḍakamāḍam with the Padmanābhasvāmi temple at Trivandrum by the commentator Arumpadavuraiāśiriyar is unconvincing. (See also K. G. Sesha Aiyar's views in *J. I. H.*, 1932, pp. 135-63.)

Āḍakamāḍam is probably a reference to the Vaiṣṇava temple that is now found in the suburb of Karūr. For it is a far cry from Trivandrum to the capital Vañji. To have carried the *prasādam* all that way would have taken several days in those times of slow communication and difficult transport. It is impossible to think that the news of the march had reached distant Trivandrum and made the temple authorities go post-haste, even to Cranganore for the sake of argument, or to Karūr, to bless that king. It is remarkable that there is no trace of such a Vaiṣṇava temple near or about Cranganore.

[3] Kuṭṭuvaṉ is apparently a title adopted by Imayavarambaṉ after he had extended his sway to the *Kuṭṭanāḍu*, and in the same way the Kuḍakkō implies that the Cēra was also the lord of the western country. It may be noted in passing that these two *nāḍus*, the Kuḍa-nāḍu and the Kuṭṭa-nāḍu, are portions of the Kaḍaṉmalaināḍu which formed a large division of the ancient Cēra empire.

[4] The implication is that they are soon to be separated from their lovers.

[5] (Sans., Māgadha.) The presence of Māgadhas and the Sūtas was a North Indian convention. Their function was to glorify the king in season and out of season. Cf. *Ar. Sās.*, Bk. X, ch. 3.

[6] The foot-soldiers were often enlisted from the Maṛavar class who were a virile and hardy tribe.

78–92 (In this manner) the monarch left Vañji, like Indra leaving his celestial city to attack the Asuras. The leaders of the army and the advance guard of his forces, which seemed to have spread to the very shores of the foaming sea, made the backs of the mountains bend (beneath their weight) and caused the plains to quake. He marched thus with his prancing steeds and decorated chariot corps, till he reached the outskirts of the blue mountain (Nīlagiri).[1] There the swaying elephants, the chariots, the horses and the veteran foot-soldiers stayed in a camp (*pāḍi*) protected by zealous guards. The king, resplendent as the sun, graced Mother Earth with his holy feet, and as he went to his great chamber he received the praises of his able warriors.

93–104 Afterwards, prompted by a desire to see this ruler of the vast earth who was like Indra[2] in wealth, saints moving in the sky left for the royal assembly and appeared with their bodies flashing like lightning. The monarch rose up and rendered them obeisance,[3] whereupon they said: 'Listen, O Cēra born in Vañji through the grace of Śiva[4] of the matted hair! We are going to the Malaya (Podiyil) hills. It is your duty to protect the learned Brahmanas who live there, O great king!' They then blessed him and departed. Soon after appeared the
105–115 dancers from the Konkaṇa country,[5] exclaiming: 'Long live the lord of the sea-girt earth!' The fierce Karunāṭar in their respective dresses and ornaments, and actresses whose dark curly hair was loosely woven with shining

[1] The army halted at the Nilgiri hills.

[2] The comparison of Śenguṭṭuvaṉ with Indra who went to attack the Asuras, shows the influence exerted by Sanskrit legends in the Tamil land.

[3] This statement is appropriate to the Purānic tradition that the Gandharvas, Yakṣas, Kinnaras and others used to fly in the air. As they were supposed to be divine beings, they were also worshipped.

[4] Here is further evidence to establish the personal religion of the Cēra King.

[5] The kingdoms of Konkaṇ and Karuṇāṭaka are under reference.

garlands, whose incipient breasts were adorned with (jewelled) chains and whose long eyes resembled dark carps, sang thus in the *pāṇivari*:[1]

'The black koels send forth their note: the bees produce the music of the *yāḻ*! The summer, when buds bloom, has come! Yet our lover has not appeared.'

Next came the people from the Kuḍagu country, with 116–121
their (dancing) girls, possessors of fine bangles and carp-like long eyes. They celebrated in song the *kuravai*[2] peculiar to winter, thus:

'O lady wearing bangles of fine workmanship! Put on your jewellery; watch the moment; the clouds gather rapidly with loud thunder-claps. The chariot in which my lover rode has returned. He has finished his work.'

The Ōvar[3] also came blessing the king: 'May our 122–124
king with the mighty sword bring his expedition to a successful end[4] and live long with his flourishing circle of friends and followers.'

The wielder of the lance that made his enemies quake 125–140
rewarded those who praised (him), in the manner ordained by the master of dances,[5] with rare ornaments of which they had no knowledge. When he rested, the gate-keeper came and reported: 'O king of the righteous sceptre, and of the lofty standard with the bow-emblem! One hundred and two actresses, and two hundred and eight accompany-

[1] *Pāṇivari* was the song sung during summer by the heroine who expected the arrival of her lover.

[2] *Kārkkuravai* is a kind of dancing and music appropriate to the winter season. Here it may be noted that at one and the same time while it was summer in Konkaṇ it was winter in Kuḍagu which bears testimony to the author's accurate geographical knowledge. It is also worth noting that this is the third kind of *kuravai* mentioned in this classic. The other two already noticed are *Ācciyarkuravai* and *Kuṉṟakkuravai*.

[3] Ōviyar, a tribe. Arumpadavuraiāśiriyar speaks of them as *ēttālar* (panegyrists). This is not convincing as panegyrists have already been mentioned.

[4] Literally, 'finish the work assigned to his sword'.

[5] An officer of the State (perhaps in charge of fine arts like music and dancing).

ing singers, and one hundred jesters who are adepts in the ninety-six modes of *pāṣaṇḍa*,[1] one hundred lofty chariots,[2] five hundred spirited elephants, ten thousand steeds with trimmed manes, twenty thousand carts laden with different kinds of merchandise[3] from the northern country unknown to other places, with their contents marked by pictographs, and lastly a thousand *kañjukas*[4] with well-coiffured heads, under the leadership of Sañjayaṉ,[5] have arrived at the gate.'

141–155 The king said: 'Let the dancing-girls, the great officials, and musicians, both vocal and instrumental, come hither along with Sañjayaṉ.' Sañjayaṉ then entered the splendid assembly hall of the righteous king, made his obeisance, and after praising him in many ways, he introduced to him in order the most distinguished officials, and also the hundred and two players, and addressed him thus: 'O king wielding the righteous sceptre! The Nūṟṟuvar Kaṉṉar[6] who have no differences

[1] Ninety-six kinds of *pāṣaṇḍas* are distinguished. There is nothing to corroborate this in Sanskrit literature. Apparently there were a number of heretical sects.

[2] The numerical strength of the army and commissariat which followed Senuguṭṭuvaṉ in his northern expedition.

[3] Here is evidence of the use of the Indus script and the Egyptian script in the ancient Tamil land, implying a large volume of trade between these countries and the far south of India.

[4] *Kañjukamākkaḷ*, literally, 'men attired in splendid dress'. From the context we gather that they were messengers of whom different kinds are distinguished. *Kañjukin* was an important character in Sanskrit dramas. He was generally an attendant on the harem, or a chamberlain, and usually an aged Brahmana. See *Vikramōr.*, Act III, sc. 1. and *Śākuntala*, Act V, sc. 3.

[5] The chief ambassador was Sañjayaṉ.

[6] It is difficult to interpret this term. The difficulty lies in deciding whether the expression stands for a certain individual or a group of individuals. If it is singular number, it may refer to King Śātakarṇi. Taking it in the plural, Pandit M. Raghava Ayyangar identifies them with the chiefs of Mālva. Considering the fact (which the *Śilappadikāram* warrants) that Nūṟṟuvar Kaṉṉar had the command of both banks of the Ganges, meaning that their sway extended to E. Mālva, and the fact of the Mālva chief being present at the consecration ceremeony of Pattiṉidēvi, it is reasonable to assume that an Andhra king is under reference, and that he was an ally of Senguṭṭuvaṉ.

with you and are quite friendly, have said: "If the expedition to the north by the Cēra king is intended to select a stone to carve the figure of a deity upon, we will take a stone from the lofty Himalayas, bathe it in the rushing currents of the Ganges, and bring it to him. We are capable of doing this." May you live long to rule over the sea-girt earth.'

The protecting king whose ocean-like army could 156–165
devour the lives of enemy-kings possessing victorious lances, said in reply: 'Bālakumara's sons, Kaṉaka and Vijaya,[1] and other northern monarchs, with unrestrained tongues[2] on the occasion of a royal banquet spoke disparagingly and in ignorance of the valour of Tamil kings. With exceeding wrath, even like the God of Death, this army marches forth.[3] Therefore instruct the Nūṟṟuvar Kaṉṉar and tell them to prepare for us a great fleet of boats in order that we may cross the sacred Ganges.'

After Sañjayaṉ had gone away, the *kañjukamākkaḷ*, a 166–171
thousand in number, who were faultless in speech, brought chips of sandalwood and pearls from the deep sea together with tributes dispatched by the Pāṇḍyan;[4] then the guardian king directed his pictographic scribes to send, through them, letters (of acknowledgement) sealed with clay, to all those kings.[5]

After (the messengers) had left (for their respective 172–181
destinations) the ruler of the sea-girt earth received the praises of the chief officials in charge of different local units, broke up his camp and marched to the holy Ganges

[1] For a probable identification, see K. G. Sesha Ayyar's article on 'The Date of *Śilappadikāram*' in the *Madras Christian College Magazine*, 1917.

[2] Cf. *Kuṟaḷveṇbā* 127.

[3] It is interesting to note that royal banquets were held, recalling modern State banquets. The *Arumpadavurai* interprets the term *virundiṉ maṉṉar* as 'new kings'. In this case the meaning is that 'Kaṉaka and Vijaya and other new kings spoke thus in a meeting'.

[4] This shows that the Pāṇḍyan king was a subordinate chieftain of Senguṭṭuvaṉ.

[5] This institution answers to the *lekhaka* of the *Arthaśāstra*.

which he crossed, on the fleet of boats supplied by the Kannar, to the northern bank where they welcomed him. Passing beyond that region also he proceeded to the *uttara*[1] country of the enemy hemmed in by a vast expanse of water, and with his army entered the camp near the battlefield.

182–196 Confronted with such a warrior, Uttaran (Sans. Uttara), Vicittiran (Vicitra), Uruttiran (Rudra), Bairvan (Bhairava), Cittiran (Citra), Śingan (Simha), Tanuttaran (Dhanurdhara), Śivētan (Śivēta), and other kings of the north, along with Kanaka and Vijaya marched at the head of a confederate army vast as the ocean, saying : 'Let us see the prowess of the southern Tamil kings.' When they advanced thus Śenguṭṭuvan inwardly rejoiced, even as a hungry lion in search of prey would rejoice at the sight of a herd of elephants, and sprang upon the different forces of the enemy decorated with *kāñci* garlands. The *pandal* of flags swallowed the sun's rays ; the earth (the battlefield) re-echoed to the sounds of the cruel drums covered with well-tanned skins, white conches, roaring drums, long horns and sweet cymbals (*pāṇḍil*),[2] reinforced by the all-pervading thunder of the royal war-drum with its hairy covering[3] seeming to devour lives given in sacrifice.

197–203 At that time the volume of dust raised by archers with bows on their shoulders, by soldiers with fierce spears in their hands, by warriors with leather shields, by mighty chariot-warriors, by elephant-men on their white-tusked elephants, and by fleet horsemen, spread over that vast

[1] What territory actually constituted this *uttara* country is difficult to say. Perhaps it is a reference to the territory north of the Ganges.

[2] A reference to certain martial musical instruments.

[3] It was the custom to have the royal drum covered with the skin of a powerful bull which had vanquished a tiger by sheer prowess. The hair was not removed from the skin. (See *Jīvakacintāmaṇi*, st. 2899 and *Maduraikkāñji*, ll. 732-3.)

region blindfolding the people and choked the clappers of the bells hanging from the necks of the war-elephants, and the loud-toned conches attached to the stately standards—which prevented them from striking more terror.

The vanguard of one army came in close contact with 204–210
the other and confusion prevailed. Heads and shoulders were cut off and separated when the archers gathered the dead bodies into heaps. The headless bodies (*kavandam*)[1] of the (soldiers) cut off by the sword, danced keeping time to the music of female ghosts, whose eyes resembled one-faced drums. Female goblins formed themselves in groups and danced drinking the blood gushing from the carcasses mixed with human flesh.

The valorous soldiers of the Arya (northern) kings 211–219
celebrated for their death-dealing chariot forces, were thus slain and piled upon the battlefield; the tops of their lofty chariots, as well as their massive fighting elephants and the groups of swift-footed horses, were destroyed and piled together in heaps[2] by the Cēra with the brilliant anklet, who pompously wore on his high crown a fitting garland of *tumbai*[3] flowers intermixed with palmyra leaves, and showed himself to the Arya kings in the battlefield like the God of Death riding fast on his buffalo[4] to swallow up all lives within a day.

The mighty spearmen Kaṇaka and Vijaya who bore 220–230
angry spears in their hands and their fifty-two able chariot-warriors who had spoken insultingly of the Tamil kings, now fell a prey to the fury of Śenguṭṭuvan. Some others dressed their hair in coiled plaits, some wore ascetic robes, some smeared themselves with ashes, some looked like anchorites seated on pedestals with peacock's feathers,

[1] See *Paṭṭiṉappālai*, l. 236 and ll. 256-60. Cf. *Matsya Purāṇa*, ch. 50.

[2] The term *nūḻilāṭṭu* means killing in large numbers and piling up the carcasses. See *Malaipaḍu*, st. 87, comm.

[3] *Tumbai* was an emblem of unique victory.

[4] Mahiṣa is the steed of the God of Death.

some as minstrels, some with musical instruments on their shoulders, and some as dancers threw away their swords and went to different regions in suitable disguises.

231–241 But those who had to guard the accoutred elephants shook with fear. These animals Śenguṭṭuvaṉ yoked like mere oxen, and using swords as sticks, he brought down the sheaf (the enemy) and by beating threshed it.[1] Him who ploughed the battle-ground with his spear, the goblins praised. They lifted with their long bangled quivering hands, the dark crowned heads of the dead and displaying them in front they sang and praised the First God in the celebrated *muṉṟērkkuravai* (comparing this battle) with that at the time of the churning of the milk-ocean, and with the battle waged in sea-swept Lankā, and also with the war when He, sea-hued, drove the chariot (of Arjuna); the *piṉṟērkkuravai*[2] consisted of a goblin-dance in that burial ground (the battlefield).

242–246 With crowned heads as the oven on which broken heads were placed as cooking vessels and shoulder-blades used as ladles, the goblin-cook fed each goblin with a belly-full of animal food. Delighted with that ghastly meal, the goblin groups said this as grace: 'Let the king wielding the righteous sceptre, who fought and won this *dharmaic* battle,[3] live long.'

247–254 Śenguṭṭuvaṉ of the mighty spear who had brought the war to a successful end said to his foot-messengers: 'Go and courteously assure our support to all those who

[1] The term *atari-tirittal* means literally 'threshing grain with cattle'. The threshing floor is compared here to the battle-ground, and the grain to the enemy ranks, and the cattle to elephants. (See *Puṟam.*, st. 371.)

[2] *Piṉṟērkkuravai* is a kind of war dance, generally danced behind the war-chariot of honour to celebrate victory in war. Similarly there was *muṉṟerkkuravai*, a kind of dance danced in front of the war-chariot of honour. In this particular case the dance of the goblins represented the *piṉṟērkkuravai*.

[3] This shows that the slaughter of non-combatants was not countenanced. When once the sword was cast off and soldiers had put on ascetic robes they were not interfered with. It may also be taken to mean that while it was a righteous war from the point of view of the goblins it was really an unrighteous war.

uphold the Vēdas in the northern region, and who lead holy lives by keeping alight sacrificial fires.' Afterwards the protecting king, who had won the battle and accomplished his object with Villavaṉ Kōdai, commanded several differently armed units of his army to secure from the golden-crested Himalayas a stone slab from which he proceeded to carve the image of the peerless Goddess of Chastity.

CANTO XXVII

NIRPPAṬAIKKĀDAI

OR

BATHING THE STONE

1–10 AFTER the stone slab brought from the renowned Himalayas in the north had been carved into the figure of the goddess Pattiṉi, the rain-bestower, it was placed on the resplendent crowns of Kaṉaka and Vijaya, who had offered battle to Śenguṭṭuvaṉ of the angry spear, the king of the shining anklet, who as if he had assumed the function of the Lord of Death in eighteen *nāḻigais*[1] swallowed up numbers of lives of the Arya kings who had not hitherto respected the prowess of the southern Tamils so that this sea-girt world might add this to the list of battles fought respectively for eighteen years,[2] eighteen months[3] and eighteen days.[4]

11–24 Śenguṭṭuvaṉ who put to death in the field of battle advancing hosts of the enemy in a single day with his army of frightful lances, came back to the banks of the mighty

[1] Sixty *nāḻigais* make one day and night. One hour is equal to 2½ *nāḻigais*.

[2] The reference is to a Dēvāsura-yuddha but we have not come across a Dēvāsura war which lasted for eighteen years, though a number of similar wars are mentioned in the Purānas.

[3] This seems to be a reference to the Rāma-Rāvaṇa-yuddha. There is no authority for the statement that the *Rāmāyaṇa* war lasted for eighteen months. Even if we take into consideration the Khara-yuddha which is said to have been fought in Hēmanta (roughly January), Rāvaṇa was slain at the beginning of the following April. This calculation gives a duration of only fifteen months. But Kambaṉ in describing the shedding of the blood of Sūrpaṇakā, the sister of Rāvaṇa, remarks that it was practically the beginning of the war between Rāma and Rāvaṇa. If this tradition is to be believed the total duration of the war may be taken as eighteen months.

[4] The reference is to the great battle fought at Kurukṣetra, the contending parties being the Kauravas and Pāṇḍavas. This duration corresponds to that cited in the epic *Mahābhārata*.

Ganges, and had the stone intended for the goddess Pattini bathed in conformity with Śāstraic rules, with the help of masters versed in ritual.[1] There, on the southern bank of the crystal-clear Ganges, the king entered the camp in a wide plain finely fitted by the Arya kings with a spacious palace,[2] artistic porches, golden islets, *pandals* beautified by flowers, private chambers, large flower-groves, lotus pools, dancing-halls and much else, to meet the needs of that highly renowned monarch.

He summoned to his presence the sons of those 25–47
warriors who :

had put an end to the ambitious enemy kings in those vast regions and made the daughters of Heaven[3] garland them in wedlock ;

had played havoc in the battlefield, and though defeated in action were not disheartened but lay with their shoulders and heads, above value, chopped off ;

had triumphed over their enemies, though but hired soldiers, by the use of spears, ere their own bodies were cut asunder in that wide battlefield ;

had dropped down dead with their swords, their ancestry highly applauded and praised in a *kuravai* dance by goblins with sunken eyes ;

had fallen dead with their fellow-soldiers, causing the demise of their wives[4] who wore sparkling jewels on their necks ;

had, as the vanguard of the army, adorned their

[1] This is another reference to the fact that the king was a follower of the orthodox school of Hinduism.

[2] The reception accorded to Senguṭṭuvaṉ by his allies in the north in honour of his victory.

[3] The reference is to *vīra-svarga*, set apart for bold warriors who remain in action to the end and give up their lives heroically. It is said that such soldiers enjoy heavenly bliss.

[4] It was the custom for wives to take their lives after their husbands had died heroically on the field. It does not necessarily mean that these ladies went to the field with their husbands: Tolkāppiyaṉār prohibited this. (See 'Porul', *sūtra* 175.)

crowns with *vāhai* wreaths in honour of having killed the front ranks of the enemy with their spears;

had fallen down with an ornamental staff fixed in each of their strong chariots and stood with blood on their bodies.

He also summoned soldiers who had taken possession of the field of battle after having cut off, so as to move even Yama to compassion, the dark crowned heads renowned for incalculable prowess, together with warriors whose breastplates had been pierced through to their backs causing wounds on their chests. The monarch who, by his great triumph, had won renown worthy of celebration (by poets) called to each of them 'Come near me' and rewarded one and all with a golden *vāhai* flower which was more than he would present even on his birthday.[1] He also decorated himself with a garland of palmyra and *tumbai*[2] flowers, befitting that great victory.

48–55 While he was thus sitting on his throne, the Brahmana Māḍalaṉ appeared before him and said: 'Long live our king! The seashore song of the lady Mādavi[3] made the crowns of Kaṉaka and Vijaya bear a weight. Ruler of the conquered sea-girt earth, may you live long!' The king replied: 'You have spoken enigmatically, and are not likely to be understood by some among these enemy kings. What did you say, O Brahmana, learned in the four Vēdas? Please explain.'

56–65 The Brahmana Māḍalaṉ then continued: 'The maid Mādavi, whilst sporting on the cool beach, had a lover's

Rewards for the sons of heroic rulers who fell on the field. The comparison of these gifts with those on the king's birthday shows that the custom was to give gifts on a lavish scale on that particular occasion. The day is known as *perumangalam*. (See *Tolk.*, 'Porul', *sūtra* 90. Cf. *Veḷḷaṉināḷ*, *Perumpāṇā.*, l. 295. See above *Sila.*, canto xxiii, l. 56.)

[2] *Tumbai* is a symbolical representation of victory. *Vāhai* represents complete victory.

[3] The implication is that but for the song, Kōvalaṉ would not have left Mādavi's house, and there would have been no tragedy and no consequent glorification of Kaṇṇaki as Dēvi, which necessitated Śenguṭṭuvaṉ's northern expedition in which Kaṉaka and Vijaya were vanquished.

quarrel (with Kōvalaṉ). Then governed by fate,[1] she sang the seashore song appropriate to her dance. This resulted not in their reunion but in their separation, and necessitated his entry with his virtuous wife into the ancient towered city of Madura, whose reigning king with his wreath of leaves attained blissful heaven as a result of the murder of Kōvalaṉ, whose wife, O lord of the Kuḍavar,[2] entered your country. And now she is being borne upon the crowned heads of the northern kings.

'Be good enough to listen also to the reason for my 66–78
coming here, O king of kings holding the illustrious spear! After going round the Podiyil hills sacred to the great sage[3] and bathing in the famous ghat of Kumari (Cape Comorin), I was returning, when, as if impelled by fate, I went into Madura belonging to far-famed Teṉṉavaṉ of the sharp sword. There when Mādari heard that the beautiful (Kaṇṇaki) had defeated the Pāṇḍyan king of the mighty army with her anklet, she proclaimed in the *tātērumaṉṟam*[4]: "O people of the cowherd community! Kōvalaṉ has done no wrong; it is the king who has erred; I have lost her to whom I gave refuge. Have the king's umbrella and sceptre fallen from the righteous path?" With these words, she threw herself into the burning flames in the dead of night.

'Kavundi, distinguished for her holy penance, waxed 79–83
wroth; but when she heard of the death of the great king renowned for his righteous sceptre, her ire was appeased and she burst out: "Was this the fate of those who joined

[1] The author seems to emphasize throughout the book the working of destiny and the fruits of past *karmā*.

[2] This may indicate that the Cēra was the lord of the western region as the Cōḷa was of the eastern (Kunakku).

[3] The sage under reference is Agastya.

[4] *Tātērumaṉṟam* was the common meeting-place of cowherds and cowherdesses, and was generally under a tree.

my company?" She took a vow to die of starvation[1] and thus gave up her life.

84–102 'I heard in full detail all this and also of the devastation that overtook the great city of Madura ruled by the Pāṇḍyan[2] of the golden car. Overcome by grief I went back to my native place, the ancient capital of the Cōḷas[3] and informed the chief men there of this. Kōvalaṉ's father heard what had happened to his son and daughter-in-law and also to the righteous monarch of Madura, and became deeply afflicted. He distributed all his wealth in charity, entered the seven Indra-Vihāras,[4] and began to practise self-denial like the three hundred monks who roam the sky, having renounced the world to obtain release from the cycle of births. The wife of him who thus renounced, unable to endure the sorrowful news of the death of her son under such tragic circumstances, died of pity. Kaṇṇaki's father also (at his fate) gave away his wealth in religious gifts, and adopted *dharma* in the presence of Ājīvakas[5] like sages engaged in penance of a high order. The noble wife of him who made these gifts gave up her good life within a few days.

103–111 'The lady Mādavi heard all this and said to her good mother: "I am in duty bound to live a virtuous life. Do not allow Maṇimēkalai to take to the life of a courtesan which leads to great suffering." Shorn of her hair with the flower-wreaths therein, she entered the Buddha-Vihāra and received holy instruction (*aṟam*).[6] These people died

[1] The practice of *sallēkana* or committing suicide by slow starvation is commended to Jainas and their ascetics in particular. Tradition says that Chandragupta Maurya starved himself to death.

[2] One title of the Pāṇḍyan king was Śeḷiyaṉ.

[3] Kāvērippūmpaṭṭiṉam.

[4] The Buddhist temple.

[5] Kaṇṇaki's father turned out to be an Ājīvaka, while Kaṇṇaki's own religion seems to have been Jainism or Buddhism. This is another proof of the non-differentiation of religious sects in the early centuries of Christian era.

[6] The great transformation in Mādavi's life is remarkable. As a courtesan her fidelity is all the more appreciable. She became a regular

because they heard this news from me; therefore I come to bathe in the holy waters of the Ganges (in order to purify myself). Long live you, O king of kings!'

At this the mighty lord of the Cēras, wearing the unfadable *vañji* garland strung with palmyra leaves and *tumbai*, asked: 'May I hear what happened in the highly flourishing Pāṇḍyan kingdom after the king's death?' Māḍalaṉ the Brahmana spoke again: 'May you live long, O king of the great world. You destroyed in a day the nine umbrellas of nine enemy kings[1] who joined together in an alliance against your brother-in-law Kiḷḷivaḷavaṉ[2] and who would neither countenance his elevation as crown prince nor listen to his commands but who caused ruin to his thriving kingdom; by this you re-established his golden wheel in its rightful place. 112–123

'O Poṟaiyaṉ who adorned thyself with a garland of palmyra leaves on the success of thy sword, held in thy right hand, in uprooting the margosa with its long tufted branches guarded by Paḻaiyaṉ,[3] be gracious and listen. The victorious Vēṟ-Šeḻiyaṉ[4] residing at Koṟkai[5] offered a human sacrifice of one thousand goldsmiths in a day to the divine Pattiṉi who had twisted off one of her breasts. And when ancient Madura lost her glory and was chafing in untold trouble owing to royal injustice, this Pāṇḍyan 124–140

Buddhist *bhikṣuṇī* by casting off her hair, the outward sign of a *sannyāsinī* She also led her daughter to that way of thinking.

[1] See also below, canto xxviii, ll. 116-7. From this it is seen that the battle was fought at Nērivāyil. See also *Padiṟṟu*, Fifth Ten, *padikam*; also *T.A.S.*, Vol. III, pp. 102-4.

[2] The reference is to Perunaṟkiḷḷi, son of Seṅguṭṭuvaṉ's mother's brother and therefore a first cousin of Seṅguṭṭuvaṉ.

[3] The lord of Mōhūr, a small but powerful chieftain of the hills. This line gives us a glimpse into the ancient practice according to which every chieftain had a guardian tree (*kāvalmaram*), and the uprooting of that tree by an enemy king amounted to the defeat of the king of the land. See *Aham.*, st. 347, ll. 3-5; and also st. 127. The reference is to the *kaḍambu* being felled by Imayavarambaṉ.

[4] Vēṟ-Šeḻiyaṉ was the ruler of Koṟkai.

[5] The Pāṇḍyan kingdom had two capitals, Madura and Koṟkai, corresponding to the Cōḻa and the Cēra.

prince of the lunar line,[1] which was celebrated for the exemplary way in which it gave protection to the people of the southern regions, mounted in succession the royal throne of Madura, like the sun mounting in the morning, with his rays crimson, the divine chariot with the single wheel[2] yoked to seven horses with tiny bells attached to their necks. May the king of our land live for all time protecting the world from æon to æon; live he in fame.'

141–161 During the time when the king sat listening to these words of the Brahmana, the wide world was enveloped in complete darkness. With the disappearance of the sun, the thick spreading twilight reddened the western sky where the shining crescent appeared. While the great monarch was gazing at the beauty of the crescent,[3] the court astrologer rose up and spoke words appropriate to the occasion: 'It is now thirty-two months[4] since we left Vañji. Long live the ruler of the earth.' Afterwards the king went along the car street of his camp, lined with strong wooden stakes and enclosed by high, curved curtains of cloth, and casting his eyes upon the hill-like tents, small and big, here and there, went beyond his private chamber down a side-lane and mounted the golden throne picturesquely decorated and beautified by the handi-

[1] That the Pāṇḍyas belonged to the lunar race is evident from more than one reference in the text. If there is any significance in this ancient tradition, prevalent as long ago as the early centuries of the Christian era, it shows that the Pāṇḍyas were not altogether of South Indian stock, purely Tamil in character, but a branch of the lunar line established in the Tamil districts long before epic times.

[2] This is in accordance with Sanskrit legends where the sun is said to ride on a chariot whose single wheel is yoked to seven horses. For details see *Viṣṇupurāṇa*, Bk. II, ch. viii, st. 2-5.

[3] The custom of everyone, from king to peasant, worshipping the moon on the second evening after new moon day was supposed to bring health and wealth. See 'The Lunar Cult in India' in *The Indian Antiquary*, September 1933.

[4] This indicates that it was two years and eight months since Senguṭṭuvaṉ had left his capital. A considerable portion of this time must have been taken in the march of his vast army when there were no means of quick transport.

work of expert artists of the palace. He sent word to Māḍalan̲ through the gate-keeper and asked him: 'Now that the princes of the great and fertile Cōḻa kingdom have died, does the reigning sovereign exercise his sway without fault and with success?'

Māḍalan̲, the peaceful Brahmana, blessed him: 'O my king, may you live long!' Then he said: 'Will there 162–176
ever be a time when the sharp spear of the Cōḻa, which, to the astonishment of the Dēvas who shine with lustrous ornaments destroyed the three fortresses (suspended from the sky),[1] swerves from its upright path? This cannot happen to the righteous sceptre of the monarch who carved and offered the flesh of his own body to a pecking kite,[2] in order to relieve its hunger and to remove the severe affliction of the dove hopping on its tiny feet. There can never be trouble even in times of adversity to the lord whose country is protected by the river Kāvēri.' At these words from Māḍalan̲, the foremost of of the learned Brahmanas, the great king and wielder of the lance, wearing the palmyra garland, became mightily pleased, and saying, 'O Brahmana Māḍalan̲ please accept', he honoured him with a gift of fifty *tulāms* of pure gold equal to his own weight.[3]

[1] See below, canto xxix, 'Ammāṉaivari', l. 4. For similar references see *Puṟam.*, st. 39; *Maṇi.*, canto i, l. 4. Later works like the *Rājarājacōḻan Ulā* (Kaṇṇi, 10) and the *Vikramacōḻan Ulā* (Kaṇṇi) refer to this incident.

[2] In the *Mahābhārata* the story goes thus: in order to test king Sibi's impartial justice Indra and Agni assumed the forms of a hawk and a pigeon respectively. The pigeon which was pursued by the hawk sought shelter from the king. The hawk demanded of the king the pigeon, its legitimate prey. The king who had promised protection to the pigeon offered to give any substitute for it. The hawk claimed the flesh of the king himself. He gladly cut off a piece of flesh and had it weighed. To his amazement the pigeon outweighed all pieces of flesh. Then Sibi himself got into the scale, whereupon Indra and Agni resumed their genuine forms and glorified his sacrificing spirit (*Vana Parva*, ch. 197). For a more or less similar version see the *Jātakas*, Vol. IV, pp. 250 ff. This forms the subject of one of the frescoes at Ajanta, though the fresco is considerably damaged. See G. Yazdani's *Ajanta*, Part I, pp. 4-7. See also N. J. Krom, *Barābudūr* (1927), Vol. I, pp. 275-7.

[3] A measurement equal to one's weight. This means that Seṅguṭṭuvaṉ's weight was equal to that of 50 *tulāms* of gold, and he must therefore have

177–191 Afterwards he gave leave to the Arya kings, the Nūṟṟuvar Kaṉṉar, to go back to their own prosperous kingdoms. Next he commanded his thousand messengers—noted for their fierce replies to haughty questions asked of them by enemy kings—to exhibit to the two great Tamil kings, the royal princes of big armies who fled for their lives disguised as ascetics, and the Arya hermaphrodite[1] distinguished for her dimpled cheeks, dark tuft, carplike long eyes tinged red at the corners, lustrous ear-rings, red mouth with white teeth and *śūḍakam* and other bangles on her shoulders resembling bamboos, swelling young breasts, slender waist which looked like lightning, and anklets on her little feet, and also (to present) the captive kings Kaṉaka and Vijaya who fought because of their ignorance of the great Tamil valour, symbolized by the blemishless palmyra (garland).

192–199 In the morning, after undisturbed sleep the bee (dwelling) in the blossoming lotuses of those vast regions watered by the Ganges, was everywhere murmuring *yāḻ*-like music. The young rising sun appeared on the lofty top of the eastern hills, spreading its wide rays. The conquering ruler of the western regions (Śenguṭṭuvaṉ), decorated his wreath of *vāhai* flowers with *tumbai* of the north, went round the famous camp city, and started in a southern direction with his victorious army.

200–209 In the many-storied mansion piercing the sky (in the city of Vañji) where the Goddess of Prosperity ever dwells, was the golden harem overspread with an artistic flowery canopy, the work of skilled hands, ornamented with hanging festoons of pearls and flowers strung in rows, and

been of large stature. This is also one of the sixteen supreme gifts enjoined on all and on the king particularly. It is clear from the Vijayanagara inscriptions that its kings performed these sixteen gifts. See Dikshitar, *Matsya Purāṇa, A Study*, pp. 95-100.

[1] For a more or less similar description of the *pēḍi* (hermaphrodite) see *Maṇi.*, canto iii, ll. 116-25. This custom of sending a *pēḍi* along with captured kings is peculiar and seems to imply that there was no difference between the *pēḍi* and the vanquished monarch.

glittering with the dazzle of diamonds and of lustrous gems ingeniously set at random in gold thread. Here shone the queen's beautiful gold bedstead, borne by its exquisite golden legs and covered with the soft down shed during the embraces of swans, worthy of the company of her lord[1] in retirement. There the queen rested, yet could not sleep (because of her separation).

At that time the maidservants who had heard of the 210–216
triumph of the chariot and sword of Śenguṭṭuvaṉ in the battlefield, and who were skilled in all modes of giving welcome news, (approached her) wishing her long life and praising her in many a song, said: '(O Lady), abandon now sorrow at the separation of your bosom-lord.' Next the small-bodied, the hunch-backed and the dwarfed waited upon her and said: 'Let Beauty reappear! The great lord is come. Dress your fragrant flowery hair with day-time ornaments.'[2]

Then was also heard the hill song (*kuṟiñjippāṇi*),[3] 217–225
'Let the path of him who returns on the fleeting elephant, decked with *vāhai* and the *tumbai* of the north, be shortened' sung by the Kuṟava maids in different ways. Waiting in their raised lofts they beheld the forester,[4] stupefied by drinking honey from honey-combs on bamboos, failing in his duty of hurling stones from slings at big elephants which trespassed and slept on the extensive millet fields.

The noisy song (*ōdaippāṇi*)[5] of the ploughmen was 226–230
heard: 'Having pulled down the great fortresses of the

[1] It may mean that two mattresses were spread one over the other on the bedstead.

[2] Wives wore no jewellery during the absence of their husbands. Cf. also *Sila.*, canto iv, ll. 47-57.

[3] Songs characteristic of the four regions into which the whole land was divided were sung, beginning with the hill song.

[4] From this we understand that forest-products were protected by the State watchmen. They lived in lofts and their chief article of diet seems to have been honey.

[5] *Ōdaippāṇi* is a song characteristic of the *marudam* region.

northern kings, the lord of the Kuḍavar, who ploughed the enemy's country with asses and sowed white millet,[1] is come; O bullocks! you need not bear tomorrow the heavy plough; for it is the king's birthday[2] when the fetters of the imprisoned will be removed.'

231–241 Beside the celebrated bathing ghat, attractive like Indra's bow in the sky, and spread with the paints, scented powders and flowers of the bathers in the cool Āṉ-Porunai, the music of the flute (*kuḻalpāṇi*)[3] was heard: 'The bowman is coming with herds of cattle from the far famed Himalayas. O cattle, you will mix with them.' This was sung by cowherds who had tied their tufts with flower-wreaths of charming *kuvaḷai* nurtured by the sucking bee, and of the sweet-smelling lotus with fully open petals, when they stood on the stem of the blossomed screw-pine, after driving the king's cattle to their watering place.

242–250 And there was the well-phrased love-song (*antimpāṇi*):[4] 'Our king Vāṉavaṉ has returned to fondle the shoulders and the swelling breasts of his youthful queen. Maidens! Let us sing the *vañji* song[5] in praise of his *tumbai* adorned with palmyra.' This was sung in the language of lovers by fisher-girls who assembled on the seashore in groups beneath the *puṉṉai* tree on the sands washed by the frothy waves playing *ammāṉai* and who gathered in their open, bangled hands, lustrous pearls taken out of conches with clefts in their right sides.

251–256 Listening attentively to these songs, the mighty (sleepless) queen (Kōpperundēvi)[6] replaced her close-fitting

[1] *Kavaṭi* may also be interpreted as cowrie.

[2] The term *veḷḷaṇi* in the text stands for the king's birthday. It was a custom for the king to dress himself in white on that particular day as a symbol of purity and grace.

[3] The song of the *mullai* region.

[4] The song of the *neydal* or the maritime region.

[5] The *vañji* song was sung in honour of victory.

[6] The name of the queen was Iḷangō-vēṉmāḷ. The poet impresses upon us that she was an ideal wife and observed vows as a chaste wife should

bangles. The conches blew. Seated on the topmost point of the swift State elephant, under the garlanded white umbrella, Śenguṭṭuvaṉ with a *vāhai* wreath on his crown entered Vañji, welcomed by its citizens in a procession of carts drawn by elephants.[1]

during the absence of her lord. She passed practically sleepless nights and having discarded her ornaments during the king's absence, put them on again when she heard that her lord was entering the capital.

[1] Elephants were yoked to vehicles and to ride on them was perhaps the privilege of royalty. A reference to the existence of such conveyances is also made in the *Pādiṟṟu.*, Fifth Ten, *padikam*.

CANTO XXVIII

NAḌUKAṞKĀDAI

OR

THE CONSECRATION

1–8 EVENING, when flowers blossom and many say their prayers, took possession of the ancient city of Vañji renowned for the wealth[1] of its great king's victory over the world, and for his conquering sword and tall golden umbrella[2] which like the moon cools the earth. At that hour maidens with shining bangles offered pretty flowers before a lighted lamp[3] burning with a white flame, and prayed: 'Long live the king of the whole world.'

9–16 Ladies with collyrium-painted eyes and with firm, round, and youthful breasts warmly[4] embraced the sword warriors who had brought the king's mission to a successful end,[5] and who wore wreaths of palmyra leaves and gold chains worked with flowers. The chests of some had been pierced by the white tusks of elephants; the chests of others had been scarred with deep wounds caused by long lances; the deep and shining chests of still others had been pierced by shooting arrows; while the jewel-decorated chests of the rest were cleft by sharp swords.

17–26 On that evening, their (ladies') oblique and passionate glances like the flower-arrows of the god with the fish flag, from under the curved dark eyelashes on their moon-like faces, amidst thick clouds of sleek hair fragrant with fumes of incense, conveyed the message (of their hearts)

[1] For similar expressions see *Padiṟru.*, st. 82, l. 16 and *Maduraikkāñji.* l. 763.

[2] The stick and the top of the umbrella were made of gold.

[3] See above, canto ix, ll. 1-3, for the *mores* of household women in their evening prayers.

[4] Cf. *Kalinga.*, Kādai., l. 35.

[5] See below ll. 133-4.

to these young warriors whose chests were adorned with jewels. They extolled the evening, saying: 'This is indeed a medicament;' and the women, whose bodies were like tender mango leaves, accorded to them a feast from the smiles of joy on their red soft lips, opening from their coral mouths in faces with carp-like dark eyes stretching to their beautiful ears.

Evening[1] also provided capital amusement to these 27–36
warriors in the shape of maidens with faultless faces, shining with beauty-spots (*tilaka*) of *kastūri*. Their curly hair and flower-wreaths, where bees still clustered, slipped in their enjoyment and they tidied themselves in front of mirrors.[2] They then gently withdrew a small well-looking lute from its ornamental case and played on the string twisted over its venerable stem, a *pālai-paṇ* which was the natural result of taking the *kural* (basic note) itself as the tonic (*kural*). Then they played the beautiful *kuṟiñji-paṇ* in the traditional mode which was the result of taking *tuttam* (the second note of the scale) as *kural*.

Evening then departed after pointing out to the people 37–40
of ancient Vañji celebrated by many, the spreading rays of the rising moon which received the homage of the world, and which resembled the face of Śenguṭṭuvaṉ, whose anklets were kissed by the crowns of vanquished monarchs, when he gave audience to his aggrieved subjects.

Then the lovers and their ladies obeyed the behests of 41–46
the god of love—the archer using arrows tipped with fine flowers—who held his sway over the moonlit terraces, groves covered with fallen flowers, dancing-halls powdered with (soft) earth, pandals with blooming flowers, white-

[1] The poet narrates how Evening acted as host to the guests, viz. the warriors who had come back from their expedition after a well-earned success. The feast consisted of the embraces of the long-separated lovers, and of singing and dancing.

[2] See *Pari.*, §21, l. 23; *Aham.*, st. 71. The use of looking-glasses was very common

legged bedsteads and canopied verandas[1] over all of which spread the cool rays of the moon.

47–50 In the centre of the ancient city with its rampart walls where flags flew, stood prominently the elegantly decorated *sabhā* hall of the golden palace[2], like Mēru standing in the midst of this vast fruitful sea-girt earth.

51–66 To see the beauty of the moon, the chaste and good queen Vēṇmāḷ came, followed on one side by lamp-bearing maidens[3] with glittering bangles who uttered benedictions of longevity; and on another side by those who played on *mṛdangams* smeared with mud and on lutes with curved pegs, and by those who sang sweet melodies (*paṇ*); on one side were dwarfs and hunchbacks who carried the paste of the musk deer and the paste of white sandalwood; and on another side eunuchs in women's clothes carried incense and other fragrances, maidens carried mattresses scattered with flowers, incense and other scents, and maidservants in the approved manner carried mirrors, clothes and ornamented vessels. Along with his queen the ruler of the sea-girt earth mounted the beautifully decorated terrace.

67–77 Then, a Śākkayaṉ,[4] a dancing expert from Paṟaiyūr,[5]

[1] The general meeting-places of the lovers are given. One feature of such places was the prevalence of cool moonlight.

[2] From this we gather that the palace was in the heart of the fortress city of Vañji.

[3] The queen's attendants and followers. The paraphernalia consisted of musical instruments, scents, flowers and clothes.

[4] The Brahmana as actor and dancer.

[5] Even today we have in Malabar a professional class of dancers and musicians who go by the the name of Śākkiyar. Mr T. K. Gopala Panikkar in his *Malabar and its Folk* (pp. 184-5), gives interesting details of the dress and the methods of these modern Śākkiyars assisted by the Nambiyārs who play the musical instruments. According to the *Divākaram* they were the Vaḷḷuvars or private secretaries to the kings, and the Kūttaśśākkiyars were a section of the Śākkiyars and were perhaps peculiar to the ancient *malaināḍu* (see *Sen Tamil*, Vol. VII, No. 1). But an epigraph of Rājēndra Cōḷa I (V. Rangachari's *Inscriptions of the Madras Presidency*, Vol. III, *Trichinopoly*, No. 824) records in his twenty-ninth year (A.D. 1041), 'a gift of land by the great assembly of Kamaravalli Caturvēdi-

which was famous for Brahmanas versed in the four Vēdas, exhibited for the king's pleasure, the dance known as *koṭṭiccēdam*[1] danced with Umā as part of Himself by the mighty Śiva, while the anklet worn on his beautiful feet tinkled : the big *paṟai* borne in his loving and graceful hand sounded : his red eyes expressed a thousand charming suggestions : and his red matted hair tossed in all directions : her *pāḍagam* did not throb : and yet her *śūḍagam* was not displaced : her waist-band did not produce any sound : her breasts did not shake ; her head jewels were not disturbed : and her sleek curls did not get loosened.

When he had finished praising the ruler of the vast 78–94
world, the latter went to the hall of audience[2] and bade enter the Brahmana Māḍalaṉ, Nīlaṉ, and other *kañjukins*, when the gate-keeper informed him of their arrival. Making obeisance to the king through the palace-officials,[3] Nīlaṉ reported : 'O king with the *tumbai* and the anklet, tokens of success in battle ! Attended by these vanquished Arya kings we went to the ancient city of Śembiyaṉ (Cōḻa) and paid our respects to him through his officers.[4] Seated

magalam to Śākkai Māṟayan Vikramaśōḻan for performing the dance (*śākkai-kūttu*) thrice on each of the festivals Mārgaḻi-tiruvādirai and Vaigāśi-tiruvādirai.' This shows that *śākkai-kūttu* was a living institution in the medieval period of the heyday of the Cōḻa empire.

[1] A kind of dance sacred to Śiva also known as *koḍukoṭṭi* or merely *koṭṭi*. Here Śiva is said to have danced with Umā on one side, that is, in Ardhanārīśvara form.

[2] The term used in the text for the hall of audience is *vettiyaṉ maṇḍapam*—literally the hall where the king sat to give audience to visitors and others. It is also known as *ōlakkamaṇḍapam*, and *perōlakkamaṇḍapam*. See *Studies in Tamil Literature and History*, p. 18.n.

[3] Here we are introduced to another detail of Tamil polity. Officials or non-officials who wished to have interviews with the king spoke to the gate-keeper who in his turn informed the king and with the latter's permission they were admitted to the royal presence. There were certain officials, perhaps of the nature of modern private secretaries, in the palace whose duty it was to introduce visitors to His Majesty.

[4] The term *tamar* has been rendered as 'officers'. It appears that visitors to a king in Tamil India were taken to his presence by special officials who, we have to infer, were appointed for the purpose of welcoming

in the ornamented *maṇḍapam* constructed (with the materials received as gifts) from the Vaccira (Vajra), Avanti and Magada kings,[1] he remarked to the commander of his chariot corps[2] occupying the front rank of the army: "It is no achievement to capture in the wide expanse of the battlefield those who, after displaying great military prowess, gave up their umbrellas and swords and fled in the disguise of non-combatants."[3]

95–108 'When we took leave of the magnanimous Cōḻa monarch with his breast adorned with a glowing garland, O lord of the righteous sceptre, we went to see the king of Madura of resounding fame. The Pāṇḍyan[4] of the mighty spear said: "This is a strange kind of victory indeed, gained by the display of exceeding passion and anger against monarchs who had abandoned the battlefield to the enemy and adopted the garb of ascetics. It is all the more strange when Śenguṭṭuvaṉ had decided to use the shaft of the far-famed white umbrella placed by the Aryan kings on the huge nape of their elephants as a *talaikkōl*[5] (a dancer's rod) signifying Jayanta, and to worship Śiva with His consort Umā at his side at Kuyilāluvam[6] on a part of the Himalayan slopes."'

them and introducing them to His Majesty. The commentator explains *śaṅkōcaparivāram* as probably meaning private officials who had nothing to do with administration.

[1] This presupposes a Cōla expedition to north India, sometime before the one undertaken by Śenguṭṭuvaṉ.

[2] From the term *talaittēr*, it can be inferred that the poet has in his mind the traditional reckoning of the army as *ratha, gaja, turaga,* and *pada.* Here *ratha* occupies the place of honour.

[3] According to the Cōḻa king, the Cēra king's action smacked of unrighteous warfare.

[4] The Pāṇḍyan's view of the capture of prisoners by Śenguṭṭuvaṉ. To him also the action of the Cēra did not commend itself.

[5] The *talaikkōl* was invariably the shaft of the enemy's umbrella seized in war.

[6] A place of worship in the Himalayas sacred to Śiva. The learned editor invites our attention to one Kuylālapuram, mentioned in a commentary on the Jain work *Nīlakēśi*, as one of the places of the Buddha's advent. It has been suggested that the scene of Śenguṭṭuvaṉ's battle lay in the north at Kōśala. See T. G. Aravamutham, *The Kāveri, the Maukharis and the Sangam Age,* p. 40.

When Nīlaṉ reported the disparaging remarks of these two monarchs Śenguṭṭuvaṉ laughed with scorn while his lotus-like red eyes sparkled like fire. (Noticing this change), Māḍalaṉ, of undiminished learning, rose up and said : 109–111

'O king of kings, may your valour live for ever ! May you also live long ! After destroying Viyalūr[1] famous for *neydal* in small bunches, where elephants sleep in the mountains dense with pepper plants, you won a decisive victory at Nērivāyil[2] over nine kings wearing *atti* garlands ; camping on the outskirts of Iḍumbil[3] with your army of lofty chariots, you fought a fierce battle on the sea pursuing the enemy for a long distance ;[4] you discomfited the Arya monarchs who advanced on the banks of the great Ganges with its heavy torrents. 112–121

'O king, wearing a long garland of victory and possessing a huge army ! O lion of kings, who knows all that can be known from great men, dismiss your wrath ! Ruler of the earth, may the days you have yet to live become more numerous than the particles of sand in the cool river Āṉ-porunai ![5] 122–126

'Ruler of the earth encircled by the deep sea, may you live long ! Pray do not dismiss my words. Listen. Even after passing through fifty years of your protection[6] 127–142

[1] Viyalūr is noted for pepper and elephants. It is also called Viyalūr and may be located somewhere in Kaḍaṉmalainādu and was once under. Naṉṉaṉ Vēṇmāḷ (*Aham.*, st. 97).

[2] The battle of Nērivāyil : see *Sila.*, canto xxvii, l. 117 ff. It was a place to the south of Uṟaiyūr.

[3] See *Padiṟṟu.*, Fifth Ten, *padikam*. This is Iḍumbātavanam, a village near Tiruttaraippūṇḍi, Tanjore Dt. It is interesting that the *Tēvāram* should refer to this place.

[4] Here is evidence of a naval expedition. Unfortunately we have no details.

[5] This is modern Amarāvatī. See *Puṟam.*, st. 11, 36, etc.

[6] This shows that either Śenguṭṭuvaṉ was aged fifty at the time of his return to Vañji from his northern expedition ; or it was fifty years since he had assumed the reins of government. The text admits of both interpretations and possibly the latter is more likely.

on this earth you do not perform religious sacrifices[1] but continue to perform the sacrifice of battle. O king, who carried out your vow with a sword in your right hand and with a garland of palmyra! Among your ancestors in this city one king distinguished himself by destroying the *kaḍambu* of the seas;[2] another exhibited great prowess by carving the bow-emblem on the Himalayas;[3] another enabled a Vēdic Brahmana in return for composing some poems, to ascend (bodily) to the higher world;[4] another commanded messengers of Death not to take away lives indiscriminately but only in a particular order; another Cēra penetrated the golden region of the high mountain in the fertile kingdom of the barbarous Yavaṉas[5].

143–154 'Yet another Cēra had the might to assail the hill fortress (*ahappa*) of an enemy after driving him away with his great army from the dire battlefield; another in that illustrious line of kings bathed in the Ayirai[6] river and in the waters brought from the two seas;[7] another brought the *Catukkabbūtam*[8] unto Vañji and offered it the sacrifice of liquor; none of these escaped the clutches of

[1] This instance of religious sacrifice and Senguṭṭuvaṉ's ready approval bears out unmistakably that the king was a true follower of the established religion of the land represented by the Vēda.

[2] *Padiṟṟu.*, st. 2, ll. 12, etc.

[3] Further evidence of an earlier expedition to north India.

[4] The reference is to Pālai Gautamaṉār. See *Paḍiṟṟu.*, Third Ten, *padikam.* Also *Sila.*, canto xxii, p. 63 ff., note. Palyāṉaiccel-keḻukuṭṭuvaṉ is under reference.

[5] The Yavaṉa country must have been somewhere in the Indus region. It is worthy of note that the learned author characterizes them as men of barbarous words. According to the Sanskritists they spoke the *mlēccha* tongue. Their kingdom is mentioned among the northern countries in the *Brahmāṇḍa Purāṇa,* ch. 16.

[6] *Padiṟṟu.*, st. 3, 10, 79, 88-90. Poṉṉāṉi is the modern name. See Pandit R Raghava Aiyangar's *Vañjimānagar*, p. 52 ff. The river takes its source from Ayiraimalai or Aivaramalai in the Ānamalais, Coimbatore District.

[7] The two seas under reference are the eastern and western seas. In other words his sway extended from coast to coast.

[8] *Catukkam* is from the Sanskrit term *Catuṣkam*. It was a feature of ancient cities. See, for example, the description of Lankā in the *Rāmāyaṇa*, 'Sundara.', ch. 53, st. 26.

death. You know well that this body is not stable. Did you not see in your battle with the Arya kings, who insulted the audacious Tamils of conquering prowess, that wealth[1] will not abide for all time with the men living in this fertile world?

'O just king, it is not necessary to point out to men 155–170
of wisdom that youth will not last for ever.[2] O protecting king, the goddess of wealth abides in your breast, for you see your own body covered with grey hairs. Even good souls in divine bodies may, it is just possible, enter human frames on earth. O honoured king, the souls of those who are born as men now may perchance be reborn as animals. Souls which cast off the bodies of animals may, it is possible, find a place in the afflicted bodies of hellish beings.[3] Men are but actors on a stage, and will have no enduring embodiment in only one fixed form.[4] That life after death will depend upon deeds[5] done in a previous birth is a significant statement which is not untrue. O king decorated with a garland of seven crowns[6] on your breast, may the discus which you hold accumulate more and more repute for your line!

'O king of the powerful sword! I have chosen (to 171–178
voice all this) not to solicit rare gifts from you. I cannot suffer to see a good soul wrapped within a good body travel the path trodden by the common people of this vast world. O king who has crossed the limits of learning![7]

[1] The author's view of wealth is explained in Sanskrit by two pregnant words *cala* and *cañcala*.

[2] By past *karmā* a god may be born as a man, a man as an animal, and an animal as a hellish being or *vice versa*.

[3] Here is the philosophic view of life. The author is against postponing things to the morrow.

[4] See *Maṇi.*, canto xii, ll. 51-2.

[5] *Ibid.*, canto vi, ll. 158-9. Belief in *karmā* and rebirth.

[6] Cf. *Padiṟṟu.*, st. 14, 16, 45 comm.

[7] Evidence which shows that Śenguṭṭuvaṉ was highly learned as befitted a Kṣatriya monarch. By the fact that he consented to do the *yajña*, it is clear that he was a member of the Kṣatriya community. If it had not been so, the Brahmana Māḍalaṉ would not have insisted on this, which was the Kṣatriya king's birthright.

You should therefore do that great and fruitful *yajña* (sacrifice which Vēdic scriptures ordain for a Kṣatriya king) with the help of sacrificial priests learned in the four Vēdas, in order that you may gain that (superior) path which gods extol.[1]

179–186 'If you say that a good deed can be done tomorrow,[2] it may chance that your good soul trained in Vēdic lore will leave your body even today. In the whole of this sea-girt world there is not one who knows how long he is to live. May you with this your wedded queen[3] live ever worshipped by monarchs wearing anklets of submission who fall at your feet! May our eminent king live long protecting the world from æon to æon!'

187–194 When the learned tongue of the Vēdic Brahmana thus ploughed and sowed seeds[4] of divine wisdom in the king's ears, those seeds sprouted forth in right time. With a desire to enjoy the fruits of the harvest of virtue, the king with the resounding anklets, commanded the presence of those sacrificial priests who had completed their studies by listening to teachers belonging to a group of traditional interpreters of the four Vēdas. They were asked to commence the festival of sacrificial rituals in the manner instructed by Māḍalaṉ.

195–206 Then he ordered the release of the Arya kings from prison and had them taken outside the ancient city of Vañji of exceeding renown, to the mansion of Vēḷāvikkō, surrounded by pools of water and cool flower-groves. They were told that they might return to their own cities on the day following the end of the religious sacrifice. He had then the pleasure of saying: 'Villavaṉkōdai! Look to their comforts as befits their royalty.' Orders

[1] The implication is that the king must perform the Rājasūya.

[2] Cf. *Aṟaneṟi*, st. 67.

[3] That the queen's presence was indispensable for the religious sacrifice is emphasized, the *dharmapatnī* of Sanskrit literature.

[4] The reference here is to the prescriptions of the *Srauta-sūtra*.

were issued to Aḻumbilvēḷ and also to *āyakkaṇakkar* :[1] 'Let all prisons[2] be vacated and cleaned, let all taxes due from the citizens of our kingdom be remitted.'

Evidencing the example of the Cōḻa king wearing the 207–235
atti garland, Pattiṉi, worshipped and prayed to by all the earth, exhibited the truth of the good old Tamil saying that the chastity of virtuous women would not be meritorious if the valiant monarch did not rule properly[3] and made him (the Cōḻa) realize it; again she made the Pāṇḍyan,[4] the guardian of the southern regions, realize that the king would not live if his sceptre swerved from justice. Further the Cēra[5] king of the western regions was made to feel that the wrath incurred by (true) monarchs would not be appeased till their sworn vows were fulfilled so as to be known to the kings of the northern regions. Pattiṉi who in raging fury had raised flames from one of her breasts and devastated the ancient city of Madura, entered our country and stood in the fresh golden shade of the cool *vēngai* branches. To that venerable lady was dedicated, by the united aid of the *dharmaic* Brahmanas, *purōhitas*, astrologers, and expert sculptors,[6] a shrine (*Pattiṉikkōṭṭam*), constructed in all its parts accord-

[1] Officials of the State, probably connected with the Department of Accounts, especially the Revenue Department.

[2] See above, canto xxiii, ll. 126-7. Cf. *Maṇi.*, canto xix, l. 161. *Jīvaka.*, canto l. 2372.

[3] Cf. *Maṇi.*, canto xxii, ll. 208-9. *Kuṟaḷveṇbā* 543, comm. by Parimēlaḻagar. The implication is that because the Cōḻa king did not reign properly, Kōvalaṉ left his wedded wife for a courtesan, and after wasting all his wealth, he had to abandon his native place for an alien country to seek a livelihood.

[4] The implication here is that the Pāṇḍyan king did not make the necessary preliminary inquiry before administering justice as evidenced by his execution of Kōvalaṉ on the mere testimony of his goldsmith.

[5] The implication in the case of the Cēra is that no Kṣatriya should take an insult from another Kṣatriya lying down. He should squarely face the situation.

[6] The *śilpins* or the sculptors were there to build the temple according to the *Silpaśāstra.*

ing to the prescribed rules[1] so that it might win the approval of the wise. Therein was planted the image of Pattiṉi, carved[2] with expert handiwork upon the stone brought from the Himalayan slopes, the residences of gods, after prayers to the god (Śiva) on the top of those hills. (The deity) was decorated with choice ornaments of exquisite workmanship, and worshipped with flower offerings. At the temple entrance were stationed (images of) the guardian deities.[3] The lion of kings who brought all north India under his control thus performed the ceremony of consecration (*kaḍavuṉ-mangalam*) and commanded the conduct of worship from day to day by sacrificial offerings and other festivities.

[1] These rules are largely found in the treatises known as the *Āgamas*. It may be that the *Āgama* school had come to stay even before the commencement of the Christian era. See P. T. Srinivasa Iyengar, *History of the Tamils*, pp. 87-8.

[2] This is evidence that Sanskrit works on the *Silpaśāstra* had come into popular usage in the Tamil land.

[3] These are called *dik-pālas* and *dvāra-pālas* in Sanskrit literature.

CANTO XXIX

VĀḺTTUKKĀDAI

OR

THE BLESSING

PREFATORY[1]

HAVING defeated the Kongus in a fierce battle and journeyed to the banks of the great Ganges, Śenguṭṭuvaṉ—son of Cēralātaṉ who alone ruled all the earth from Cape Comorin to the Himalayas,[2] and of the daughter of the Cōḻa of the illustrious solar race—remained at Vañji in a wrathful mood. At that time several saints of the north came there, and reported to him that the northern kings who had gathered together on the occasion of the marriage[3] of a certain princess unanimously derided the prowess of the kings of the southern Tamil regions, who had once opened war on them and carved on the Himalayan slopes their distinctive emblems of bow, fish and tiger. In disparagement they said: 'Perhaps there were then no crowned kings here as powerful as ourselves.' Like a wheel that has been set revolving by a stick, the decision to take a stone from the Himalayan slopes for the image (of Kaṇṇaki) received confirmation as it enabled Śenguṭṭuvaṉ to vanquish the kings of Aryavarta. When he had accomplished this he stayed for some time on the banks of the Ganges as an honoured guest, but he made some of them bear the Himalayan Śilā-deity[4] on their crowned

[1] Here is a summary in prose of the gist of the whole story. With the closing of the last canto ending with *mangalam*, the drama comes to an end. Cantos xxix and xxx read like the *Uttarakāṇḍam* of Vālmīki's *Rāmāyaṇa*.

[2] See *Padiṟṟu.*, st. 43.

[3] *Svayamvaram* or selection of a husband by the bride was a common form of marriage among the ancient Kṣatriyas.

[4] The term in the text is *aṇanku*.

heads after bathing it, according to tradition, in the holy Ganges. Thus he appeased his exceeding indignation. He entered the city of Vañji and enshrined with ceremonious consecration the idol of Kaṇṇaki, whose breast was responsible for a revolution, in a temple which was worshipped by many crowned kings of the earth offering tributes.

Soon after this, Māśāttuvāṉ[1] became an ascetic, having heard from the gracious Brahmana an account of the inconsolable mourning of Kaṇṇaki, who had shed tears from the carp-like eyes in her moon-like face, and whose dark dusty tresses had fallen over her back as she condemned the God of Righteousness for the injustice done to Kōvalaṉ resulting in his death at the hands of a detestable person; whereupon she had stood with flowing tears before the king, who died of his unjust act. His aged wife too gave up her life.

On hearing this (account) the nurse, the chief maid, and Dēvandi[2] who had sought refuge with the deity Śāttaṉ, became sorely vexed and went together to see Kaṇṇaki in the great city of Madura, and there heard of the havoc caused by her cast-off breast. They then repaired to the cowherdess Aiyai, the daughter of Mādari, who ceased to live after the loss of her refugee; and all of them took the route along the Vaigai, and ascending the lofty hill,[3] entered the palace of king Śenguṭṭuvaṉ who had enshrined the Lady of Chastity, and addressed him on their relationship (to Kaṇṇaki) thus:[4]

[1] Cf. *Maṇi*, canto xxviii, l. 73.

[2] News spread to Puhār of the disaster which had overtaken Kaṇṇaki and her husband. Dēvandi, Kaṇṇaki's nurse, and the maid then left for Madura to see their distressed friend.

[3] The hills under reference may perhaps be the Paḻni hills near modern Diṇḍigul. Paḻni is still an important place of pilgrimage to Malayali Hindus.

[4] The three who left Puhār for Madura saw Śenguṭṭuvaṉ and each spoke to him about the greatness of their friend.

SPEECH OF DEVANDI

'Know me! I am the companion of that deity protected by the three crowned kings, who was born in the northern Himalayas[1] and bathed in the swift flowing tide of the Ganges, and whose shoulders are adorned with bangles. Know me as the companion of the lady of the Cōḷa country.'

SPEECH OF THE NURSE

'Know me as the nurse of the lady with long eyes, who did not show her anger towards the modest and fair Mādavi[2] but who went clasping her beloved husband's hand to the dreadful forest where even a potful of water could not be found in the wells. Please know that I am the foster-mother of the lady of cool Puhār.'

SPEECH OF THE CHIEF MAID[3]

'Know me as the companion of the lady with the golden bangles who had nothing to say to the mother who gave her birth, nor even a word for the nurse who brought her up, nor for me either, but followed her husband remembering only her duty as a true wife.[4] Know me, a companion of the lady of Pūmpuhār.'

LAMENTATION OF DEVANDI[5]

'I have done no penance. I did not realize the implication of your bad dream on the day I heard it. O, what

[1] The stone for the image was taken from the Himalayas. According to *Vāstu* literature images were also made of earth and wood. But by the time of the *Silappadikāram*, *śila* or stone must have taken their place.

[2] As Kaṇṇaki's difficulties were indirectly due to Mādavi, it would have been natural for her to be angry. But Kaṇṇaki's righteous temperament did not allow her to do more than consider how resistless are the decrees of fate.

[3] *Aṭittōḻi* is, according to the grammatical treatise *Tolkāppiyam*, the daughter of a nurse who serves as the companion and maid of the daughter of the house.

[4] See above, canto xv, ll. 143-4.

[5] All the three now address the image of Kaṇṇaki.

have I done? On the day when your mother heard of the havoc caused by your cast-off breast, O lady with the beautiful tresses of hair, she died of grief. O, did you hear, friend, your mother-in-law also died? O, did you hear that, friend?'

LAMENTATION OF THE NURSE

'Māśāttuvāṉ heard of the harm done to Kōvalaṉ by that wretched man, and the consequent death of the protecting king. Losing heart, he preferred death to life and after making several gifts he took to asceticism.[1] Did you hear that, mother? O, did you also hear, mother, of the renunciation of Mānāikaṉ?'

THE CHIEF MAID'S LAMENTATION

'Mādavi heard of the death of your beloved and of the extreme suffering to you, the lover, and of the crying for shame by common folk, and lost heart. She went to the holy saints living under the *bōdi* tree,[2] gave away in charity all her wealth, and became a nun. O companion, did you hear that? O companion, did you also hear of the renunciation of Maṇimēkalai?'

LAMENTATION OF DĒVANDI POINTING TO AIYAI[3]

'This unmarried girl is the daughter of the old lady[4] who gave up her life saying: "I enter the fire. I was not able to protect the refugee entrusted to me by her (Kavundi) of doubt-free vision." Do you see, friend, Aiyai of the lovely teeth? Do you see, friend, this fair daughter of your aunt?'[5]

1 Māśāttuvāṉ and Mānāikaṉ took to an ascetic life. Life as householders had no more charm for them.

2 The term *bōdi* tree is significant as it proves that both Mādavi and her daughter Maṇimēkalai became Buddhist *bikṣuṇis* or nuns.

3 Dēvandi now addresses Aiyai who followed her and her companions from Madura to the sacred hill.

4 The term Avvai or Auvai here is one of respect.

5 Māma and Māmi (uncle and aunt) are terms still generally used by Tamilians today when addressing elderly men and women. This form of address has thus been the custom from ancient times.

ŚENGUṬṬUVAṈ SPEAKS

'What, what is this? O, what is this? What is this? O! I see in the sky the marvellous sight of a lightning-like figure with golden anklets,[1] waist-band, bangles on her arms, golden ear-rings set with excellent diamonds and other ornaments of superior gold.'

Kaṇṇaki showed her divine form to Śenguṭṭuvaṉ and exclaimed:

'The Pāṇḍyan is blameless. He is now a good guest in the palace of the king of gods. I am his daughter.[2] I am going to sport on the hill of Veṇvēlāṉ (Skanda); friends, please come with me there, all of you.'

SPEECH OF THE MAIDENS OF VAÑJI[3]

'Maidens of Vañji, O maids with waists like *vañji*-creepers, O maids whose feet are dyed with lac, who form the retinue of the conquering monarch, all of you, come!

'Come, all of you, and sing about her who devastated the city of Kūḍal with her breast and discomfited the king with her anklet. Let us all sing about the daughter of Teṉṉavaṉ. She came to our country whose king spoke these words of praise: "Pāṇḍyan monarchs would not live if their just sceptre deviated from its path."

'About that beautiful damsel all of us shall sing. Come along, all of you, we shall sing about the Pāṇḍyaṉ's daughter.'

[1] Kaṇṇaki was seen by Senguṭṭuvaṉ in the air in the form of a goddess.

[2] Here Kaṇṇaki calls herself the daughter of the Pāṇḍyan king. As the latter was the cause of her transformation into a goddess she claims the Pāṇḍyaṉ as her father. The Veṇvēlāṉ hill cannot be Sengōḍu as the commentator has it. Nor can it be Senguṉṟam, if Vañji is to be identified with Karūr in Coimbatore district. This hill is also known to the Sangam classic, *Kalittogai* (st. 27). But it is difficult to venture a conjecture as to its identification. Probably the reference is to the chain of Palṉi hills (see R. Raghava Aiyangar's *Vañjimānagar*, p. 128).

[3] Group worship by the people of Vañji.

THE SPEECH OF THE GROUPS OF MAIDS

'We said that she was our king's daughter. She said that she was the creeper-like daughter of the king of the Vaigai.[1] We shall praise the Vāṉavaṉ (Cēra). Let the gods praise the king of the Vaigai.'

PRAISE (AND BLESSING)

'Long live the king who surrendered his life[2] to the tears of the sorrow-stricken maiden prompted by pre-ordained fate!

'Long live the old dynasty[3] of kings reigning over the people of Madura encircled by the constantly flooding Vaigai! Live long!

'Long live the king[4] who made the tall-crowned monarchs of northern regions bear on their heads the (stone) image yielded by the king of mountains (the Himalayas)!

'Long live the king and his ancient[5] dynasty at Vañji encircled by the Āṉ-porunai in continual floods! Live long!

'All of us shall sing to the king of the Kāvēri regions.[6] Let us sing of Puhār, O girls with flower-decked tresses!'

[1] This is in accordance with Kaṇṇaki's own claim to be the daughter of the Pāṇḍyan.

[2] As has already been shown this points to the high sense of justice that actuated the Pāṇḍyan monarch. The king here stands euphemistically for the king's line.

[3] This shows that the Pāṇḍyan dynasty had a much more ancient history than we would ordinarily imagine.

[4] This is in praise of Śeṅguṭṭuvaṉ who made Vijaya and Kaṉaka carry the stone intended for the image.

[5] The reference is to king Neḍuñjeḻiyaṉ.

[6] It is worthy of note that each of these three Tamil kings lived on the banks of a river. The Āṉ-porunai for the Cēra, the Kāvēri for the Cōḻa, and the Vaigai for the Pāṇḍya show the truth of the theory that ancient kingdoms and civilizations rose and flourished on important river beds. It bears out the antiquity of Tamil culture also.

AMMĀNAI SONG[1]

'O Ammāṉai! who is that strong man who reigned over the sea-girt world and guarded the tall fortress of the king of gods? That powerful person who guarded the tall fortress, O Ammāṉai, know to be the Cōḻa king who pulled down the three fortresses suspended from the heavens. O Ammāṉai, sing of Puhār, the capital of the Cōḻa!

'O Ammāṉai, who is the conquering king[2] praised in heaven for weighing himself and offering flesh from his own body, for the sake of a dove? That king who cut off his flesh, O Ammāṉai, was the king[3] to whom (on a previous occasion) a cow appealed for justice. O Ammāṉai, we shall sing of Pūmpuhār, that king's capital!

'O Ammāṉai, who was he that planted the emblem of the strong tiger on the northern Himalayas when the elephants at the eight cardinal points[4] looked on with unwinking eyes? O Ammāṉai, he who carved his tiger-emblem on the northern Himalayas was the conquering monarch who with grace brought all the eight directions under one umbrella. Let us sing, O Ammāṉai, of Pūmpuhār of that king.

'O Ammāṉai, what is the object of the maidens with handsome ornaments, singing in their homes holding wooden balls in their hands? The object of singing (thus) in their houses is, O Ammāṉai, that their garlanded king should embrace their full-grown and alluring breasts. If

[1] This section of the *Ammāṉai* song, consisting of three stanzas of five lines and one stanza of six lines, is sung in praise of the Cōḻa monarch who had his capital in Puhār. *Ammāṉai* is a wooden ball. The game of *ammāṉai* is still current among the womenfolk of the Tamil land.

[2] The reference is to Sibi Cakravarti.

[3] The allusion is to Manunītikaṇḍa Cōḻaṉ.

[4] *Aṣṭadiggajas* in Sanskrit Literature. Legend has it that the universe lies balanced on the tusks of elephants, each elephant supporting a quarter of the world. Here it alludes to the extensive conquests of the king.

our king so embraces such full-grown and alluring breasts, we will sing of the romantic city of Puhār, O Ammāṉai !'

THE (KANDUKA) BALL SONG[1]

'O girl shining like a golden creeper ! With golden necklaces glittering and in harmony with the repeated tinkling of our lightning-like girdles, let us run in all directions and strike the rebounding ball saying : "Long live the Pāṇḍyan, long live he." Let us strike the ball saying : "Long live he who wears Indra's garland on his chest."

'Let us go, come, sit and move about in front, behind and everywhere, as if the lustrous creeper-like lightning of the sky had descended to the earth. Let us run and strike the rebounding ball saying : "Long live the Pāṇḍyaṉ, long live he." Let us strike the ball saying : "Long live he who wears Indra's garland on his chest."

'The rebounding ball did not stay in our palms : nor did it rise up heavenward leaving the vast earth. Let us go and strike the ball, saying : "Long live the Pāṇḍyaṉ, long live he". Let us strike the ball saying : "Long live he who wears Indra's garland on his chest." '

THE (ŪŚAL) SWINGING SONG[2]

'Seated on the ornamental swing suspended by ropes, let one of us standing close to Aiyai stretch out her hands and, beating the single time-beat, sing of our king who first destroyed the *kaḍambu*. Shall we not swing ourselves in the swing rolling our palm-like oval eyes? Shall we not swing ourselves in the swing singing about the carving of the cruel bow?

'Singing about the heroism and valour of the mountain king Poṟaiyaṉ, our Cēra, who ungrudgingly gave immense

[1] This section of *Kandukavari* (or play with balls), consists of three stanzas of four lines. Each is sung in praise of the Pāṇḍyan king reigning at Madura.

[2] This section of *Ūśalvari*, consisting of three stanzas of five lines each, is in praise of the Cēra king reigning at Vañji.

quantities of food[1] in the war fought between the five (Pāṇḍavas) and the hundred (Kauravas), shall we not swing in the swing causing our cloud-like tresses to wave? Shall we not thus swing singing about the way in which the *kaḍambu* was destroyed?

'Shall we sing to the glory of our king, the lord of men, who protects the earth as far as Cape Comorin, abounding in heavy large stones, with his bow, fish and tiger flags, including the fertile country of the Yavaṉas of barbarous speech?[2] Shall we not swing in the swing bending our lightning-like waists? Shall we not sing of the prowess of him who carved the bow-emblem?'

VALḶAIPPĀṬṬU OR THE PESTLE SONG[3]

The maidens of Puhār[4] gathered together under the shade of the flowering *kāṉci* tree to pound valuable pearls (as rice) using sweet sugarcane as their pestles, singing in praise of Śembiyaṉ's strong chariot and his discus ensign and his garlanded shoulders wide and broad. That alone is song. That song alone is the song which is sung by these damsels (of Puhār).

The damsels of lofty-towered Madura[5] pound with coral pestles, pearls celebrated by poets, singing in praise of the fish-emblem of the Pañcavaṉ[6] whose shoulders shine with the garland of the king of the gods. That alone is song. That song alone is the song which eulogizes the margosa garland of the Pāṇḍyan.

[1] See above, canto xxiii, l. 55: cf. *Puṟam.*, st. 2.

[2] Another reference to the extensive conquests of the Cēra king. He was not only the overlord of the Tamil kingdom but carried conquests to the very north, including the Yavaṉa country. For the Yavaṉas, see *Padiṟṟu.*, second *padikam*. It is interesting to note that the Yavaṉas spoke a harsh tongue.

[3] This section is praise to all the three principal Tamil Kingdoms, the Cōḷa, the Pāṇḍya, and the Cēra.

[4] Puhār was noted for sugarcane and corals of great value.

[5] Madura was noted for superior pearls and coral.

[6] Pañcavaṉ is another term for the Pāṇḍyan.

The damsels of Vañji[1] who pound priceless pearls with pestles of white ivory in sandalwood mortars, sing of the worldwide fame of the garlanded Cēra for the destruction of the *kaḍambu* after crossing the waves. That alone is song. That song alone is the song in praise of the palmyra garland, which enraptures the heart.

Now, it is difficult for those who do not worship the auspicious feet of Poṟaiyaṉ[2] of the great bow, to bless our lord of the great earth. Our king's illustrious daughter (Kaṇṇaki) spoke benedictory words : 'May our Śenguṭṭuvaṉ live long.'[3]

[1] Vañji was noted for elephants, sandalwood and also pearls Thus all the ancient Tamil kingdoms were rich in pearls.

[2] Poṟaiyaṉ is another term for the Cēra.

[3] The section appropriately ends with Kaṇṇaki giving her blessing to Śenguṭṭuvaṉ.

CANTO XXX

VARANTARUKĀDAI

OR

THE BOON

THE great king who had subdued the north saw with his own eyes the divine form of Kaṇṇaki. He looked well at Dēvandikai and asked her : 'Who is that Maṇimēkalai for whom you cried out your heart? What were the grounds for her renunciation? Please tell me that.' 1–5

Dēvandikai blessed the king: 'May the king's fame grow without diminution! May the country shower plenty!' She then narrated to him the great renunciation[1] of Maṇimēkalai, celebrated among the group of dancers, with handsome waist ornaments. She began by saying that her dark tresses had grown in luxuriance so as to be divided into (the usual) five plaits, and her cool eyes delightfully red in the corners had acquired a new charm of which she was unconscious. (Continuing her description of Maṇimekalai she said :) Within her tender coral lips, her pearl-like teeth were not fully grown; her lovely breasts had developed; her bosom had broadened; her slender waist became narrower and her pretty *alkul* had widened; her two thighs were rounded; her shapely tender feet, unable even to bear (the weight) of ornaments, became glossy to the view. Yet men of noble families did not recognize her as a professional dancer because the dancing master had not initiated her into that art. 6–21

[1] Maṇimēkalai, the lovely daughter of the courtesan Mādavi and Kōvalaṉ, renounced her worldly life at an impressionable age, and overcame all temptations. She performed such miraculous works as inspired the poet Sāttaṉār to compose an epic recording her life and career.

22–28 'At that time Mādavi's good mother[1] asked her daughter: "What is your intention? What am I to do?" Then Mādavi called Maṇimēkalai to her, saying: "Come here, my dear modest daughter," and removed her locks[2] with the flower-wreaths thereon, thus making the bodiless god fling to the bare ground his flower dart and his bow of sugarcane. She was admitted to the Buddhist Sangha to follow their *dharma*.

29–37 'When the king and his citizens heard this they felt as sorry as one who had dropped a priceless gem into the deep sea. The well-spoken saint[3] said very kindy: "The lovely girl expressed to me her wish for renunciation." Because that fair maiden changed her fair appearance despite her youthful age, I lamented.'

38–46 After speaking thus to the king, Dēvandikai became god-possessed,[4] and the flower wreaths on her locks fell loose behind her; her brows began to quiver; her coral lips shut to; her white teeth were set in a strange smile; her words were not normal; her lovely face perspired; her fair eyes reddened and her hands were lifted up in a threatening manner. Then she moved her legs and rose from her seat. Unrecognized by many was her understanding. She was in a state of bewilderment. With parched tongue she spoke inspired words before the king of the blossoming *kuṟiñji* region.

47–58 'Among the modest, good, and beautiful womenfolk who have come here to see the installation of this goddess, there are the twin girls born to the handsome wife of Araṭṭaṉ Seṭṭi, as also the little daughter of Śēḍak-

[1] The name of Mādavi's mother was Citrāpati. She reproached Mādavi for having failed in her duty, of initiating Maṇimēkalai into the art of dancing.

[2] The Buddhist *bhikṣuṇi* was expected to cast off all her adornments and shave her head. See above, canto xxvii, ll. 107-8.

[3] The saint under reference is Aṟavaṇa Aḍigaḷ. See S. K. Aiyangar's *Maṇimēkalai in its Historical Setting*, pp. 221-30.

[4] It was the god Śāttaṉ who entered into the person of Dēvandikai and served as the medium between the god and man.

kuḍumbi,[1] engaged in the service of the Lord reposing upon the Divine Serpent in the Golden Temple (Āḍakamāḍam). Near the temple of Mangalā-Dēvi[2] there is a sky-high hill on the red crests of which stands a big bow-like rock with many pools. From their midst issues forth water, with white stones like small mustard seeds, and red stones resembling *murukku* flowers which seem like dissolved rice flour.

'As those who bathe in those pools will gather know- 59–70
ledge of their past births, I[3] brought that water and handed it over to you, O Brahmana Māḍalaṉ, when you were sitting at the portal of that temple and said: "Receive this. It is meant that you should preserve it. Are you not keeping it in that pot within your string-bag (*uri*) in your hand? As that water will not lose its divine quality so long as the sun and the moon exist, if you now sprinkle it upon these three little girls you will find them remembering their past births. Know me to be Pāśaṇḍaṉ,[4] appearing within the person of this Brahmana lady."'

At this Śenguṭṭuvaṉ was lost in wonder, and turned 71–87
towards Māḍalaṉ when he said with good cheer: 'Hear this, O king! Let all your ills disappear. Lady Mālati once offered milk to the child of her co-wife when fate pursued her and death cut short its life. Mourning inconsolably, and utterly downcast for the child, she prostrated herself, asking for grace, before Pāśaṇḍaṉ (Śāttan) who

[1] A member of the *Arcaka* community.

[2] Dr Swaminatha Aiyar in a note says that the allusion is to Kaṇṇaki. Pandit Raghava Aiyangar examines this and locates the place as the Durgā temple in the village Mangalam, some nine miles to the north-west of Vṛddāchalam (*Cēraṉ Senguṭṭuvaṉ*, p. 8, n. 2). It is interesting to note the name Maṅgalādēviammaṉ occurring in an epigraph (*Ep. Rep.* 420 of 1907) to whom the king of Kērala assigns certain lands as gifts.

[3] I, referred to above, stands for Sāttaṉ.

[4] See above, canto ix, l. 15, where the term *pāśaṇḍaśśāttaṉ* occurs. In the light of this passage it is reasonable to assume that the word Pāśaṇḍaṉ stands for the god Sāttaṉ.

came to her in the form of her child[1] and said: "Mother, give up your great grief" and removed her affliction. He who performed this miracle (Śāttaṉ), grew up well tended under the fostering care of his mother (Mālati) and her co-wife in the ancient family of the Kāppiyas.[2] He then married Dēvandikai by going round the fire. And after living with her for eight years, he showed her his youthful divine form and disappearing said: "Come to my temple."[3]

88–95 'When I was in the temple of Mangalā-Dēvi, this god appeared before me in the form of a Brahmana and gave me this string-bag with the pot in it and asking me to keep it safe, went away. But he never appeared before me again. I took it away with me. Just now, the All-Wise appeared in the person of the Brahmana lady and said to me: "Sprinkle that water." O king, let us, therefore, sprinkle it over these damsels and know the truth.'

96–103 When he had thus sprinkled it, the knowledge of their previous births rose up in their minds and (the mother of Kaṇṇaki) began to sob thus:[4] 'O my daughter, O my helpmate! Without even caring for me who sympathized with you because your celebrated husband misbehaved towards you, you went to an alien city alone but for the company of your husband, and suffered exceeding trouble. O my dearest! Will you not come and relieve me of my great sorrow?'

[1] The account smacks of mythology. It is said that God Himself came to Mālati in the form of her deceased child, grew up in her house, was married, and after a brief period as a householder, returned to His shrine.

[2] Dr Swaminatha Aiyar identifies Kāppiyakkuḍi with a village south-east of Shīyāli. Pandit M. Raghava Aiyangar is of opinion that the reference is to the family of Kāppiyas, perhaps Kāvyagōtra. If the latter construction be accepted, we are reminded of the grammatical treatise *Tolkāppiyam* whose author was evidently a Kāppiyaṉār, a member of the family or *gōtra* of that name.

[3] See, for details, canto ix, ll. 5-36.

[4] The mother of Kaṇṇaki, now born as one of the twin daughters of Araṭṭaṉ Seṭṭi.

Another (the mother of Kōvalan̲) said.[1] 'O, you betook yourself away in the dead of night alone and in misery, with my good daughter-in-law staying with me. Grieving over your departure, I began to rave. I can no more endure this. Will you not come to me, my son?' 104–107

The third (Mādari) said:[2] 'I left for the bathing ghat of the Vaigai of fresh floods. When I came back I heard (the news) from the youngsters of the famous ancient city. I did not see you in my house. O my dear, my dear, where have you hidden yourself?' 108–111

In this manner the three young bangled girls with lisping mouths, lamented again and again and sobbed and wept, uttering their elders' words before the warlike king with golden jewels on his chest. When the king of the *pōndai* garland and victorious anklet looked at the face of Māḍalan̲, the Brahmana wearing the sacred thread on his chest, he blessed him: 'O king of kings. long may you live!' and spoke what he remembered: 'These three were, in previous births, much attached to the devoted wife of Kōvalan̲ who seized the must elephant's tusk to release (from its clutches) a Brahmana suffering deep sorrow, and thus attained the form of a celestial; but they could not follow her to the other world as they had performed no other act of virtue. Because of their excessive attachment born of heartfelt love towards the lovely lady (Kaṇṇaki) like the golden creeper, who fearlessly approached this ancient great city of Vañji, these two were born[3] as twins, to the great satisfaction of the good and modest wife of Araṭṭan̲ Šeṭṭi; and this elderly cowherdess (Mādari) who in her previous birth was devoted to the charming lady (Kaṇṇaki) 112–135

[1] The mother of Kōvalan̲, born now as one of the twin daughters of Araṭṭan̲ Seṭṭi

[2] Mādari, the cowherdess, now born as the daughter of a Brahmana *arcaka*.

[3] Here the poet brings out the great Hindu ideal that detachment and not attachment leads to salvation with no more rebirths.

and performed a *kuravai* dance has now been born as the little daughter of Śēḍakkuḍumbi in the service of Lord Viṣṇu.[1]

136–140 'It is not strange that people who do good things attain heaven and people who have worldly minds are re-born, and that good and bad deeds have their own reward and that those born should die, and those dead should be re-born. Those are ancient truths.[2]

141–146 'You who were born through the grace of Him who rides on the sacred Bull[3] and have won distinction as a king in this wide world, saw, clear as an object held in the palm of your hand, the fruits of righteous deeds and the forms of holy people. Live long from æon to æon protecting the earth! Live long, gracious monarch.'

147–154 Pleased with what the Brahmana Māḍalaṉ said, the king endowed[4] grants to the temple of the ever-youthful Pattiṉi who had twisted off her breast and thereby raised flames which enveloped the noisy *kūḍal* of the great Pāṇḍyan kingdom, much celebrated in poetical themes. He further ordered the conduct of daily festivals by instructing Dēvandikai to offer flowers, perfume and incense.

155–164 The monarch of the world circumambulated the shrine thrice and stood proffering his respects. In front of him the Arya kings[5] released from prison, kings removed[6]

[1] The *kuravai* dance is sacred to Viṣṇu and hence Mādari was born in a family devoted to the service of Viṣṇu.

[2] The great truth that was taught by Kṛṣṇa on the battlefield of Kurukṣētra to Arjuna. The *Gītā* says:

Jātasya hi dhruvō mṛtyuh dhruvam janma mṛtasya ca.

[3] Another statement to testify that Śenguṭṭuvaṉ's religion was Śaivism.

[4] The evidence of epigraphy shows that this custom of endowing temples was practised by all Hindu kings in all periods of Indian history.

[5] The Arya kings are Kaṉaka and Vijaya.

[6] Cf. *A.S.I.*, 1905-6, p. 170.

from the central jail, the Kongu ruler of the Kuḍagu, the king of Mālva and Kayavāgu (Gajabāhu),[1] the king of sea-girt Ceylon, prayed reverentially to the deity thus: 'Please grace our countries by your presence just as you have done this auspicious day, a fête-day at Imayavaramban's sacrifice.' Then a voice from the welkin issued forth: 'I have granted the boon.'

At this Śenguṭṭuvan, the other kings and their valorous 165–182
armies praised the deity in pregnant words as if they had gained salvation (*vīḍu*).[2] Then with the seeker of truth, Brahmana Māḍalan, and with kings of low-sounding anklets who bowed at his feet, Śenguṭṭuvan entered the sacrificial hall.[3] I[4] also went in. Afterwards Dēvandikai stood up before me god-possessed. She came to me, and said: 'In the artistic Audience Hall of the ancient city of Vañji, when you were seated by your father's side, you frowned upon the astrologer who predicted indications of your succeeding to the throne, so as to relieve the affliction of Śenguṭṭuvan famous for his chariot[5] forces and his fragrant *kongu* garland. You then went away to the Guṇavāyirkōṭṭam[6] and standing before eminent saints (*paṭiyōr*) you renounced all thought of the burdens of this earth in order to secure the kingship of

[1] Here is evidence that Gajabāhu introduced the Pattiṉi cult into Ceylon and this cannot be untrue as we are still able to trace remains of this cult to-day. See Appendix Iv.

[2] *Viḍu* stands for *mokṣa* in Sanskrit.

[3] This is definite evidence that Śenguṭṭuvan was a follower of the Vēdic religion. The following line throws welcome light on the personal religion of Iḷangō-Aḍigaḷ also. If he had been converted to the Jaina faith he would not have attended the sacrifices performed according to Vēdic rules, with the help of the Vēdic Brahmanas.

[4] I stands for the author, Iḷangō-Aḍigaḷ.

[5] We have to understand that Śenguṭṭuvan had not only a powerful elephant corps but also a strong chariot force.

[6] The story of how Iḷangō-Aḍigaḷ became an ascetic is told by Pattiṉi whose spirit is said to have entered Dēvandikai.

the vast realm afar-off and of eternal bliss, incapable of approach by even the faculty of reason.[1]

183–202 'O distinguished and good people, you have now heard with distinctness the auspicious and benevolent words of the daughter of the gods (Kaṇṇaki) who proclaimed my story (through Dēvandikai). Rise above pleasure and pain in accordance with the approved course of conduct.[2] Know God, and serve those who have known Him. Fear speaking falsehood. Avoid tale-bearing. Refrain from meat-eating and abjure injury to any living being. Give gifts and perform the prescribed penances. Do not forget the good done to you. Despise bad friendship. Do not give false evidence, and never depart from words of truth. Do not fail to join assemblies of people learned in *dharma*. Strive ever to escape the meeting-places of the unrighteous.

'Avoid other people's wives, and give succour to those who are dying. Protect the household virtues, but reject what is bad. Abstain immediately from drinking, theft, lust, falsehood and useless company. Youth, wealth and the body are impermanent.[3] You cannot escape from the days allotted to you: nor can you avoid what will happen. So seek the best help to the land of your final destination (Heaven). Do all this, O dwellers on this wide prosperous earth.'

[1] These lines seem to be at once a reproduction of the great philosophic truth where occur the following:

यतो वाचो निवर्तन्ते । अप्राप्य मनसा सह ।

Taitt. Āraṇ. 8. 4. 1 and 8. 9. 1.

आनन्दं ब्रह्मणो विद्वान् । न बिभेति कुतश्चनेति ।

Taitt. Up. 2. 4. 1 and 2. 9. 1.

[2] This line and the following are a categorical list of *dharmas* to be observed by all persons irrespective of caste or creed. This the Hindus call *Sanātana Dharma*—what we may term the ethical aspect of Hinduism. This portion of the canto shows strong influence of the teaching of the *Kuṛal*.

[3] The fundamental teaching of Hinduism is that nothing goes with the dying man except his righteous or unrighteous deeds.

Kaṭṭurai

Of the three crowned monarchs, the garlanded ruler (Śenguṭṭuvaṉ) of the western kingdom of undiminished glory was born in the line of the Cēras. His virtue, martial valour and achievements, the glory of his ancient flourishing city, its gorgeous, unceasing festivals and the appearance of Dēvas, the wealth of the subjects abiding in his kingdom of unceasing prosperity, their abundance of provisions, songs and dances with their well-defined inter-relationships, his army of sword-warriors who achieved decisive victory in battles by righteous methods, his success in pursuing the enemy (at a long distance) in the expansive foaming sea,[1] and his expedition to the banks of the holy Ganges—all these deeds which form a part[2] of his career, are narrated in the Vañjikkāṇḍam.

[1] This shows that Śenguṭṭuvaṉ had an equally formidable naval force.

[2] The author here acknowledges that only a part of the career of the Cēra monarch is given. He did not furnish a full account of his life as the contents did not warrant it.

NŪṞKAṬṬURAI

OR

EPITOME OF THE EPIC

So ends the *Śilappadikāram,* which really ends with the contents of the story in the *Maṇimēkalai*[1]. In the manner in which lofty hills are reflected in a mirror, it expresses the essence of the cool Tamil country bounded[2] by the Kumari, Vēngaḍam and the eastern and western seas, in its two quarters of pure and impure Tamiḻ[3] comprising the five regions (*tiṇais*) where dwell men and gods devoted to duty and to the common practice[4] of *dharma*, *artha*, and *kāma*; and it deals in chaste language expressive of good sense in flawless rythm, with *aham* (love) and *puṟam* (war)[5], and with worthy songs (*pāṭal*), *eḻāl,*[6] *paṇ*, *pāṇi, arangu,*[7] *vilakku,* and *āḍal*[8] and other things which were in conformity with established rules of the well-known forms of *vari, kuravai* and *śēdam*[9] couched in perfect and understandable Tamiḻ.

[1] The epic *Maṇimēkalai* is a continuation of the *Silappadikāram.*

[2] For the boundary limits of *Tamiḻagam* see *Vīraśōḻiyam*. Kumari is Cape Comorin and Vēngaḍam the Tirupati Hills.

[3] Two kinds of Tamil were in vogue.

[4] The *Silappadikāram* is itself a treatise on the *Trivarga* which is *dharma, artha* and *kāma.*

[5] This presupposes a period when anthologies of the *Aham*. and *Puṟam.* have been collected under different heads and used as books.

[6] *Eḻāl* is another term for *yāḻ.*

[7] *Arangu* is drama.

[8] *Āḍal* represents different kinds of dances.

[9] *Sēdam* according to the *Tamil Lexicon* is an element in dancing. It may perhaps refer to the *Koṭṭiccēdam.*

APPENDIXES

Appendix I

USE OF SANSKRIT WORDS AND THE DATE OF THE EPIC

Below is given a transliteration of Canto iv, 'Antimālaiśśiṟappucceykādai'. This canto has been chosen at random to show roughly the percentage of Sanskrit words in the text. The Sanskrit words in this canto are all italicized for the sake of easy reference. A counting of the total words in the canto furnishes the number 288. Out of these, thirty-two, or eleven per cent, are Sanskrit words. In other words, for every eight Tamil words we meet with one Sanskrit word. Sanskrit expressions form one-ninth of the text. This shows clearly that the author of the *Śilappadikāram* lived centuries before the authors of the *Tēvāram* and *Divyappirabandam* in which the percentage of Sanskrit words is very much higher. We know definitely that these were compositions extending from the fifth to the tenth century A.D., and it is reasonable to assume that the *Śilappadikāram* must have been composed very much earlier than the fifth century A.D. As it would take some considerable length of time to raise the percentage of Sanskrit words from 11 per cent to 30 per cent, we cannot be far wrong if we assign the composition of the epic to the second century A.D.

ANTIMĀLAIŚŚIṞAPPUCCEYKĀDAI

Virikadir parappi *yulaka*muḻu tāṇḍa
Vorudaṉit tikiri yuravōṟ kāṇe
Nankaṇ vāṉat taṇinilā virikkun
Tingaḷañ śelvaṉ yāṇḍuḷaṉ kolleṉat
Tiśaimukam paśantu śemmalark kaṇkaṇ
Muḻunīr vāra muḻumeyum paṉittut
Tirainī rāṭai yirunila maḍantai

Yaraiśukeḍut talamvaru mallaṟ kālaik
Kaṟaikeḻu kuḍigaḷ kaidalai vaippa
Vaṟaipōku kuḍikaḷo ḍorutiṟam paṟṟi
Valampaḍu tāṉai maṉṉa rilvaḻip
Pulampaṭa viṟutta viruntiṉ maṉṉariṟ
Rāḻtuṇai tuṟantōr taṉittuya reytak
Kādalarp puṇarntōr kaḻimakiḻ veytak
Kuḻalvaḷar mullaiyiṟ kōvalardammoḍu
Maḻalait tumbi vāyvait tūda
Vaṟukāṟ kuṟumpeṟin tarumbupodi *vāśañ*
Śiṟukāṟ śelvaṉ maṟukiṟ ṟūṟṟa
Velvaḷai makaḷir *maṇi*viḷak keḍuppa
Mallaṉ mūdūr mālaivan tiṟutteṉa
Viḷaiya rāyiṉum pakaiyaraśu kaḍiyuñ
Śerumāṉ ṭeṉṉar *kula*muda lākali
Nandi vāṉattu veṇpiṟai tōṉṟip
Puṉkaṉ mālaik kuṟumpeṟin toṭṭip
Pāṉmayiṟ ṟiriyātu pāṟkadir parappi
Mīṉara śāṇḍa veḷḷi viḷakkat
Tilvaḷar mullaiyoḍu *mallikai* yaviḻnda
Palpūñ śēkkaip paḷḷiyuṭ polintu
Śendukirk kōvai śeṉṟēn talku
Lantukiṉ *mēkalai* yaśaintaṉa varunda
Nilavu*ppayaṉ* koḷḷu neḍunilā muṟṟattuk
Kalaviyum pulaviyum kādalaṟ kaḷittāng
Kārva neñcamoḍu kōvalaṟ ketirik
Kōlan koṇḍa *mādavi* yaṉṟiyun
Kuḍatiśai marunkiṉ Veḷḷayir taṉṉoḍu
Kuṇatiśai marunkiṟ kāraki ṟuṟantu
Vaḍamalaip piṟanda vāṇkēḻ vaṭṭattut
Teṉmalaip piṟanda *candaṉa* maṟukat
Tāmaraik koḻumuṟit *tātu*paḍu śeḻumalark
Kāmaru kuvaḷaik kaḻunīr māmalarp
Paindaḷirp paḍalai parūkkā *ḻārañ*
Śundaraśśuṇṇat tukaḷoḍu maḷaiyic
Cindupu parinda śeḻumpūñ śekkai

Mandamā rutattu mayankiṉar malintāng
Kāviyan koḻuna rakalat toṭunkik
Kāviyan kaṇṇāṟ kaḻittuyileyta
Vañceñ śīṟaḍi yaṇiśilam poḻiya
Meṉṟuki lalkuṉ mēkalai nīngak
Konkai muṉṟiṟ *kunkuma* meḻutāṇ
Mangala vaṇiyiṟ Piṟitaṇi makiḻāḷ
Koḍunkuḻai tuṟandu vaḍinduviḻ kādiṉa
Ṭingaḷ vāṇmukañ śiṟuviyar piriyac
Cenkaya ṇeḍunka *ṇañcaṉa* maṟappap
Pavaḷa vāṇuta *ṟilaka* miḻappat
Tavaḷa vāṇakai kōvala ṉiḻappa
Maiyirun *kūnda* ṉeyyaṇi maṟappak
Kaiyaṟu neñcattuk kaṇṇaki yaṉṟiyum
Kādalarp pirinda mātar nōdaka
Vūtulaik kuruki ṉuyirttaṉa roḍungi
Vēṉiṟ paḷḷi mēvādu kaḻindu
Kūdirppaḷḷik kuṟunka ṇaṭaittu
Malayattāramu maṇimut tāramu
Malarmulai yākat taḍaiyādu varundat
Tāḻik kuvaḷaiyoḍu taṇśen kaḻunīr
Viḻpūñ cēkkai mēvādu kaḻiyat
Tuṇaipuṇa raṉṉat tūviyiṟ śeritta
Viṇaiyaṇai mēmpaṭat tirundutuyil peṟā
Tuḍaipperun koḻunaro ḍūdaṟ *kālat*
Tiḍaikkumi lerindu kaḍaikkuḻai yōṭṭik
Kalankā vuḷḷam kalankak kaḍaiśivantu
Vilankinimir neḍunkaṇ pulambumut tuṟaippa
Vaṇṇa meṉṉaḍai naṉṉīrp poykai
Yāmba ṉāṟun tēmpodi naṟuvirait
Tāmaraiś śevvāyat taṇṇaṟaṟ kūndaṟ
Pāṇvāy vaṇḍu nōdiṟam pāḍak
Kāṇvaru kuvaḷaik kaṇmalar viḻippap
Puḷvāy *muraśa* moḍu poṟimayir vāraṇattu
Muḷvāyś *śanka* muṟaimuṟai yārppa
Vuravunīrp parappi ṉūrtuyi leḍuppi

Yiravut talaippeyarum vaikaṟai kāṟu
Maraiyiruḷ *yāmattum* pakalum tuñcār
Viraimalar vāḷiyoḍu karuppuvil lēndi
Makara velkoḍi maindaṉ ṟiritara
Nakaran kāva ṉaṉiśiṟan tatuveṉ.

FOURTH 'TIRUVĀYMOḺI-PUKAḺUNALLORUVAṈ'

(*From Divyappirabandam*)

1 Pukaḻum nal oruvaṉeṉko? Poruvilśīrp *pūmiye*ṉko?
Tikaḻumtaṉparavaiyeṉko? Tīyeṉko? *Vāyuve*ṉko?
Nikaḻum *ākāśame*ṉko? Nīḷśuḍariraṇḍumeṉko?
Ikaḻvil ivvaṉaittumeṉko? *Kaṇṇaṉa*ikkūvumāṟe
2 Kūvumāṟaṟiyamāṭṭēṉ kuṉṟaṅkaḷaṉaittumeṉko?
Mēvuśīrmārīyeṉko? viḷanku*tārakaikaḷe*ṉko?
Nāviyal *kalaikaḷe*ṉko? *jñāṉa*nallāviyeṉko?
Pāvuśīrkka*ṇṇaṉ* emmāṉ *Pankayakkaṇṇaṉaiye*
3 *Pankayakkaṇṇaṉe*ṉko? *Pavaḷa*ccevvāyaṉeṉko?
Ankadiraṭiyaṉeṉko? *Añcaṉavaṇṇeṉe*ṉko?
Śenkadirmuḍiyaṉeṉko? Tirumaṟumārvaṉeṉko?
*Śankucakkaratta*ṉeṉko? *Cātimāṇikka*ttaiye.
4 *Cātimāṇikkame*ṉko? *cavi*koḷpoṉ *muddame*ṉko?
*Cātinalvayirame*ṉko? Taviviḷśīrviḷakkameṉko?
*Ādiyam cōdi*ēṉko? *ādiyam Puradaṉe*ṉko?
Ādumil *kālatendai accutaṉ amalaṉaiye.*
5 *Accutaṉamalaṉe*ṉko? aḍiyavarviṉaikeḍukkum
Naccumāmarundameṉko? nalankaḍal*amudame*ṉko?
Accuvaikkaṭṭiyeṉko? aṟuśuvaiyaḍiśileṉko?
Neyccuvaittēṟaleṉko? kaṉiyeṉko? Pāleṉkēno?
6 Pāleṉko? nāṉku*vēdappayaṉe*ṉko? *Śamayanīti*
Nūleṉko? Nuḍangukeḷviiśaiyeṉko? Ivaṟṟuḷnalla
Mēlanko? viṉaiyiṉ mikka*payaṉe*nko? *kaṇṇaṉe*ṉko?
Māleṉko? *māyaṉe*ṉko? vāṉavar*ādi* aiyye.
7 Vāṉavar*ādiye*ṉko? Vānavar*daivame*ṉko?
Vāṉava*bhōgame*ṉko? vānavaramuṟṟumeṉko?
Ūṉamilśelvameṉko? ūṉamil*śuvargame*ṉko?
Uṉamil *mōkkame*ṉko? Oḷi*maṇivaṇṇaṉ*aiye.

Oḷimaṇivaṇṇaṉeṉko? oruvaṉeṉṟettaniṉṟa 8
Naḷiramaticcaḍaiyaṉeṉko? nāṉmukakkaḍavuḷeṉko?
Aḷimakiḻandu *ulakamellām* paṭaitta vaiyētta niṉṟa
Kaḷimalarttuḷavaṉ emmāṉ *kaṇṇaṉaimāyaṉaiye.*
*Kaṇṇaṉaimāyaṉ*taṉṉaik kaḍalkaḍaintu *amudam*koṇḍa 9
Aṇṇalai *accutaṉai aṉantaṉai, aṉantaṉ*taṉmēl
Naṇṇiṉaṉkuṟaikiṉṟāṉai jñālamuṇḍumiḻnda mālai
Eṇṇumāṟu aṟiyamāṭṭēṉ yāvaiyum yavarumtāṉe.
Yāvaiyum yavarumtāṉāy avaravar*śamayam*tōṟum 10
Tōyvilaṉpulaṉaintukkum śolappaḍāṉ uṇarviṉ *mūrti*
Āviśēruyiriṉuḷḷāl ādumōr paṟṟilāda
*Pāvaṉai*yadaṇaikkūḍil avaṇaiyum kūḍalāme.
Kūḍivaṇḍaṟaiyum taṇtark kondalpol *vaṇṇan*tannai 11
Māḍalarpoḻil kurukūr vaṇ *Śaḍagōpaṉ* śoṉṉa
Pāḍalōrāyirattuḷ Ivaiyum orupattumvallār
Vīḍila *bōgam*aiti virumpuvar *amarar*moyaitte.

Appendix II

ASTRONOMICAL DATA AND THE DATE OF THE *ŚILAPPADIKĀRAM*

In commenting on the first three lines of Canto x of the *Śilappadikāram*, Aḍiyārkkunallār furnishes some interesting astronomical data as to the commencement and duration of Indra's festival, the sea reverie of Kōvalaṉ and Mādavi, and the date on which Kōvalaṉ and Kaṇṇaki left Puhār for Madura. The texts in question give only a hint as to the time of starting for Madura; but collecting the details as given in the *Maṇimēkalai*, and in 'Kaḍalāḍu-kādai', Aḍiyārkkunallār has done some valuable research which deserves our close examination and scrutiny. As I have remarked in the footnote on the three opening lines of Canto x, the late L. D. Swamikannu Pillai put the date to severe test and came to the conclusion that the premises were incorrect. I felt the subject required further investigation, and with the aid of my friend Mr P. R. Chidambara Aiyar of the Kodaikanal Observatory, I have been able to arrive at a more or less satisfactory conclusion.

Let me first state what Aḍiyārkkunallār has to say. The full moon day in the month of *Cittirai*, during which the festival of Indra commenced, fell on a Saturday. The festival was celebrated for four weeks. It ended on the twenty-eighth day of the month of *Vaikāśi* during the sea reverie when Kōvalaṉ suspected Mādavi's attitude towards him and *vice versa*. This resulted in their misunderstanding and consequent separation. According to Aḍiyārkkunallār's calculation, this day of misunderstanding (*ūḍutal*) was a Monday, the thirteenth *tithi* of *Pūrvapakṣa* when the ruling asterism was *Anuṣa*. The very next day, i.e. the twenty-ninth day of *Vaikāśi* (which was a Tuesday and the fourteenth *tithi* of the *Pūrvapakṣa*), during the asterism

Keṭṭai, very early in the morning, before the sun rose but when the moon had disappeared, Kōvalaṉ and Kaṇṇaki set forth for Madura. Aḍiyārkkunallār remarks that that was a particularly inauspicious time and led to the death of those who started at that particular hour.[1]

In a later Canto[2] Aḍiyārkkunallār tells us in an informing note that the very day when the outskirts of Madura were reached by Kōvalaṉ and Kaṇṇaki was the last day of the month of *Āṉi*. As we have already seen, according to that commentator the couple left Puhār for Madura on the 29th of *Vaikāśi*, and if his calculation is to be believed, it took a full month and a little more for the travellers to reach Madura. If they had started on the 29th of *Vaikāśi* which was a Tuesday, and if they reached the outskirts on the last day of *Āṉi*, then it must have been a Thursday. We hear in a still later Canto[3] that Madura was destroyed by fire on a day of Bharaṇi-Kṛttikai. *Aṣṭamī* during the dark fortnight in the month of *Āḍi*, on a Friday about midnight. An attempt has been made, rightly, to reject Mr Swamikannu Pillai's theory of 756 A.C.; for, his calculations do not seem to satisfy any of the data furnished either by the text or the commentary.[4] Evidently the burning of Madura took place on the first of *Āḍi* which was a Friday. On the last day of *Āṉi*, they were Mādari's guests for the day and in the evening Kōvalaṉ went with the anklet into the city and was executed. Immediately Kaṇṇaki met the king and cursed that the city be consumed by flames.

While we are discussing the date of the *Śilappadikāram* from an astronomical viewpoint, it is better to say a word

[1] See also his commentary on ll. 5-6 'Kaḍalāḍukādai'.

[2] xiii, 'Purañcēriiruttakādai', ll. 30-7, and especially l. 36.

[3] xxiii, ll. 133-7.

[4] See K. G. Sankar's article in *Q.J.M.S.*, Vol. VIII, pp. 34-60. But his theory of 157 A.C. also does not cover all astronomical details.

about the reference to Friday in the epic. Years ago when Indological researches were in their infancy, Dr Fleet suggested that India borrowed weekdays from Greece about A.D. 400 and put them to popular use not earlier than A.D. 800. Granting that India is a borrower in this respect, she need not necessarily be indebted to the Greeks who were themselves borrowers and perhaps had no knowledge of weekdays before the first century A.D. A more reasonable suggestion would be that borrowing had taken place direct from the Chaldeans whose intercourse with India from at least the time of Darius (500 B.C.) cannot be disputed. The use of weekdays in ancient Hindu literature is not rare. The *Purāṇas*, like the *Matsya* (ch. 93, ll. 10-20) and *Viṣṇu* (Bk. I, ch. 12), refer to planets in the order of weekdays. The *Vaikhānasa sūtra*, which cannot be later than the second century B.C., mentions the *Budhavāra*. Besides, we perform the *arghyam* every day in weekday order during our *sandhya* prayers. This has to be traced to the *Pariśiṣṭas* of *Āśvalāyana Gṛhyasūtra*. It may be contended that the *Pariśiṣṭas* are held to be later than the texts of the *Gṛhyasūtra*. Even if this position were accepted, that portion cannot be later than by one or two centuries. These facts, among others, show the ancient use of weekdays in the Hindu calendar and the reference to Friday cannot be taken as an argument to assign a later date for the composition.

Proceeding to work upon the data given by Aḍiyārkkunallār, and by bringing the evidence of the Gajabāhu synchronism to clinch it, we find the year A.D. 174 answers nearly perfectly. In this year the first of *Cittirai* was a Tuesday, and would be 16 March in the Gregorian calendar. The following table may clarify our position :

174 A.D.

1st *Cittirai*	=	16 March (Tuesday)
First new moon in the year	=	4·7997
		20.7997 March (Saturday)
Duration from new moon to new moon	=	29.5306
		50·3303
Days in the month	=	31
First new moon in *Vaikāśi*	=	19·3303 (April, Monday)
Interval to full moon	=	14·7653[1]
		34·0956
Days in the month	=	30
Full moon day (May)	=	4·0956 (Tuesday) in *Vaikāśi*

This Tuesday the fourth of May in A.D. 174 coincides with *Kēṭṭai nakṣatram* in the early morning. What we have to note here is that *Paurṇima* and not *Caturdaśi* ends early in the forenoon on Tuesday. There is the *Keṭṭai nakṣatram* before sunrise on·that day. In questions of chronology from an astronimical standpoint, there is bound to be a certain amount of uncertainty. This is largely due to the different *Siddhāntas* or systems followed by different schools of thought, such as the *Sūryasiddhānta*, the *Āryasiddhānta*, *Vākya*, etc. What system was in use in the age of Iḷangō-Aḍigaḷ, the author of the epic, it is rather difficult to determine. But for our purpose, there

[1] If we substract the interval in *tithi* 14.7653 from 19.3303, we get 4.5650, when occurred the full moon in April, on a Sunday.

is indicated the astronomical fact that on the early morning in question the moon had set before the sun rose, although it is difficult to know, in the absence of accurate data, what was the actual interval between the setting of the moon and the rising of the sun.

As to whether *sauramāna* or *cāndramāna* was in vogue at the time, there is no room for doubt, since the word *Cittirai* (which is the one used by Aḍiyārkkunallār) has always meant the solar month, the corresponding lunar month being known as *Caitra*. As the text of Aḍiyārkkunallār is clear in the use of the expression *Cittirai* and not *Caitra*, it can be easily conceded that the commentator used the *sauramāna* method of reckoning. I am aware that we should not rely entirely on the astronomical combination as evidence in itself. For the argument is that, as the event took place at a particular time of day when a particular astronomical combination was prevailing, a certain number of cycles of the moon in its two aspects, viz. *tithi* and *nakṣatra*, must coincide with a certain number of revolutions of the sun, along with a certain number of weeks, and multiples of the hours in a day. This will be the L.C.M. of the sidereal period of the moon, the synodic period of the moon, the solar year, the week, the hours in a day. As one is not divisible by the other, roughly the product of all these quantities has to be taken to be the period that would elapse before the same *tithi* and *nakṣatra* on the same day of the week could be expected to occur again at that particular hour of the day in that particular part of the year. This can by no means be a short period. This particualr case, one may say, would only recur after some centuries. We can therefore easily set aside 756 A.C. fixed by the late Swamikannu Pillai.

My object in examining the data furnished by Aḍiyārkkunallār was to see whether it would supplement other inferable historical facts which have led us to fix the age of the composition of the *Śilappadikāram* in the second half of the second century A.D. Our examination has proved beyond doubt that the astronomical data given by Aḍiyārkkunallār are very strong contributory evidence for fixing the date as the second century A.D. The details furnished by the commentator fit in with the year A.D. 174, and this date fully satisfies the Gajabāhu synchronism as Gajabāhu had ascended the throne three years earlier in A.D. 171.

APPENDIX III

MUSIC IN THE *ŚILAPPADIKĀRAM*[1]

THE ancient Tamils possessed a highly developed system of music. This is evident from a perusal of the Tamil classics. Their musical culture was at a high level. Works dealing exclusively with the science of music were written during the Śangam period, but they were lost long ago. The *Śilappadikāram* of the second century A.D. throws a flood of light on the music of the Tamils. Music in Tamil nomenclature is *iśai*. An etymological interpretation is furnished by Aḍiyārkkunallār in the closing lines of his elaborate commentary on Canto iii, l. 26.[2] Those who practised music were styled *Pāṇar* and sometimes *Perumpāṇar*. These expressions occur frequently in the epic. There was a community, which included flutists and drummers, whose hereditary occupation was music. Even a section of Brahmanas and Ambaṇavar took to music as a profession. We get more interesting details of *paṇ* if we turn to Aḍiyārkkunallār's gloss to ll. 160-7 of Canto xiv. Four divisions of *paṇ* were distinguished. These are *Pālai*, *Kuṟiñji*, *Marudam* and *Śevvaḻi*, suggesting at once a classification after the regions, in other words, specific melody types. The different musical pieces were brought under some classification or other. One classification was tenfold : *śenturai*, *veṇṭuṟai*, *perumdēvapāṇi*, *śiṟudēvapāṇi*, *muttakam*, *peruvaṇṇam*, *āṟṟuvari*, *kāṇalvari*, *virimuraṇ*, and *talaipōgumaṇḍilam*.[3] Almost all these pieces of music are found referred to

[1] I am indebted to Sri P. Sambamurti, Lecturer in Music, University of Madras, for helping me in writing this appendix. I have also drawn upon two lectures on 'Ancient Tamil Music' by Swami Vipulananda, reported in *The Hindu* on 25 and 26 February 1936.

[2] p. 105 of the Tamil edition.

[3] This is found in Sikaṇḍiyār's *Iśainuṇukkam*. See text, p. 190.

directly or indirectly in the epic. For example, *śenturai* and *venṭurai* are implied in Canto iii, l. 29. *Perumdēvapāṇi* and *śiṟudēvapāṇi* are used in ordinary music as also in *nāṭakat-tamiḻ* or dramatic compositions. While *perumdēvapāṇi* is used in praise of Baladeva, *śiṟudēvapāṇi* was used in praise of caste *būtas*.[1] Examples of *āṟṟuvari* are the three songs on the Kāvēri in Canto vii. The whole of Canto vii is entitled 'Kāṉalvari'. This epic helps us to understand the nature of their fundamental scale, the resultant scales that they obtained by the modal shift of tonic, the *rāgas* that they used, the musical forms in vogue at that time, the instruments that they used in concerts, the types of dances cultivated and many other useful details relating to their art. 'Arangēṟṟukādai' and 'Ācciyarkuravai' are two cantos containing a mine of information relating to Tamil music.

THE ŚUDDHA-MĒLA (FUNDAMENTAL SCALE)

The ancient Tamils used a scale of twenty-two *śrutis*. In other words they recognized and used as many as twenty-two notes in the *sthāyi* or octave. This is exactly the number of notes that a refined ear can distinguish and use in a *saptaka*. The terms *alaku* (அலகு) and *mātra* (மாத்திரை) are used as the equivalent of *śruti*. It was the scale of just intonation that they used. The notes of their foundation scale (*śuddha-mēla*) had the following *śruti* values :

4 4 3 2 4 3 2

The figure 4 is the equivalent of a *catuśśruti interval* (9/8, major tone); the figure 3 is the equivalent of a *triśruti interval* (10/9 minor tone); and the figure 2 is the equivalent of *dviśruti interval* (16/15, semitone). In the series : 4 4 3 2 4 3 2, each figure signifies the value of the interval between the note it stands for and

[1] Canto iii, l. 107.

its previous note. Thus in the *śuddha* scale of the ancient Tamils there were three *catuśśruti intervals* (3 major tones), two *triśruti intervals* (2 minor tones) and two *dviśruti intervals* (2 semitones). There was a *Catuśśruti interval* between *ni* and *sa* (i.e. between *tāram* and *kural*), between *sa* and *ri* (i.e. between *kural* and *tuttam*), and between *ma* and *pa* (i.e. between *uḷai* and *iḷi*). There was a *triśruti interval* between *ri* and *ga* (i.e. between *tuttam* and *kaikkiḷai*) and between *pa* and *dha* (i.e. between *iḷi* and *viḷari*). The *dviśruti interval* existed between *ga* and *ma* (i.e. between *kaikkiḷai* and *uḷai*) and between *dha* and *ni* (i.e. between *viḷari* and *tāram*). That is expressed in modern terminology thus :

4	4	3	2	4	3	2
(ṇi) sa	ri	ga	ma	pa	dha	ni
$\frac{9}{8}$	$\frac{9}{8}$	$\frac{10}{9}$	$\frac{16}{15}$	$\frac{9}{8}$	$\frac{10}{9}$	$\frac{16}{15}$
catuśśruti interval	*catuśśruti* interval	*triśruti* interval	*dviśruti* interval	*catuśśruti* interval	*triśruti* interval	*dviśruti* interval

$$\frac{9}{8} \times \frac{9}{8} \times \frac{10}{9} \times \frac{16}{15} \times \frac{9}{8} \times \frac{10}{9} \times \frac{16}{15} = 2$$

In other words, the frequencies of the notes figuring in the *śuddha* scale were :

s	r	g	m	p	dha	n	s
1	$\frac{9}{8}$	$\frac{5}{4}$	$\frac{4}{3}$	$\frac{3}{2}$	$\frac{5}{3}$	$\frac{16}{9}$	2

Representing these facts in a more visual manner, the *svarasthānas* of the Tamil *śuddha* scale will appear in the following places :

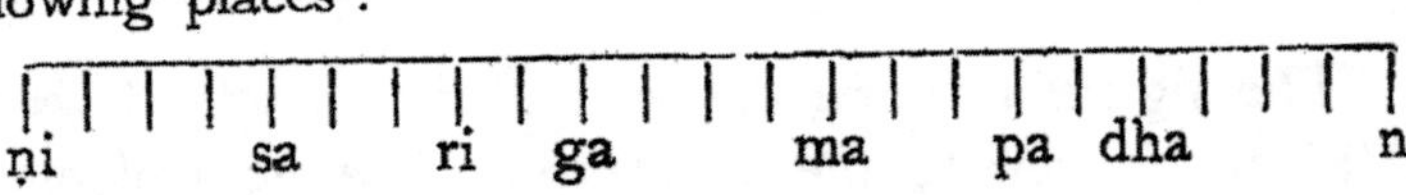

This scale approximates to the modern *harikāmbhōji mēla* and so it follows that the *śuddha* scale of the ancient Tamils was *harikāmbhōji*.[1]

[1] *Harikāmbhōji* takes the same notes as the major scale of European music except that B flat takes the place of B natural.

It is interesting to note that the *śuddha* scale of Bharata had the following *śruti* values :

4 3 2 4 4 3 2

It is evident from this that the tonic note of the Tamil scale was the fourth note or the *madhyama* of the scale of Bharata. The fourth note of Bharata's scale when taken as the tonic results in *harikāmbhōji*. We may say that the *śuddha* scale of the ancient Tamils was the *madhyama mūrchana* of *ṣaḍja grāma* just as the modern *śankarābharaṇa* is the *niṣāda mūrchana* of *ṣaḍja grāma*. In other words, the *śuddha* scale of Bharata is the *pañcama mūrchana* of the *śuddha* scale. That *harikāmbhōji* is the *śuddha-mēla* of the ancient Tamils is a fact not hitherto noticed by many scholars. An analysis of *paṇs* reveals that a substantial number of them are in *rāgas* which are either derivatives of *harikāmbhōji* or are in *rāgas* which use a majority of *svaras* belonging to the *harikāmbhōji* scale. One merit of this scale is that the notes[1] figuring therein can be sounded pure and that one can stand on them for a length of time. There are other interesting facts in support of *harikāmbhōji*. The following *śloka* gives the names of the animals and birds whose cries approximated to the pitch of the *sapta svaras* :

षड्जं मयूरो वदति गावस्त्वृषभ भाषिणः ।
अजाविकन्तु गांधारं क्रौंचः क्वणति मध्यमम् ॥
पुष्पसाधरणे काले पिकः कूजति पंचमम् ।
धौवतं हेषते वाजो निषादं बृंहते गजः ॥

Tamil books associate the following animals and birds with the *sapta svaras* : வண்டு (beetle), கிளி (parrot), குதிரை (horse), யானை (elephant), குயில் (cuckoo), பசு (cow) and ஆடு (goat).

[1] It is evident that these notes could not have belonged to one and the same octave.

The fact that the notes of the *śuddha* scale were compared to the cries of certain animals and birds is proof that our ancients had a conception of absolute pitch.

Name of the Svaras	Sanskrit List	Tamil List
Sa	Peacock	Beetle
Ri	Cow	Parrot
Ga	Goat	Horse
Ma	Heron	Elephant
Pa	Indian nightingale	Cuckoo
Dha	Horse	Cow
Ni	Elephant	Goat

A perusal of the above table reveals the fact that all except two are animals common to both lists. Since the *ṣaḍja grāma* is the *pañcama mūrchana* of the Tamil *śuddha* scale, it will be found that the lists of animals and birds also agree in a corresponding manner except that the beetle and the parrot take the place of the heron and the cuckoo of the Sanskrit list. This list supplies more evidence to show that the *śuddha* scale of the Tamils was the *harikāmbhōji* scale, viz. the *madhyama mūrchana* of the *ṣaḍja grāma*.

Rāgas

By the modal shift of tonic, seven *mūrchanas* or scales were derived. They are named: *cempālai*, *paḍumalaip-pālai*, *śevvaḻippālai*, *arumpālai*, *kōḍippālai*, *viḷarippālai* and *mērcempālai*. The initial (tonic) notes of these scales progress in the *avarōhaṇa krama* (downward series). The use and application of the seven *pālais* are seen in Canto iii, ii. 59-60 and ll. 70-1, and the commentary of Arumpadavuraiyāśiriyar thereon. It is said that when

Mādavi sang, she well observed the four *śātis*: *ahanilaimarudam*, *puṟanilaimarudam*, *aruhiyaṉmarudam* and *perukiyaṉmarudam* and had an eye to the threefold *iyakkam* which may be rendered high, low, and middle pitch (Canto vii, ll. 35-44). The distinction of *alakus* or *śrutis* has been tabulated as follows:

Cempālai	...	4	4	3	2	4	3	2
Paḍumalaippālai	...	2	4	4	3	2	4	3
Śevvaḻippālai	...	3	2	4	4	3	2	4
Arumpālai	...	4	3	2	4	4	3	2
Kōḍippālai	...	2	4	3	2	4	4	3
Viḷarippālai	...	3	2	4	3	2	4	4
Mērcempālai	...	4	3	2	4	3	2	4

Four main *pālais* are referred to which correspond to derivative *grāmas*, and fresh scales were derived by the process of modal shift of tonic in each case. *Sampūrṇa rāgas* (heptatonic scales) were called *paṇ* (பண்) and *varja rāgas* (transilient scales) *tiṟam* (திறம்).

நிறைந்த நரம்பு நிகழும் பண்ணெனல்
குறைந்த நரம்பு திறமெனக் கொள்க

Tiṟam is also used in the sense of an *auḍava rāga* (pentatonic scale). *Paṇṇiaṟṟiram* signified a *sodara rāga* (hexatonic scale) and *tiṟattiṟam* signified a *svarantara rāga* (a scale with four notes).

Instrumental music

Music was always associated with dancing in ancient times. It is no wonder therefore that all the information we are given about ancient Tamil music is in connexion with the dances of Mādavi and the group dance recounted in a later canto of the *Śilappadikāram*. The treatment of music as a separate art, i.e. independent of its relation to dancing, is found only in later works.

A remarkable feature of the education of an actress, which began in her fifth year, was a thorough training in dancing and music. Among other things the young girl was trained to sing songs composed in foreign languages and to play on the *yāḻ*, the drum, and the flute. In addition to the drummer, lute player and flutist, there was the musician of honour or chief musician, and a composer of songs who improvised pieces suitable to all occasions. This bears great testimony to the creative mind of the composer. From the fact that a separate music master is mentioned we have to assume that this composer may or may not have been a musician himself, for it is said that verses composed by him were set to music by the musician. There is an elaborate description of the harpist and the harp in ll. 70-94 of 'Arangēṟṟukādai'. The passage in question has been rendered difficult of correct interpretation by Aḍiyārkkunallār's not commenting on these lines except to give a few short notes, most of which are copied from the commentary of Arumpadavuraiyāśiriyar. But with the materials available, it seems fairly certain that *śakōḍayāḻ* was the kind of harp generally used on the stage by a debutante. It had fourteen major strings. The flute usually preceded the harp. In other words the song was started by the flutist and followed by the harpist. Then there was the beating of the *maddalam*, the *kuḍamuḻavu* and the *iḍakkai*, one following the other. *Iḍakkai* was a musical instrument used for keeping time. Sometimes one and the same song was played on the harp and the flute at one and the same time.

Thus we see that instruments in those times were used for accompaniments. The three great instruments, viz. *vīṇa*, *vēṇu* and *mṛidangam*, have their parallels in the *yāḻ*, *kuḻal* and *maddalam* of the Tamils. Since the range of the human voice was three octaves the compass of the stringed and wind instruments used for accompaniments was also of the same range. The three octaves were respectively called the *mandaviśai* (lower octave or the *mandra sthāyi*), *samaniśai* (middle octave or the *madhya sthāyi*) and *vallisai* (higher octave or the *tāra sthāyi*). The strings of the *yāḻ* were tuned to notes of absolute pitch and the instrument itself was played on open strings. It is evident that in addition to metallic strings of different varieties and thickness and density, gut must also have been used. Conclusions based solely on the lengths of the strings of the *yāḻ* in the absence of data relating to their nature, cross section, and density must necessarily be incorrect. The strings of the *yāḻ* were named after the notes to which they were tuned. This facilitated the playing of different *rāgas* by the modal shift of tonic. In the absence of facilities for the introduction of *gāmakas*, we have to conclude that the *yāḻ* produced only pure notes. The basic melody was played by the *yāḻ* player and the melody was adorned by *gāmakas* from the flute which also repeated the melody in the higher octave. In a medallion from the Amarāvati sculpture preserved in the archaeological gallery of the Madras Government Museum we see a woman playing the *yāḻ*, indicating that the instrument was very popular during the time of the *Śilappadikāram* and the centuries preceding it.

Varieties of Yāḻ. Mention has already been made of the *śakōḍayāḻ* which was usually a stage instrument. Among other kinds referred to are the *pēriyāḻ* as opposed to *śiriyāḻ*. The first was a large harp consisting of twenty-one strings while the second was a small harp with seven strings. Among the different varieties of *yāḻ*, these two seem to be very ancient. But in the early centuries of the Christian era we find reference to *makarayāḻ* distinguished by seventeen strings and *śakōḍayāḻ* with fourteen strings. These *yāḻs* or harps were early in use. Here and there we meet with descriptions of them and of how they were sometimes inlaid with gems and kept in decorated cases. In other Śangam classics, like the *Porunarāṟṟuppaḍai*, *Malaipaḍuka-*

ḍām and *Kallāḍam*, we find descriptions of *yāḻ*. One gathers from all these that the *pēriyāḻ* was a pretty instrument and was portable. Its twenty-one strings represented the three *sthāyis* of seven notes each.

The *yāḻ* and the *vīṇa* are not identical instruments. The former had no frets. The term *vīṇa* has been used by some writers to mean stringed instruments generally but latterly it has come to denote a stringed instrument with frets. Māṇikkavāśakar says: 'இன்னிசை வீணையர் யாழினர் ஒருபால்' and so it is clear that there were two distinct instruments. The *yāḻ* was a majestic and beautiful instrument and must have produced impressive and melodious music. It became obsolete some eight centuries ago. It ceased to be in use the moment the fretted *vīṇa* with its great musical possibilities appeared on the firmament of South Indian music.

The instrumentalists of those days seem to have reached a high standard of playing. Their finger technique, the skill with which they displayed the *ghana naya bhāvas*, the wonderful command that they possessed over their instruments and the artistic finish of their performances are all echoed in the *Śilappadikāram*. The performers had their allotted seats on the stage.

Parallel ideas

There are many parallel ideas in the ancient works on music in Tamil and Sanskrit. The similarities in the values of the *śruti* intervals and the names of animals and birds whose cries approximated to the seven notes have already been referred to. *Ni* was the first note in the *yāḻ* and it was to this same note that the string of the *vīṇa* was tuned in ancient times. The classifications of *svaras* into *vādi, samvādi, anuvādi* and *vivādi* have their correspondence in *iṇai* (இணை), *kiḻai* (கிளை), *naṭpu* (நட்பு), and *pakai* (பகை) notes.

It is a pity that the beautiful musical system of the ancient Tamils is now lost. Even in the time of Aḍiyārk-kunallār it was quite forgotten. Some of the ancient *paṇs* are however still used in the recitals of the *Tevāram* hymns.

Appendix IV

THE PATTIṈI CULT THROUGH THE AGES

In Ceylon, more than in India, the Pattiṇi cult has continued for a long time. In the march of years many legends have grown round the origin and career of Kaṇṇaki, and the Sinhalese tradition is very different from what obtains in South India. In Ceylon Pattiṇi has been regarded as Durgā with as many as eight Kāḷis waiting in attendance on her. She causes and cures epidemics like smallpox, and so prayers are offered at her shrine.[1] One mode of prayer was the worship of the anklet symbol (*śilambu*) which was placed in a decorated vessel with the figure of a cobra moulded on it. There are works in Sinhalese entitled *Śalamba Kathava* and *Pattiṇi Pidima* dealing with the career of Pattiṇi and the ritual of offering prayers to her.[2] The cult has become so popular that in one district alone, Jaffna, there are as many as a dozen temples to Pattiṇi. Many miraculous deeds are attributed to her. It is not possible nor necessary to give all details concerning the cult in an appendix like this. One such miraculous deed was that when she planted her foot on a rock, there gushed forth a fountain of water.

H. Parker, the author of *Ancient Ceylon*, refers to this cult in more than one place. In the last portions of his book he records a tradition that Kaṇṇaki was reborn a demoness and entered Ceylon with two sons of the Pāṇḍyan king, notwithstanding the stout opposition from the four guardian deities of the island. We are told that this tradition has given rise to what is known as the Fire-Walking Ceremony conducted every year in her honour.[3]

[1] H. Parker, *Ancient Ceylon*, pp. 151, 161.
[2] *Cey. Ant.*, Vol. I, No. 2. p. 128.
[3] Parker, op. cit., pp. 632-3.

Still another interesting story current in certain parts of Ceylon is that Kaṇṇaki was a daughter of the Pāṇḍyan King. Astrologers predicted that she would be the ruin of the Pāṇḍyan kingdom. The King who believed this put his daughter in a box and left it afloat on a river. Two members of the Vaiśya caste, who were merchants by profession, noticed this box and had it rescued. The names of these merchants were Maṉakkar and Māśāttar. The former adopted her as his daughter and the latter's son married her in course of time.[1] This tradition has special interest for us in South India as the Kōvalaṉ drama is still shown on the stage and very popularly attended. The Tamil dramatic representation has more or less adopted this Ceylonese tradition in its delineation of the early life of Kōvalaṉ and Kaṇṇaki.

This now leads us to inquire into the different turns which the epic episode of Kaṇṇaki has taken in South India.[2] One is the association of this Pattiṉi cult with the Draupadī Ammaṉ festival, Draupadī being the chaste queen of the five Pāṇḍava brothers. Tradition affirms that she is one of the five *kanyaṣ* whose names are daily remembered so as to keep the torchlight of morality ever burning throughout the length and breadth of this land. Tamil tradition refers to Draupadī as *aḻiyāta pattiṉi*, the eternal Pattiṉi or an incarnation of chastity. Later tradition has confounded the Kaṇṇaki cult with the Draupadī cult, and the whole thing has been treated as the Pattiṉi cult in general. Draupadiyammaṉ Utsavam is a popular festival in Tamil India today, and in some places this is connected with a fire-walking ceremony.

That the Pattiṉi cult was once prevalent throughout South India is seen from the fact that even to the present day festivals in her honour are celebrated in a village on

[1] *Cey. Ant.*, Vol. VIII, No. 3. p. 252.

[2] See M. Raghava Aiyangar's *Cēran Seṅguṭṭuvan*, pp. 141-4: *Arāiycci-toguti*, pp. 238-40.

the outskirts of the town of Negapatam (Tanjore District) underneath a tree; in the region of Āṟṟūr (Madura District); and among the primitive Toda tribes in the Nilgiris. Still more interesting is the story contained in a popular book entitled *Kovalankadai* attributed to a certain Pugaḻēndiyār. This is probably a composition of 300 or 400 years ago. There is a similar version in a manuscript in the Malayāḷa country, showing some agreement with the *Kovalankadai*. It is said that the Bhagavatī worshipped in Chengaṇūr or Tricchengaṇūr in Malabar was none other than *Kaṇṇakidēvī*, who took the role of a Kāḷi, popularly known as Durgādēvī, and finally settled in Tiruvoṟṟiyūr, the northern limit of the city of Madras. She became known there as Vaṭṭapuriyammaṉ. There is a separate shrine to this deity in the northern *prākāra* of the famous Tiruvoṟṟiyūr temple, and every year a festival is held in her honour lasting for fifteen days. Local tradition affirms that in ancient days a goldsmith was regularly offered to this deity in connexion with this festival. But once a goldsmith poet praised the goddess in suitable terms and extracted a promise that an animal would thereafter be substituted. One conspicuous feature of this festival is that on the last day, the special *pandal* erected for the sacrifice is fired, as a symbolical representation of the burning down of Madura city by Kaṇṇaki. This only demonstrates how the cult spread from one part of the land to the other, from Malabar to Coromandel.

Much more interesting is the tradition by which the Bhagavatī enshrined at Cranganore goes by the name of Oṟṟaimulaicci, the goddess with one breast. How and when this metamorphosis of the Pattiṉi cult into the Bhagavatī and Kāḷi cult of a demoness took place, it is difficult to say at this distance of time. Though the text of the *Śilappadikāram* does not give us any hint on this point, yet by the time of Arumpadvuraiyāśiriyar, this transformation had become an accomplished fact. He says in one place that Kaṇṇaki was born as Durgā. This is due to the fact, to hazard a guess, that as Kāḷi worship was popular in the Tamil land from the earliest times, the Pattiṉi cult had in course of time been intimately associated with it.

Whatever may have been the later developments of the cult, it is certain that immeditely following the foundation of the first shrine to Pattiṉidēvi by Śenguṭṭuvaṉ in the second century A.D., it was introduced into countries outside the Tamilnāḍu, like Ceylon and Malva, and became a universal cult not only in South India and Ceylon but also in some part of the Deccan.[1]

[1] Yet another distorted version of the story is found in M. Frere's *Old Deccan Days* (published in 1868 by John Murray, London) in a tale called 'Chandra's Vengeance'. Kōvalaṉ is called Koila, and Kaṇṇaki is Chandra. The story goes that Koila, son of a sowkar, was captivated by a dancing-girl called Moulee and had won the garland by which he became her husband. After dire circumstances, Koila and his wife reached Madura where an old milk-seller offered them hospitality. A jeweller of that place who had deprived the Rani of a bangle, accused Koila of stealing it and had him cut in twain. Chandra set fire to the city although the old milk-seller advised her to spare the *purwari* (residences of low castes). Then she sewed the two halves of the dead body and prayed to Siva to give it life. Koila was resurrected and returned home with Chandra. (This is a version of the story told to Frere in Goa by an *ayah*. The *ayah* herself had heard it from her grandparents who were living in Calicut.)

Index

Āḍakamāḍam, a temple near Karūr, 295, 295n., 339
Ādimandaiyār, or Mandi, daughter of Karikāla, 251n.
Ādiśēṣa, 293n.
Aḍiyārkkunallār, 59, 63n., 68, 70, 71, 73, 74, 77n., 92n., 103n., 107n., 110n., 119n., 156n., 17n., 181n., 187n., 189n., 191n., 194n., 207n., 210n., 212n., 223n., 226n., 236n., 239n., 242n., 246n.
Āḍukōṭpāṭṭuccēralātaṉ, son of Kuḍakkō-Neḍumcēralātaṉ and Vēḷāvikkōmāṇḍēvi, 11, 12; ruled over Kuṭṭanāḍu, 14
Agastya, lived in Podiyil Hill, 46, 58, 145, 189n.; curse of, 97, 97n.; cursed Ūrvaśi, 123; his tradition in South and Greater India, 210n.
Agni, 51; tested Sibi, 311n.
Ahalyā, 252n.
Ahanāṉūṟu, 11, 14, 23, 24, 33, 64, 66, 67
Ahavaṟpā or *Ahaval* (blank verse), 9
A History of Fine Art in India and Ceylon, 16n.
Aimperumkuḻu, 36, 103n., 117, 117n.
Ayirāṇi, same as Indrāṇi 125n.
Airāvata, white elephant of Indra, 116n., 183; temple of, [illegible] worship of, 50
Aiyai, daughter of Mādari and an attendant of Kaṇṇaki, 5, 50 179n., 184, 219, 220, 221, 228, 229, 239n., 328, 330
Aiyai, Koṟṟavai, 180n.
Aiyaikōṭṭam, the temple of Korṟavai, 179n.
Aiyaikumāri, worshipped by the Maṟavar, 179n.
Aiyaṉār, temple of, identified with Sātavāhana's temple by Aḍiyārkkunallār, 152, 152n.
Aiyangar, Dr S. K., 15n., 74n., 103n., 248n., 338n.
Aiyangar, Raghava, Mahāvidvān R., 44, 213n., 284n.
Aiyangar, Raghava, Pandit M., 12, 35n., 40n., 44, 48, 90n., 114, 117n., 210n., 283n., 298n., 322n., 339n.
Aiyangar, Srinivasa, M., 12n.
Aiyangar, Srinivasa, P. T., 9n., 14n., 24n.
Aiyar, Ramaswami, M. S., 60n., 98n.
Aiyar, Sesha, K. G., 235n., 295n., 299n.
Aiyar, Swaminatha, Dr V., 11, 69, 74, 99n., 101n., 154n., 163n., 172n., 213n., 214n., 252n., 339n.
Āiykalaippāvai, other names of, 179n
Ājivaka, sect, 47, 52
Akrūra, 228n.
Ālamarśelvaṉ (Dakṣiṇāmūrti), 266
Ālavāi, 253n.
Aḻumbil vēḷ, a Vēḷir chieftain, 37, 290, 290n., 325
Aḻvārkālanilai, 117n.
Amarāvati, 122, 122n.
Ambaṇavar, 191n., 192n.
Ammāṇai, 333, 333n., 334
Aṇangu (Bhadrakāḷi), 247
Ancient Ceylon, 16n.
Ancient India, 15 n.
Andhras, 26, 28
Anduvaṉ, father of Selvakkaḍungo, 12
Aṉporunai (Amarāvati), a river in the Cēra country, 43, 321, 332, 332n.
Antari or Sakti or Āiykalaippāvai, 179n., 188
Āpya, goddess of wild tribes, 179n.
Aṟakkaḷam, Hall of Justice, 41
Ārāiccimaṇi, 263n.
Araiśu-kaṭṭiluṟuñjiya, a title of Neḍuñjeḻiyaṉ, 271n.
Arangam, a name for Srirangam, 171, 171n.
Araṭṭaṉ Seṭṭi, 338; Kōvalaṉ's mother and Kaṇṇaki's mother born as the twins of, 340n., 341
Aṟavaṇaḍigaḷ, 121n., 221n., 338n.
Aṟavōṉ (Buddha), 156

Ardhanārīśvara, 319*n*.
Aṟivaṉ, 158, 171
Āriyappaḍaikaḍanda Neḍuñjeḻiyaṉ, 262*n*.
Āriyappaḍaitanda Neḍuñjeḻiyaṉ, 32, 33
Arjuna, 257, 259*n*., 302, 342*n*.
Āṟṟuvari (river song), 8
Arthaśāstra of Kauṭalya, 20, 81*n*., 116, 161*n*., 201*n*., 202*n*., 209*n*., 223*n*., 269*n*., 290*n*., 292*n*., 295*n*., 299*n*.
Aruhaṉkōil, 68
Arumpadavurai, a commentary on the *Silappadikāram*, 70, 189, 205*n*., 207*n*., 226*n*., 239*n*., 247*n*., 257*n*., 277*n*., 299*n*.
Arumpadavuraiyāśiriyar, 70-1, 203n., 241*n*., 270*n*., 289*n*., 295*n*.
Aruṇagiri Svāmigal, 277*n*.
Arundati, 88, 90, 90*n*., 120
Aryan culture, traces of, in the epic, 64f.
Aryan kings released from prison 342*n*.
Āryavarta, kings of, spoke in disparagement of the Tamil kings, 327
Aśōdai (Yaśodā), 221, 236
Aśoka, patronage of different sects by, 52; inscriptions of, 198*n*.
Aṣṭākṣara, 63, 177*n*.
Āṭakamāṭam, temple of, identification of, 48
Avanti, 26, 114, 320
Āyakkaṇakkar, 325
Ayirai, river, 322, 322*n*.
Ayodhyā, condition of, on Rāma leaving it, 193, 193*n*.
'Ayodhyā', 213*n*.

Baladēva, also called Valiyōṉ (Balarāma), 66, 117, 117*n*., 199
Bālakumāra and Vijaya, identification of, 28; sons of, spoke disparagingly of the Tamil kings, 299
Balarāma, the white god (Baladēva), 47, 229, 231, 234*n*.; temple of, 151, 151*n*.; worship of, 50, 175*n*.
Baleokourous, a corrupt form of Bālakumāra, 28
Bairavaṉ, 300
Bāṇa, dance of Viṣṇu after the destruction of, 124, 125
Bāṇāsura, see Bāṇa, 58, 125, 125*n*.
Bandikōśikaṉ, 192*n*.
Bangaḷar, conquest of, 34, 289, 289*n*.
Banerji, R. D., 34*n*.
Bāratam, of Perumdēvaṉār, 3
Barataṉ, Kōvalaṉ in his former life, 6, 269
Baratasēnāpatiyam, 71
Barataśēnāpatiyār, 59
Bārati (Kāḷi), dance of, 124
Barbaras, 179*n*.
Bavakāraṇi, a pond, 175
Bhagavat Gītā, 162*n*.
Bhāgavatapurāṇa, 113*n*., 124*n*., 188*n*., 221*n*., 232*n*., 233*n*., 235*n*., 236*n*., 237*n*.
Bhairavaṉ, 26, (Bairavaṉ), 300
Bhandarkar, Prof. R. G., 50, 117*n*.
Bharatanāṭyaśāstra, 59
Bhārati, S. S., on Marumakkattāyam, 12
Bhogabhūmi, 65
Bodhāyanagṛhyasūtra, 88*n*., 90*n*.
Bōgabūmi, 154
Bow, emblem of the Cēra, 228, 322
Brahmā, 183, 183*n*, 185, 189*n*., 257, 280; son of Viṣṇu, 200*n*.; Vedic sacrifices ordained by, 118*n*.; dance before, 124
Brahmāṇḍa Purāṇa, 49, 172*n*., 187*n*., 322*n*.
British Museum plates of the Pallavas, 10
Buddha, 47; (*Aṟavōṉ*), 156; sect of, 51
Burgess and Natesa Sastri, 22*n*.
Būtams, four, desertation of Madura by, 256-9
Būtacatukkam, 32, 51, 115

Cakravāḷa mountain, 144
Campāpati, see Puhār, 122
Cāmuṇḍi, one of the seven Lokamātas, 247*n*., 248*n*.
Cāmuṇḍi, of the Mysore kings, 261*n*.
Candirakam, 193*n*.

Candra, 64

Cape Comorin (see Kumari), 335

Cāraṇa, met the Kôvalaṉ party, and talk of, 163-6

Cāraṇar, a class of divinities, 157, 171, 216, 216n., 217

Catukkabūtam, 120n., 322n.

Caturmukha, 164n.

Cēḍi, city of the Vidyādharas, 122, 122n.

Celkeḻukuṭṭuvaṉ, 65

Cendil, 277, 277n.

Cengōḍu, 277, 277n.

Cera kings, earned the titles of Puhār-śelva, and Imayavaramba, 31

Cēralātaṉ, father of Iḷangō, 12, 66, 67, 283n. 327

Cēraṉ Śenguṭṭuvaṉ, 35n., 210n., 283n., 339n.

Cēra kingdom, 30-1

Cēranāḍu, extent and division of, 43

Cēras, early history of, can be carried back to an epoch before the Mahā bhārata war, 11

Ceylon, 7; relations of South India with, 35

Chastity, seven women of, at Puhār, 251-3

Chronology of the Early Tamils, 9n.

Citra (see Cittiraṉ), 300

Cittira, 100.

Cittiramaṭattutuñjiya Naṉmāraṉ, a Pāṇḍya title, 271n.

Cittiraṉ (Citra), 26, 300

Citrāpati, Mādavi's mother, 65, 338n.

City god, temple of, 151

Cōḻa kingdom, 31-2, 46

Cōḻa Manakkiḷḷi, son of Karikāla and father of Naṟcōṉai, 12, 24; Cōḻa princess, mother of Śenguṭṭuvaṉ, 327

Cōḻas, genealogical list of the early rulers of, 25

Commerce, 39

Confederacy of the northern kings, battle with Śenguṭṭuvaṉ, 300-2

Cranganore, 44

Cūḍāmaṇi, 163n.

Cupid, fish-bannered prince, 109, 119, 120, 145, 147, 150, 203; sufferings caused by, 200

Dakkiṇaṉ (Dakṣiṇāmūrti), 266

Dakṣa, daughters of, married Kaśyapa, 247-8n.

Dakṣiṇāmūrti (Ālamarśelvaṉ), a form of Śiva, 266, 279

Damayanti, 201, 201n.

Dances, kinds of, 49, 55, 57, 58, 104, 104n., 124-5, 148-9, 275f.: characteristics of, 205ff.: two schools of, 97, 97n., 98n.

Das, A. C., 116n.

Daśaratha, 193n., 200

Dāruka, 248, 248n.

Death, punishment for a thief, 249

Dēvandi, wife of the Brahman, 62; talk with Kaṇṇaki, 153-4; dream of Kaṇṇaki narrated to, 245; went to Madura and then to Śenguṭṭuvaṉ, 328-330.

Dēvandikai, wife of Sāttaṉ, 340; told Śenguṭṭuvaṉ of Maṇimēkalai's story, 337; god-possessed, 338ff.; ordered to offer flowers to the temple of Pattiṉi, 342; address of, to Iḷangō Aḍigaḷ, being god-possessed, 343, 343n.

Dēvayāni, daughter of Indra, married by Subrahmaṇya, 270n.

Dēvi, worship of, as Koṟṟavai, 49

Dhanurdhara (see Taṉuttaraṉ), 300

Dharmaśāstras, 57

Diamonds, kinds of, 207

Dikshitar, V. R. R., 8, 20n., 33n., 36n., 39n., 103n., 117n., 152n., 174n., 178n., 183n., 210n., 211n., 249n., 254n., 277n., 312n.

Divākaram, 51, 152n., 318n.

Divyaprabandham, [illegible]

Dramaturgy, two branches of, 99, 99n.

Dress and ornaments, 126-7

Durgā (Māyavaḷ), 125, 194, 183, 183n., 185n., 186n., 270n.; worship of, 58; anxiety of, for justice, 267

Duryodhana, 257n.

Dvārakā, 235

Eiyṉar of the Maṟavar tribe, 56, 174, 180, 181, 181n., 182, 182n., 184, 185, 186n., 187, 187n., 188

Elements of Hindu Iconography, 89*n*.
Eṇpērāyam, 36, 117, 117*n*.
Erakam, Svāmimalai, 49, 277, 277*n*.
Ermangalam, sung by ploughmen, 162
Eṭṭi, a title conferred on merchants, 39
Eṭṭi Sangamaṉ, a merchant of Madura, 40
Eṭṭiśāyalaṉ, a title of merchant princes, 216, 216*n*., 217
Eṭṭuttogai, 66
Evil omens, signs of, 63, 160
Evolution of Hindu Administrative Institutions in South India, 74*n*.

Festivals, in honour of the Lady of Chastity, 81; sacred to Indra, 3
Fire cult, 65, 253
Fires, three, 257, 257*n*., 265, 265*n*.
Flags of the Tamil kings, 37, 38, 162, 290

Gajabāhu, king of Ceylon, 7; synchronism of, 14f., 35; built a temple for Pattiniḍēvi, 16
Gajabāhu II, 15*n*., 16
Gajabāhukagāmani, same as Gajabāhu, 15
Gandharvas, 296*n*.
Gangā, in the hair of Śiva, 295
Gangar (Konkaṇar), the people of Gangavāḍi, 18, 35; conquest of, 289, 289*n*.
Gauri, see Kavuri, 183
Gōkula, 232, 235
Goldsmith, of the Pāṇḍyaṉ State, machinations of, for causing the death of Kōvalaṉ, 223-7
Gōpāla, Sanskrit variant of the name Kōvalaṉ, 213
Gopalan, R., 10
Gopinatha Rao, T. A., 89*n*.
Gṛhya sūtras, 57, 65
Guṇanūluṭaiyār, 59
Guṇavāyiṟkōṭṭam, 343

Hair, dressed in five plaits, 135, 158, 214, 286
Hanumān, 262*n*.
Hara, 185
Hari, 185
Hariharacaturanga, a manuscript on war by the minister of Pratāparudra, 21
Harṣa, worshipped Sun, Buddha and Śiva, 52
Head offerings, *Talaibali*, 113, 113*n*., 181
Himalayan crests, the marks of the three Tamil kings on, 228
Hiragaḍahalli plate, 10
Hiraṇyakaśipu, killed by Narasimha, 236*n*.
Hindu Administrative Institutions, 36*n*., 103*n*., 153*n*., 176*n*., 254 *n*., 293*n*.
History of the Tamils, 9*n*., 14, 15*n*., 24*n*., 47, 74, 210*n*., 226*n*.
History of India, by Jayaswal, 26
History of the Tamil Language, 99*n*.
Human sacrifice, 187*n*.
Humped bull, coming in front, a bad omen, 223
Hunter, W. W., 59

Iḍumbātavanam, 321*n*
Iḍumbil, 321
Iḷamcēral Irumpoṟai, son of Kuṭṭuvaṉ (Perumcēral) Irumpoṟai and Vēṇmāl-Anduvaṉ Celḷai, 11, 12, 13
Ilam kiḷḷi (Nalam kiḷḷi), 31
Iḷampūraṇar, see Uraiyāśiriyar, 8, 9*n*.
Iḷañcēṭcenni, 46
Iḷangō (Iḷango-Aḍigaḷ), 202*n*.
Iḷango-Aḍigaḷ, the author, son of Cēralātaṉ, brother of Senguṭṭuvaṉ, account of, 3, 13, 55, 58, 66-9, 80, 181*n*.; became an ascetic, 14; no Jain, 52; conduct towards, 38; praise of Karikāla by, 21f.; address to Dēvandikai by, 343
Ilangō vēḷ, 283*n*.
Iḷango Vēṇmāḷ, queen of Senguṭṭuvaṉ, 283, 283*n*.; attended council meetings, 37; amusements of, 38
Iḷañjēṭcenni, 25

Iḷamjeḻiyaṉ (see Veṟṟivēṟceḻiyaṉ), younger brother of Āriyapaḍaitanda Neḍuñjeḻiyaṉ, and father of Neḍunjeḻiyaṉ, 32, 33; the Pāṇḍyan king, 7
Iḷañjimaṉṟam, 115
Iḷan-Kōśar, 81
Ilavandikai, the king's park, 157
Ilavandikaippaḷḷi, a pleasure resort of Seṅguṭṭuvaṉ, 38
Ilavantikaipaḷḷituṉjiya Naṉmāraṉ, a Pāṇḍya title, 271*n.*
Imayavaramba, a title of the Cera kings, 31, 293
Imayavarambaṉ, date of, 17; and the Yavanas, 27; felled Kaḍambu, 209*n.*; elder brother and Palyaṉaicelkeḻukuṭṭuvaṉ, 265*n.*
Imayavarambaṉ Neḍumcēralātaṉ, son of Udiyaṉ Cēral, 11, 12, 13; father of Seṅguṭṭuvaṉ, 19; contemporary of Karikāla, 24; invasion of, over the north, 23; wounded by Karikala at Veṇṇi, 13
Imayavarambaṉ, a title of Seṅguṭṭuvaṉ, 19
Indirakāḷiyam, 71
Indra, 47, 51, 58, 64, 66, 94, 123, 125*n.*, 156, 172, 201, 202, 276, 283*n.*, 334; father of Jayanta, 97, 97*n.*, 102; father of Dēvayāni, 270*n.*; tested Sibi, 301; festival of, 53, 120*n.*, 122, 116ff.; his festival, introduced by Tuñjaiyileṟinda-toḍittōṭśembiyaṉ at Pūmpuhār, 120*n.*; worship of, 123; garland of, worn by the Pāṇḍyaṉ king, 195*n.*
Indrāṇi, worship of, 58; dance of, 125
Indravihāras, 308
Interregnum, after Neḍuñjeḻiyan's death, 38
Iṟaiyaṉār Ahapporuḷ, 8, 103*n.*
Irrigation, vessels used in, 161
Irukkuvēḷ, 283*n.*
Irumśolai, a name of Tirumālkuṉṟam, 175*n.*
Irungōvēḷ, 283*n.*
Iśai, 1, 99*n.*
Iśaippāṭṭu, 2
Iśaittamiḻ, the epic belongs to the class of, 59
Iṭṭaśiddi, a pond, 175
Iyal, 1, 99*n.*
Iyengar, Srinivasa, P. T., 73, 126*n.*

Jaina, 47; practices of, 52; temples of, in Puhār, 118
Jayankoṇḍāṉ, the author of *Kalingattuparaṇi,* 72
Jayanta, Indra's son, misbehaviour of, at Indra's court, 58; curse of, 97*n.*; represented by the *talaikkōl,* 102, 320
Jayantanūluṭaiyār, 59
Jayaswal, K. P., 26
Jīvakacintāmaṇi, 103*n.*, 108*n.*, 146*n.*, 215*n.*, 300*n.*
Justice, 41-2

Kaḍalpiṟakōṭṭiya Seṅguṭṭuvaṉ, 11
Kaḍalpiṟakōṭṭiya Vēlkeḻu Kuṭṭuvaṉ, a title of Seṅguṭṭuvaṉ, 18
Kaḍamba, destroyed by Cēralātaṉ, 283
Kaḍamba, of the sea, overthrowing of, 235, 235*n.*, 291
Kaḍambaṉ, 278
Kaḍambu, felled by Imayavarambaṉ, 266, 266*n.*, 309*n.*, 322, 334, 335, 336
Kaḍiyalūr Uruttiraṉ Kaṇṇaṉār, author of *Paṭṭiṉappālai,* 22
Kailāsa, the abode of Śiva, 122, 279, 279*n.*
Kākandi, a name of Kāvēripaṭṭiṉam, 87*n.*
Kaḷam, common dancing hall, 55
Kaḷangāykkaṇṇi Nārmuḍiccēralātaṉ, son of Cēralātaṉ and Vēḷāvikkōmāṉ Padumaṉdēvi, 11, 12
Kaḷavu marriage, 56
Kāḷi, 248, 253*n.*; dance of, 124; a name of Koṟṟavai, 179*n.*
Kāḷidāsa, 89*n.*
Kalinga, kingdom of, 268
Kalingar, history of, 34, conquest of, 289
Kalingattupparaṇi, 72, 264*n.*

Kalittogai, 138*n*., 150*n*., 167, 181, 189*n*., 201*n*., 219*n*., 230, 279*n*., 282*n*., 331*n*.
Kalpa tree, worship of, 50
Kalpanāmaṇḍitīkā, 29
Kāma, 157; dance of, 125; Kōvalan compared to, 96
Kāmākṣī, worship of, 49
Kamsa, 58, 124, 188, 188*n*., 237*n*.
Kaṉaka, 332, 342*n*.; gave battle to Seṅguṭṭuvaṉ and was defeated, 7, 26, 300, 301; carried the stone slab for the image of Pattiṉi, 304, 306, 306*n*.; sent back, 312; spoke disparagingly of the Tamil kings, 299, 299*n*.; identification of, with Kaniṣka, 28, 29
Kanakasabhai, 15, 27, 44, 68
Kāṉalvari (sea song), 8
Kāṉappērtanta, an attribute of Ukkirapperuvaḻudi, 33
Kāñcī, 30; worship of Kāmākṣī at, 49; mentioned by the twin epics, capital of the northern viceroyalty of the Cōḻas, 10; boundary of the Cōḻamaṇḍalam, 32; birth-place of Urvaśī, 97*n*.
Kandaṉ (Subrahmaṇya), 171*n*.
Kandaṉpaḷḷi, 171, 171*n*.
Kāṇḍāvaṉam, 259, 259*n*.
Kandukavari (song sung by girls while playing with balls), 9
Kaṉika, identified with Kaniṣka, 28, 29
Kaniṣka, 26, 28, 29
Kāñji (Noyyil), a river in the Cēra country, 43
Kañjukamākkal, 37
Kaṇṇaki, heroine of the story, 1, 2, 3ff., 50, 52, 77, 79, 88, 89, 90, 90*n*., 120, 180, 182, 182*n*., 191, 200*n*., 219, 219*n*., 220, 220*n*., 306, 307, 339*n*., 344; parents of, Ājīvikas, 52, 308; looked like Ratī, 166; compared to Piṉṉai, 221; sorrow of, 108; at Uṟaiyūr, 167, 171; attracted to Madura, 32, 156, 157, 158, 179, 179*n*., 195, 197; dream of, described to Dēvandikai, 62, 153-4; returned to, by Kōvalaṉ, 154-5; lodging with Mādari, 215, 217; grief of, at the death of her lord, 239, 239*n*., 240, 240*n*., 241, 241*n*., 242, 243, 244, 244*n*., 245; dream of, 246; communication of the same to the king, 247; representations to the king, 248-9; curse of, 38; spoke to the seven women of chastity, 251-3; destroyed the city, 253-4; victory of, over the Madura king, 261*n*.; went up to Heaven, 270; story of, narrated to the Cēra king by the hill tribes and Sāttaṉ, 285ff.; stone for the image of, from the Himālayas or the Podiyil hill, 287ff., 327; image of, bathed in the Ganges, 39; carving of the image of, 64; deification of, 275f.; consecration of a temple to, 328, 329*n*.; remission of taxes at the time of the consecration of the temple of, 39; greatness of, magnified by the Dēvas, 281, 282; divine form of, seen by Seṅguṭṭuvaṉ, 331, 337; mother of, born as a daughter of Araṭṭaṉ Seṭṭi, 339, 339*n*.
Kaṇṇar, see Nūṟruvar Kaṉṉar, 300
Kaṇṇeḻuttu, 39
Kaṉṉi, see Kaṉyākumāri, 132, 253*n*.
Kaṉyākumāri, 132, 132*n*.
Kapilapura, a city in Kalinga, the capital of Kumāra, 34, 268, 268*n*.
Kapilar, Sangam poet, a contemporary of Iḷangō, 9, 68
Kāppiyas, family of, 340
Karandai, 186*n*.
Karikāl-Peruvaḷattāṉ, see Tirumāvaḷavaṉ
Karikāla, 90, 210*n*., 251; a posthumous child and son of Uruvappahrēr-Ilañjēṭceṉṉi, 21-2; wounded Imayaramban at Veṇṇi, 13, 22; construction of the embankments of the Kāvēri by, 22; invasion of, over the north, 23; and Cēran Seṅguṭṭuvaṉ, 24; had nothing to do with Trilocanapallava or Cāḻukya Vijayāditya, 24; date of, 22ff.; contemporary of Imayavarambaṉ, 14; embankment of the Kāvēri by, 35; justice of, 36; overlordship of, acknowledged by Avanti, Vajra and Magadha, 26;

celebrated the first freshes of the Kāvēri, 129, 129*n*., 130, 132*n*.
Karikālaccōḻaṉ, 46, 90*n*.
Karikālvaḷavaṉ, see Karikāla, 22
Kariyamāḷ, 253*n*.
Kāriyāṟu, a river in the Cēra country, 43
Kāriyāṟu, battle of, where Neḍumkiḷḷi was killed by Nalamkiḷḷi, 31
Karkaṭaka pose, 232, 232*n*.
Kārkkuravai, a kind of dance, 297*n*.
Karavaṭam, a treatise on theft, 63
Kaṟpu marriage, 56
Kārttikai, wife of Vārttikaṉ, 267, 267*n*.
Karuṇāmṛtasāggaram, 231
Karunāṭar, 34; conquest of, 289
Karūr, Cēra capital? 48, 235*n*., 294*n*.
Karuvūr, was Vañji, 44, 235*n*.
Kaśyapa, 248*n*.
Kaṭṭiyar, 35; conquest of, 289, 289*n*.
Kauravas, hundred, 238, 304, 335
Kauriyar, a title of the Pāṇḍyan king, 209, 209*n*.
Kauśikaṉ, the Brahman, 4, 243*n*.; address of, to Kōvalaṉ, 192ff.
Kauṭalya, 293*n*.
Kavāṭapuram, 45
Kāvēri, 2, 4, 166, 168, 172, 172*n*., 251, 252*n*., 287, 311, 332; construction of its embankment by Karikāla, 22; first freshes of, celebrated by Karikāla, 129, 129*n*., 130, 157; description of the movement of, 160-4; a town adjoining it, 183; songs about, sung by Kōvalaṉ, 131-6
Kāvidimākkaḷ, officers in charge of the finance department, 39
Kāvirippūmpāḍḍattupaṭṭiṉam, a town near Kāvēri, 216*n*.
Kāvēripaṭṭiṉam, a capital of the Cōḻa kingdom, became prominent under Karikālaccōḻaṉ, 46, 209*n*., 308*n*.; other names of, 87
Kavundi or Kāvundi, a Jain Saint, 4, 5, 190, 194, 209, 217, 219, 214, 330; talk of, with Kōvalaṉ, 157ff.; outfit of, 160; accompanied Kōvalaṉ to Madura, 160f.; talk with the Cāraṇa, 163f.; reply of, to the Brahmana, 177, 177*n*.; talk of, 199, 200, 201; address to Mādari, 215ff.; died of starvation, 307-8
Kavundi Aḍigaḷ (Kavundi), a Jain Sannyāsini, 48
Kavundippaḷḷi, residence of Saint Kavundi, 157
Kavuri (Gauri), 183
Kayavāhu (Gajabāhu), 15; prayer of, to Pattiṉi, 343, 343*n*.
Kiḷḷivaḷavaṉ Perunaṟkiḷḷi, son of Peruviṟarkiḷḷi, 25, 31; brother-in-law of Seṅguṭṭuvaṉ, 309; conduct of, 38
Kinnaras, 296*n*.
Kīrandai, story of, 264
Koḍuhūr, devastated by Seṅguṭṭuvaṉ, 18
Koḍumbai, see Koḍumbāḷūr, 174
Koḍumbāḷūr, 174*n*.; Vēlir chiefs of, 283*n*.
Kōl, 101, 102
Koḷu, a custom among the young girls of the cowherd community, 230, 230*n*.
Koṅgaṉ, a title of the Cera king, 30
Kongar (Gangas), defeated by Seṅguṭṭuvaṉ, 18
Kongiḷamkōśar, see Kōśar, 33
Kongu, ruler of, prayer to Pattiṉi, 343
Kongumaṇḍalam, 7
Kongus, defeated by Seṅguṭṭuvaṉ, 327
Kongudēsarājākkaḷ, see Kongar, 18
Konkaṇ, battle of, 289, 289*n*.
Konkaṇa, dances of, 296
Konkaṇar, conquest of, 289*n*.
Kōpperundēvi, the great Paṇḍyan queen, [illegible]
Koṟkai (Kavāṭapuram), quondam capital of the Pāṇḍyas wherefrom Veṟṟivēṟceḻiyaṉ was ruling, 7, 32, 45, 81, 247, 247*n*., 309, 309*n*.; a port of the Pāṇḍya kingdom, 262, 262*n*
Koṟṟavai, Goddess of victory, 47, 49, 59, 179*n*., 180*n*.; the deity of the Cēras, 44; temple of, 270
Kōśar, the Satyaputras of the Aśokan inscriptions, 33f.
Kōśikaṉ, 192*n*.
Kothaimangalam, 44
Kōṭṭam, 64, 69

Koṭṭiccēdam, a dance, danced by Śiva with Umā, 319
Kōvalaṉ, a Vaiśya merchant, son of Māśāttuvaṉ, 49, 52, 53, 63, 64, 65, 71, 77, 78, 79, 119, 143, 144, 145, 147, 150, 190, 245, 270, 337*n.*; parents of, Buddhists, 52; lived in Puhār, 89, 90, 92ff.; compared to Kṛṣṇa, 221, 221*n.*; looked like Kāma, 166; an observer of the vows of the Śāvakas, 220; story of, 1, 2, 3ff.; earlier life of, 6; good deeds of, 209-12, 341; captivated by Mādavi, 105; life with her, 107, 126-30; attracted to Madura, 32; proceeded to Madura with Kaṇṇaki, 154f.; played odes to the Kāvēri, 131-7; at Uṟaiyūr, 167, 171; talk of, with a Brahmana, 171ff.; talk of, with the forest deity in the guise of Vasantamālā, 178; proceeded to Madura, 179, 179*n.*; talk with Kauśikaṉ, 193-4; proceeded to Madura, 195; reached Vaigai, 197; talk with Kavundi, 199ff.; at Madura, 210ff.; dream of, 213-4; went out with the anklet to sell it, 221, 222, 223; killing of, 227; miscarriage of justice in the case of, 42; result of his death, 328; curse in his previous birth, 269; story of, narrated by Māḍalaṉ to Śeṅguṭṭuvaṉ, 307ff.; mother of, born as a daughter of Araṭṭaṉ Seṭṭi, 340, 341*n.*
Kṛṣṇa, 47, 48, 175*n.*, 188*n.*, 189*n.*, 228*n.*, 229*n.*, 230*n.*, 232, 232*n.*, 233*n.*, 234*n.*, 236*n.*, 257*n.*, 342*n.*; married to Piṉṉai, 49; worship of, 50, 58; dance of, 59; Kōvalaṉ compared to, 221, 221*n.*
Kṣatriya būtam, 257
Kūḍal, see Madura, 82, 195, 250, 253*n.*, 281, 331, 343; destruction of, 254
Kuḍakkoccēral Iḷaṅgō, 77, 78, 79
Kuḍakko Neḍumcēralātaṉ, father of Āḍukōṭpāṭṭuccēralātaṉ, 12
Kuḍamalai, 182
Kuḍavanāru, a river in the Cēra country, 43
Kuḍavar, lord of, the Cēra king, 313
Kuḍavar, Śeṅguṭṭuvaṉ, lord of, 307
Kuḍavar kō, 282*n.*
Kuḍavarkōmāṉ, a name of the Cēra king, 30
Kuḍavarkōmāṉ Neḍumcēralātaṉ, father of Śeṅguṭṭuvaṉ, 12
Kūlavāṇikaṉ Śāttaṉ (Śāttanār), see Śāttaṉ, 52, 80
Kūlavāṇikaṉ Śittalai Śāttaṉār, a Saṅgam celebrity, and the author of *Maṇimēkalai*, 9, 67, 68
Kumāra, king, ruled at Kapilapuram, 34, 268, 268*n.*
Kumari, a port in the Pāṇḍyaṉ kingdom, 172, 172*n.*, 181*n.*, 183, 185, 188, 262, 262*n.*, 346; sea, 145
Kumari hill, swallowed by the sea, 44
Kuṇavar kō, 282*n.*
Kuṇavarkōmaṉ, ruled over the Cōḻa kingdom, 31
Kuṇavāyil, 77
Kuṇavāyiṟkōṭṭam, the residence of Iḷaṅgō, 67, 68, 77*n.*
Kuṇavāyiṟkoṭṭam Aruhaṉkōil, 73
Kuṇḍūrkūṟṟam, 171*n.*
Kuravai, dance, 2, 5, 229, 277, 282 282*n.*
Kuṟavas, 280
Kūṟṟam, district, 42
Kuru, 209*n.*
Kuṟuntogai, 203*n.*, 251*n.*, 289*n.*
Kuṭṭuvaṉ, a Cēra title, 43
Kuṭṭuvaṉ, a title of the Cēra king, 30, 43
Kuṭṭuvaṉ, a title of Imayavarambaṉ, 295, 295*n.*
Kuṭṭuvaṉ Cēral, son of Śeṅguṭṭuvaṉ, given to Paraṇar as a gift, 12, 13
Kuṭṭuvaṉ (Perumcēral) Irumpoṟai, father of Iḷamcēral, 12, 13
Kuyilāluvam, a place of worship in the Himalaya, sacred to Śiva, 320 320*n.*; battle of, 26

Lady of Chastity, festivals in honour of, 81
Lakṣmī, 58, 118*n.*, 119, 172, 183, 232, 261*n.*, 286; dance of, 125; Kaṇṇaki compared to, 213

Lankā, 302, 322*n.*
Leyden Grant, 22
Linga Purāṇa, 39
Literary Tamil, traits of, 9
Lute, descriptions of the sounds of, 131

Mābōdi, 51
Māḍalaṉ, the Brahmana astrologer, of Talaiccengāṉam, 7, 17, 19, 39, 339-342, 343; gifts to, by Śenguṭṭuvaṉ, 20, 311; told the Kōvalaṉ party of the good deeds of Kōvalaṉ, 209ff.; told the story of Kōvalaṉ to Śenguṭṭuvaṉ, 306-10; reported to Śenguṭṭuvaṉ about the slight offered to him by the Cōḻa and Pāṇḍya kings and asked the king to perform Vedic sacrifices, 319; account of the three ladies by, 341
Mādari, cowherdess of Madura, 5, 50, 52, 65, 219, 231, 232, 234, 239*n.*, 307, 328, 341; worshipped Kṛṣṇa and Kavundi Aḍigaḷ, 48; host of Kaṇṇaki, 215, 217, 218; turn of, to supply milk to the palace, 228; born as the daughter of Śēḍakkuḍumbi, 341-2, 342*n.*; talk with the Kōvalaṉ party, 214
Mādavi, a charming courtesan of Puhār, 2, 3, 4, 55, 65, 79, 121, 155, 144, 145, 146, 147, 149; born of Urvaśī's line, 123; attainments of, 97f.; charms of, 118; music and dance by, 103-4; sale of the garland of, 104-5; captivation of Kōvalaṉ by, 105; life with Kōvalaṉ, 107, 126-30; songs of, 131, 137, 138-43; stay in her summer retreat, 145; condition of, on Kōvalaṉ's departure and her letter to him, 192-3; birth of Maṇimēkalai to, 210-11, 337*n.*; story of, her seashore song made Kaṉaka and Vijaya bear weight, 306-7; turned a Buddhist, 308, 309, 309*n.*, 329, 329*n.*, 330; false story of, told by the forest nymph to Kōvalaṉ, 178ff.; her yielding Maṇimēkalai to a Buddhist saint, 214
Madhyadeśa, topography of, 217*n.*
Madura, the Pāṇḍyan capital, 1, 2, 4, 5, 6, 7, 45, 55, 63, 71, 77, 78, 79, 80, 145, 177, 178, 209, 214, 219, 219*n.*, 243, 245*n.*, 275, 281, 285, 307, 308, 309, 310, 328, 332, 335; capital of Āriyappaḍaitanda Neḍuñjeḻiyaṉ, 32, 33; thirty leagues from Puhār, 158, 159*n.*; way to, description of, 159ff., 195ff.; goddess of, 269; four temples of, 253; life in, 196; dancing girls of, 224; description of 201-8, 218; Kōvalaṉ and Kaṇṇaki start for, 155; destruction of, prediction about, 268; blazing of, 259ff.
Maduraikkāñji, 65*n.*, 74*n.*, 81*n.*, 109*n.*, 161*n.*, 189*n.*, 201*n.*, 202*n.*, 218*n.*, 227*n.*, 263*n.*, 286*n.*, 316*n.*
Madurāpati, the family deity of the Madura king, description of, 261, 261*n.*, 262, 263
Māgada, poets, 65, 295, 295*n.*
Magadha, 26, 114, 320
Mahābhārata, 8, 201*n.*, 209*n.*, 237*n.*, 248*n.*, 259*n.*, 304*n.*
Mahākāḷī, a name of Koṟṟavai, 179*n.*
Mahālakṣmī, called Kāmakṣī at Kāñcī, 49
Mahāmāyā, 247*n.*
Mahārājakanikalekha, 29
Mahāvaṁśa, 15, 15*n.*, 35
Mahiṣāsura, 261
Mahiṣāsuramardanī, 183*n.*, 261*n.*
Mahiṣāsuramardanī (Koṟṟavai), 247*n.*, 248*n.*
Maiyurkiḻāṉ, 12, 12*n.*
Makkattāyam, 12
Malainādu, 7, 30
Mālati, story of, 151-3, 339-40
Malaya (Podiyil hill), 296
Malva, 7, king of, an ally of Śenguṭṭuvaṉ, 26; present at the consecration of Pattiṉidēvi, 298*n.*; the ruler's prayer to Pattiṉi, 343
Māṉāikaṉ, 330, 330*n.*
Maṉakkiḷḷi, son of Karikāla, 25, 31
Maṉappāḍu, 278*n.*

Māndaraṉ Cēral king, a name of Palyāṉaicelkeḻu Kuṭṭuvaṉ, story of, 264-6

Maṇḍōdari, 287*n*.

Mangalādēvi, temple of, 339, 340

Maṇivaṇṇaṉ (Viṣṇu), temple of, 156

Maṇimēkalai, a *mahākāvya*, 8; written by Kūlavāṇikaṉ Sittalai Śāttaṉār, 9, 67; speaks of Kāñcī, 10; a continuation of the *Śilappadikāram*, 346, 346*n*.; 51, 52, 53, 77*n*., 221*n*., 240*n*., 269*n*., 325*n*., 328*n*.

Maṇimēkalai, daughter of Mādavi, naming of, 210-11; given to the Buddhist saint, 214; renunciation of, 330*n*., 337, 337*n*., 338; entertained Aṟavaṇaḍigaḷ, 221*n*., left Puhār for Maṇipallavam, 32; stayed in Puhār for five years and returned to Vañji, 17

Maṇimēkalai, the deity, cursed that Puhār be swallowed by the sea, 121*n*.; the guardian deity of the sea and the family deity of Kōvalaṉ, 121*n*.

Maṇipallavam, 32

Mānkāḍu, Brahman of, talk with Kōvalaṉ, 172ff.

Manmatha, God of Love, 154, 154*n*.

Maṉṟam, 42, 53

Maṉṟappodiyil, 78

Maṉunītikaṇḍa Cōḻaṉ, 38, 249*n*., 264 333*n*.

Māraṉ, Cupid, 145, 145*n*.

Maṟavar, worshipped Aiyaikumari, 179*n*.

Maṟavars or Eiyṉar, 56, 180, 184*n*., 295.; worshipped Aiyaikumari, 179*n*.

Māriveṇkō, 33

Marriage, types of, 56-7; of Kōvalaṉ and Kaṇṇaki, 65

Marumakkattāyam and the Cēras, 12ff.

Maruvūrppākkam, a division of Puhār, 111, 112, 113, 128*n*.

Māśāttuvaṉ, father of Kōvalaṉ, 88, 88*n*., 215*n*., 249; became an ascetic, 328, 330, 330*n*.

Mativāṇar, 59

Mativāṇar-nāṭakattamiḻnūl, 71

Matsya Purāṇa, 28, 39, 39*n*., 97*n*., 119*n*., 125*n*., 179*n*., 301*n*., 185*n*., 187*n*., 189*n*.

Matsya Purāṇa, a study, 312*n*.

Māvaṉkiḷḷi, 31

Maya, 92, 92*n*., 115

Mayamatam, a work on architecture, 203*n*.

Māyavaḷ, dance of, 125

Māyavaṉ (Kṛṣṇa), 229, 231, 232, 233, 234, 237

Mayidavolu plate, 10

Māyōṉ, Kṛṣṇa, 47, 58

Menon, Acyuta, C., 248*n*.

Mōhūr, Seṅguṭṭuvaṉ's success in the naval battle of, 18

Moon God, worship of, 50; temple of, 152

Mucukunda, 32, 113, 113*n*., kept watch over Amarāvati, 122, 122*n*., of Puhār line, 53

Muhavai song, 162

Murugaṉ (Subrahmaṇya), 2, 7, 47, 278; married Vaḷḷi, 49; worship of, 58, 151

Murugavēḷ Kuṉṟam, a hill sacred to Muruga, 7

Music, 146

Musical treatises, 71

Music, South Indian, 59ff.

Muśiri, a port of the Cēra country, 43

Muttūrkkūṟṟam, 171*n*.

Naccinārkkiṉiyar, 74, 114*n*., 117*n*., 189*n*., 199*n*., 241*n*., 253, 253*n*.; division of the Tamil land into four provinces by, 43

Nāḍu, division of the empire into, 42

Nallanduvaṉār, 66

Nalamkiḷḷi (Iḷamkiḷḷi), 31; son of Peruviṟarkiḷḷi, 25

Namaśivāya, 176*n*.

Naṉmāraṉ, a title of Iḷamjeḻiyaṉ, 33

Naṉṉaṉ Vēṇmāṉ, the Vēḷir chieftain defeated by Seṅguṭṭuvaṉ, 17

Nappiṉṉai, 229*n*.

Nārada, Vedic bard, 123, 188, 234

Narasimha, an avatār of Viṣṇu, killed Hiraṇyakaśipu, 236, 236n.
Nārāyaṇa, 177n., 238
Naṟcōṇai, daughter of Cōḻan Maṇakkiḷḷi, wife of Kuḍavarkōmāṉ Neḍumcēralātaṉ and mother of Senguṭṭuvaṉ, 12, 13, 24, 25
Nārmuḍiccēral, 235n.
Nārmuḍiccēralātaṉ, ruled in north Kongu, 14
Naṟṟiṇai, 64, 182n.
Nāṭakam, 1
Nāṭakanūl, 64
Nāṭṭiyanaṉṉūl, 104n.
Nāṭkōl, 63
Neḍiyōṉ (Viṣṇu), 117, 257
Neḍumāl, 239
Neḍumkalniṉṟamaṉṟam, 115
Neḍumkiḷḷi, son of Maṇakkiḷḷi, ruled at Uṟaiyūr, 25; father of Perumkiḷḷi and uncle of Senguṭṭuvaṉ, 31
Neḍumuḍikiḷḷi, the Cōḻa king, 120n.
Neḍunalvāḍai, 151n.
Neḍuñjeḻiyaṉ, of Talaiyālangāṉam fame, son of Iḷamjeḻiyaṉ, 33, 63, 81n., 332; conquests and achievements of, 45, 271-2; proclamation of, 40; ordered the execution of Kōvalaṉ, 32; his brother's garland stolen by a thief, 226-7; sense of justice of, 36
Neḍuvēḷ, a name of Cupid, 203; hill sacred to, 270, 270n.
Neḍuvēḷkuṉṟam, hill reached by Kaṇṇaki, 50
Nērivāyil near Uṟaiyūr, battle at, 18, 19, 321
Nerūr, 44
Nigranthas, temple of, 152; sect of, 68
Nīla, a messenger of Senguṭṭvan, 37 319, 320
Nīlagiri, 296, 296n.
Nīli, wife of Sangamaṉ, 188, 269
North India, condition of, in the early centuries of the Christian era, 25ff.
Nūṟṟuvar Kaṇṇar, 27ff., 312; ordered to prepare a fleet to cross the Ganges, 298, 298n., 299, 299n., 300
Omens, bad, 223, 228, 229, 246
Orutandai or Orūtandai, 12
Oṭṭakūttar, 72
Ovar, Ōviyar, a tribe, 297, 297n.
Ōviyanūl, 64
Oviyar, see Ōvar, a tribe, 297, 297n.

Padiṟṟuppattu, 14, 15, 17, 18, 19, 24, 27, 65, 67, 282n., 316n., 327n., 322n., 323n., 335n.; list of eight kings in, 11
Pahṟuḷi, river, swallowed by the sea, 44, 172n.
Pālai Gautamaṉār, 65, 265n., 322
Paḷaiyaṉ, the Lord of Mōhūr, 309, 309n.
Pallavas, not mentioned by the twin epics, 10; not come to power at the beginning of the Christian era, 29-30
Paḷḷi, used to denote a Jaina temple, 64, 199n.
Palmyra, garland of, 294, 297, 306, 309, 311, 312, 322, used by the Cēras
Palyāgaśālai-Mudukuḍumi, 65
Palyāṉai-celkeḻu-kuṭṭuvaṉ, younger brother of Imayavarambaṉ, 11, 12, 13, 65, 265, 266n., 322n.; proclamation of, 268
Pañcabāratiyam, 64
Pañcākṣara, sacred to Siva, 63, 176n., 177n.
Pañcamantra, the Pañcākṣara and Namaśivāya of the Jains and representing the first letters of Pañcaparamoṣṭins, 160n.
Pañcamarapu, 71
Pañcanamaskāram, see *Pañcamantra*, 160n.
Pañcaparameṣṭins, Jaina Yogins, 157n., 160n.
Pañcatantra, 211n., 212n.
Pañcavaṉ, a title of the Pāṇḍyaṉ king, 247, 247n., 335
Pāṇḍavas, 237, 238, 304n., 335
Pandithar, Abraham, 60n., 231n.

Pāṇḍu, 209*n*.
Pāṇḍya, sceptre of, swerved from the righteous path, 227, 241; became bent, 243
Pāṇḍyaṉ king, acknowledged ruler by all the kings of Jambūdvīpa, 228; wore a margosa garland, 225*n*., wore Indra's garland, 195
Pāṇḍyaṉ kingdom, 32-3, 44, 46
Pāṇḍyaṉ umbrella and sceptre, fall of, 249; king, death of, 249-50
Pāṇḍyas, ancestry of, 190, 190*n*., 191*n*.
Paṉikkar, Gopala, T. K., 318*n*.
Paṟaiyūr, 318
Paraṇar, a Sangam poet, 9, 9*n*.; contemporary of Iḷaṅgō, 67, 68; gifts to, 12, 20; praise of Seṅguṭṭuvaṉ by, 17, 19
Parāśara, account of, 264-8
Parimēlaḷagar, 218*n*.
Paripāḍal, 66, 89*n*.
Pārvatī, 280
Pāṣaṇḍa, ninety-six modes of, 298, 298*n*.
Pāṣaṇḍa gods, worship of, 50, 152*n*.
Pāśaṇḍaṉ (Sāttaṉ), 339
Pāṣaṇḍas, heretical sects, 51
Paśupatikōil, 49, 294*n*.
Paṭṭavarttaṉam, the Cēra State elephant, 294*n*.
Paṭṭimaṇḍapam, 114, 114*n*.
Paṭṭiṉam, a name of Kāvēripaṭṭiṉam, 87*n*.
Paṭṭiṉappākkam, a division of Puhār, 112, 112*n*., 113, 129*n*., 163
Paṭṭiṉappālai, 22, 132, 154*n*., 301*n*.
Pattiṉi, goddess, the date of the consecration of, 14; grants to the temple of, by Seṅguṭṭuvaṉ, 342; stone slab for the carving of the image of, carried by Kaṉaka and Vijaya and bathed in the Ganges, 304-5; 1,000 goldsmiths sacrificed to, 309
Pattiṉi cult, 15; Seṅguṭṭuvaṉ, the originator of, 69
Pattiṉidēvi, 37; release of prisoners at the time of the consecration of, 39; consecration of, 298*n*.
Pattiṉikkaḍavuḷ, a name for Kaṇṇaki, consecration of a temple to, 7, 81
Pattiṉikkōṭṭam, temple to Pattiṉidēvi, consecrated by Seṅguṭṭuvaṉ, 325-6
Pāṭṭuḍaicceyyuḷ (Campu), 3
Pattuppāṭṭu, 66, 111*n*.
Pāvaimaṉṟam, 116
Periplus, 46
Periyapurāṇam, 174*n*.
Pēriyār, R., same as Poṉṉāṉi, 284
Perudaṇam, 205*n*.
Perumakaṉ, an epithet for Arhat, 163, 163*n*.
Perumcēralātaṉ (Imayavaramban Neḍumcēralātaṉ), wounded at Veṇṇi by Karikāla, 13
Perumcēral, son of Selvakkaḍuṅgō and Vēḷāvikkōmāṉ Padumaṉdēvi, 12
Perumcēral Irumpoṟai, 11
Perumdēvaṉār, author of the Tamil *Bāratam*, 3
Perumkāppiyam (mahākāvya), 1
Perumkiḷḷi, 31; built a temple for Pattiṉikkaḍavuḷ, 81
Perumpāṇāṟṟuppaḍai, written by Uruttiraṉ Kaṇṇaṉār, celebrates Iḷamtiṟaiyaṉ, 10
Perunāḷ, king's birthday, 38
Perunaṟkiḷḷi, same as Perumkiḷḷi, the Cōḷa king at Uṟaiyūr, 7, 25, also called Kiḷḷivaḷavaṉ, 33, 309*n*.; king at Uṟaiyūr when the temple of Kaṇṇaki was established at Vañji, 32
Perumdēvi, the queen, 247
Peruviṟarkiḷḷi, died on the battlefield with Neḍumcēralātaṉ, 25
Pillai, Sivaraja, K. N., 9*n*., 210*n*.
Piṉṉai (Nappiṉṉai), 229, 231, 233, 234, 234*n*.; Kaṇṇaki compared to, 221, 221*n*.; dance of, 59
Piṉṟērkkuravai, a kind of war dance, 302, 302*n*.
Piṭāri (Cāmuṇḍi), 247*n*.
Pliny, 45
Podiyil, hill (Malaya), sacred to Agastya, 46, 87, 97, 107*n*., 145, 204, 210*n*., 287, 296

Poduviyal, a branch of dramaturgy, 99, 205
Poṉṉāṉi, river, also called Periyār, 284*n.*
Poṉṉi (Kāvēri), 251
Poṟaiyaṉ, a title of the Cēra king, 30, 266, 266*n.*, 309, 334, 336
Poṟaiyaṉ Perumdēvi, daughter of Orutandai or Orūtandai, wife of Anduvaṉ, and mother of Śelvakkaḍungo, 12
Porunai, 266
Prabhākaravardhana, worshipped the sun, 52
Pratāparudra, 21
Proclamation of Palyāṉaiśelkeḻu Kuṭṭuvaṉ, 268
Ptolemy, 28, 46, 87*n.*
Puhār, the capital of Karikālaccōḻaṉ; ruled over by Māvaṉkiḷḷi or Kiḷḷivaḷavaṉ, 2, 3, 24, 31, 53, 77, 87, 87*n.*, 88, 92, 122, 123, 133, 145, 145*n.*, 163, 248, 253, 235, 264, 328, 329, 332, 333, 333*n.*, 334, 335; approximates to the modern city of Madras, 115; description of the streets in, 127-9; Indravihāra of, 51; life at, 106-7, 110-19; sung about by Mādavi, 138-9; condition of, after Kōvalaṉ left the place, 192ff.; ruin of, by the erosion of the sea, 32; section on, contents of, 168
Puhārśelva, a title of the Cēra kings, 31
Pulindas, 179*n.*
Pūḻiyaṉ, a title of the Cēra kings, 30, 43
Pūmpuhār (see Puhār), 82, 120*n.*, 329, 333
Puṟanāṉūṟu, 11, 22, 23, 33, 64, 66, 67,
Puṟañcēri, 198*n.*

Rāhu, 119
Rājasūyamvēṭṭa Perunaṟkiḷḷi, 65
Rājendra Cōḻa, 318*n.*
Rājyavardhana, a Buddhist, 52
Rāma, 304*n.*, went to forest under his father's command, 193, 193*n.*; conquest of Ceylon by, 237*n.*
Ramanayya, Dr N. V., 24*n.*
Rāmāyaṇa, 8, 20, 137*n.*, 175*n.*, 200*n.*, 203*n.*, 213*n.*, 214*n.*, 237*n.*, 250*n.*, 252, 262*n.*, 286*n.*, 287*n.*, 322*n.*, 327*n.*
Ranganatha temple at Karūr, 48
Rati, Kaṇṇaki, compared to, 96
Rāvaṇa, 286*n.*, 287*n.*, 304*n.*
Release from prison, 342
Religion, of royalty, cosmopolitan, 15, 52
Religious data in the epic, 47f.
Revenue of the State, 40
Rewards for the sons of heroic rulers who fell in battle, 305-6
Rig Vedic Culture, 116*n.*
Royal amusements, 38
Rudra (Uruttiraṉ), 300
Rural amusements, 161-2

Sabhā, 42
Sabhā hall, in the heart of Vañji, 318
Sabaras, 179*n.*
Śaivism, 48
Śākkayaṉ, a dancing expert, 318, 319
Śākkayar, account of, 318*n.*, 319*n.*
Śakti, other names of, 179*n.*
Śāliṉi, born of the Maṟavar family, 180, 181, 182*n.*, 184*n.*, 190; the prophecy of, 183
Samaṇa sect, 52
Samari, 183
Sambandar, 253*n.*
Samudragupta, 23
Sangam, works, epoch, date of, 8ff., 23
Śangamaṉ of (Singapuram), 78; story of, 268-9; killed by Barataṉ (Kōvalaṉ), 6
Sañjayaṉ, the chief ambassador of Śenguṭṭuvaṉ, 37, 298, 298*n.*, 299
Śankara, K. G., 89*n.*
Śankari, 188
Saravaṇai, 278
Śaravaṇam, a pond, 175

Saravaṇappūmpaḷḷi, 278
Sarasvati, 183, 261*n*.
Śāsta, temples of, 51
Sastri, Krishna, H., 10, 24*n*.
Sastri, Nilakanta, 15*n*., 24*n*., 45*n*., 103*n*., 114*n*., 210*n*.
Sastri, Seshagiri, 15*n*.
Sastri, Subrahmaṇya, V. G., 99*n*.
Śātakarṇi, 298*n*.
Śātakarṇi and the Nūṟṟuvar Kaṇṇar, 27ff.; refers to Yajñaśri Sātakarṇi or Pulumāyi, 28
Śatrughna, 20
Śātta, caravan trade, 178*n*.
Śāttaṉ, a heretical sect, 51
Śāttaṉ story of (Pāṣaṇḍaṉ), 339, 340; learned Pāṣaṇḍaṉ, temple of, 152, 152*n*.; worship of, 50
Śāttaṉ, author of the *Maṇimēkalai*, 77-80; narrated the story of Kaṇṇaki, 285-6
Śāttaṉār, a poet, 7, 337*n*.
Saturn, 160
Śāvakas, Jaina householders, 216, 216*n*., 217
Śeḍakkuḍumbi in the service of Viṣṇu, father of Mādari, 339, 342
Śeḻiyaṉ, a title of the Pāṇḍya king, 247, 247*n*.
Sellāndi Ammaṉ, temple of, the meeting place of three Tamil kingdoms, 46
Selvakkaḍuṅgō-Vāḻiyātaṉ, son of Anduvaṉ and Poṟaiyaṉ Perumdēvi and father of Perumcēral, 11, 12, 13
Sembiyaṉ, an epithet for the Cōḻa king, 91, 91*n*., 144, 319
Śeṅguṭṭuvaṉ, son of Kuḍavarkōmāṉ-Neḍumcēralātan, and Naṟcōṇai, and brother of Iḷaṅgō, 12, 32, 33, 66, 67, 77, 81*n*., 266*n*., 271*n*., 298*n*., 317, 327, 331, 332, 336, 336*n*., 343, 343*n*.; married Iḷaṅgō Vēṇmāḷ; father of Kuṭṭuvaṉ Cēral, 12; paternal and maternal lines of, 13; Paraṇar's reference to, 9*n*.; an orthodox Hindu, 48, 52, 68, 69, 69, 294*n*.; amusements of, 38; military establishment of, 40, not a contemporary of Karikāla, 14; officers of, 37; march of, to the Himālayas, 41, 292ff.; an ally of the kings of Avanti, Vajra and Magadha, 23; and Karikāla, 24, 24*n*, 25; northern expedition of, 7, 26f.; battle of, on the Ganges 54; battle with the confederacy of the northern kings, 300-2; conquests of, 289-90, 291; period of his northern expedition, 16-17; rewards of, to the sons of those who fell in battle, 305-6; talk with Māḍalaṉ, 306ff.; heard that his success was lightly spoken by the Cōḻa and Pāṇḍya kings, 319-20, 321; was advised to perform sacrifices, 322-4; made *tulābāradānam*, 39; presentation of, to Māḍalaṉ; gave leave to all to go back to their homes, 311-12; return to the capital, 313, 315; released the Aryan kings, and remitted taxes, 324-5; relations with Ceylon, 35; spoken to by Dēvandi, Mādari, Aiyai, 328ff., saw Kaṇṇaki's divine form, 331; achievements of, 17-18, 345, 345*n*., an estimate of his character, 19ff.
Seyiṟṟiyaṉār, 59
Śēyōṉ, Murugaṉ or Vēlaṉ, 47
Sibi Cakravarti, 248*n*., 249*n*., 264*n*., 311*n*., 333*n*.
Śilappadikāram, 11, 12, 16, 18, 23, 25, 27, 29, 31, 32, 34, 37, 43, 47, 48, 50, 51, 52, 53, 61, 64, 66, 70, 79, 137*n*., 174*n*., 175*n*., 182*n*., 183*n*., 195*n*., 217*n*., 230*n*., 242*n*., 253*n*., 264*n*., 269*n*., 282*n*., 285*n*., 298*n*., 313*n*., 329*n*.; meaning and contents of, 1-2, 346, 346*n*.; the form of, 2-3; the story of, 3-8; its place in the Śangam works, 8-10; commentaries on, 70, 71, 72, 73, 74
Śilambāṟu, 175
Silātala, worshipped by Kōvalaṉ and Kaṇṇaki, 157, 163
Siṃha, see Śingaṉ, 300
Śingaṉ (Siṃha), 26, 300
Śingapura, a city in Kalinga, 34, 78; Capital of Vasu, 268, 268*n*.
Sirudaṇam, 205*n*.

Sirumalai, a hill, 174, 203
Sītā, 197n.
Sīttalai Sāttanār, 285n.
Śiva, 47, 66, 69, 93, 117, 181, 183n., 185n., 248, 251n., 258, 294, 296, 319, 320; dance of, 124; his burning of Cupid, 119, 119n.; temple of, 199; worship of, 58
Śivakāśi, 265n.
Śiva Sri Pulumāyi, 28
Śivētan (Śivēta), 26, 300
Skanda, 331
Smith, V. A., 16n.
So fortress, 237, 237n.
Some Aspects of the Vāyu Purāṇa, 210n.
South India, political condition of, at the beginning of the Christian era, 29f.
Somakuṇḍam, 154
Somatīrtham, at Tiruvenkāḍu, 154n.
Spring, a friend of Cupid, 145, 147, 150; minister of king Sun, 173
Śrīkōil, outside Puhār, 118
Śrīrangam, also called Turutti, 163, 172n.
Stage, description of, 101f.
Studies in Cōḷa History and Administration, 24n., 210n.
Studies in Tamil Literature and History, 8, 103n., 117n., 191n. 203n., 209n., 249n., 319n.
Subrahmaṇya, 66, 88n., 89, 94, 117, 171n., 270n., 275n., 277, 278; cock flag of, 199; dances of, 124, 125, 125n.; places of worship of, 49; hill sacred to, 270n.
Suddhāṉandappirakāśa, a musical treatise, 97n., 101n.
Suḷḷiyāṟu, a river in the Cēra country, 43
Sun, cult of, 241n.
Sun God, worship of, 50, 52, 64; king, 173; temple of, 156
Superstitions, 62f.
Sūra, destruction of, 124
Sūryakuṇḍam, 154
Sūryatīrtham, at Tiruvenkāḍu, 154n.
Sūta, 65, 295, 295n.
Svāmimalai, 277n.
Svāyambhuva, 164n.
Takkayāgapparaṇi, 72
Talaiccengāṉam, Talaiccengāḍu, near Kavēripaṭṭiṉam, 209n.
Talaiccengāḍu same as Taliccengāṉam, 209n.
Talaikkōl, represented by Jayanta, 53, 58, 102, 103, 205, 320
Tambirāṉ, a technical term for king, 247n.
Tambirāṭṭi, a technical term for queen, 247n.
Tamil country, boundaries of, 145, 346; divisions of, 43
Tamil Studies, 12n.
Tangāl, identified Tiruttangāl, near Śivakāśi, 265, 265n. 267, 267n.
Taṉuttaraṉ (Dhanurdhara), 26, 300
Tāranātha, 28, 175n.
Tarunilaikkōṭṭam, temple of the Kalpaka, 116
Temples, to different deities, 151-2
Teṉṉavaṉ, the ruler of the southern region, 171, 204, 243, 247, 307, 331
Teṉṉavar Kōṉ, 282n.
Tēvāram, 10, 209n., 253n., 321n.
The Chronology of the Early Tamils, 19, 210n.
The Kāveri, the Maukharis and the Sangam, 320n.
The Mauryan Polity, 20n., 201n.
The Matsya Purāṇa, 277n., 280 n.
The Pallavas of Kāñci, 10
The Pāṇḍyan Kingdom, 45, 103n.
Thieves, eight aids employed by, 225-6
Thomas, F. W., 28
Tiger, emblem of the Cōḷa king, 228n.; carved on the Himālayas, 235
Tiruccendūr, 49, 270n., 278
Tiruccengōḍu, 49, 270n.
Tirukkarūr, identified with Vañji, 44
Tirukkuṟaḷ, 95, 107n.
Tirumāl, 236, 237
Tirumālirumśōlai, a name of Tirumālkuṉram, 175n.
Tirumālkuṉram, a hill near Madura, 175, 175n.
Tirumāvaḷavan, a title of Karikāla, 22
Tirumuḍangai, temple at, 253
Tirunallāṟu, temple of, 253n.

Tirupati hills, 123, 145, 173n.
Tirupparankunram, 270n.
Tiruttangāl, same of Tangāl, 265n.
Tirutturappūṇḍi, 321n.
Tiruvaḍuvūr, 253
Tiruvālavāi, temple of, 253n.
Tiruvarangam, 171n.
Tiruvilaiyāḍal Purāṇam, 172, 214n., 238n.
Tolkāppiyam, 47, 56, 64, 66, 162n., 175n., 221n., 251n., 329n.
Tolkappiyaṉār, 175, 212n.
Toṇḍamāṉ Iḷam-Tiraiyaṉ, a Tiraiyar chief and a Cōḷa viceroy at Kāñcī, 10
Toṇḍi, a port of the Cēra country, 43, 204n.
Tōriyamaḍandai, an aged dancing girl, 206
Toṭaimlaicceyyuḷ, 1
Town life, 53-5
Treasure trove, belonged to the discoverer, 40
Tributes of hill tribes, 284-5
Trilocana Pallava, 24 24n.
Tripura, 58
Trivandrum, 48
Trivikramavatār, 177n., 236n.
Tulābāradānam, made by Śenguṭṭuvaṉ to Māḍalaṉ, 39, 311
Tunes, fourteen, of music, 146, 147
Tuñjiyileṟinda-toḍittōṭ-śembiyaṉ introduced Indra's festival at Pūmpuhār, 120n.
Turner, W. J., 60
Turutti, refers to Śrīrangam, 172, 172n.

Udaya hill, 110
Udiyaṉcēral, a Cēra king, 11
Ugra Pāṇḍyaṉ, 172n.
Ujjain, 123
Ukkirapperuvaḷudi, a contemporary of Perunarkiḷḷi and Cēra Mārivenkō, 33
Umā, 185n., 319, 320; kept time while Śiva danced,, 124; in the form of Mahiṣāsuramardhanī, 261n.
Uragapuram, see Uṟaiyūr, 46
Uraippāṭṭu, 8
Uṟandai, 145, 145n.
Uraiyāśiriyar (Iḷampūraṉar), 8
Uraiyiḍaiyiṭṭa Pāṭṭuḍaicceyyuḷ (Campu), 3
Uṟaiyūr, a capital of the Cōḷa kingdom, 4, 7, 18, 46, 81, 167, 171, 171n.; became important on the destruction of Puhār, 32; ruled by Maṇakiḷḷi and Neḍumkiḷḷi, 25, 31
Uruttiraṉ, 26
Uruttiraṉ (Rudra), 300
Uruttiraṉ Kaṇṇaṉār, author of *Perumpāṇāṟruppaḍai*, 10
Urvaśī, 58; cursed by Agastya, 97, 97n.
Ūśalvari (song to accompany swinging), 9
Uttara, see Uttaraṉ, 300
Uttaragautta, origin and life of his son, 216
Uttaraṉ, 300
Uttiraṉ, 26

Vaccira (Vajra), 320
Vaccirakkōṭṭam, a temple, 116
Vacciranāḍu, 114
Vaḍukar, 34
Vaḍuku, a kind of dance, 104, 104n.
Vaḍuvar, worshipped Aiyai-Kumari, 179n.
Vaigai, 2, 4, 46, 201, 239, 270, 271, 332, 341; description of, 196ff.
Vaiṣṇavism, 48
Vaiśya-bhūtam, 257-8
Vaitālikas, 295
Vajra, 26
Vajra, temple of, 151; worship of, 50

Vajrakōṭṭam, 53
Vaḷavaṉ, the Cōḷa king who carved a tiger on the Himalayas, 235
Vaḷaivāṇaṉ, king of Nāganāḍu, 120n.
Vāliyōṉ, (Baladēva), 117
Vaḷḷi, 275, 275n.; Kuṟava girl, 281
Vaḷḷuvars, the Private Secretaries of kings, 318n.
Vānavaṉ, refers to Śeṅguṭṭuvaṉ, 314, 332
Vañjanai, 100
Vañji, 145, 235, 241, 283, 296, 310, 312, 317, 322, 324, 328, 334n., 336
Vañji, ruler of, Karikāla's son-in-law, 22; spies at, 37; left for by Aṟavaṇa Aḍigaḷ, 121n.; Śeṅguṭṭuvaṉ returned to, 315, 316
Vañjikkāṇḍam, contents of, 345
Vañjikkaruvūr, capital of the Cēra kingdom, 14, 30, 43, 287n.; identification of, 44
Vañjikkōṉ, 252
Vañjimānagar, 44, 284n., 322n.
Vankanasikatissa, 15
Vāraṇam, Uṟaiyūr, 167, 171
Vārāṇasi, Benares, 216
Varōttama, a nymph, account of, 175f.
Vārttikaṉ, story of, 266-7
Varuṇa, a sea-god, 47, 51, 64, 133n.
Vasantamālā, maid of Mādavi, 130, 147, 149, 149n., 150; communicated news of Kōvalaṉ to Mādavi, 193
Vasantamālā, forest deity in the guise of, talk with Kōvalaṉ, 178ff.
Vāsiṣka, 29
Vasiṣṭha, 189n.
Vasu, king, ruled at Singapuram, 6, 34, 268, 268n.
Vāsudeva, worship of, at Tirumālkuṉṟam, 175
Vāsudeva-Kṛṣṇa, 183n.
Vāsuki, 183, 236
Vedic deities, worship of, 51
Vēḷāḷa Bhūtam, 258-9
Vēlāṉ, 278; 278n.
Vēḷāvikkō, mansion of, 325
Vēḷāvikkōmāṉ, 13
Vēḷāvikkōmāṉdēvi, wife of Kuḍakkō-Neḍumcēralātaṉ and mother of Āḍukōṭppāṭṭuccēralātaṉ, 12
Vēḷāvikkōmāṉ Padumaṉdēvi, wife of Śelvakkaḍuṅgō and mother of Perumcēral, 12
Vēlaṉ, 47
Vēlaṉpāṇi, 284, 284n.
Vēḷappārppāṉ, 192n.
Vēḷir chiefs, 283n.
Vēlkeḻu Kuṭṭuvaṉ, another name for Śeṅguṭṭuvaṉ, 19
Veḷiyaṉ-Vēṇmāḷ Nalliṉi, wife of Udiyaṉ Cēral, 11
Vēḷḷiambalam, 78
Veḷḷiṭaimaṉṟam, 115n.
Veṇbā, 9
Vēnkaṭam, Tirupati, 173, 346
Veṇkuṉṟam, 277
Veṇkuṉṟu, 49
Vēṇmāḷ, 318
Vēṇmāḷ-Anduvaṉ Ceḷḷai, daughter of Maiyūrkiḻāṉ and mother of Iḷam-Ceral, 12
Veṇṇi (Veṇṇil), 13; identified with Kōyilveṇṇi near Mannargudi, 13n.
Veṇvēlāṉ (Skanda), 331, 331n.
Vēṇmāḷ (Iḷaṅgō Vēṇmāḷ), wife of Śeṅguṭṭuvaṉ, 12, 13
Venus, 160
Veṟṟivēṟceḻiyaṉ, of Koṟkai, 32; sacrificed 1,000 goldsmiths, 81
Vēr Seḻiyaṉ, (Veṟṟivēṟceḻiyaṉ), ruler of Koṟkai, offered 1,000 goldsmiths, 309; as a sacrifice to Pattiṉi, 309n.
Vēttiyal, a branch of dramaturgy, 99
Vēṭṭuvavari (hill song), 8
Vibhāvari, a name of Aiyaikumari, 179n.
Vibhāvari, story of, 185n.
Vicittiraṉ, 26, 300
Vidyādhara, 211; description of the Indra festival by, to his wife, 122ff.
Vijaya, son of Bālakumāra, 28, 35, 332; gave battle to Śeṅguṭṭuvaṉ but was defeated, 7, 26, 300, 301; carried the image of Pattiṉi, 304, 306, 306n.; sent back, 312; released from prison, 342; spoke disparagingly of the Tamil kings, 299, 299n.; identification with Vijayakīrti of Khotān, 28, 29
Vijayāditya, Cāḷukya, 24
Vikramacōḷa, a paraṇi on, 72

Village administration, 42-3
Village life, 55-6
Villavan Kōdai, minister of Senguṭṭuvan, 37, 289, 302, 324
Vīṇa, kinds of, 61
Viṇṇavarkōmān Viḷunūl, a work attributed to Indra, 175*n*.
Viṣṇu (Neḍiyōn), 66, 69, 117, 125*n*., 145, 156, 172, 177*n*., 183, 183*n*., 284, 295; father of Brahmā, 200*n*.; dance of, 124, 125, 125*n*; temple of, 199; served by Sēḍakkuḍumbi, 242, 342*n*.
Viṣṇu Purāṇa, 189*n*., 221*n*., 228*n*., 229*n*., 235*n*., 236*n*., 237*n*., 310*n*.
Viyalūr, the capital of Nannan Vēnmān, 321, 321*n*.; occupied by Senguṭṭuvan, 17
Wilhelm Geiger, 15
Women, drinking habit of, 161; life of, 54-5
Warfare in the period, 40-1
Yakṣas, an ancient ruling tribe in South India, 214, 296*n*.; early history of, 175*n*., 176*n*.
Yāḷ, varieties of, 99*n*.
Yama, 120, 179
Yamunā, 233
Yaśōdā, 236*n*.
Yavanas, 27, 110, 322*n*., 335; swordsmen, 201*n*.